Wilfried Zeisler

The Belle Époque Life in Paris
Olga Paley and Paul of Russia

First edition in English, with a new chapter
on Princess Natalie Paley by Megan J. Martinelli

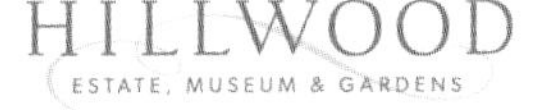

mare & martin

My dear Olga, what an admirable nature is yours and how simply and delightfully "You" you always are! One flaw though: you like to flatter your friends, but is that a flaw?

Alexander A. Polovtsov to Olga von Hohenfelsen (Paley)

I am averse to satire and mockery when it comes to my friends, or those I consider to be friends. Is it kindness or indifference – I do not know – but I do feel real pain at not being able to take the side of my friends; and who can fight against you, when you start attacking!!

Olga von Hohenfelsen (Paley) to Robert de Montesquiou

Epigraphs

Alexander A. Polovtsov to Olga von Hohenfelsen (Paley), 1909, GARF, F. 613, op. 1, D. 391, L. 6; Olga von Hohenfelsen (Paley) to Robert de Montesquiou, 1909, BNF, NAF-15155-FF 29-30.

Acknowledgments by Wilfried Zeisler, 2018

Access to rare family albums has made the documentation for this book particularly rich. I would like to thank Mme Mercedes Romanoff for her generous hospitality.

This book would not have been possible without the help and support of many individuals, colleagues, and friends, not to mention the invaluable collaboration of various institutions around the world, in particular the Russian archive centers in Moscow and St. Petersburg, from which most of the sources used in this book originate. We would like to thank them all for their contributions to this book, in particular:

In Great Britain:

Christie's, London

Alexis de Tiesenhausen, Helen Culver-Smith, Aleksandra Babenko

Royal Collection Trust, London

Caroline de Guitaut, Stephen Patterson, Karen Lawson, Alex Buck

National Gallery, London

Ceri Brough

In the United States:

Hillwood Estate, Museum & Gardens, Washington, DC

Kate Markert, Liana Paredes (†), Abby Stambach, Jennifer Levy, Elizabeth Blackwood, Jaime McCurry

Museum of Russian History, Holy Trinity Seminary, Jordanville, NY

Michael Perekrestov

Frick Art Reference Library, New York

Eugenie Fortier

Getty Research Institute, Los Angeles

Sally McKay

Christie's, New York

Casey Rogers

Virginia Museum of Fine Arts, Richmond

Barry Shifman

In France:

Archives départementales de la Haute-Saône, Vesoul

Georges Rech

Musée de la mode et du costume, Palais Galliera, Paris
Alexandra Bosc, Dominique Revellino, Sophie Grossiord
Musée des arts décoratifs, Paris
Audrey Gay-Mazuel, Sophie Motsch
Musée du Louvre, Département des objets d'art, Paris
Jannic Durand, Anne Dion-Tenenbaum, Frédéric Dassas, Marie-Elsa Dantan
Boucheron, Paris
Claudine Sablier-Paquet
Cartier, Paris
Renée Frank, Aude Barry, César Imbert
Chaumet, Paris
Béatrice de Plinval, Michael Lepage
Delisle, Paris
Jean-Michel and Jean Delisle, Pauline Monnet
Givaudan, Paris
Martine Uzan, Cyril Tika
Tassinari & Chatel, Paris
Carole Damour
Louis Vuitton Malletier, Paris
Florence Lesche, Marie Wurry, Bleu-Marine Massard

In Russia:
State Museum of Tsarskoye Selo
Iraida Bott
Pushkin State Museum of Fine Arts, Moscow
Julia Ustinova

In Switzerland:
Fondation Zoubov – Musée d'art et d'histoire (MAH), Geneva
Jean-Yves Marin, Marie-Laure Monney, Rachel Schaerer, Janeth Cadena

Thanks also to:
Dominique d'Arnoult, Cyrille Boulay, Ludmila Budrina, Dorothée Cailleux, Kyra Cheremeteff, Nicolas End, Rebecca Graham, Jérôme Lamy, Catherine de Leusse, Stéphanie Routier, Cynthia Sparke Coleman, Christophe Vachaudez.

Acknowledgments by Megan J. Martinelli, 2024

I am very grateful to Deputy Director and Chief Curator Dr. Wilfried Zeisler and Executive Director Kate Markert of Hillwood Estate, Museum & Gardens for entrusting me with yet another princess, and such a compelling, enigmatic one at that. At Hillwood, my work was made possible thanks to the Archives and Special Collections team: Jason G. Speck, Head of Archives and Special Collections, Kendall Aughenbaugh, Digital Services Archivist, and Kitty Bell, Library and Archives Technician. I wish to thank my colleagues within my own department, Collections, especially Rachel Burns, Exhibitions & Collections Project Manager, Diana Brazil, Collections and Curatorial Coordinator, Sabine Fisher, Collections Manager, Mackenzie Witter, Assistant Registrar, Manuel Diaz and Manuel Rouco, Conservation Technicians, and Jon Meo, Preparator.

Outside of Hillwood, I am appreciative of the generous research and introductions shared by independent Natalie Paley scholar Beatrice Cotte. I recognize the kindness and trust of Jack and Molly Macauley, who shared with me and Wilfried their personal collection and memories of "Aunt Natasha" for both this research and the accompanying 2025 special exhibition, *From Exile to Avant Garde: The Life of Princess Natalie Paley*. I am so thankful to Natalie Paley's biographer, Jean-Noël Liaut, for his scholarship into Princess Paley, and his willingness to engage and contribute to this project.

The staff at Yale University's Beinecke Rare Book and Manuscript Library welcomed both Wilfried and me on two occasions, exactly a year apart, to study scores of material. Moira Fitzgerald and John Monihan were especially helpful. I would also like to thank the teams at the University of Bristol Theater Collection and the Cadbury Research Library at the University of Birmingham for accommodating my research requests in March 2024.

Wilfried and I owe a particular expression of gratitude to the Hillwood Board of Trustees for their support.

FOREWORD

Marjorie Merriweather Post started collecting art seriously after 1914, when at age twenty-seven she inherited the Postum Company on her father's death. She was a discerning collector from the beginning, with a keen interest in finely crafted decorative objects, and she came into her wealth at an opportune time. She was attracted to pieces that had a story to tell, especially if it related to royalty. After the revolution in 1917, many Russian nobles were forced to flee the country, taking their valuables, and selling them to survive; jewelry and small decorative objects of high value were favored since they could be tucked into garments or luggage. Later, the Soviet government sold off many of the treasures they left behind: furniture, exquisite dinnerware, dressing table sets, and other precious things. Marjorie Post began collecting objects with Romanov provenance during this period as they became available on the market in Europe and America.

Her interest in Russian art was furthered during her time in the Soviet Union as the wife of Joseph Davies, who served as ambassador there in 1936-38. She was given access to the shops where the government continued selling what remained of many of the treasures it had confiscated from the church, the imperial family, and the aristocracy to raise hard currency. By the time of her death in 1973, she had amassed many hundreds of Romanov pieces – Fabergé eggs and small decorative objects and icons that had populated exquisite aristocratic interiors, as well as porcelain and glass sets that had been used on the tables of many palaces and residences of the royal family and would later grace her own.

Wilfried Zeisler, Deputy Director and Chief Curator, Hillwood Estate, Museum & Gardens, has explored the Romanov family's acquisitions and interests over his scholarly career, as part of his investigation into the Russian aristocracy's purchases of French objets d'art and luxury goods in the late nineteenth and early twentieth centuries. In 2018, he published (in French) *Vivre la Belle Epoque à Paris: Olga Paley et Paul de Russie* (Paul being the uncle of the last emperor of Russia, Nicholas II, and Olga his morganatic wife), delving into the couple's creation of their homes in France and later in Russia, where they strove for eighteenth-century perfection. He documents their avid acquisitions at some of the most important French houses: fashion at Paquin and at Worth, jewelry at Cartier, porcelain at l'Escalier de Cristal, luggage and trunks at Vuitton, and many more. The first section of the present volume is this work translated into English.

During Zeisler's study of Olga and Paul's life in Paris, he got to know the family of some of their descendants and the owner of a significant family collection of Romanov material taken out of Russia after the revolution; later, this collection became available for purchase. Hillwood Estate, Museum & Gardens was an attractive potential repository to the owners because, thanks to Marjorie Post's many Romanov acquisitions, it could provide a larger context for the precious family heirlooms that they wanted to keep together, and the material would be professionally cared for in a beautiful museum environment. Like Olga Paley, Marjorie Merriweather Post created exquisite interiors populated with the finest eighteenth- and nineteenth-century furniture and decorative arts, so it was fortunate happenstance that these objects might find a permanent home here. Happily, Hillwood's Board of Trustees enthusiastically agreed to the purchase, and in 2022, Hillwood acquired a trove of materials descended from Olga Paley and her daughters Irina and Natalie, as well as other members of the Romanov family. That group of objects is the nucleus of the exhibition *From Exile to Avant-garde: The Life of Princess Natalie Paley*, curated by Wilfried Zeisler and Megan Martinelli, Hillwood's Curator of Textiles, Apparel, Jewelry, and Accessories, and it provides the occasion for publishing this material.

To develop the exhibition, Martinelli and Zeisler delved deeply into the story of Natalie Paley and her intriguing circle of friends in American and European archives and libraries, discovering captivating details of the life of this beautiful and enigmatic émigré and bringing them to a broader audience in both the exhibition and this publication. In the second part of this volume, Martinelli extends the story of the Paley family beyond Olga's charmed Parisian life and her tragic return to her native land just before the First World War and the Russian Revolution, with the women's escape from Russia and Natalie's eventual migration to the United States. It is a riveting story, full of boldfaced names that make this absorbing saga come alive. Martinelli has brought her expertise in fashion and jewelry to bear on the choice of additional loans to the exhibition that flesh out the story and bring to life the arresting glamour of the Paley women. Researching Natalie Paley's personal photograph albums and the papers of her second husband, John C. Wilson, at the Beineke Rare Book and Manuscript Library, Yale University; the Mainbocher collection and Valentina collection at the Costume Institute, Metropolitan Museum of Art; and in Great Britain, the Noël Coward Collection at the University of Birmingham and the personal papers of Oliver Messel at the University of Bristol, Martinelli has found clear evidence of Natalie Paley's business acumen, especially at the fashion house of Mainbocher. Martinelli also discovered the depth of Paley's personal contributions to the circle of creatives who were her companions in the 1930s and 1940s, determining that she was not only a muse and a beautiful face but also a creative figure and tastemaker during this vibrant period.

Hillwood has continued to enlarge its Romanov holdings and especially those closely related to the branch of the family associated with Grand Duke Paul, with additions to the archives and special collections of letters by Olga Paley and Natalie's sister Irina Paley, as well as documents linked to their brother, the poet Prince Vladimir Paley, who was murdered at age twenty-one by the Bolsheviks. Recently, Hillwood was also presented with a Mainbocher dress that Natalie Paley owned, given by her biographer, Jean-Noël Liaut (see pl. 67). With the major 2022 acquisition, later purchases, and gifts, building on the many acquisitions of Marjorie Post, who was keenly interested in preserving the legacy of the Romanovs, Hillwood now has the largest assemblage of this Romanov/Paley material outside of Russia. To fully understand the Paley story, you must come to Hillwood to study it. We very much hope future scholars will further investigate the history we have begun to explore with this publication and exhibition.

We are grateful for the support of many Hillwood donors who have made possible the numerous facets of this project over several years. Their generosity has enabled the Romanov acquisitions, the Paley exhibition, Martinelli's and Zeisler's extensive research travel to develop a deeper understanding of these brave and fascinating women, and the translation and publication of the present volume. Most especially, I wish to thank Hillwood's Board of Trustees, who profoundly understand the importance of continuing to build on Marjorie Post's legacy, and her fascination with objects that reveal history, through significant acquisitions and exhibitions that expose our ever-expanding audience to the lives and times of figures whose stories may otherwise have been forgotten.

Kate Markert
Executive Director,
Hillwood Estate, Museum & Gardens

INTRODUCTION

My research work led me to develop an early interest in the destiny of Grand Duke Paul of Russia (1860-1919) and Countess Olga von Hohenfelsen (1865-1929), better known as Princess Paley, and, in particular, that of their collection. As a teenager, I picked up Princess Paley's *Souvenirs de Russie*[1] in a bookshop, while collecting memoirs and biographies about imperial Russia. A few years later, I again came across her name and references to her Russian palace and the collection she had built in Paris at the beginning of the twentieth century, which she mentioned in her *Souvenirs*. In the course of my research at the École du Louvre and the Sorbonne, I discovered the significance of this collection for the history of taste, the decorative arts, and Franco-Russian relations in the early twentieth century. I began to retrace its history by perusing the auction catalogs listing the various works of art constituting it, dispersed at several sales at Christie's London in July 1929. Then, in 2004, during a research trip to Russia, I was finally able to consult the guide to this collection, kept in the State Hermitage Museum library and published in the aftermath of the Russian Revolution, when the Paley Palace was transformed into a museum. Summary, but illustrated and precise, it reflected the spirit of a taste that was formed between Paris and St. Petersburg by two representatives of Franco-Russian high society on the eve of the First World War, and whose Parisian ties remained. Their Boulogne-Billancourt mansion, now home to the famous Cours Dupanloup, still exists and retains much of the interior decor they had planned.

In Russia, I roamed the streets of Tsarskoye Selo, the imperial resort on the outskirts of St. Petersburg, in search of the Paley Palace, which at last appeared to me hidden beneath its Soviet makeup. I trawled through the archives of the Hermitage, where I came across the 1919 file listing the main works, most of which are to be found ten years later in Christie's sales. As part of my dissertation, I pursued this research further, gathering new documents from the State Historical Archives, the National Archives of Art and Literature in St. Petersburg, and those of the Russian Federation in Moscow, as well as a number of articles published by Russian colleagues.[2]

The archives of the Russian Federation proved to be the richest in surprises, especially the Grand Duke Paul holding. It contains personal

1 Paley 1923.

2 Antifeeva and Tshistikov 2000, 335-40.

documents, correspondence, some of his diaries, and administrative and accounting records, revealing a wealth of previously unpublished information on his personal and public life, as well as on the history of the Tsarskoye Selo palace and its collections built in Paris. A further surprise in 2010 was my discovery of a Paley holding containing the same types of documents. In particular, there was Princess Paley's diary from 1902 to 1914.[3] Written in Paris, it provides an invaluable record of her life during this period. It takes the form of small diaries, several of which bear the label of the Girbal printing house, 420-422, rue Saint-Honoré, Paris. Not only is this diary unpublished, but it does not seem to have been consulted since the 1950s. Perhaps it has never really been read since it was lost. I like to think that this collection, containing this diary and many other personal papers, is the one that the princess described in 1923 as

> my most precious treasure, the six hundred letters the grand duke had written me over the last twenty-five years. All our documents, all our passports and birth certificates, everything of any value to us had been deposited in this place that seemed so safe.[4]

The princess here refers to the Austrian embassy in St. Petersburg, which was plundered in 1918 after the fall of the Austro-Hungarian Empire.

These documents added a whole new dimension to the subject. Coupled with more traditional sources, such as press clippings, public and private archives of some of the princess's suppliers, and family archives of her Parisian relations, they provided a firsthand account of life during the Belle Époque, the very name of which is still the object of study.[5] Written in Russian, but with numerous passages in French, the diary conveys the cosmopolitanism of the international elite of the time, the *grand monde* described by Alice Bravard.[6] This document is also a worldly work that plunges us into the universe of Marcel Proust, since most of Princess Paley's relations had fed the naturalist imagination of the writer, who even mentions her in *À la recherche du temps perdu*. Evenings, dinners, concerts, and other outings punctuate the family's daily life and tell the story of Parisian life in the Belle Époque. The social aspect is not limited to friendships and social events. The countess had dealings with jewelers, couturiers, and milliners, as well as with her decorator, merchants, and antique dealers, as she was closely involved in furnishing her residences. A study of the diary provides a panorama of the Paris art market,

3 GARF, F. 613, op. 13-27. References to Olga's diary (including partial or complete date) are usually mentioned in the text, not in a note form.

4 Paley 1923, 260-61.

5 Dominique Kalifa, *La Véritable Histoire de la Belle Époque* (Paris: Fayard, 2017).

6 Bravard, 2013.

little studied for this period, and its art industries. As with social relations, its analysis demonstrates the importance of a network in the construction of exchanges. By following the countess's Parisian activities day by day, we understand how such a network was built, and the complexity of the relationship with the various players involved in building a collection. When it comes to taste, mentors play a fundamental role. First there was Alexis de Hitrov (Khitrovo) (1848-1912), the loyal Russian friend and collector, who spent part of his time living in Paris, and whose role in the art market deserves to be studied. He was followed by Boni de Castellane (1867-1932). The mentor doubles as decorator, both sharing their address books with the connoisseur who then chooses furniture, other objects, and artworks. The real involvement of the client can be seen in this diary, whether it be the furnishing of a house, the creation of a work of art, or the design of a piece of jewelry.

In terms of the history of taste, when I took up my curatorial duties at Hillwood Estate, Museum & Gardens in Washington, DC, in 2014, I was surprised by the similarities between the collection built in Paris by a Russian aristocrat in the early twentieth century and that of an American business executive, Marjorie Merriweather Post (1887-1973), built up from the late 1910s on. Post assembled a collection of eighteenth-century French art, rather traditional in the local history of taste, and Russian art, a nearly unique case. She shared other tastes with Olga von Hohenfelsen, for porcelains, jewels, and fine and ornamental stones. These similarities may be seen as an illustration of the history of taste and collecting as a function of gender,[7] or of the persistence throughout the twentieth century of the taste of the cosmopolitan elite, lying between decoration and collection.

The collection built up by Olga von Hohenfelsen, with the backing and financial support of Grand Duke Paul, is similar to more prestigious Parisian examples, all of which testify to the success of French art of the eighteenth century, whose well-documented process of rediscovery was affirmed in the splendor of the Second Empire.[8] Indeed, we might mention the case of the countess's compatriot Baron Basile de Schlichting, whose donation to the Musée du Louvre "suffices to testify to a magnificent collector's lesson: it is a timely reminder that, in the ineffable Paris of the years 1900-1914, almost everything was in Paris, or flowing into Paris."[9]

While the nature of the collection was different, and more abundant and diverse in terms of art and periods, Schlichting's very precise collector's notebook[10] cites many of the suppliers and antique dealers Olga frequented

7 Charlotte Gere and Marina Vaizey, *Great Women Collectors* (London: Philip Wilson, 1999). See also Verlaine, 2013.

8 Vogtherr, Preti, and Faroult, 2014.

9 Jacques Foucart, "La Collection Schlichting," in Centorame and Andia 2005, 215.

10 Musée du Louvre, documentation du Département des objets d'art.

at the same time, including Laurent, Taburet, Stettiner, and Guiraud. This provides a panorama of the antiques art market in Paris at the beginning of the twentieth century. These dealers were among the earliest purveyors of antiques of the eighteenth century, particularly objets d'art, and were among the suppliers of Count Moïse de Camondo (1860-1935). His collection, though richer, can also be compared in terms of taste to that of Olga von Hohenfelsen.

The collection that serves as the benchmark for the entire period, establishing the eighteenth century as the absolute model of aristocratic and Parisian taste, is of course that of Jacques Doucet, which was completely dispersed in 1912.[11] This collection reflected the preferences of numerous players in the world of taste, including the society surrounding Countess von Hohenfelsen. A major customer of Parisian taste, notably that of Doucet, Olga was immersed in this world. Her couturier Worth, of whom she was an intimate, was also known for his art collection, particularly of porcelain.[12] Certain suppliers, such as Georges and Henri Pannier, owners of l'Escalier de Cristal, were close to Doucet and other collectors of eighteenth-century art.[13] Finally, decorator Georges Hoentschel (1855-1915), who oversaw the installation of the countess's mansion in Boulogne, had also worked for Doucet, "knowing how to give patiently collected objects the decorative framework that suited them, and not hesitating to combine the real with the counterfeit."[14] This association is a fundamental element in the history of taste during a period dominated by an obsession with stylistic perfection, a quest for an ideal that was possible because the Parisian art industries had preserved the ancestral know-how that had made them successful, producing works that were not ashamed of their historical models.

While Countess von Hohenfelsen's collection may not be the most perfect example of the broader history of taste in Paris, its transfer to Russia instead marked a pivotal moment in the local history of taste and collecting. In terms of decoration, this was not the first time a complete collection had been put together in Paris and then transferred to Russia. In the nineteenth century, examples include the apartments of Grand Duke Michael and Grand Duchess Elena Pavlovna in the 1820s and the Yusupov Palace in St. Petersburg in the late 1850s. Closer to Olga's time, there were also the furnishings of some palaces,[15] such as the Leuchtenberg or Gortchakov residences in St. Petersburg, which bear witness to the international success of Parisian decoration. However, the Paley Palace and its collection, with

11 Georgel, 2016.

12 Worth sale, Paris, Drouot, April 24, 1899. Probably the collection of his father, Charles.

13 Annick Masseau and Didier Masseau, "Jacques Doucet et les frères Pannier," in Georgel 2016, 64-66.

14 Anne Forray-Carlier, "Les Demeures XVIIIe siècle de Jacques Doucet," in Georgel 2016, 72.

15 Zeisler 2014b, 134-40.

its refined, orderly taste, was something quite new. Many members of the imperial family, however accustomed to Paris and aware of the latest trends, as well as some of the most renowned collectors and art lovers of the time, understood that this ensemble represented a new stage in the history of Russian taste. In his *Memoirs*, Grand Duke Gabriel speaks of the "great taste" of this house: "Uncle Paul had a very beautiful study furnished in wood and raspberry-colored fabric. On the magnificent desk, there were few objects, not like in my parents' or my own home."[16] The emperor himself dared not compare his new palace at Livadia in the Crimea with that of the countess: "The princess has the most beautiful house in the world in Tzarskoïé [*sic*], a veritable museum. How do you expect her to tell you what she thinks of our house, where we've thrown together a jumble of things we liked and which has no style?"[17]

In the aftermath of the Revolution, the importance of the collection and the palace was recognized, and although it was brand-new, for a time it was home to the Museum of French Art and History. While the taste embodied by the Doucet collection was propagated and maintained throughout the twentieth century, its Russian equivalent, symbolized by the Paley Palace or the little-known Olive collection, is all the more interesting in that its model was brought to a sudden halt by the Revolution, then by the Soviet regime.

On the subject of Doucet, Chantal Georgel notes:

> And it is as if, deep down, these successive homes [...] were more than just a showcase for works and objets d'art: they were the heart of Jacques Doucet's life project, the "milieu," in the Vidalian sense of the term, in which he could blossom in symbiosis with these works-artifacts that, at the same time as he invested in them morally, nourished him, humanly first of all.[18]

Indeed, in addition to the interdisciplinary notions nurtured by the study of the countess's diary and her collections, it recounts lives that belong to their time. They are the story of an extraordinary couple, perhaps ahead of their time, who renounced their respective families and the glitter of court life to live a love in exile. This diary traces the life of a woman and mother in search of independence, often embodying the myth of the Parisian woman shaped by the times. She was confronted with the burning issue of divorce, at the heart of a more or less open society. The subject was kept quiet in Paris. The grand duke's prestige no doubt had a lot to do with it. This unique destiny was written in the equally extraordinary context of the alliance between the

16 Grand Duke Gabriel 1955, 119.

17 Paley 1923, 12.

18 Chantal Georgel, "Qui êtes-vous Monsieur Doucet?," in Georgel 2016, 18.

Republic and the Empire, which shared an unprecedented degree of mutual passion and fascination.

The period known as the Belle Époque has its darker side, however, in Russia as in France. Olga was a Russian citizen who, prior to her exile in Paris, had lived in an empire where state anti-Semitism had developed since the reign of Alexander III, manifesting itself in violent pogroms and population movements. In her *Souvenirs* covering the period of the end of the war and the Revolution, Olga repeatedly expresses her feelings about the Jews she meets. At the heart of the Revolution, she went to the Cheka, the early Soviet secret police, to negotiate the release of her imprisoned son, and she describes her interlocutor: "Small, stocky, with twisted legs, a large head, curly blond hair. Small eyes, hidden behind pince-nez, hooked nose, full lips, ironic, evil smile. The repulsive type of the bad Jew, the evil Jew."[19]

Her Paris diary gives little information about her political convictions, but her friendships and commitments place her in a rather conservative aristocratic milieu, albeit one that was curious and tolerant when it came to art and morals. The Dreyfus affair predates the countess's diary. Olga von Hohenfelsen frequented the Parisian Jewish elite analyzed by Cyril Grange[20] from a distance and did not seem particularly close to it. Many of her suppliers, however, were Jewish.

A study of the diary and all the archives and documents consulted and compiled for this book reveals an aspect of life and collecting in Paris at the beginning of the twentieth century, and of cultural transfers between France and Russia during the same period, while adding a chapter to the history of the branch of the Romanovs born of the union between Grand Duke Paul and Countess von Hohenfelsen. This branch produced strong personalities from the artistic and cultural world, several of whose members have been the subject of biographies: Natalie Paley, muse, actress, and fashion icon;[21] Vladimir Paley, a young poet and martyr;[22] and, more recently, Michael Romanov.[23] The latter, a direct descendant of Emperor Nicholas I through his father and mother, "always said that Princess Paley, his maternal grandmother, had genetically 'saved' him."[24]

19 Paley 1923, 185.

20 Grange 2016.

21 Liaut 1996.

22 Jorge F. Saenz, *A Poet among the Romanovs: Prince Vladimir Paley (1897-1918)* (Richmond, CA: Eurohistory, 2004).

23 Toscano 2014.

24 *Ibid.*, 11.

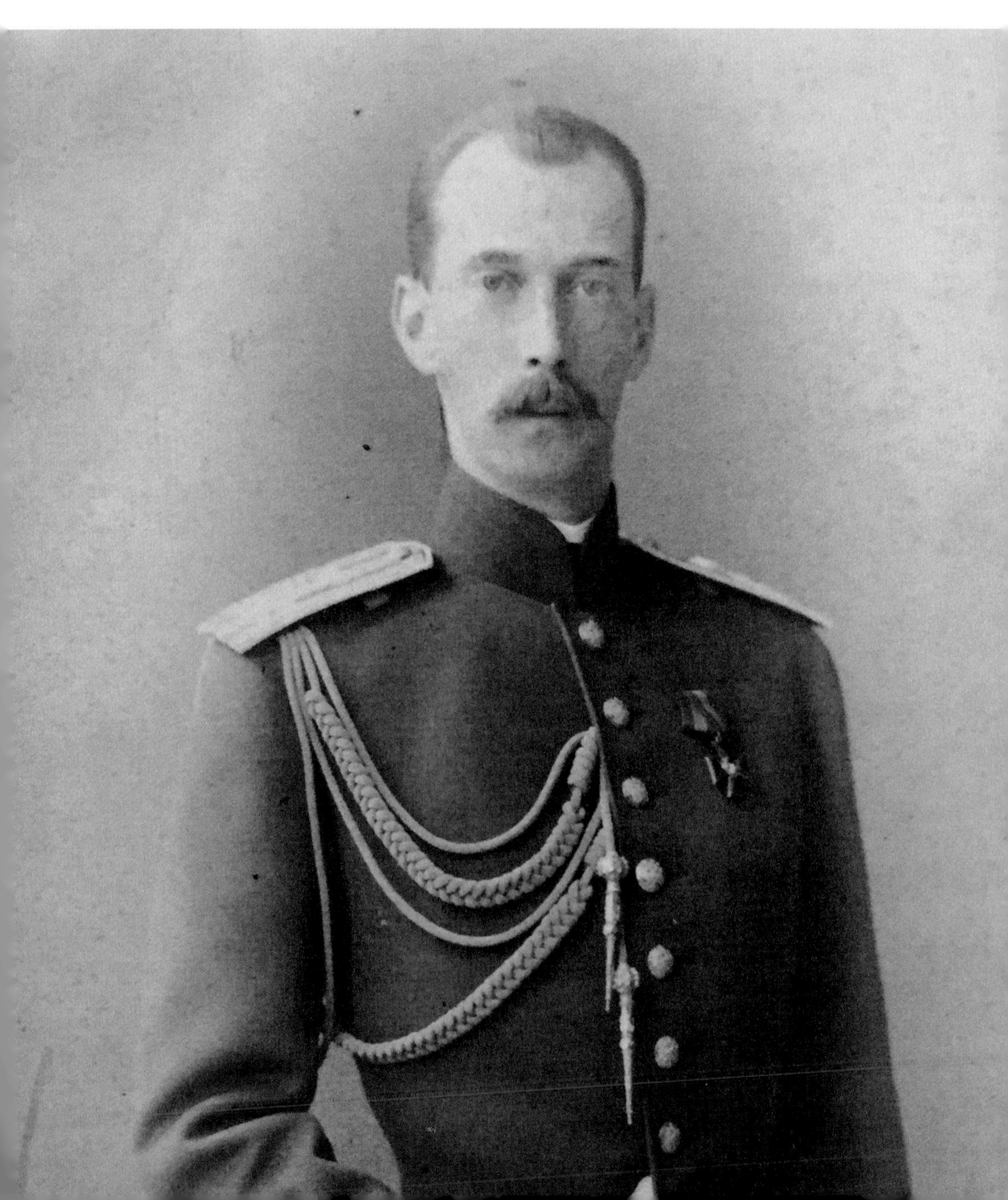

A COUPLE AHEAD OF THEIR TIME?

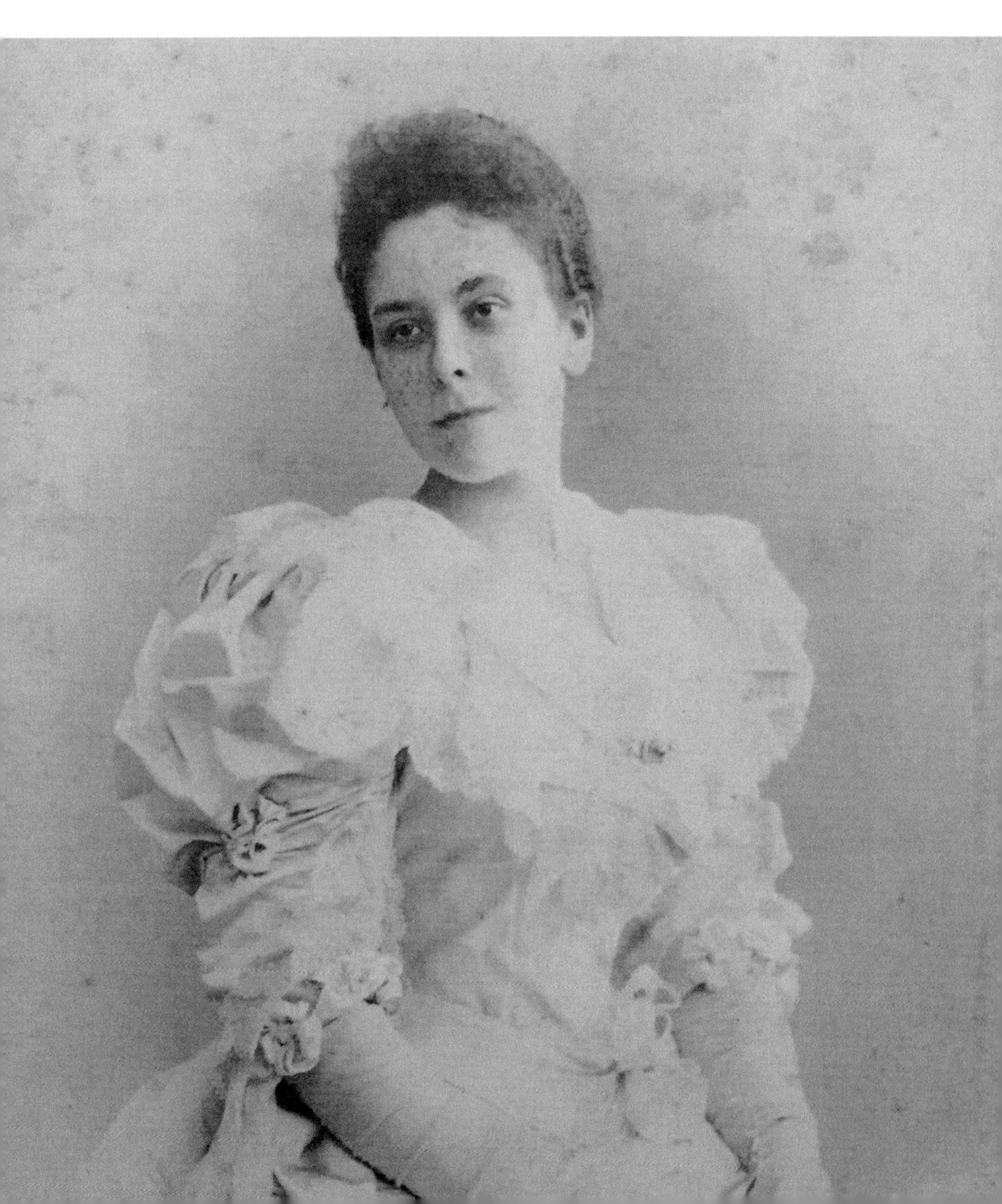

Born in St. Petersburg in 1865 into a wealthy family of Hungarian nobility, Olga Karnovich – better known by her successive names Olga von Pistohlkors, Countess von Hohenfelsen, then Princess Paley – became a figure of Belle Époque Paris thanks to her destiny (fig. 1). The Karnovich family was allied to some of the great names of the Russian nobility, such as Cheremetev, Schakovskoy, and Uvarov, and included several high-ranking officials in the service of the Court. Olga's father, Valerian Gavrilovich (1823-1891), was chamberlain and deputy director of the State Property Ministry Department of General Affairs.[1] Beautiful, elegant, and ambitious, young Olga was highly appreciated in the Court entourage. In 1884, early in the reign of Emperor Alexander III, she married Erich A. von Pistohlkors (1853-1935), an officer in the Imperial Guard regiment (fig. 2). The wedding was one of the capital's social events and was attended by the influential Secretary of State Alexander Polovtsov *père* (1832-1909).[2] An intimate

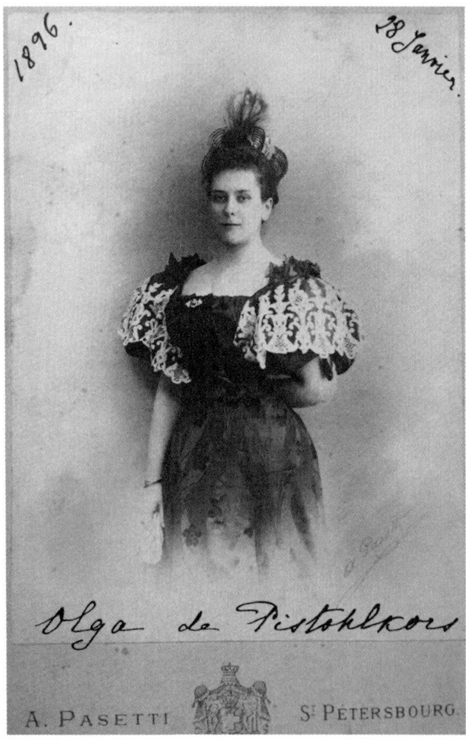

Fig. 1 Studio A. Pasetti, St. Petersburg. Olga von Pistohlkors, January 28, 1896. Photograph. Private collection.

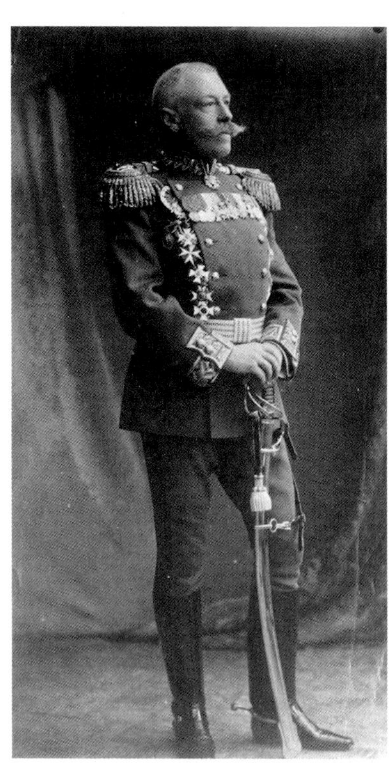

Fig. 2 Erich A. von Pistohlkors, ca. 1900. Photograph. Georges von Pistohlkors Archives, Holy Trinity Orthodox Seminary / Museum of Russian History, Jordanville.

1 Ferrand 1993, 134.

2 Polovtsov 1966, 1:230.

portrait of Olga from this period was commissioned from the fashionable painter and academy professor Konstantin Makovsky (1842-1915). At the height of his Russian career, Makovsky had already painted many members of the imperial family; the late Emperor Alexander II had acquired several of his works.[3] Signed and dated 1886, the painting shows Olga in a thick fur-trimmed housecoat, a bouquet of fresh flowers in her bodice, presumably there to conceal her pregnancy. With a symmetrical face, thin colored lips, straight nose, rosy cheekbones, and brown hair, she stares at the painter and illuminates the neutral background of the painting (pl. 1). She is a Petersburg beauty.

In addition to her charm, Pistohlkors's position facilitated Olga's entry into high society. She frequented the circles surrounding the powerful Grand Duchess Vladimir (1857-1920), the emperor's sister-in-law, whose palaces in Petersburg and Tsarskoye Selo had become the focal points of Petersburg social life. As early as 1894, when her husband was promoted to aide-de-camp to Grand Duke Vladimir (1847-1909), Olga began an affectionate correspondence with the grand duke,[4] while her exchanges with the grand duchess were more formal and worldly. Olga frequented the most sought-after salons in Petersburg, including that of Countess Marie Kleinmichel (1846-1931), a well-known hostess of high society. As proof, even Grand Duchess Vladimir, who did not appreciate some of the rumors the countess was spreading about one of her close friends, Madame Peters, asked Olga for advice: "If she wishes to continue in my good graces, I beg you to make it clear to her that all she has to do is undo the harm caused by her too-fast tongue, and as she is not lacking in wit, I have no doubt that she will know how to undo it."[5]

Emperor Nicholas II, who mentions the Pistohlkors couple in his diary as early as 1894, only occasionally met Erich von Pistohlkors, probably in what today would be considered a professional context. On the other hand, Olga, whom everyone called "Mama Liolia," quickly became part of the imperial family's inner circle, as evidenced by her presence at a joyous dinner in town on July 31, 1894, attended by Baron Konstantin Hartong, Grand Duke Nicholas (heir to the throne, as the future Nicholas II), the Vladimir family, the French ambassador Montebello and his wife, General Peters and his wife, the Obolenskys, Grand Duke Paul, and his friend and cousin Grand Duke Konstantin, who tells of having flirted a little with Olga.[6]

3 Wendy Salmond, Russell Martin, and Wilfried Zeisler, *Konstantin Makovsky: The Tsar's Painter in America and Paris* (Washington, DC: Hillwood Estate, Museum & Gardens in association with D. Giles, 2015).

4 GARF, F. 613, op. 1, D. 426.

5 GARF, F. 613, op. 1, D. 438, L. 30.

6 Nicholas II 2011-13, 1:165.

This social life also provided an opportunity for the young woman to socialize with many of the officers introduced to her by her husband, a cavalry captain in the same regiment as Grand Duke Paul (pl. 2). The youngest sibling of the future Emperor Alexander III, Paul was pampered by his mother, Empress Maria Alexandrovna (1824-1880). When he was born, his father, Emperor Alexander II, renamed the Cossack fort of Koryakovsky, on the banks of the Irtysh in Kazakhstan, Pavlodar in his honor. Grand Duke Paul, like his brother Sergei (1857-1905), received a very thorough education under the guidance of Admiral Dimitri Arseniev (1832-1915), as Countess Kleinmichel recalls in her memoirs.[7] She also paints a glowing portrait of the grand duke:

> Anyone who knew Grand Duke Paul knows what a noble, upright, and loyal character he had. His essentially harmonious nature rejected excess and lack of taste wholeheartedly. Very simple and very kind, extremely polite with everyone around him, he never lost his natural air of dignity, and although he did what he could to make people forget he was a grand duke, others were unable to forget that.[8]

The grand duke's military education also included the arts, in particular theater, music, and dance, which were complemented by several official and private stays abroad: in Germany (his mother was born Marie von Hessen und bei Rhein), in France (in Paris and on the Côte d'Azur), and in Italy. This last tour was organized to keep Paul away from his first love, Countess Vera Miloradovich, whose husband, a general, was constantly complaining to the emperor about the indecent situation.[9] A few photographs from family albums bear witness to Paul in his youth (fig. 3). And then, in 1881, Alexander II was assassinated.

Back in Russia and pursuing his military career under his brother's rule, the grand duke married Princess Alexandra of Greece (1870-1891) in 1889. She died prematurely in childbirth, leaving the young widower with two little children, Maria (1890-1958) and Dimitri (1891-1942). Meanwhile, by this time, Olga von Pistohlkors had already given birth to four children: Alexander (1885-1944), Olga (1886-1887), Olga (1888-1963), and Marianna (1890-1976). By the social standards of the time, she was an accomplished woman and wife. As for Grand Duke Paul, he was renowned for his charm, and for being a good dancer and excellent actor. The future Queen Maria of Romania (1875-1938) left a precise description of the thirty-one-year-old grand duke:

7 On the grand duke's youth and military training, see Dimitri Matlin, "Grand Duke Pavel Alexandrovich: 1860-1919," in Bott 2013a, 8-9.

8 Kleinmichel 1927, 242-43.

9 Matlin, "Grand Duke Pavel Alexandrovich," in Bott 2013a, 10.

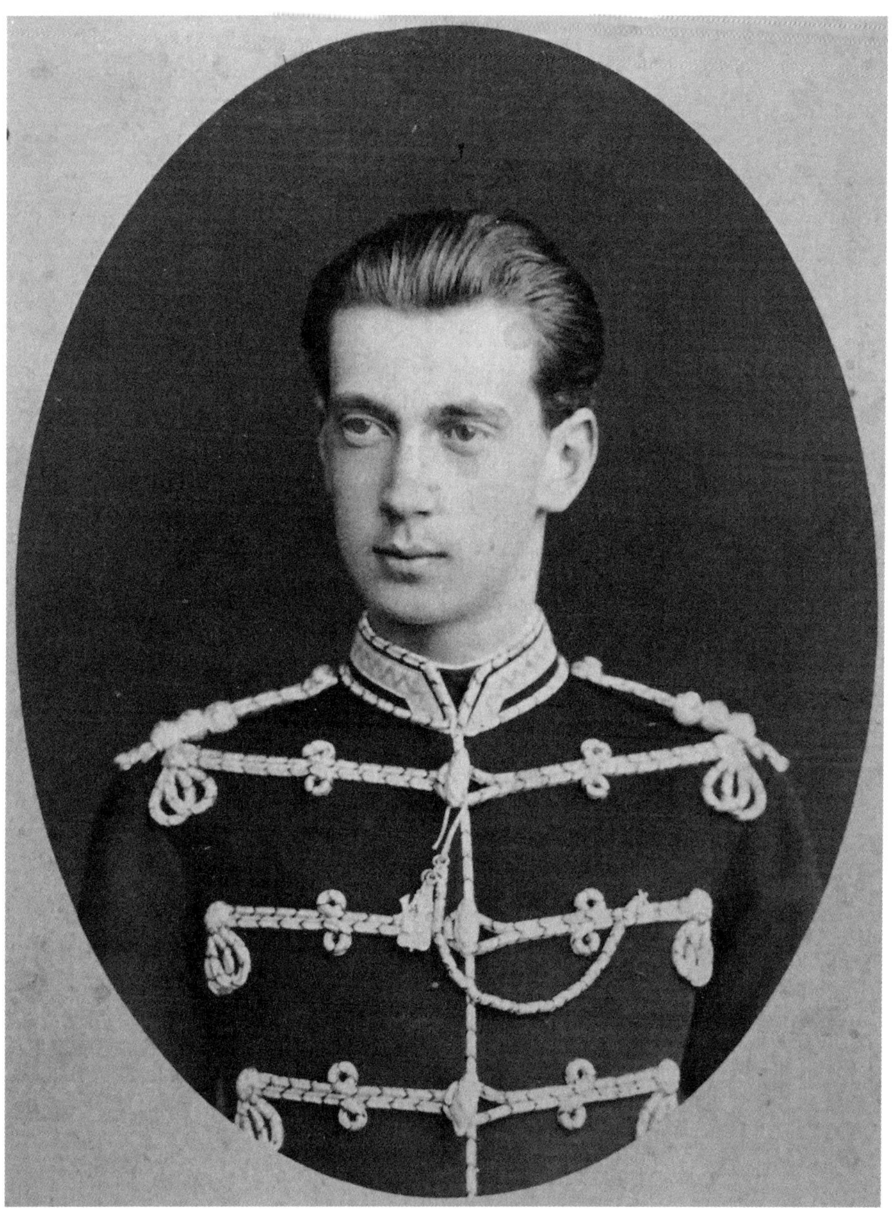

Fig. 3 Studio Levitsky, St. Petersburg. Grand Duke Paul Alexandrovich, ca. 1877. Photograph. Private collection.

> Uncle Paul stood out from his brothers for his more delicate appearance and admirably slim waist. Darker, more seductive, with extremely soft brown eyes, he had his mother's admirable hands. [...] Tall and slender, like a marble column, with luminous eyes and a caressing voice, he was full of understanding and benevolence, always ready to defend the weak, always fair, a charming comrade, cheerful and intelligent.[10]

By this time, the grand duke, devastated by the tragedy he had suffered, had become very close to the inner circle of Grand Duke Nicholas, who became emperor in 1894. The following year, Empress Alexandra told her brother, Ernest, Grand Duke of Hesse: "Paul often dines and lunches with us."[11]

Olga charmed Grand Duke Paul, making him forget the misfortune that had recently befallen him. The circumstances of their first meeting remain unclear, even if their respective positions meant they frequented the same circles, notably that of Grand Duchess Vladimir, where their romance blossomed. Only part of their correspondence is preserved in Russian archives, and it does not begin until 1899.[12] Nevertheless, we learn from that correspondence that Olga had been in a relationship with the grand duke, whom she affectionately nicknamed "Pucia," since 1893. It was at Krasnoye Selo, on the outskirts of St. Petersburg, the Russian army's famous training ground, that it all began, as Olga recalls in French in a missive she sent to the grand duke in 1899:

> I'm in Tsarskoe [*sic*] for you, we'll see each other, we'll love each other, we'll *have* each other! If Krasnoe is the *cradle* of our love, Tsarskoe is its *bed*. That's where you've come back to me, definitively and *for ever*![13]

It would be nice to imagine that the photograph signed and dated "Pavel / Tsarskoye Selo, 1893," preserved in the family albums, is the portrait the grand duke exchanged with Olga during one of these first encounters (fig. 4). This hypothesis is all the more appealing given that the photograph opposite it is of Olga and bears these handwritten words: "My thoughts, my feelings and my songs and my strengths. All are for you!" Taken from Tchaikovsky's fashionable romance after a text by Aleksey Apukhtin (1880), the stanza from which this extract is taken begins with "Whether my days be serene or sad, whether I disappear wasting my life, I'm sure of it to the grave" (fig. 5).

10 Marie de Roumanie 2014, 185-86.

11 Kleinpenning 2010, 225. Letter dated October 9/21, 1895. See also 188, 226.

12 GARF, F. 644, op. 1, D. 141-149.

13 GARF, F. 644, op. 1, D. 141, L. 42. Letter dated May 13, 1899.

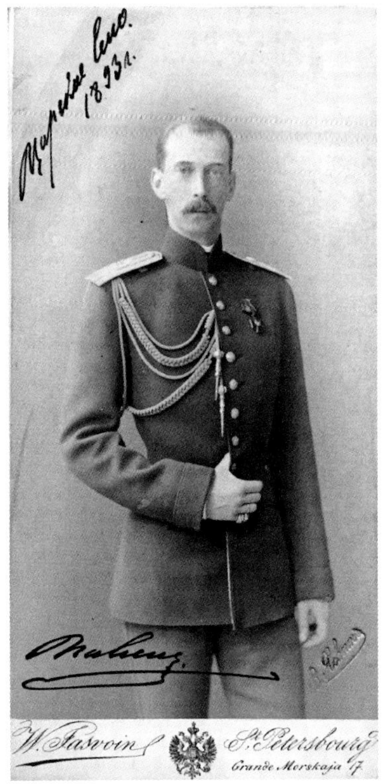

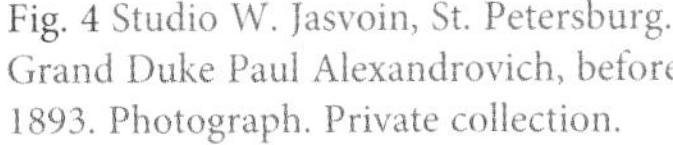

Fig. 4 Studio W. Jasvoin, St. Petersburg. Grand Duke Paul Alexandrovich, before 1893. Photograph. Private collection.

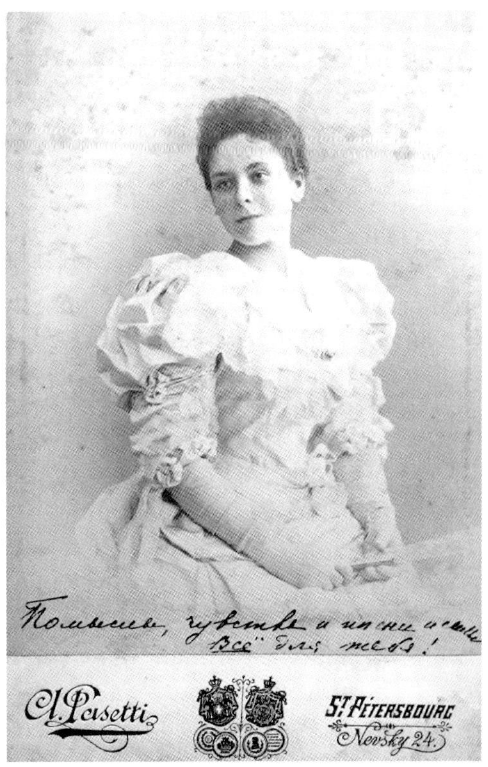

Fig. 5 Studio A. Pasetti, St. Petersburg. Olga von Pistohlkors, before 1893. Photograph. Private collection.

Their first child, Vladimir, was born in 1897, and this brought the adulterous relationship out into the open, even though it could hardly have been unknown to those close to the grand duke. In the eyes of the times, Olga found herself in a situation that genealogist and historian Jacques Ferrand rightly calls "indecent and disagreeable,"[14] particularly in relation to her husband and their children, whom she was accused of abandoning. The reference that immediately springs to mind is Tolstoy's heroine: Anna Karenina, who also belonged to the best of Petersburg society, was plunged some twenty years earlier into a comparable situation, which the author depicts with great naturalism. Forced into bitter negotiations with her husband, she cannot obtain a divorce without giving up her son.

From the point of view of the imperial family, the relationship between Olga von Pistohlkors and Grand Duke Paul posed several problems. Apart from the fact that she was a married woman (and even if she obtained a divorce), her status and rank prohibited any marriage with a member of

14 Ferrand 1993, 136.

the imperial family. The case of Grand Duke Michael Mikhailovich – who, having married Sophie von Merenberg in 1891, lost all his privileges and was forced into exile for life – certainly served as a precedent, but it did not help establish a satisfactory solution for the couple. Grand Duke Paul's deeply religious character could only add to his torment, unable to come to terms with his situation vis-à-vis his family and society. Morals had begun to evolve; but even if adventures outside marriage were tolerated, wanting to make them official required a certain courage in the heart of a society governed by norms stronger than the law. Far from being forced to commit suicide like Anna Karenina, Grand Duke Paul's mistress rebelled against social convention by urging him to take responsibility. Faced with yet another social humiliation, she wrote to him in 1900:

> Pucia, be a man, have courage where you need it, go higher and explain yourself once and for all, without secrecy and without fear. What more do you have to fear than what's happening? That is, that your indifference and carelessness to the affronts I endure cause me to suffer. Even if they spurn you, they will appreciate your moral courage to stand up for the woman you've loved for 7 years and who's being hurt thanks to you!

And to implore him further:

> Save me from the social downfall into which you are dragging me and my children![15]

Faced with this situation, and with the support of Grand Duke Vladimir, who was close to his younger brother Paul and had taken a liking to the unfortunate wife of his aide-de-camp, Pistohlkors agreed to the divorce. But the divorce still had to be authorized by the sovereign, and negotiations with Emperor Nicholas II (Grand Duke Paul's nephew) and influential family members were in vain. Olga reproached the grand duke for this for the umpteenth time, as this extract from a letter she wrote to him in 1901 suggests:

> You're right: one doesn't place "one's *mistress*, that abject being" next to one's children and brother, and Grand Duke Alexei, who has too much courage of his opinion, is wrong to keep Balletta next to the others. You see, I don't put myself on the same level as this lady. I don't mind: but you've deceived me again, you've lied to me again. That's what's so painful in my heart and what I'll never be able to console myself for! I'd tell you that any bad deed toward me was bad luck for

15 GARF, F. 644, op. 1, D. 141, L. 11. Letter dated January 27, 1900.

> you. The punishment came swiftly this time, for you fell ill almost immediately. May the good Lord preserve you from any further suffering and inspire you with a little more affection and sincerity.[16]

With his brother Vladimir as intermediary, Grand Duke Paul persevered and finally obtained the emperor's permission for Pistohlkors to divorce, in exchange for Paul's promise not to marry.[17] But then, despite the ban, despite the open opposition of several family members including the imperial couple and Grand Duke Sergei and his wife (who was the empress's sister), despite painful exchanges[18] (Grand Duke Sergei confided to his diary that his brother "causes one terrible pain"),[19] and, above all, despite his word, Grand Duke Paul eloped with the woman he wanted to make his wife. The lovers met secretly in Livorno, Italy, and were officially united in the Greek church there on September 27, 1902.[20] The scandal was immense, not only because it affected the imperial family, but especially because it revealed to Russian high society the emperor's lack of authority and his inability to enforce his decisions, even within his own family. How could this man, already criticized for being weak, govern one-sixth of the world's landmass when he was unable to impose the law in his own home? An analysis of the correspondence, diaries, and other memoirs, which all refer to the affair, reveals the way in which Nicholas II took advice from all the members of his family, who did not share the same opinion – far from it – before making any decision, whether private or public. In response in this case, the emperor was initially very severe, applying to Grand Duke Paul the sentences that his father, Alexander III, known for his authority, had imposed on Grand Duke Michael in 1891.

In addition to the disappointment his actions caused through his having lied,[21] Grand Duke Paul was stripped of his official functions and duties and forbidden to return to Russia, where his property was confiscated. Custody of his children was withdrawn: Maria and Dimitri, as well as their share of the inheritance, were placed under the guardianship of Grand Duke Sergei and his wife, Grand Duchess Elizabeth (1864-1918), who had requested it.[22] Grand Duke Sergei, who had been very close to his brother, felt betrayed and wrote of his deep bitterness in his diary on October 4: "And on top of that,

16 GARF, F. 644, op. 1, D. 143, L. 65. Letter dated November 29, 1901. Elizabeth Balletta, a famous actress at the Imperial Theater in St. Petersburg, had a long affair with Grand Duke Alexei Alexandrovich, one of Grand Duke Paul's brothers.

17 Maylunas and Mironenko 1996, 211.

18 Nicholas II 2011-13, I:643.

19 Efimov and Kovalskaya 2009, 567 (in French).

20 Nicholas II 2011-13, 1:701.

21 Efimov and Kovalskaya 2009, 586.

22 After Grand Duke Sergei's death in 1905, the children were the direct responsibility of the emperor.

he had given his word to the emperor not to marry! It's terrible!" even speaking of a "nightmare."[23] Nevertheless, both he and his wife pitied Grand Duke Paul, holding Olga largely responsible; the grand duchess called her a "devious, amoral" woman,[24] and Grand Duke Sergei dubbed her a "succubus."[25] The judgment of the dowager empress, the widow of Alexander III, was equally harsh about her brother-in-law:

> I kept hoping it was not true, that he was not going to marry, that his love for his children would prevail, but unfortunately he forgot everything, all his basic duties, his children, his country, his service, his honor, everything; he sacrificed everything for this stupid woman who is not worth it.[26]

A morganatic marriage is one thing, but breaking one's duty and one's word is quite another. Relations between Grand Duke Paul and his family became all the more tense as it soon became apparent that everything had been meticulously premeditated with a view to the sanctions he risked. Indeed, the aim was to obtain a divorce by any means necessary. Faced with the threat of exile, the grand duke had taken precautions and by August had arranged to have three million rubles at his disposal at a bank in Berlin.[27] While a comfortable material situation was assured for the grand duke and his morganatic wife, their respective families were particularly affected. Deprived of their children from their previous marriages, Paul and Olga wandered for several weeks before deciding to settle in Paris, where, far from the Court, they were able to blossom freely. The marriage being irrevocable, in 1904 Olga was granted a title of nobility by the Bavarian Court through the intervention of Grand Duke Paul. Henceforth, she would be known to the Parisian world as Countess von Hohenfelsen. Grand Duke Nicholas Mikhailovich (1859-1919) sarcastically christened his cousin "Paul von Hohenfelsen."[28] At the time of the Franco-Russian Alliance, Paris welcomed these new Russian nationals with open arms:

> She [Olga] soon made friends, for the morganatic marriage heated people's imaginations, and the grand duke was pitied for his exile, but admired the woman who had chained him. The mystery of their love was revealed to Parisians.[29]

23 Efimov and Kovalskaya 2009, 611.

24 *Ibid.*, 612.

25 *Ibid.*, 614.

26 Maylunas and Mironenko 1996, 212.

27 Efimov and Kovalskaya 2009, 614.

28 Vogel 2005, 711.

29 Chambrun 1941, 223.

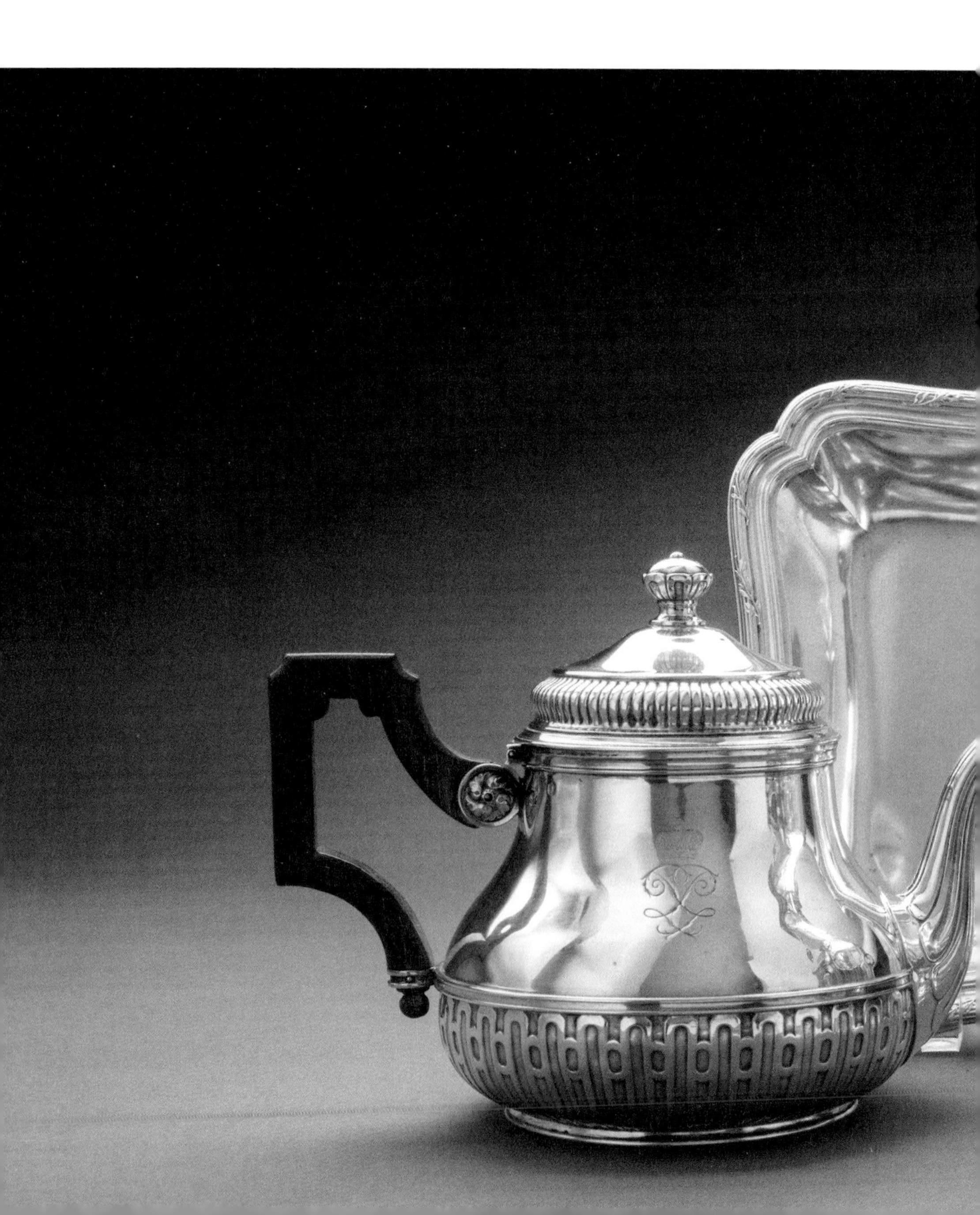

SETTLING IN PARIS

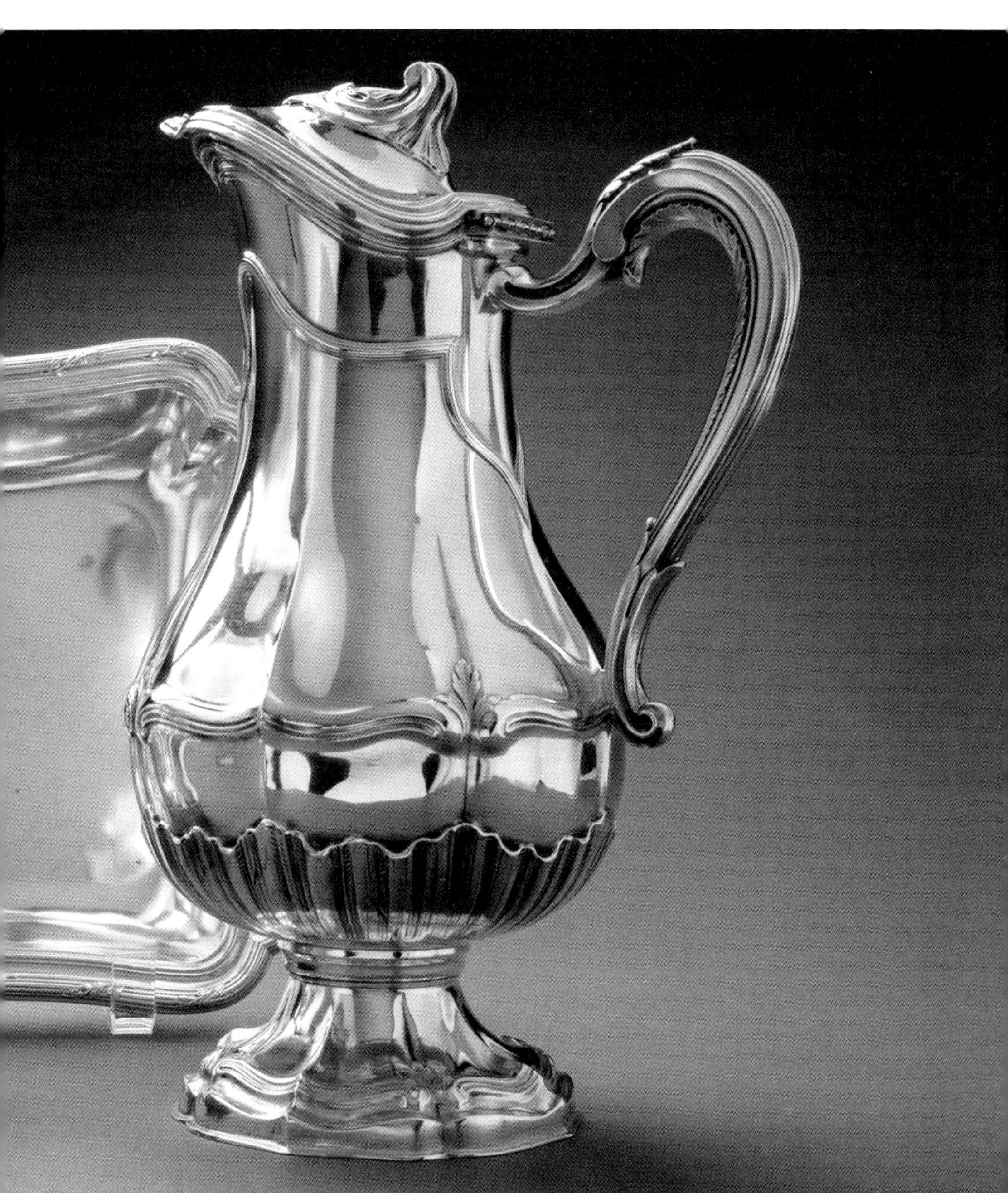

While the couple secretly prepared for their wedding, Olga distanced herself from the Court and left Russia, perhaps with the aim of avoiding suspicion. Both her diary and correspondence bear witness to months of wandering around Europe as the scandal of her union with Grand Duke Paul unfolded in Russia. In the first volume of her diary in exile, we learn that Olga left St. Petersburg at the beginning of 1902 for a long journey that began in Italy, with a stay in Florence from February to May, followed by a period in Germany and then a short sojourn at the Ritz in Paris, where she arrived at the beginning of September. After the couple got married in Livorno, they settled for a longer period in Florence. Olga wrote in her diary: "The weather is mild and calm, and so is my soul… We leave tonight. May God grant us a pleasant stay in Florence! I adore my Paul."[1]

The honeymoon continued until April 1903 in the idyllic setting of what Olga called the Villa Boutourline in Florence, most likely the place known today as the Villa Careggi, which, with its gardens, dates back to the fifteenth century. They then traveled to the Ritz in Paris and subsequently to Germany in late spring. As the summer drew to a close, they decided where to settle. The time for negotiations had passed, and the penalties promised by the emperor had been confirmed. A return to Russia was thus impossible for the time being, so the couple chose France as their new home.

In addition to the traditional appeal of the City of Lights to the Russian and international elite, the choice of Paris was all the more appropriate given the large Russian colony living there; it would allow the couple to keep in touch with their compatriots. Grand Duke Vladimir and his wife regularly made Paris their home, staying at the Hôtel InterContinental on rue Castiglione,[2] which was particularly well placed in the heart of Parisian luxury, while Grand Duke Alexei Alexandrovich (1850-1908) had rented an apartment on avenue Gabriel since 1896. Paris was also the summer retreat of the collector Alexis de Hitrov (fig. 6). Close to the imperial family, Hitrov was court master to Grand Duke Vladimir between 1897 and 1901. It was probably during this period that he befriended Olga. Hitrov, like his peers in Paris, was a patron of the luxury goods and art industries. He is as well-known for the costume parties[3] he hosted at 43, avenue du Bois, and for the receptions he later organized in his apartment at 50, avenue Marceau, as for his collection of eighteenth-century French art and British portraits.[4] This taste was shared by the great Parisian art lovers of his time, such as Madame Édouard André, whom Olga met in 1904 at the latest.

1 GARF, F. 613, op. 1, D. 13, L. 152.

2 Pascal Boissel and Marc Gaillard, "L'Hôtel InterContinental," in Centorame and Andia 2005, 227-28.

3 *L'Art et la mode*, no. 51 (1886): 611.

4 P. Weiner, "La Collection de feu A. Z. de Hitrovo à Saint-Pétersbourg," *Starye Gody* (December 1912): 3-36.

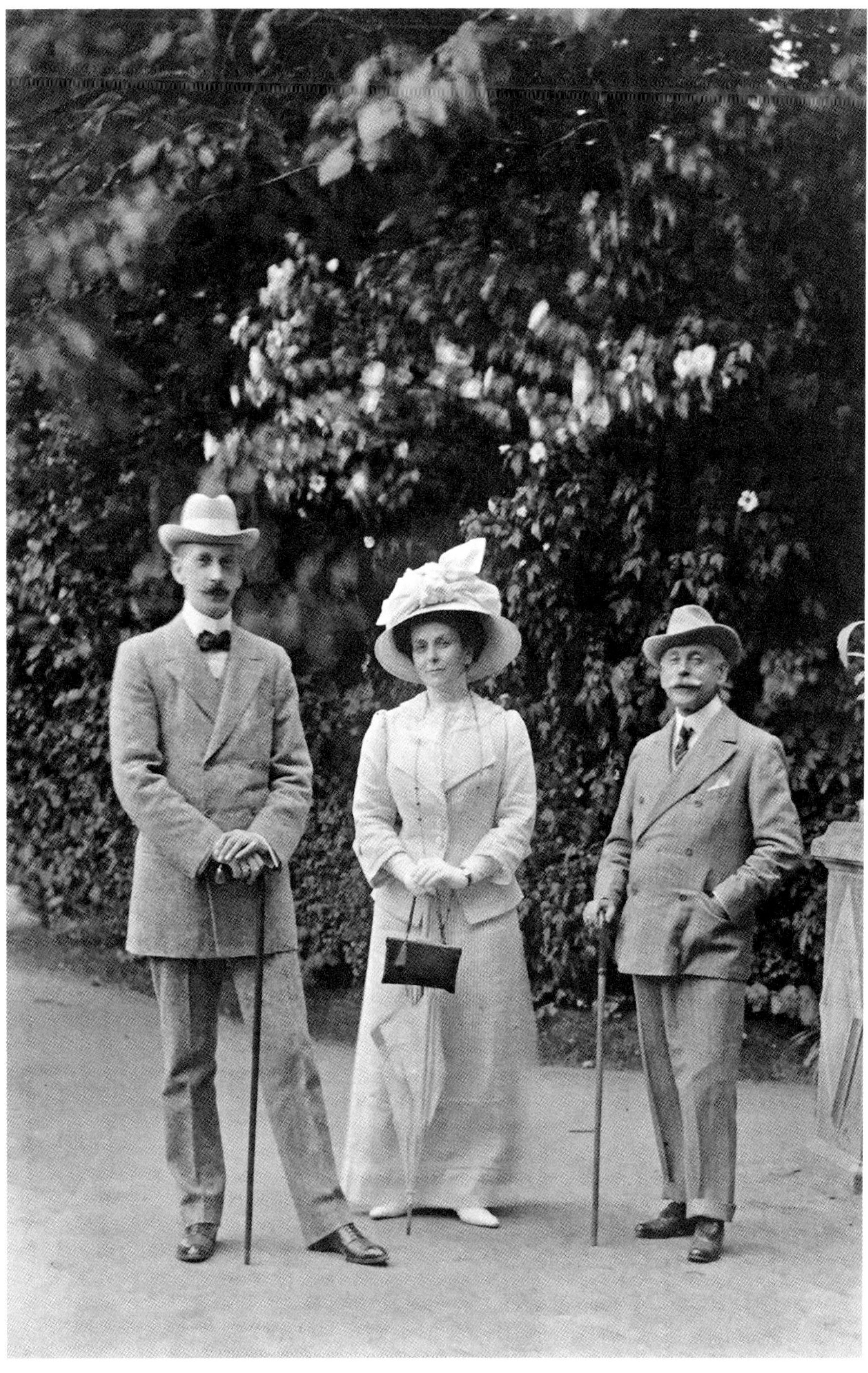

Fig. 6 Countess von Hohenfelsen, Grand Duke Paul and Alexis de Hitrov, ca. 1912. Photograph. Private collection.

As the Orient Express bore the newlyweds to Paris,[5] the city was immersed in the Russophile euphoria of the Franco-Russian Alliance. Russia had become extremely fashionable since the various agreements concerning it had been ratified in the 1890s. Being a member of the imperial family in Paris, a city that the grand duke had visited many times, provided a master key to perfect social integration, something that Olga desperately wanted: here, she would be able to be treated like a grand duchess, a status forbidden to her in Russia.

As soon as she arrived, she appeared with the name "H.I.H. the Grand Duchess Paul of Russia" in the order books of the famous Lyon silk manufacturer Tassinari & Chatel.[6] From the firm, she ordered meters of taffeta to decorate the apartment the couple had just moved into at 11, avenue d'Iéna. This address appears on the letterhead of her correspondence as early as September 9/22, 1903. *Le Figaro* described the apartment as a "very elegant mezzanine floor."[7] And *Les Modes* added that the countess "only opens her salons to intimates."[8] The neighborhood was extremely fashionable. Opposite, at no. 10, was the mansion built for Prince Roland Bonaparte between 1892 and 1899, while Olga's new address was in the same block as the mansion of Charles Ephrussi, famous collector and owner of the no less famous *Gazette des beaux-arts*.

Decorating it correctly was a priority, and in keeping with the social norms of the time, this task fell to Olga, who spent her whole life practicing this art, in a very diligent and committed way. Her library included Henry Havard's monumental *L'Art dans la maison: Grammaire de l'ameublement* (1884),[9] "a work halfway between a practical manual and a treatise on aesthetics"[10] on how to present one's home interior, a bible that every good mistress of the household should own and consult. In the chapter on "Settling In," Havard writes:

> Now that we are in possession of a general education, complete enough to enable us to decorate an apartment and arrange furnishings, without fear of committing too many heresies, it seems that we could not make better use of our freshly acquired science than to apply the whole of our new knowledge to the various rooms that make up a dwelling.[11]

5 GARF, F. 613, op. 1, D. 15, L. 21.

6 ATC, Livre de commissions, September 16, 1903.

7 *Le Figaro*, February 18, 1905.

8 *Les Modes*, no. 50 (February 1905): 10.

9 TsGALI, F. 254, op. 1, D. 5, L. 56.

10 Rossella Froissart Pezone, "Henry Havard," in Philippe Sénéchal and Claire Barbillon, eds., *Dictionnaire critique des historiens de l'art actifs en France de la Révolution à la Première Guerre mondiale*, http://www.inha.fr/fr/ressources/publications/publications-numeriques/dictionnaire-critique-des-historiens-de-l-art/Havard-henry.html.

11 Havard 1884, 319.

From this period on, Olga's diary is full of information about this first Parisian move and her decorating requirements, as suggested by the "very urgent" note on her order placed with Tassinari & Chatel. Back in 1892, Olga and Pistohlkors had already called on this firm for their Petersburg furnishings (see pl. 29). Well-informed about Parisian taste and commerce by her peers in Russia and her French connections, Olga knew to whom to turn in order to arrange the details of the decoration of the family apartment. As early as September 1903, for example, she visited Cuvillier, an important commission agent with connections to several grand dukes, as well as the watchmaker Planchon and lamp maker and bronze artist Gagneau, both of whom had been supplying Russian customers with numerous objets d'art since the 1880s.[12] It was from the latter's stock that the sconces for the bedroom were selected. In addition to silks and bronzes, choices had to be made with regard to the furniture for each room. For this, they called in a famous decorator and manufacturer of fine furniture, Jansen, successor to the cabinetmaker Zwiener, who had supplied sumptuous pieces for the imperial palace in Gatchina.[13] The series of Louis XV – style giltwood sofas and armchairs, trimmed with green damask, that Olga sold in 1923 was probably part of this first Parisian furnishing.[14] Olga also visited the Parisian cabinetmaking district, la rue du Faubourg Saint-Antoine, and notably Krieger's, but found nothing, and had to satisfy herself with ordering a table from the Louvre.[15] In her diary, she also mentions the Paris branch of Maple (established at 5, rue Boudreau), a British furniture institution that Grand Duke Paul knew very well. In 1897-99, the firm had refurbished part of the apartments in his Petersburg palace in modern taste. These were known as "the English rooms" and comprised a lounge, billiard room, study, and adjoining lavatory.[16]

Among the Russian court's long-standing and privileged suppliers in Paris was one of the temples of luxury, the famous l'Escalier de Cristal store, located since 1872 at the corner of la rue Scribe and la rue Auber.[17] This store, where Grand Duke Paul had been a customer since 1881, had a way of operating inherited from the ancien régime (before the French Revolution), whose taste had been shaped by the merchants of luxury (*marchands merciers*). L'Escalier de Cristal was one of their most brilliant heirs in the nineteenth century. Offering its clientele tableware, a variety of objets d'art, and a selection of furniture that was constantly renewed in line

12 Zeisler 2014b, 344.

13 *Ibid.*, 358.

14 Paley sale, Paris, December 5, 1923, lot 76.

15 This is probably a reference to the Magasins du Louvre, which had a furniture department like most department stores of the time.

16 RGIA, F. 526, op. 1, D. 218, L. 42-51.

17 Zeisler 2014b, 341.

with changing trends, this business heralded what is now known as a concept store, although the goods produced exclusively or selected by the Pannier family, who had run the business since 1852, never included clothing. The Pannier brothers, Henri and Georges, who had taken over from their father in 1885, personally took care of their best customers, and one of them was among the first people the countess turned to when she sought to refurbish her new apartment.

Crockery and other items required for the move were selected from specialist stores in Paris or ordered from abroad. Some of the tableware and glassware was chosen from stocks at the large E. Bourgeois porcelain and glassware depot on rue Drouot, while the silverware was ordered from the famous goldsmith on rue de la Paix, André Aucoc.[18] A gilded porcelain tea service with green festoons was delivered in June 1903 by Thomas Goode & Co., supplier to the British court. Local and foreign courts had been turning to this London institution for elegant tableware since 1827, the year of its establishment.[19]

All that remained was to install and arrange everything. These were times for experimentation and exchange, which Olga shared with her friend of impeccable taste, the collector Hitrov. On September 3, 1903, the family friend, with whom she maintained a correspondence in French, was at the home of the countess and the grand duke; the discussion revolved around the furniture and objects Olga was "arranging," while evoking her suppliers: Jansen, Maple, *L'Escalier de Cristal*, Tassinari…

This Parisian home, which was far more modest than the grand duke's palace in St. Petersburg, was nevertheless the couple's first home, where they were able to live and watch their family grow. Two daughters, Irina and Natalie, were born there, in 1903 and 1905 respectively.[20] With her mother visiting her regularly, and helped by a home-school teacher, Hortense Judlin, Olga led a happy family life with the grand duke and his loyal aide-de-camp, Captain Alexander Efimovitch, the couple's neighbor at 26, avenue d'Iéna.[21]

However, this Parisian harmony was soon disrupted by tragic events in Russia: the war with Japan and the ensuing first revolution. In this regard, the Parisian society press commented on the situation for the countess: "for some time now, painfully moved by the misfortunes that have befallen Russia, she [Olga von Hohenfelsen] has kept away from society events, in an intimacy that general respect strives not to disturb."[22]

18 *Ibid.*, 326.

19 GARF, F. 644, op. 1, D. 271, L. 1, 2.

20 GARF, F. 644, op. 1, D. 3 L. 1, 2. Birth certificates.

21 Ferrand 1993, 7.

22 *Le Figaro*, February 20, 1905.

As a patriot, Olga offered her help by sending several parcels to imperial charities. On March 14, 1904, she wrote in her diary the full text of the telegram she received from Tsarskoye Selo: "Her Majesty Empress Alexandra Feodorovna has commanded me to convey her sincere thanks for the clothing for the wounded; we received the boxes yesterday. Princess Elizabeth Obolensky."

In addition to expressing her commitment, this betrayed her desire to win the empress's good graces. In 1905, Russia was plunged into the chaos of revolution. In her diary, Olga transcribed the contents of a telegram received from Grand Duchesses Maria Pavlovna (Grand Duke Vladimir's wife, sometimes called "Maria Pavlovna the Elder"; Grand Duke Paul's daughter Maria also came to be known as Grand Duchess Maria Pavlovna) and Elizabeth Feodorovna (married to Grand Duke Sergei), demonstrating the imperial family's anxiety in the face of upheaval: "Hopefully new ministry will restore calm. Were notified last minute. Impossible to give more precise details. Fondly, Maria."

A few months earlier, in February, the entire Parisian press had reported on the spectacular assassination of Grand Duke Sergei in Moscow, which illustrated the atmosphere in Russia at the time. The grand duke's death was not only violent but also had a double impact on Grand Duke Paul, who lost both his brother, with whom he had never been able to make peace, and the guardian of his children. Such was the tragedy within the imperial family that Emperor Nicholas II authorized his uncle to return for the funeral and restored to him the titles, ranks, and functions that Paul had lost since his marriage. The grand duke's presence was all the more important as he brought with him a package his brother had entrusted to him thirteen years earlier, containing his last wishes regarding the location of his tomb and the uniform he wished to wear there.[23]

The Parisian press nevertheless noted the humiliation suffered by Olga, who accompanied her husband but was forbidden to cross the Russian border.[24] Grand Duke Paul arrived in Russia angrily, as numerous witnesses revealed. He reproached the emperor for having once again changed his mind.[25] In practical terms, it was Olga who was deemed guilty and was condemned. The unexpected confirmation of her status as an exile for as long as she was married to the grand duke made Paris the couple's main place of residence. The notion of a long period of residence here, implying a grand-ducal lifestyle, and the concomitant growth of the family, probably made it clear to the couple of the need for a more imposing residence.

23 Maylunas and Mironenko 1996, 260.

24 See *L'Aurore*, February 20, 1905; *Le Temps*, February 20, 1905; *Le Radical*, February 21, 1905; *La Croix*, February 21, 1905; *Le Petit Parisien*, February 22, 1905.

25 Maylunas and Mironenko 1996, 267.

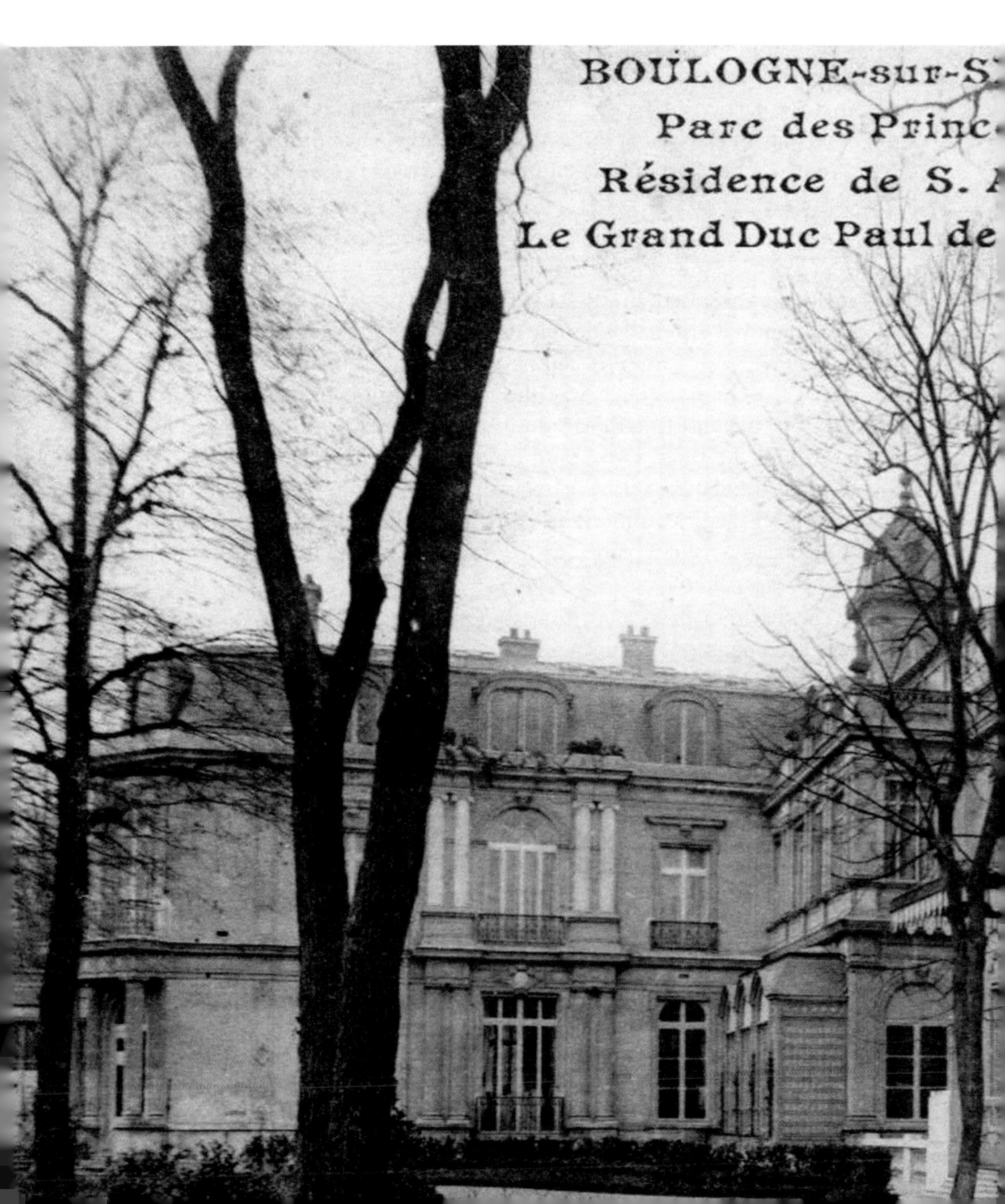
BOULOGNE-sur-S
Parc des Princ
Résidence de S. A
Le Grand Duc Paul de

A NEW ADDRESS: THE YUSUPOV MANSION AT THE PARC DES PRINCES

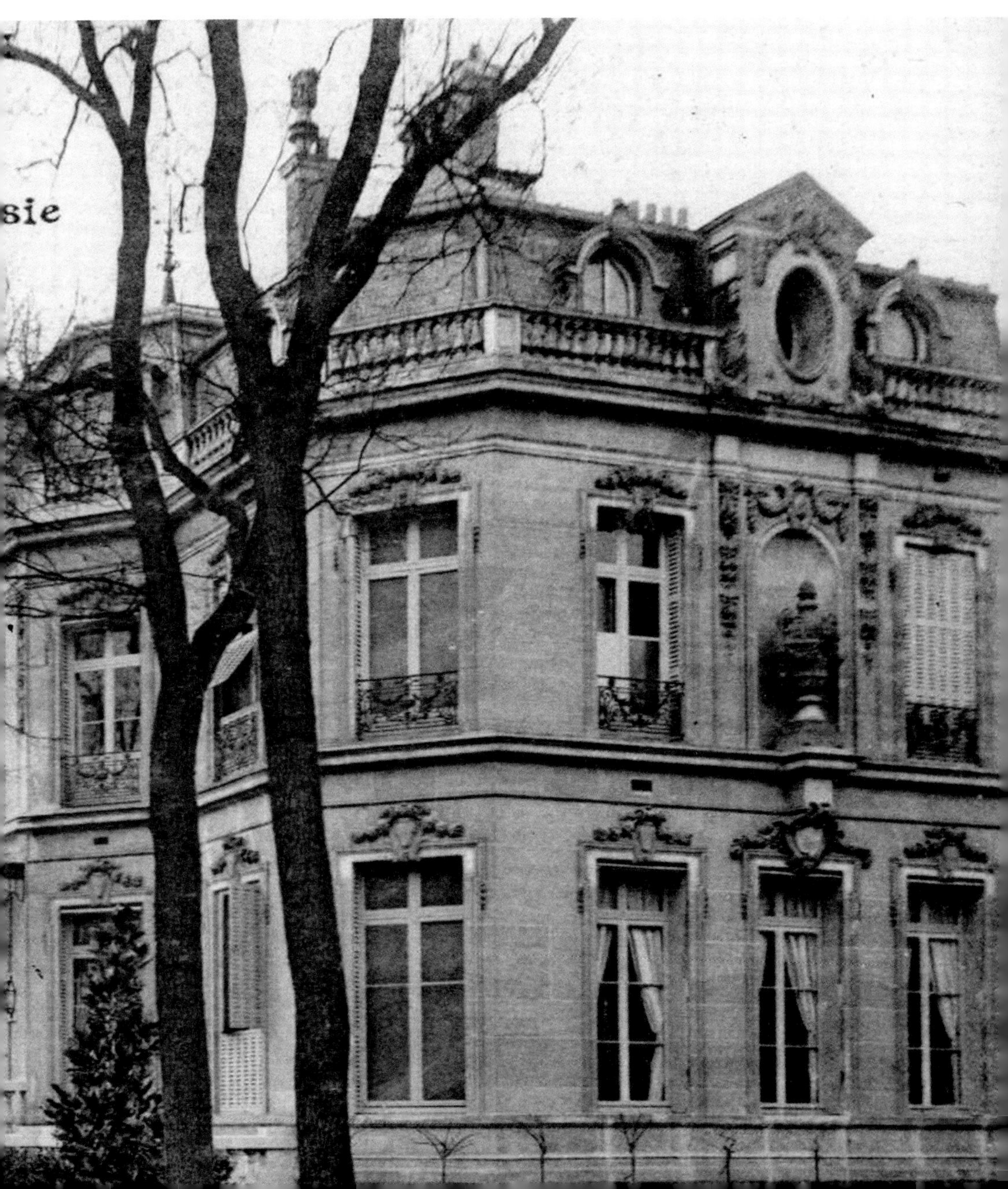

Le Figaro announced in its society columns on February 8, 1907:

> H.I.H. the Grand Duke Paul of Russia and the Countess von Hohenfelsen inaugurated their magnificent home on le boulevard Victor-Hugo, in Boulogne, with a dinner to which they had invited only close friends. The guests were Prince and Princess Baryatinsky, comte and comtesse R. de Leusse, Mr. and Mrs. de Bénardaky, comte and comtesse Brevern de La Gardie, Miss Vassiltchikov, comte de Turenne, comte Kutaisov, Mr. de Etter, Mr. Dubois de L'Estang and Colonel Efimovitch. The dinner was not followed by a reception.[1]

One can imagine the elegance of the evening, in the house's dining room, at the foot of an Aubusson tapestry placed above the fireplace, everyone seated at a table richly laid with silverware acquired beginning in 1903 from the Parisian goldsmiths Aucoc and Risler & Carré (pl. 3). The last deliveries from this order were made in 1907, in time for the inauguration. This precious crockery, perfectly cataloged in the archives, consisted of 168 silver plates and 60 vermeil dessert plates by Aucoc, tea sets, and other accessories, all complemented by cutlery and decorative pieces, which were probably older and from Russia, some by the Petersburg silversmith Gratchev. The elegant Louis XVI flatware from Risler & Carré was presented in an oak case bearing the crowned monogram of the grand duke.

The history of the mansion that was to become the couple's home, today the Cours Dupanloup, is relatively well documented (fig. 7). This house, like the ceremonial crockery, is a typical example of the lifestyle of Parisian and Russian high society during the Belle Époque. The grand-ducal history of the residence began in 1905. In August, while the countess was staying in Germany, Efimovitch searched for a house for the couple in Versailles or Chantilly. These options were highly aristocratic and reflected a keen interest in the France of the ancien régime. At the time, Versailles was the refuge or holiday resort of the great names of elegant society, foremost among them Robert de Montesquiou (1855-1921), as evidenced by the construction of the luxurious Trianon-Palace between 1908 and 1910 by the architect René Sergent.[2] The Third Republic also received Emperor Nicholas II with great pomp in the palace of the kings of France during his official visit in 1896. However, Versailles appears to have been quickly dismissed for lack of opportunity, and efforts were concentrated on Chantilly, another fashionable location. At the end of the nineteenth century, before the château was bequeathed to the Institut de France in 1886 and the death of the duc d'Aumale in 1897, a number of grand dukes and celebrities had been regular guests at the estate,

1 The event is also mentioned in the columns of *Le Gaulois*.

2 Gendre 2003.

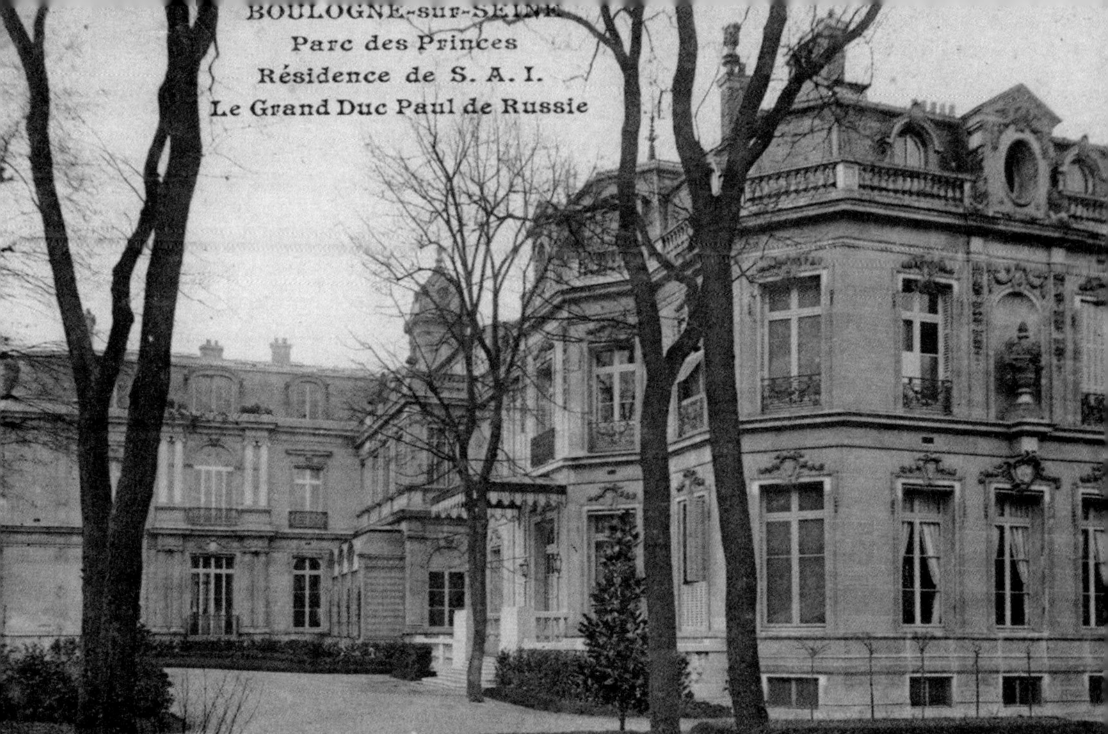

Fig. 7 Residence of Grand Duke Paul Alexandrovich and Countess von Hohenfelsen (former Yusupov mansion) in Boulogne-Billancourt, ca. 1905. Postcard. Private collection.

giving them the opportunity to admire its priceless collections and take part in major hunting expeditions.

Back in Paris in September, the couple went to Gouvieux, a town near Chantilly, accompanied by Efimovitch, who received a Bréguet watch from the countess, presumably to thank him for the property searches he had undertaken. In November, *Le Figaro* announced that the grand duke, the countess, their children Vladimir and Irina, and Captain Efimovitch "are shortly expected in Chantilly."[3] Autumn also saw Olga scouting out other locations around Paris, and in October she mentioned a mansion in the Parc des Princes. Several visits followed, and after one she wrote in her diary: "the garden is fine." Following another visit, Olga met the famous decorator Georges Hoentschel on November 27,[4] presumably to discuss the design of the house.

This was not the house's first "Russian period". The Hôtel Yusupov, as the countess called it in her diary, was built in 1860-61 by the architect Antoine-Martin Garnaud – his final work – on a plot of land acquired in 1859 by Princess Zinaida Ivanovna Narishkina (1809-1893), widow of Prince Boris N. Yusupov (1794-1849) and the new wife, since 1861, of Count Charles de Chauveau (1829-1889). The mansion, surrounded by modest gardens and a

3 *Le Figaro*, November 3, 1905.

4 Kisluk-Grosheide, Krohn, and Leben 2013.

few outbuildings, is a perfect example of the suburban holiday architecture that developed around Paris during the reign of Napoleon III. Its ashlar facade is decorated with sculptures from a variety of sources, mainly borrowed from the reign of Louis XVI, and is a fine example of eclectic architecture. Under the enlightened direction of its first owners, who were both enthusiasts and collectors, the house demonstrated a quest for excellence in terms of decoration. The initial layout was the result of a collaboration with the upholsterer and decorator Jules Duval[5] (1827-1887), whose company was later joined by that of the famous furniture manufacturer Krieger. Awarded the *Légion d'honneur* in 1879, Duval participated in the Great Exhibition in London (1851) and the Paris Expositions (1855, 1867, 1878), winning numerous awards and international recognition, as demonstrated by some of the commissions he received from Grand Duke Vladimir of Russia in 1883.[6] Duval worked with the finest representatives of the Parisian art industries, and some of the textiles were supplied by his regular collaborator Braquenié. The marble work came from Dupuis & Parfonry, a leading Parisian firm in this field, while the decorative paintings were the work of Jules Petit. As for the decorative bronzes for the furniture, most came from Chaumont, Morizot, Chabrié, and Paillard, all firms with a well-established reputation.

At the cutting edge of Parisian taste during the Second Empire, the Yusupov mansion consisted of a three-story main building, with the ground floor containing the reception rooms, vestibule, dining room, several drawing rooms, and other study rooms. A large room with a return gallery, known as the Salon Henri II, housed Princess Zinaida Ivanovna's collection of antique tapestries, including a Flemish piece from the fifteenth century and others from the Louis XIII and Louis XIV periods. A first renovation was carried out in 1871, following the Franco-Prussian War and the troubles of the Commune. The entire house was then restored under the direction of architect Paul Murison between 1885 and 1887. After Princess Yusupov's death in 1893, the mansion and its contents were inherited by her family living in St. Petersburg, in particular Prince Nicolas Yusupov (1883-1908), the eldest son of her granddaughter Zinaida Nikolaevna (1861-1939).

In 1905, Countess von Hohenfelsen and Grand Duke Paul discovered a residence that had been empty for more than ten years. Once it was acquired, Georges Hoentschel was entrusted with the task of bringing it up-to-date. Hoentschel's career[7] is a typical example of a success story from the Third Republic. From a relatively modest background, he became the director of the Leys decorating maison, which was well established in the Parisian furniture

5 Arch. Nat. LH 883/70.

6 Zeisler 2014b, 102.

7 Daniëlle Kisluk-Grosheide and Ulrich Leben, "Georges Hoentschel and His World," in Kisluk-Grosheide, Krohn, and Leben 2013, 19-41.

world and worked for the greatest names in French and international aristocracy. On the death of his father, Hoentschel had come under the protection of his mother's cousin Ernest Leys, head of the family firm, which was based on le boulevard de la Madeleine. In 1892, Hoentschel took over the management, and he gradually became one of the most prominent artistic figures in Paris, working for the duc de Gramont, his friend Robert de Montesquiou, the comtesse de Ganay, the king of Greece, the emperor of Japan… To this list, we must now add Countess von Hohenfelsen and Grand Duke Paul for their Boulogne home. The first meetings between the countess and the decorator took place toward the end of 1905, when Hoentschel was at the height of his career, having designed the pavilion for the new Musée des arts décoratifs in Paris and exhibited as far afield as the United States. Exchanges between the two increased and lasted until 1907. They involved a number of other people, including the friend, adviser, and collector Hitrov, who accompanied Olga to antique and other dealers throughout 1906 to find elements that would harmonize with the decor Hoentschel designed as a tribute to eighteenth-century France. In April, Hitrov was asked to find "decorative panels" for the future dining room. A few days later, he took Olga to two antique dealers to see some Gobelins tapestries. Hitrov, the countess, and the grand duke met a few days later at Hoentschel's to look at the panels and textiles before going on to the antique dealers, including Stettiner.

Of Polish origin, Henri Julius Stettiner (1842-1913) was listed in 1905 at 8, rue de Sèze, as specified in his advertisements, which describe his specialties: antique paintings, furnishings and tapestries, as well as objets d'art and curios.[8] It was at this time that he sold some Sèvres porcelains to Count Moïse de Camondo.[9] The family business was taken over by his children Alphonse (1876-1966), Oscar (1878-1948), and Adèle (1880-1963), of Franco-British nationality, under the name Stettiner & Cie, and disappeared in the throes of the Second World War after the gallery closed in 1939. The Stettiner family's assets suffered the same tragic fate as many other Jewish businesses in Paris.

During the Belle Époque, the Opéra district was home to many of the antique dealers and merchants to which Countess von Hohenfelsen turned to furnish and decorate her new house. One of them was Laurent-E. Perdreau Successeur (known under this name in 1894). Under the name Laurent, this firm of "Curiosities, Works of Art – Antique Furnishings – Snuffboxes and Miniatures"[10] was established in 1891 at 2, rue Meyerbeer.[11] In 1886, Paul

8 *Portraits peints et dessinés du* xiii*e au* xvii*e siècle*, exh. cat. (Paris: Bibliothèque nationale, 1907), 209. See also *Les Arts*, no. 39 (March 1905).

9 Legrand 2016, 30, 34.

10 Advertisement. *L'Art*, no. 713 (February 1st, 1894).

11 RGIA, F. 468, op. 13, D. 197, L. 3.

Eudel mentioned this renowned firm in his work on the world of curiosities and published a few biographical details. Since the beginning of the nineteenth century, Laurent, which had kept its name despite a succession of owners, had been one of the illustrious showcases of the Palais-Royal, the heart of the Parisian luxury market. The house was first taken over by Goupy, then in 1857 by the merchant Guénot, nicknamed "the Lazare Duvaux of our century"[12] in reference to one of the greatest merchants of luxury during the reign of Louis XV, whose ledger had just been published by Louis Courajod in 1873. At the time, the house counted the most important collectors among its clients, including the Rothschilds, and expanded its activities. Initially known for selling "gold miniatures, fans, boxes and *bonbonnières*,"[13] the company expanded into the antique furniture trade. In partnership with his son-in-law Perdreau, Guénot, who came from a Parisian dynasty of merchants and goldsmiths, developed the business by renting a new space on rue Meyerbeer. Around 1882, the historic shop in the Palais-Royal was sold and Laurent moved its business to the new fashionable district, following the example of many other artistic and commercial institutions in the Palais-Royal, such as l'Escalier de Cristal and the jeweler Frédéric Boucheron, which had moved to the corner of la rue Auber and la rue Scribe in 1872 and to la place Vendôme in 1893 respectively. By the time the countess and grand duke came to Laurent, its clientele already included Emperors Alexander III and Nicholas II,[14] as well as several grand dukes.

On May 16, 1906, the couple admired some Gobelins-covered furniture at Laurent's (fig. 8). Laurent's bill came to 25,000 francs, a considerable sum for the time.

The search did not stop there, and the tour of antique dealers and merchants continued, interspersed with meetings and lengthy discussions with Hoentschel, the suppliers, and the inescapable Hitrov. With Hitrov, indeed, Olga went to Taburet, as she called it in her diary, to see a piece of Directoire furniture (from the late 1790s) and to Lévy for a chandelier, probably the antique dealer L. Lévy, who specialized in the eighteenth century; the sale of his collection held in the wake of his death took place in 1917.[15]

Boin-Taburet, located at 3, rue Pasquier, was founded by Émile Taburet (1823-1880), who distinguished himself in the curiosities trade. In 1879, he passed the business on to his son-in-law, goldsmith Georges Boin (1849-1911), who also sold antiques, particularly goldsmiths' and jewelers' pieces.[16] At the beginning of the twentieth century, the company distinguished

12 Eudel 1886, 219.

13 *Ibid.*, 220.

14 RGIA, F. 468, op. 13, D. 1878, L. 2.

15 Sale Paris, Galerie Georges Petit, June 18-19, 1917.

16 Zeisler 2014b, 329.

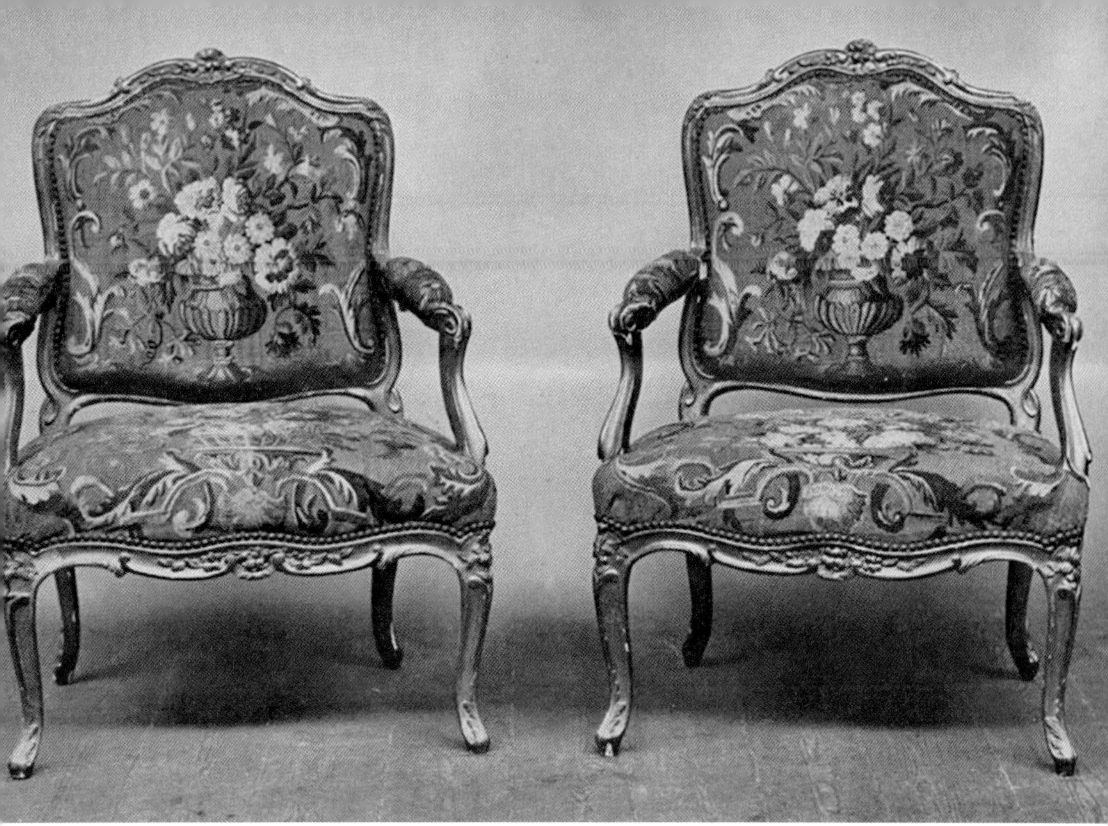

Fig. 8 Armchairs from a suite in gilded wood, covered in tapestry, France, Louis XV period. This suite probably corresponds to the one acquired from the antique dealer Laurent-Perdreau. Current location unknown. Hillwood Estate, Museum & Gardens, Archives and Special Collections, Washington, DC.

itself in this field: "the sale of antiques, furniture, porcelain, bronzes, engravings, Louis XIV, Louis XV and Louis XVI paintings, as well as collectible items of all styles, of which the largest assortment can be found at the gallery."[17] (fig. 9).

Olga had visited the Taburet galleries as early as 1899. In 1903, after receiving a gift from the store, the very next day, October 27, she rushed into the shop that was to become one of her favorite addresses. On December 21, 1905, for example, she wrote in her diary that she had seen "splendid objects" at Taburet.

In addition to the antique works that would give the countess's residence its aristocratic cachet, research – always undertaken in close discussion with the decorator, as demonstrated by the regular entries in Olga's diary – was carried out among the great contemporary manufacturers. They were able to produce works that harmonized perfectly with the style of *antique objets d'art*, with the aim of creating veritable period rooms as were displayed in the decorative arts museums or retrospective exhibitions of the time.

17 *La Ville lumière* 1909, 441.

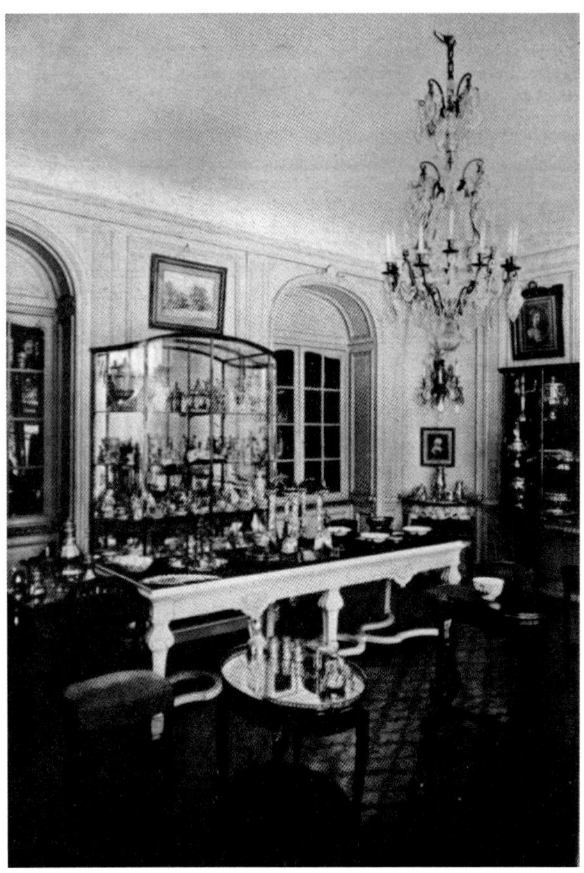

Fig. 9 Interior of the Boin-Taburet galleries, rue Pasquier, Paris. *La Ville lumière* 1909, 440. Private collection.

Many of these suppliers also worked regularly for the Parisian interior design scene, in particular with Hoentschel, as did the carpet and tapestry manufacturer Braquenié. In May 1906, the couple chose a Savonnerie carpet from there. In addition to its illustrious history dating back to 1824, Braquenié was well-known in Russia, an argument that was bound to win over the countess and the grand duke. The same was true of the lamp maker and bronze artist Gagneau, some of whose lights adorned the palaces of the emperor in Gatchina and Grand Duke Vladimir in St. Petersburg.[18] Georges Gagneau (1824-1909), associated with the family business since 1867, was a regular collaborator of Hoentschel, as was the bronze artist Vian, whose workshops the countess visited in December 1906; she settled some invoices from the company a few months later, in April 1907. Henri Vian (1858-1904) had taken over the management of his father's business in 1874, and in 1889 he won a gold medal at the Paris Exposition. Vian was located at 5, rue de Thorigny, a district with many workshops linked to the bronzes

18 Zeisler 2014b, 333-44.

industry.[19] There was the workshop of Hazart (14, rue Saint-Gilles), a bronze maker descended from a dynasty of sculptors, which the countess visited on the same day as that of the furniture manufacturer Sormani (10, rue Charlot), dubbed "the thousand and one nights of furniture" at the Paris Exposition in 1900.[20] At Hazart, Olga noticed "magnificent bronzes."

Finally, it was to Hoentschel's regular collaborator Hippolyte Eugène Ternisien (1852-1923) that she went with Hitrov in January 1907 to order furniture. Ternisien was an upholsterer and one of Hoentschel's long-standing friends,[21] and it is not surprising to see him lending a hand on a piece that Hoentschel designed. After taking over from his father, Félix Alfred, a decorative upholsterer associated with the Fraysse upholsterer (Hippolyte's mother, Sophie, was a Miss Fraysse) Ternisien distinguished himself at numerous national (Bordeaux, 1895; Rouen, 1896) and international (Brussels, 1897; Liège, 1905) exhibitions.[22] Ternisien, like Hoentschel, had counted Braquenié among his suppliers since the Second Empire.

To decorate the reception areas, the countess turned to antique dealers and the best upholsterers and manufacturers of the day, who were often linked to one another by matrimonial or business alliances, reflecting the importance of networks in the Paris art industry. For the service areas, she sought out more commonly produced objects, as shown by her purchase of furniture for the concierge's lodge from the Aux Trois Quartiers shop in October 1906. Established around 1829 on le boulevard de la Madeleine, Aux Trois Quartiers was one of the "department stores" that revolutionized urban commerce in the nineteenth century. Organized by department, these stores offered a wide variety of products, from fashion to home decoration, often available by catalog.

By early 1907, work was progressing, deliveries were increasing, and the house was taking shape. Although the couple received a few friends on an occasional basis, the official inauguration took place in February, as announced in *Le Figaro*.[23] The effervescence of the preparations can be felt in the short entries in the countess's diary. On January 14, she made some final orders and purchases from the framer Dupré, Maple, and Gagneau. On January 31, Olga was with Hitrov, and until one o'clock in the morning she arranged the porcelain in the showcases. This demonstrates the owner's involvement in the final layout of the interiors a decorator designed. The next day, while continuing to arrange the display cases, she drew up the invitations and had them sent out, probably on the stationery of her new residence, "2, avenue Victor Hugo (Parc

19 Arch. Nat. LH 270450.

20 Quoted in Zeisler 2014b, 355.

21 Kisluk-Grosheide, Krohn, and Leben 2013, 31.

22 Arch. Nat. LH 257656.

23 *Le Figaro*, February 8, 1907.

des Princes) / Boulogne-sur-Seine," stamped with her monogram OH under a countess's crown, most probably the work of the prestigious engraver Stern, a firm founded in 1834 and established in the passage des Panoramas. The day after this first grand dinner, following breakfast, Olga arranged the furniture in the drawing room, which had had to be rearranged to accommodate the brilliant company. This event also marked the end of the mission entrusted to Hoentschel, as recorded in Olga's diary on February 15: "Today I went to the bank and drew 50,000, which I took to Hoentschel." This is probably the last installment of the decorator's bill, whose services were far from cheap. In 1906, Olga had simply commented on this note: "it's a lot." Be that as it may, the customers seemed satisfied. The grand duke's recommendation to the couple's friend comtesse Edmond de Pourtalès in 1908 bears witness to this:

> Dear countess and friend, I would like to write to you again to say how pleased I am with the work carried out by Monsieur Georges Hoentschel on our Boulogne s. S. property. He has brought to it perfect taste, admirable execution and has been surprisingly punctual in these times of unemployment and strikes. I am happy to be able to recommend him to our goodwill. I kiss your dear hands and I remain, countess, your affectionate and devoted Paul.[24]

In the mansion at Boulogne-sur-Seine, the decorator's work, enhanced by the taste of the mistress of the house, was constantly enriched by new acquisitions that mingled with the collections that the countess and the grand duke already owned.

24 Archives de la ville de Strasbourg, 5 MW 197. Letter dated April 7, 1908. Document provided by Ulrich Leben, December 22, 2012.

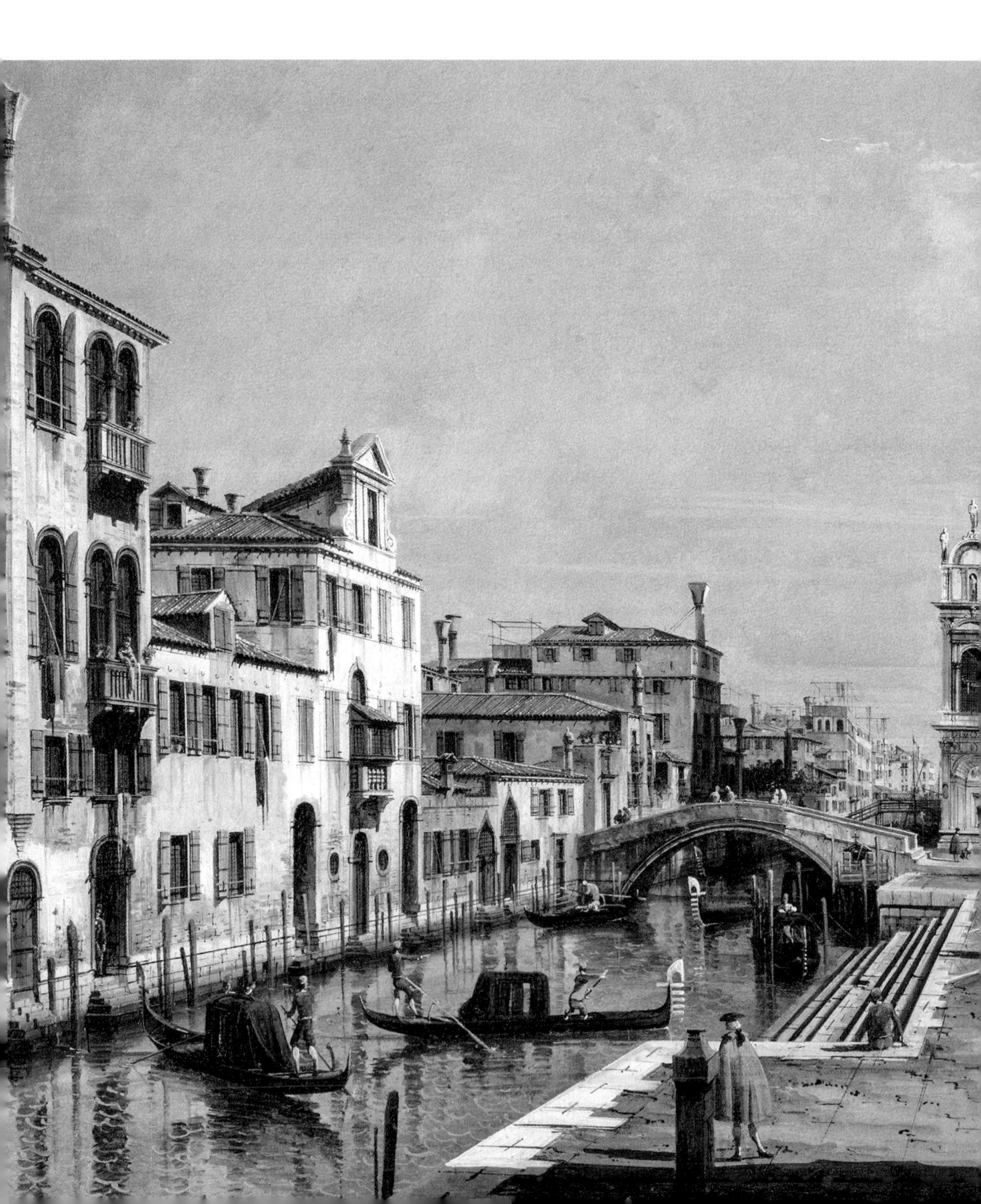

AT THE HEART OF THE PARIS ART MARKET: DEALERS AND CLIENTS, ARTISTS AND PATRONS

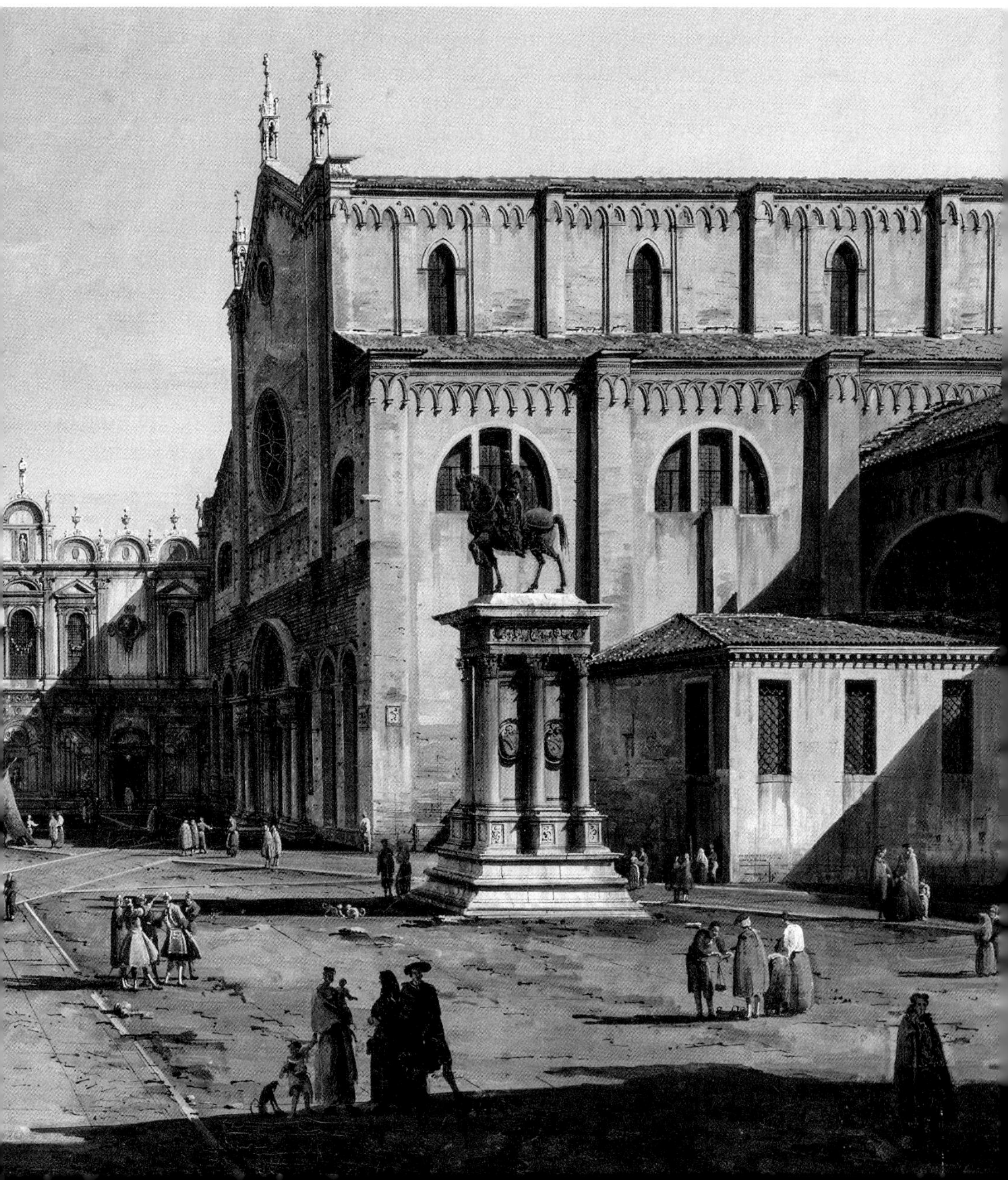

Olga von Hohenfelsen had been living in Paris for four years and was now established in a large house. She explored the Paris market in order to add to her art collection, especially as, at the time, "Paris was the most dynamic place in the European art trade."[1] Her taste was particularly standardized and in keeping with her milieu. As the fittings designed by Hoentschel demonstrate, it was above all the eighteenth century that the countess admired, since it had come back into fashion at the end of the Second Empire as an idealized model of aristocratic taste. Exhibitions, the market, decoration – everything was geared toward this taste. As far back as 1899, when she was staying in Paris, Olga had expressed her interest in antique art in her correspondence with Grand Duke Paul.

In 1899, she visited Taburet, Roger, and Mme Guiraud. While Roger remains an unidentified name in the art market, Mme Guiraud certainly refers to the antique dealer of the same name, a family business run by Louis Guiraud (1878-1955) and his brother Lucien (1886-1954) at the beginning of the twentieth century.[2] Established at 1, quai Voltaire and 5, rue de Téhéran, the company had been founded by their father, Émile-Sylvain Guiraud (1852-1936), originally known for his talents as a wood gilder. The dealer and collector René Gimpel noted in 1918 that Guiraud's wife, Caroline-Christine Hermann (1859-1924), probably the Madame Guiraud mentioned by Olga, had great taste.[3] As Gimpel's writings and other sources indicate, Guiraud specialized in eighteenth-century art. A few years before Olga's visit, in 1897, when Grand Duke Paul's brother Alexei had a new apartment to furnish in Paris, he chose two tapestry-covered types of armchairs called bergères from this dealer for 5,000 francs, as well as two antique cane knobs, one of them in Louis XV gold for 1,100 francs.[4]

During her stay in 1899, Olga was also introduced to the art market by a local connoisseur, Kergorlay, probably comte Pierre de Kergorlay (1847-1919), collector and builder of the mansion of the same name in Paris at 9, rue de l'Amiral d'Estaing, designed by the architect Paul-Ernest Sanson. Olga was very happy to have met him because, as she confided to her diary, he knew everything about everything, and took her to see several masterpieces in antique shops. She reported enthusiastically to the grand duke about her visit: "I saw such paintings and objects!" and continued: "And to think that you spend outrageous amounts of money on modern objects when there are marvels from the past century! A painting by Lancret (admittedly for 180,000 francs) but what a marvel! And Watteau, Boucher, Greuze."[5]

1 Gabet 2011, 23.

2 *Les Donateurs du Louvre* (Paris: RMN, 1989), 225.

3 Gimpel 1963, 16.

4 RGIA, F. 526, op. 1, D. 355. L. 1-13. Invoice of November 15/27, 1897.

5 *Ibid.*, L. 36. Letter dated April 9/21, 1899.

Olga explicitly criticizes the grand duke's taste for Salon art, no doubt referring to his major acquisitions from the famous gallery Boussod, Valadon & Cie, successors to Goupil & Cie, a regular supplier of art to the Russian court and the great collectors of the period.[6] The grand duke's choices showed that he focused on artists with undeniable commercial success. In 1887, his first acquisition from the gallery was a painting by Jean-Jacques Henner (1829-1905), *Dans la Bibliothèque*, for which he paid 4,000 francs.[7] Although Henner had developed his own aesthetic approach to art, which kept him at a distance from the academicism and naturalism triumphant at the Salon, his career was a successful one, crowned by numerous official distinctions awarded by the authorities of the Second Empire and then by the Third Republic.

In 1894, the grand duke acquired *The Reception for Napoleon I on the Isola Bella in the 5th Year of His Reign* by François Flameng (1856-1923) for 35,000 francs[8] (pl. 5). Flameng was a portrait painter much appreciated by the international elite. He even spent time in Russia, where he received numerous commissions.[9] As a painter, he had made a name for himself by depicting historical genre scenes set in the eighteenth century or from the story of Napoleon, a subject of interest at the Russian court. Several members of the imperial family collected works linked to the history of the French emperor, in particular Grand Duke Nicholas Mikhailovich and Emperor Nicholas II, who owned an entire cycle glorifying Napoleon, by Flameng,[10] encouraging the first manifestations of the neo-empire in the entourage of the Russian imperial family. In addition to the painting *Isola Bella,* Grand Duke Paul had assembled a series of engravings by Flameng in Boulogne, depicting episodes taken from the life of Napoleon; these were set in mahogany and bronze frames.[11] The grand duke also owned a watercolor by Flameng of a Venetian scene.[12]

In addition, the grand duke had a taste for academic subjects, of which Jean-Léon Gérôme (1824-1904) was a leading exponent.[13] At the Russian court, Gérôme's works won over Emperor Alexander III and Grand Duke Sergei, two brothers of Grand Duke Paul.[14] In 1895, Grand Duke Paul bought

6 Penot 2017, 270.

7 The J. Paul Getty Trust, Goupil & Cie / Boussod, Valadon & Cie Stock Books, Book 11, Goupil no. 18192, p. 181, row 12.

8 *Ibid.*, Book 13, Goupil no. 22557, p. 112, row 7; Paley sale, Paris, December 5, 1923, lot 14; Sotheby's New York, October 12, 1994, lot 110.

9 Page 2016, 25-26, 138-43.

10 This series, which adorned the emperor's personal apartment in the Winter Palace, is now in the State Hermitage Museum.

11 Paley sale, Paris, December 5, 1923, lots 2-5.

12 *Ibid.*, lot 9.

13 Ackerman 2000.

14 *Ibid.*, nos. 172.2, 253, 328, 334, 385, pp. 264, 290, 312, 314, 330.

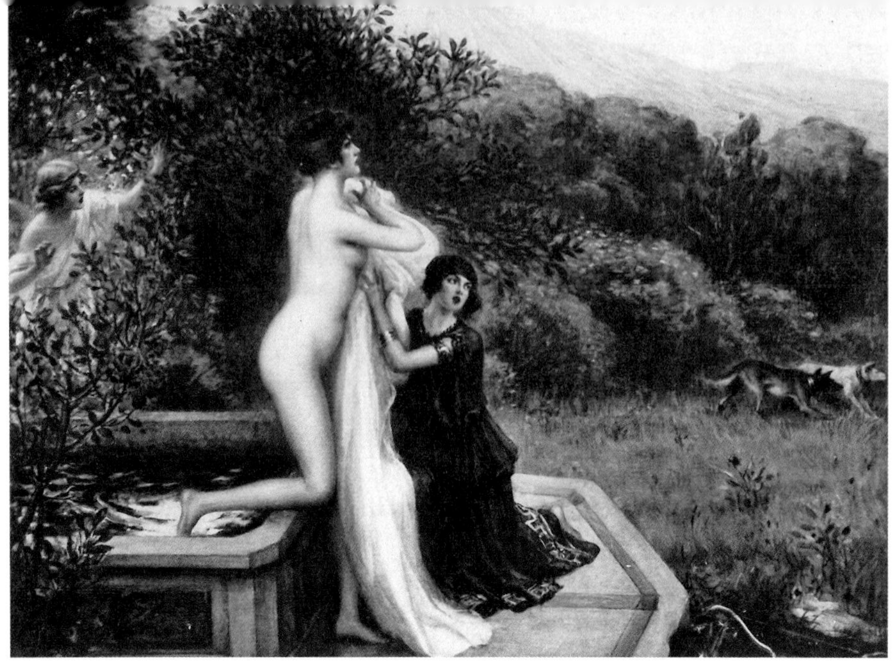

Fig. 10 Albert Lynch, *Diana*, ca. 1897. Postcard. Private collection.

a version of *Diana and Actaeon* by Gérôme for 12,000 francs;[15] this was a subject close to his heart (pl. 6). In 1897, he bought another *Diana*, by Albert Lynch (1851-1912), another very fashionable artist, for 4,000 francs[16] (fig. 10).

The same year, he paid 10,000 francs for a genre scene, *Après la pêche*, by Édouard Detaille (1848-1912).[17] Detaille shared with Flameng a body of work of Napoleonic subjects, which were very fashionable at the end of the nineteenth century and a great success in Russia. In 1884, the artist, known for his military subjects, had been invited to the Russian court by Alexander III; he received several commissions and was visited by a number of grand dukes.[18] The collections of Grand Duke Paul, which included a watercolor from 1884, *Cossacks in the Urals*, reflected this stay and Detaille's reputation in Russia.[19]

Olga took this taste in the opposite direction. She radically shifted her choices toward the eighteenth century, which the grand duke approved of. From 1901 on, his taste for art began to evolve, as illustrated by his acquisitions from the famous dealer Thomas Agnew & Sons.[20] Founded by Thomas

15 The J. Paul Getty Trust, Goupil & Cie / Boussod, Valadon & Cie Stock Books, Book 14, Goupil no. 24214, p. 86, row 11; Ackerman 2000, no. 428, p. 342, private collection, Sotheby's, New York, November 8, 2013, lot 17.

16 The J. Paul Getty Trust, Goupil & Cie / Boussod, Valadon & Cie Stock Books, Book 14, Goupil no. 25057, p. 142, row 13.

17 *Ibid.*, Book 14, Goupil no. 24770, p. 123, row 11.

18 Robichon 2007, 52-59.

19 Paley sale, Paris, December 5, 1923, lot 8.

20 NGA27/14/2/4, F. 683.

Agnew in 1817, this art market institution specialized in old masters. The dealer had a prestigious address in Bond Street, London, and a wide network of agents and offices around the world, notably in Paris. At the London gallery, the grand duke chose a portrait of Empress Catherine II (Catherine the Great),[21] then attributed to Lampi, which appeared to have come from a British collection. This attribution could be due to Agnew, who had also noted in pencil in the margin of the acquisition register the name Drouais followed by a question mark. Work by the French artist François-Hubert Drouais at the Russian court was well-known at the time, as was that of the Austrian artist Johann Baptist Lampi the Elder. This portrait may have been a version of Lampi's famous version in the Hermitage. However, the only portrait of Catherine II mentioned in Grand Duke Paul's collections is a version after the composition by the Russian painter Mikhail Shibanov, dated 1787-89, now in the British Royal Collection[22] (pl. 7). This is most likely the work supplied by Agnew & Sons. At the Paris branch of Agnew & Sons, in 1908, the grand duke chose another major item for his collection:[23] the painting *View of the Church of San Giovanni and Paolo* in Venice by Bernardo Bellotto[24] (1722-1780), a nephew of Canaletto (Michele and Donald D'Amour Museum of Fine Arts, Springfield, Massachusetts) (pl. 8).

The collection built up in Paris was the main preoccupation of the countess, who relied on the sound advice of her mentor Hitrov. He had probably used the same dealers and suppliers for his own collection. His name appears in the registers of the Agnew & Sons gallery.

Motivated by the refurbishment of her new home, which had led her to frequent the Paris art market, Olga continued to make acquisitions from the great antique dealers of the time. Édouard Larcade (1875-1945) was one of these.[25] He was the founder of a prestigious dynasty of dealers whose trade flourished at the beginning of the twentieth century. In 1922, his gallery, which sold "*objets d'art ancien – Chine – tableaux*,"[26] was located at 140, rue du Faubourg Saint-Honoré. In association with Hoentschel, Larcade's clients included many French art lovers, including the Camondos, and Americans, as well as international museums. On March 15, 1907, the countess paid another visit to the antique dealer, where she had admired objects on February 28 and March 13. This time she was accompanied by Hitrov. The visit was a success, and she left with a Hubert Robert that she described as "ideal" for

21 NGA27/1/1/9, no. 9388. Acquired by Grand Duke Paul on October 25, 1901.

22 Paley sale, Christie's, London, June 21, 1929, lot 49; RCIN 400964.

23 NGA/14/4/1, F. 302.

24 NGA27/1/10, no. 2161, June 22, 1908 (25,000 francs); Paley sale, Christie's, London, June 21, 1929, lot 18. Bowron 2001, 60.

25 *Les Donateurs du Louvre* (Paris: RMN, 1989), 247.

26 Advertisement, *La Renaissance de l'art français et des industries de luxe*, July 1922.

13,000 francs and a Jean-Baptiste Perronneau for 6,000 francs (pl. 9). Robert was one of the most representative artists of the eighteenth century, whose works combined the Enlightenment's admiration for antiquity with a taste for nature, magnified by sumptuous landscapes and genre scenes flanked by monumental ruins. The painter had been the darling of Russian collectors until the early years of the nineteenth century,[27] and his paintings continued to adorn the picture rails of the Stroganov and Yusupov families and the imperial family, starting with Emperor Alexander III, who owned several in the Anichkov Palace. At a time when eighteenth-century taste was triumphant in the elegant salons of the international elite, a Hubert Robert was a must-have for Countess von Hohenfelsen. The one she bought from Larcade might have been the large-format painting of washerwomen at a fountain, also in Boulogne. It was probably around the same time that the collection was enriched by another work by Robert: a bridge with figures, *Bridge with Washerwomen*,[28] now in the collections of the Palazzo Barberini in Rome[29] (Galleria nazionale d'arte antica) (pl. 10). The art dealer Arthur Tooth & Sons, 155 New Bond Street, London, used it in an advertisement in October 1907.[30] Was it perhaps acquired at the same time as the Bellotto purchased from Agnew in 1908? The Tooth Gallery was founded in London in 1842 by Charles Tooth, a renowned framer, then managed by his son Arthur (1828-1900). Specializing in modern and, occasionally, historic paintings, it remained a family business until its closure in the 1970s.[31]

The Perronneau purchased from Larcade was an oval portrait of a young man with powdered hair and wearing a brown jacket.[32] Perronneau was one of the great portrait painters of the eighteenth century and the subject of a publication in the *Gazette des beaux-arts* in 1903 by the art historian and man of letters Maurice Tourneux, who had distinguished himself with his book *Catherine II et Diderot*.[33] At the time of the Franco-Russian Alliance, this was one of a series of scholarly editions on Franco-Russian cultural exchanges, reinforcing and justifying the union between the Third Republic

27 Moulin 1999.

28 Paley sale, Christie's, London, June 21, 1929, lot 41, *The Bridge*, 28 × 36 in.

29 Lorenza Mochi Onori and Rossella Vodret, *Galleria Nazionale d'arte antica: Palazzo Barberini* (Rome: L'Erma di Bretschneider, 2008), 230. See also Ekaterina Deriabina, "Hubert Robert et les collectionneurs russes," in Moulin 1999, 107.

30 *The Burlington Magazine* 12, no. 55 (October 1907).

31 Thomas M. Bayer and John Page, "Arthur Tooth: A London Art Dealer in the Spotlight, 1870-1871," *Nineteenth-Century Art Worldwide* 9, no. 1 (Spring 2010). A study of part of Tooth's archives at the Getty Research Institute might reveal more about the history of this painting. However, Sally McKay has found no trace of this work there.

32 Paley sale, Christie's, London, June 21, 1929, lot 38, 23 ½ × 19 1/2 in. Information shared by Dominique d'Arnoult, author of *Jean-Baptiste Perronneau, un portraitiste dans l'Europe des Lumières* (Paris: Arthena, 2014).

33 *Diderot et Catherine II* (Paris: Calmann Lévy, 1899).

and the Russian Empire through historical sources. Portraiture was also a widely studied genre at the beginning of the twentieth century. An exhibition of Russian historical portraits organized by Sergei Diaghilev in St. Petersburg in 1905 had been preceded by a 1902 project orchestrated by Baron Nicolas Wrangel and Alexander Benois, which Diaghilev judged as "amateurish."[34] This new interest had established the portrait as one of the principal artistic expressions of the Russian eighteenth century and had given rise to numerous publications on the subject and on the artists of the period.[35] Old master portraits were in vogue in Russia, and the grand duke's brother, Grand Duke Sergei, had assembled a large collection of them.[36] As early as the 1880s, Grand Duke Paul himself had begun acquiring historical portraits, which can be seen in the interiors of his palace shown in a series of photographs taken in the 1890s (figs. 11, 12). All these factors had certainly played a decisive role in shaping the countess's taste for this art and for the eighteenth and nineteenth centuries, especially as Diaghilev had, as early as 1898, presented the famous portrait of the grand duke by Valentin Serov (see pl. 2) at his exhibition of Russian and Finnish artists, organized on the premises of the Baron von Stieglitz museum-school.[37] This painting, considered one of the important works in the exhibition, belonged at the time to the regiment of the grand duke, who had certainly been consulted in connection with this loan. Moreover, during the couple's years in Paris, Diaghilev was a regular visitor to Boulogne. Winnaretta Singer (1869-1943) remembers: "Among these guests, I often met a tall, energetic-looking young man, with a white streak in the middle of his thick black hair, who was none other than the great Sergei Diaghilev."[38]

During this period, the countess never missed an art exhibition or auction linked to the eighteenth century, her favorite period. In 1906 (on May 22), together with Grand Duke Paul and their son, Vladimir, she had visited an exhibition of eighteenth-century works of art at the Bibliothèque nationale. The catalog gives the details of the items on display, which included miniatures, engravings, prints, medals, engraved stones, and Sèvres biscuit ware.[39] The event, which brought together what the countess had admired at the dealers and sometimes what she already owned, was judged by her to be "marvelous." The next day, she admired the collection of novelist

34 Vladimir Kruglov, "Sergei Diaghilev's 'Russian Years,'" in Petrova 2009, 18.

35 On this subject, see Petrova 2009, 59-69.

36 Part of this collection is conserved in St. Petersburg, in the State Russian Museum and the State Museum of the History of the City of St. Petersburg.

37 Petrova 2009, 31.

38 Singer 2000, 48.

39 *Exposition d'œuvres d'art du XVIIIe siècle à la Bibliothèque nationale : Miniatures, gouaches, estampes en couleurs françaises et anglaises 1750-1815, médailles et pierres gravées 1700-1800, biscuits de Sèvres* (Paris: E. Lévy, 1906).

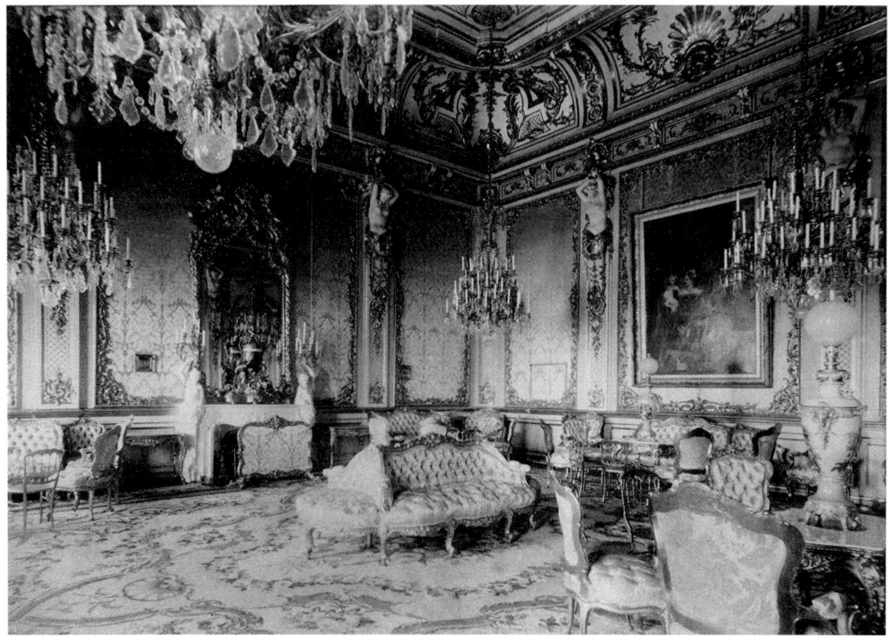

Fig. 11 Drawing room of the palace of Grand Duke Paul Alexandrovich on the English Embankment in St. Petersburg, ca. 1891. Georges von Pistohlkors Archives, Holy Trinity Orthodox Seminary / Museum of Russian History, Jordanville.

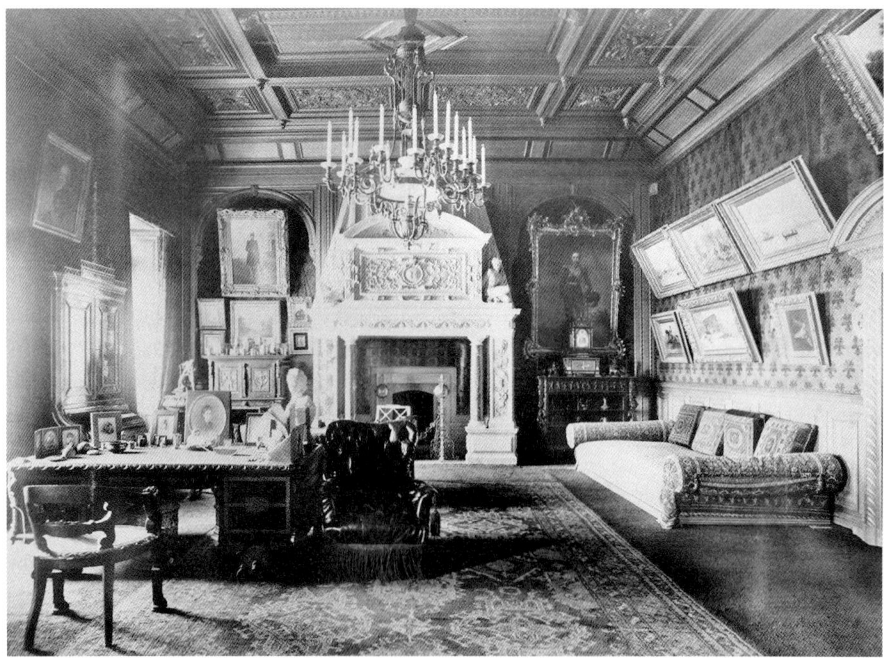

Fig. 12 Study of the palace of Grand Duke Paul Alexandrovich on the English Embankment in St. Petersburg, ca. 1891. Georges von Pistohlkors Archives, Holy Trinity Orthodox Seminary / Museum of Russian History, Jordanville.

and playwright Paul Meurice (1818-1905), which was about to be auctioned at the Hôtel Drouot.[40] She was undoubtedly attracted by its collection of seventeenth- and eighteenth-century objets d'art, including earthenware and porcelain, sculptures by Clodion, various chairs and tapestries in the style of those Olga collected.

On June 17, 1907, this time with Hitrov, after buying a tapestry and screen from Laurent for the dining room, she went to the Georges Petit gallery on rue de Sèze to see the Fragonard and Chardin exhibition, which she described as "magnificent." The gallery, named after its founder, an art expert and dealer, was one of the most famous in Paris, hosting exhibitions of a wide range of art, both old masters and contemporary, and prestigious sales, including the 1912 sale of Jacques Doucet's collection of eighteenth-century art. The gallery's elegant premises attracted the best society, who flocked to the preview evenings.[41] The exhibition Olga admired was a work of philanthropy organized by the Chardin and Fragonard Committee and the magazine *L'Art et les artistes*. Their aim was to raise funds to erect a monument to Chardin for the "benefit of the cancer charity and the arts orphanage."[42] Henri de Rothschild was chairman of the committee, whose members included many representatives of the artistic world, including the painter Léon Bonnat; Georges Cain, curator of the Musée Carnavalet; Pierre de Nolhac, curator of Versailles; and collectors such as Baron de Schlichting,[43] a compatriot of Countess von Hohenfelsen, and David David-Weill. The exhibited works came mainly from private collections, including those of the emperor of Germany, the painter François Flameng and, of course, Henri de Rothschild, perhaps the most generous lender at the event – all role models for Olga.

Another eighteenth-century artist who came to prominence during the Belle Époque was Elisabeth Vigée-Lebrun, portraitist to Queen Marie-Antoinette. The painter's career was closely linked to Russia, where she entered the service of the Court and high society in the aftermath of the French Revolution. In 1909, on the lookout for new publications on the subject, Olga even gave Pierre de Nolhac's *Vigée-Lebrun*, a 1908 edition of which she had in her library, as an Easter present. The books in the countess's home testify to her taste and her desire to collect – in like manner to most art lovers and collectors – publications and documents on her favorite subjects, ranging from general works on France and the eighteenth century to monographic or more specialized works. The library included *Album des peintres de l'école française*

40 Maître Paul Chevallier, Hôtel Drouot, Paris, May 25, 1906.

41 Pierre Pinchon and Cécile Thézelais, "La Galerie Georges Petit," in Centorame and Andia 2005, 212-13.

42 *Exposition Chardin et Fragonard* (Paris: Imp. Georges Petit, 1907).

43 Jacques Foucart, "La Collection Schlichting," in Centorame and Andia 2005, 214-15.

(1885); *La France artistique et monumentale*, edited by Henry Havard (1892); *La Reine Marie-Antoinette* (1890); and *Histoire du château de Versailles* (1899-1900) by Nolhac. Several books reflected an interest in old master painting, as illustrated by *Les Chefs-d'œuvre de la peinture italienne* by Paul Mantz (1870), *Honoré Fragonard* by Baron Roger Portalis (1889), *François Boucher: Premier peintre du roi* by Nolhac (1907), and *Thomas Gainsborough* by Sir Walter Armstrong (1909). Other works indicating a taste for the decorative arts included Havard's monumental *Dictionnaire de l'ameublement* (1887-90), Charles Blanc's *Grammaire des arts décoratifs* (1882), the catalog of the 1900 *Exposition rétrospective de l'art décoratif français*, and Ris-Paquot's two-volume *Histoire générale de la faïence ancienne* (1876).[44]

The countess was not content with seeking out works by the great French painters of the eighteenth and nineteenth centuries. She had also developed a taste for the decorative arts in general, and ceramics in particular. Indeed, porcelain from the eighteenth century, especially soft-paste porcelain, was an essential part of Belle Époque collecting, and Olga was a great lover of it. As early as 1899, she bought a pair of Louis XVI soft-paste vases in Paris for 1,000 francs.[45] Olga's diary rarely gives precise details of the purchases she made in this field; it often confines itself to simply mentioning the purchase when she was "antiquing" in France and abroad. In 1908, during a visit to Germany, she described her morning walk and her visit to the local antique dealers, from whom she bought various porcelains, giving only the names of the factories, Ludwigsburg and Frankenthal, whose early productions were prized by collectors.

Another aspect of the taste of the time was that for jades and gems from the Far East. Olga collected a number of these small objects, fashioned from fine or ornamental stones. She appreciated them as much as the animals produced in the same spirit by the Russian workshops of the time and crystallized in the astonishing creations of Fabergé the jeweler, of whom she was a client. Olga acquired jades and other gems, lacquers, and porcelain from the Far East almost systematically from Madame Langweil, a key figure in the Paris art market in this specialty.[46] Florine Langweil (1861-1958), née Epstein, came from a modest family in Alsace. Coming to work in Paris in 1881, she met and married Austrian antique dealer Charles Langweil (1843-1920), who left her with two children and a business in debt. In 1893, she decided to take over the business, which she developed and made profitable. The company, established at 4, boulevard des Italiens, then 26, place Saint-Georges (1903), became one of the best addresses in Paris for Chinese and Japanese art. After retiring from

44 TsGALI, F. 254, op. 1, D. 5, L. 7-9, 56.

45 Probably the pair of vases by Taillandier; Paley sale, Christie's, London, June 6-7, 1929, lot 37, acquired by Ben Simon.

46 Arch. Nat. LH 19800035/1742/2392.

business in 1913, Madame Langweil moved to la rue de Varenne and devoted her fortune and energy to charitable work, particularly in her native Alsace. A leading specialist in Far Eastern art, she was curator of the Far Eastern objets d'art section of the Strasbourg and Colmar museums, to which she donated part of her collection between 1920 and 1923.[47] Her shop, one of the most renowned in Paris, was frequented by major French and foreign collectors and art lovers, including Jacques-Émile Blanche, Georges Clémenceau, Raymond Koechlin, Louis Metman, John Pierpont Morgan, and Grand Duke Alexei.

Olga's inclinations, which became clearer as she came to know the Parisian market, influenced Grand Duke Paul's own choices when it came to giving her a present. In addition to the traditional jewelry and fashion accessories she received for Christmas and New Year's gifts, she now regularly added works of art from the eighteenth century to her growing collection. In 1910, she wrote in her diary, "Pucia has given me a lot," and listed the gifts she had received. Many of the objects came from antique dealers she had visited during a stay in Germany, such as Drey and Steinharter, both based in Munich.

Drey was a family business located at Max-Josef-Strasse 2, Maximiliansplatz. Founded in 1860 by Aaron S. Drey, the gallery seems to have been renowned for its antique porcelain. The company had international branches with addresses in London, run by Aaron's son Franz (Francis) Drey, and Amsterdam, and it enjoyed an international clientele including Count Moïse de Camondo.[48] The business was liquidated by the Nazi authorities in 1936, and Aaron's son Siegfried was forced into exile, but the name survived through his grandson Paul Drey (1885-1953), who had set up shop in New York in 1920.[49] As for Adolf Steinharter, he is mentioned at Briennerstrasse 4 in 1897 and seems to have ceased trading around 1918, when his estate was liquidated.[50] Among the gifts Olga received that were bought from Drey were a sedan chair and a porcelain fountain with an "Old Saxony yellow background." The sedan chair symbolized the aristocratic *art de vivre* during the eighteenth century and was a frequently displayed decorative element in the homes of the Belle Époque. As for porcelain from Saxony, the cradle of the European porcelain industry, it was one of the countess's most sought-after

47 "1996: Société d'Histoire de Wintzenheim," *Revue d'Alsace*, 135 | 2009, online October 1st, 2012, accessed April 2024, https://journals.openedition.org/alsace/937.

48 Legrand 2016, 27, 34.

49 Frits Scholten, *The Robert Lehman Collection: European Sculpture and Metalwork* (New York: Metropolitan Museum of Art, 2011), X, https://cdn.sanity.io/files/cctd4ker/production/c9adc480423fb247aa9d9c30ebcbddbf6650dbf2.pdf.

50 *Nachlass Kommerzienrat Adolf Steinharter München: Antiquitäten, alte Möbel, Lüster, Gobelins, Teppiche usw.* Versteigerung in der Galerie Helbing in München Dienstag, den 28. Mai und Mittwoch, den 29. Mai 1918 (auction at Galerie Helbing in Munich Tuesday, May 28, and Wednesday, May 29, 1918).

pieces. At the same time, she received a tea caddy of the same origin from the dealer Steinharter.

The grand duke demonstrated his generosity and attachment with other gifts of a similar nature, including an antique French four-color gold box and a display case from *L'Escalier de Cristal* to showcase the collections. Over the course of the nineteenth century, the display case, the ultimate showpiece, took on increasingly luxurious forms, sometimes becoming a piece of ceremonial furniture for displaying a variety of objects. In view of the number of products made by *L'Escalier de Cristal* and the most important cabinetmakers of the Belle Époque, the display case was a favorite choice. The company supplied several to the Russian imperial family, some of which are still in use in the Hermitage Museum.[51] The one given to Countess von Hohenfelsen was in eighteenth-century style, more precisely in the Louis XVI style, decorated with cassolettes and foliage.

The list of gifts does not end there. We may also mention a drawing and a pastel said to be by Boucher, *The Young Sinner* and *Young Girl with Cat*, which, although they have not been located, seem to have been attributed to this artist (particularly the second work) because of the popularity the great masters of the eighteenth century enjoyed around 1900; an attribution that might be called into question today.[52]

By around 1910, Countess von Hohenfelsen had a mansion fitted out by a renowned decorator, a showcase for a constantly evolving collection; all that was missing was a portrait of the mistress of the house, Olga's only concession to contemporary art. The artist she chose appeared in her diary for the first time in 1907: Pascal Dagnan-Bouveret[53] (1852-1929), one of the leaders of the naturalist movement, with whom she kept up an extensive correspondence (pl. 11).

A pupil of Gérôme and Alexandre Cabanel, Dagnan-Bouveret made his debut at the Salon in 1875 and enjoyed considerable success with foreign clients, particularly Americans, with his genre scenes, Breton subjects, and portraits. In Russia, his art proved popular with the collector Sergei Tretyakov in 1882 and 1888[54] and Emperor Alexander III.[55] In 1906, Dagnan-Bouveret

51 Tatiana B. Semenova, *Istoria Ermitazhe v zerkale vitrin* (St. Petersburg: State Hermitage Museum, 2014), 108, 112, 116.

52 Paley sale, Christie's, London, June 21, 1929, lots 8 and 9. The model for the drawing is probably the one engraved by Gilles Demarteau.

53 Concerning the artist, see Weisberg 2002. See also Sassi 2009.

54 The J. Paul Getty Trust, Goupil & Cie / Boussod, Valadon & Cie Stock Books, Book 10, Goupil no. 15863, p. 198, row 1; Book 12, Goupil no. 19176, p. 61, row 10.

55 Rifat Gafifullin, "Katalog kartin Aleksandra III i Marii Fedorovny v Gatchinskom dvortse," *Imperator Aleksander III i Imperatritsa Maria Fedorovna*, conference proceedings, St. Petersburg, no. 154, 2006, 220. *The Watercolourist in the Louvre*, 1881 (State Hermitage Museum), acquired through the painter Alexei Petrovich Bogoliubov and the collector Sergei

even became an honorary member of the Imperial Academy of Fine Arts in St. Petersburg. The few entries in the countess's diary and, above all, her correspondence provide rare information about the relationship between the painter and his patron. The first letter the countess received, dated April 26, 1907, details the way in which the countess and Dagnan-Bouveret came to know each other: "My friend Mr. J. Worth has informed me of the conversation you had with him about your portrait."[56]

Olga was an important customer of the fashion house founded by Charles Frederick Worth (1825-1895), and Jean-Philippe Worth (1856-1926), son and successor with his brother Gaston-Lucien (1853-1924), seems to have been the perfect intermediary – especially as Dagnan-Bouveret had painted Jean-Philippe's portrait in 1889. On April 20, Olga wrote in her diary: "discussed my portrait by Dagnan-Bouveret with Jean." And Dagnan-Bouveret thanked her for "the opportunity you offer me to satisfy His Highness the Grand Duke who had kindly asked me a few years ago for a painting,"[57] another factor in favor of this choice. An appointment was then made in the painter's studio to plan the work and the many sittings that would henceforth punctuate the countess's weekly schedule. No fewer than sixty-one sessions were needed to create the portrait.[58] Some were devoted to details of the painting, such as the arrangement of the arms and hands, for which two sessions would suffice,[59] or the coat and furs.[60] Occasionally, the painter would clearly state his opinion in response to his model's suggestions. In a somewhat sarcastic tone, Dagnan-Bouveret sent a pneumatic letter on the subject of color choices:

> Madam, do you see me using the blues, golds and vermillion with which God has endowed butterflies?... If I used such tones to paint your face, Boissier would claim the picture for the top of a chocolate box!... See you tomorrow, Madam, with the most respectful compliments of your painter.[61]

Olga often spent the morning, or even several hours, in "her" painter's studio, exchanging ideas with the artist, sometimes over lunch, or with visitors

Tretyakov from Boussod, Valadon & Cie in May 1889 for 4,500 francs, was given to Empress Maria for her birthday. In the Gatchina palace, this painting adorned the empress's study.

56 GARF, F. 613, op. 1, D. 156, L. 1.

57 To date, no trace of another commission seems to have been documented. Perhaps Dagnan-Bouveret has the wrong grand duke.

58 GARF, F. 613, op. 1, D. 156, L. 34. Letter dated June 11, 1909.

59 *Ibid.*, L. 6. Letter dated November 11, 1907.

60 *Ibid.*, L. 13. Pneumatic letter dated January 16, 1908.

61 GARF, F. 613, op. 1, D. 156, L. 8. Pneumatic letter dated October 16, 1907. Boissier was a famous Parisian confectioner founded in 1827.

such as a close friend, the writer Paul Bourget (1852-1935). Olga wrote on June 17: "During the session Bourget arrived and disturbed us terribly; he was incredibly witty." On July 3, Grand Duke Paul and their daughter Irina also attended a sitting. The artist showed the portrait in progress, and Irina commented: "It is *maman* to perfection,"[62] Olga's diary reported. A complicity developed with the painter during the long sessions, which were also an opportunity to inspect the other works in progress, on which Olga gave her opinion. In one of his letters, Dagnan-Bouveret commented on the advice he had received about the portrait of someone referred to as "l'Américaine": "She is not beautiful, but she seems kindhearted," and he continued: "As you see, I did not want to take your very mischievous recommendations into consideration."[63] These exchanges served to flatter the countess while at the same time highlighting the artist's merits when he reported the comments of certain visitors about Olga's portrait, such as those of Mesdames de Béarn,[64] de Cossé,[65] and Bartet,[66] as well as some of his fellow artists: "There is distinction, beauty,..., charm, etc. here."[67]

Countess René de Béarn (1869-1939), who was close to Olga, may well have played a part in shaping her taste. A patron of the painter, she posed for him in 1899 and commissioned a number of works from him, which she displayed in her private mansion on rue Saint-Dominique, rebuilt by the architect Walter-André Destailleurs in the French eighteenth-century taste. This included an eclectic collection of Symbolist and earlier art, particularly from the eighteenth century, which also adorned her other homes.[68]

The painter informed Olga of Worth's reaction: "He seems very pleased with what I've done with you." Worth judged its expression "enigmatic and intimate," and the artist concluded: "On seeing it again, I have to say that it didn't displease me."[69] At the beginning of 1908, the portrait was nearing completion. Against a neutral background, the countess in a fur coat, seated on a sofa with its back visible, poses with grace, her hair up, her hands

62 This anecdote left a lasting impression on the countess, who recalled it in a letter she sent to the painter on November 10, 1919, when she had left Russia, where she had abandoned her diary. Archives départementales de la Haute-Saône, Vesoul; Fonds Dagnan-Bouveret, correspondance (23) Princess Paley.

63 GARF, F. 613, op. 1, D. 156, L. 4. Letter dated August 3, 1907.

64 Dagnan-Bouveret painted this portrait in 1899.

65 *The Portrait of Madame la Comtesse de Cossé* by Dagnan-Bouveret was sold in Toulouse, March 20, 2015, lot 89. Another portrait of the countess is in the Musée d'Orsay collection, inv. RF 29115.

66 The actress Julia Bartet (1854-1941), whose portrait was presented by the artist at the 1894 Salon (SNBA). Her portrait (pastel) by Dagnan-Bouveret was sold by Ève, Paris, Drouot, May 19, 2015, lot 103.

67 GARF, F. 613, op. 1, D. 156, L. 4. Letter dated August 3, 1907.

68 Her château in Fleury-en-Bière and her villa in Hyères; Rousset-Charny 1990, 141.

69 GARF, F. 613, op. 1, D. 156, L. 6. Letter dated November 11, 1907.

crossed, wearing an elegant white dress adorned with precious pearls, a long necklace, and a bodice brooch. It was first exhibited in March 1908 at the "cercle,"[70] where it was presented against a cherry background. This was the annual exhibition of the Cercle de l'union artistique, and *Le Gaulois* gave an account of the "very impressive" opening in its "Bloc-notes Parisien."[71] The most successful portraits were of the journalist Henri Rochefort by Marcel Baschet and of the wine merchant Daniel Guestier by Léon Bonnat.

> But [...] there is a circle around the portrait of a ravishing woman by Mr. Dagnan-Bouveret. This time, the master has done something sombre, with a delicacy of touch that is not reminiscent of his old style. – Who is the sitter? The name is whispered in our ears. Why shouldn't we say it? It is the portrait of the Countess von Hohenfelsen, wife of the Grand Duke Paul, who, as is known, lives in Boulogne.[72]

After it was exhibited, Dagnan-Bouveret explained:

> The portrait returned to my studio an hour ago. I was tempted to ask it about everything it had heard during the month of the exhibition, but as I know that in general it could only be words of flippancy, ignorance or pretension, I refrain from any questions. This time, if you will allow me, dear Madam, I will present it to the general public at the Salon.[73]

It was the only work the artist presented at the 1908 Salon.[74] On its return, retouching details of the hands necessitated further sessions before final delivery.[75]

The countess was certainly satisfied, and in 1910 it was the grand duke's turn to pose for the artist.[76] Given his status and schedule, only a few sessions were required. Dagnan-Bouveret used a mannequin for the details of the uniform. The work was completed much more quickly, in just a few weeks, as the drawing was enhanced with pastel colors.[77] Finally, on January 20, 1911, the artist wrote: "Indeed, it is always rather painful to mix questions of art and friendly relations with the inevitable question of money."[78]

70 *Ibid.*, L. 25. Letter dated April 4, 1908.

71 *Le Gaulois*, March 2, 1908.

72 *Ibid.*

73 GARF, F. 613, op. 1, D. 156, L. 25. Letter dated April 4, 1908.

74 SNBA, no. 280, *Portrait de la comtesse H.*

75 GARF, F. 613, op. 1, D. 156, L. 29. Pneumatic letter dated July 5, 1908.

76 *Ibid.*, L. 37. Letter dated November 5, 1910.

77 *Ibid.*, L. 39. Undated letter.

78 *Ibid.*, L. 41-42. Letter dated January 20, 1911.

He set the price of a portrait of the grand duke at 5,000 francs and another portrait of the countess, a drawing, at 3,000 francs, bringing to three the number of works he produced for the couple.[79]

In 1912, Dagnan-Bouveret's work sparked a debate between Olga and the aesthete Robert de Montesquiou. She was reacting to the publication that year of his book *Têtes d'expression*, which he devoted a chapter to Dagnan-Bouveret's drawings. Montesquiou was highly critical of "Bouveret's drawings; this denomination says enough about what it means, namely that I don't need to admire them, just as they don't need my cult. What bothers me is that a person whom I love and admire professes an immoderate taste for them."[80]

Olga felt targeted and replied:

> My modesty will never allow me to recognize myself in the person "whom you love and admire" and who, in spite of this, had herself painted and even drawn by Dagnan. As far as I am concerned, I am your friend, and I mean that sincerely, but I do not know who, among your other friends, has had the same fondness for the Master's paintings as I. On this point, we will never agree, and it is better for our friendship never to speak of it.[81]

In addition to these artistic commissions and acquisitions, the couple invested their fortune in numerous projects affecting their Parisian home. As the countess's stepdaughter and Grand Duke Paul's daughter, Grand Duchess Maria Pavlovna (who had the same title and name as Grand Duke Vladimir's wife), noted: "The house, surrounded by a garden, wasn't very big at first, but every year a new room was added."[82]

A little exaggerated, this statement certainly refers to the renovation work carried out by Hoentschel, above all to the extension of the outbuildings undertaken from 1907 on. The countess asked the architect Maurice-Prosper Bersia-Tourette[83] (6, place de Valois) to construct her outbuildings, including a residential pavilion, caretaker's lodge, stables, and sheds, as well as accommodations for the servants.[84] The plans drawn up in October 1907 envisaged

79 The drawing is almost certainly one held in a private collection. In her correspondence with the artist, the countess mentions the creation of "three beautiful works." Archives départementales de la Haute-Saône, Vesoul, Fonds Dagnan-Bouveret, Correspondance (23) Princesse Paley. Postcard, January 11, 1914.

80 Robert de Montesquiou, *Têtes d'expression* (Paris: Émile Paul, 1912), 5.

81 Olga von Hohenfelsen (Paley) to Robert de Montesquiou, November 2, 1912, BNF, NAF-15166-FF 107-110.

82 Marie de Russie 1937, 50.

83 Bersia-Tourette was a student at the École des Beaux-Arts in Paris in the 1880s.

84 Archives municipales, Boulogne-Billancourt, 208.W.218, permit application dated May 12, 1908.

new buildings to replace and unify the old outbuildings. Built opposite the existing house, they were an extension of its wing, with which they harmonized. With their ashlar facade, the new spaces are arranged on either side of an elegant rotunda, set against the neighboring plot. Their style is classic and characteristic of Belle Époque architecture, borrowing the taste of the eighteenth century, and in particular that of Ange-Jacques Gabriel. The extension also made it possible to add a new winter garden with elegant wooden trellises, a "classic" of the period (figs. 13, 14). Olga visited the city's greenhouses on several occasions to draw inspiration from them and, with her landscape gardener Étienne Berthier[85] (10, rue Dosne), to choose the plants she wanted. Even though these were outbuildings, the countess was heavily involved in the project and in discussions with the various parties concerned, including Delisle.[86] This young firm, which specialized in lighting and bronze, is still in business and owned by the same family, and it probably supplied the lanterns and other lighting for the new wing.

As the refurbishments drew to a close, two sphinxes, acquired from Kraemer on April 19, 1909, for 14,000 francs, provided the perfect backdrop. Now one of the oldest galleries in Paris in the hands of the same family, Kraemer was founded in 1875 by Lucien Kraemer, who had left his native Alsace after the German annexation of 1871. Initially based on rue de Penthièvre, the gallery moved to 2, rue Tronchet in the 1880s, and it was to this address that the countess went in 1909. Collectors and connoisseurs from all over the world, including Rothschild, Camondo, Castellane, and Vanderbilt, were among the important clients of this dealer specializing in antique art, as the heading on the old invoices states: "Tapestries, antique furniture, curiosities & paintings." In 1928, Raymond Kraemer, Lucien's son, moved the family business to a luxurious mansion at 43, rue de Monceau, the current address of this Parisian institution dedicated to the art of the eighteenth century.[87]

In just a few years, Countess von Hohenfelsen and Grand Duke Paul had established a house in Paris that was characteristic of the Belle Époque and its penchant for the glory of the ancien régime, viewed with nostalgia by the Parisian *grand monde* and whose survival the couple, as Russian subjects, embodied.

85 GARF, F. 613, op. 1, D. 79, L. 1. Berthier was an alumnus of the École nationale d'horticulture de Versailles. Michel Boulet, ed., *Les Enjeux de la formation des acteurs de l'agriculture 1760-1945*, conference proceedings, ENESAD, 1999 (Dijon: Éducagri, 2000), 288.

86 Zeisler 2014b, 340.

87 See http://www.kraemer.fr/.

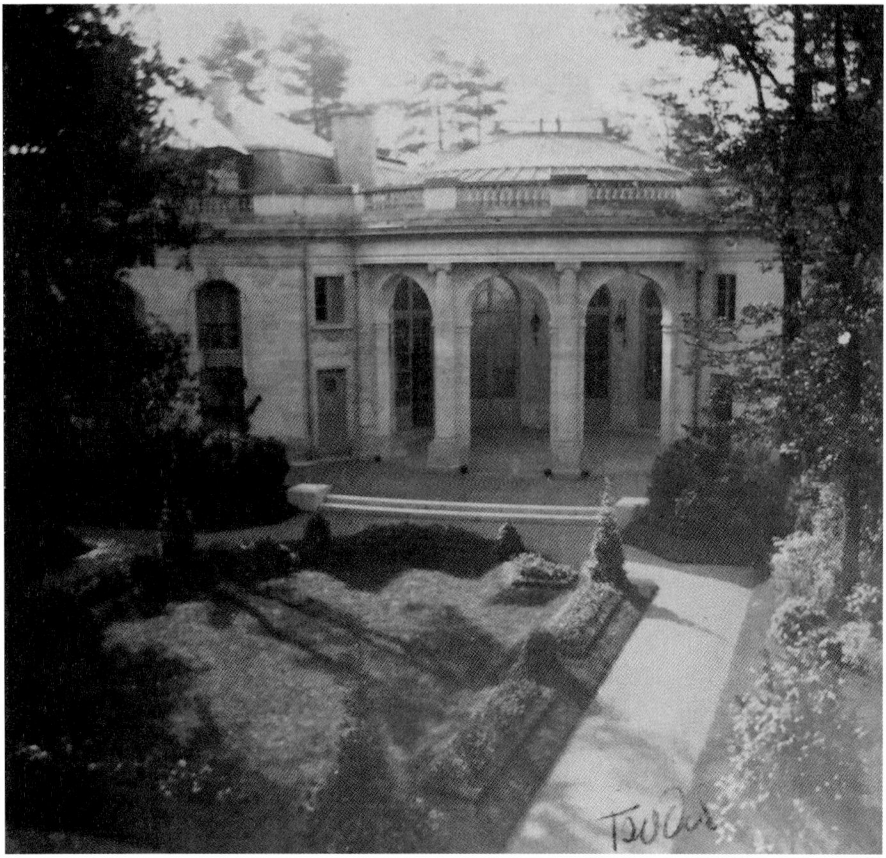

Fig. 13 View of the rotunda and new outbuildings, residence of Grand Duke Paul Alexandrovich and Countess von Hohenfelsen (formerly the Yusupov mansion) in Boulogne-Billancourt, ca. 1908. Photograph. Private collection.

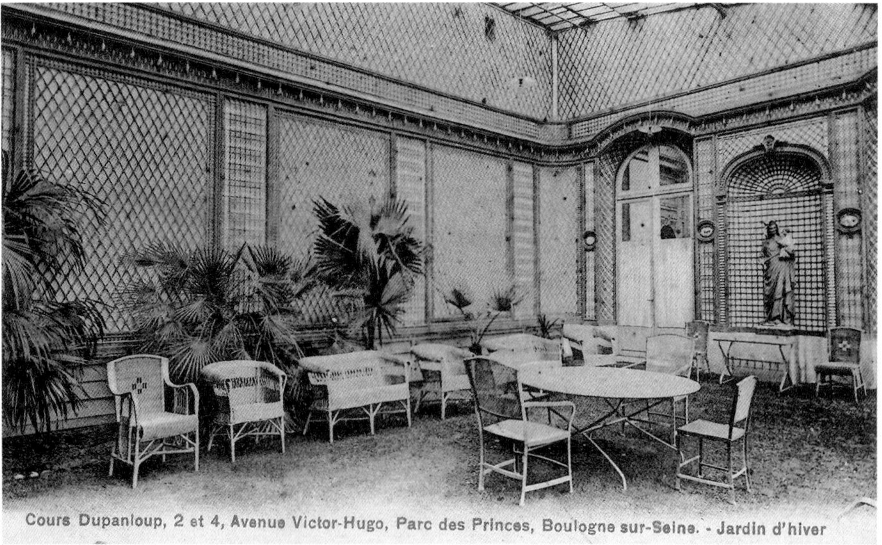

Fig. 14 Winter garden at the Cours Dupanloup, former residence of Grand Duke Paul Alexandrovich and Countess von Hohenfelsen (before that the Yusupov mansion) in Boulogne-Billancourt, after 1923. Postcard. Private collection.

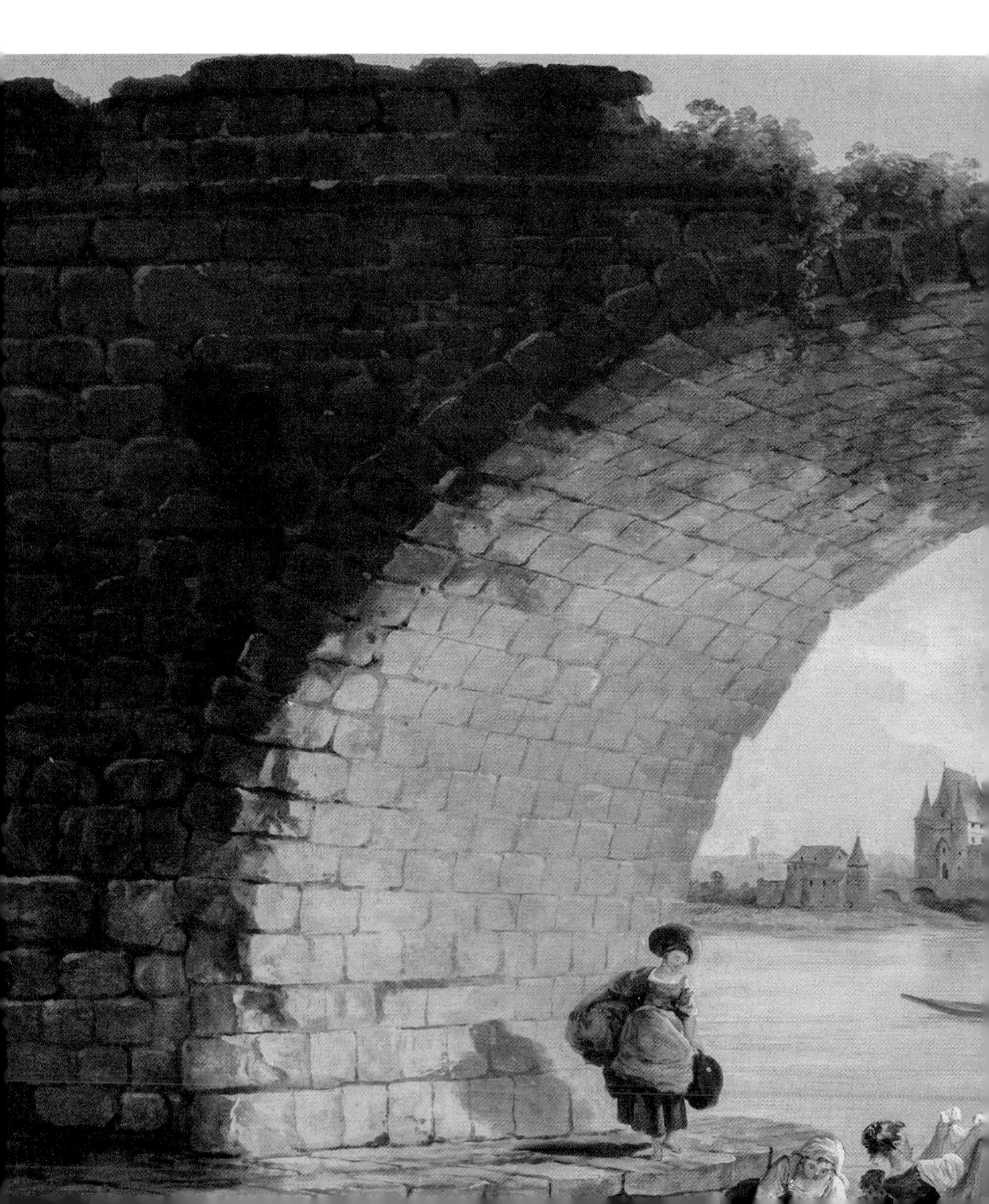

THE MANSION AND THE COLLECTION IN 1911

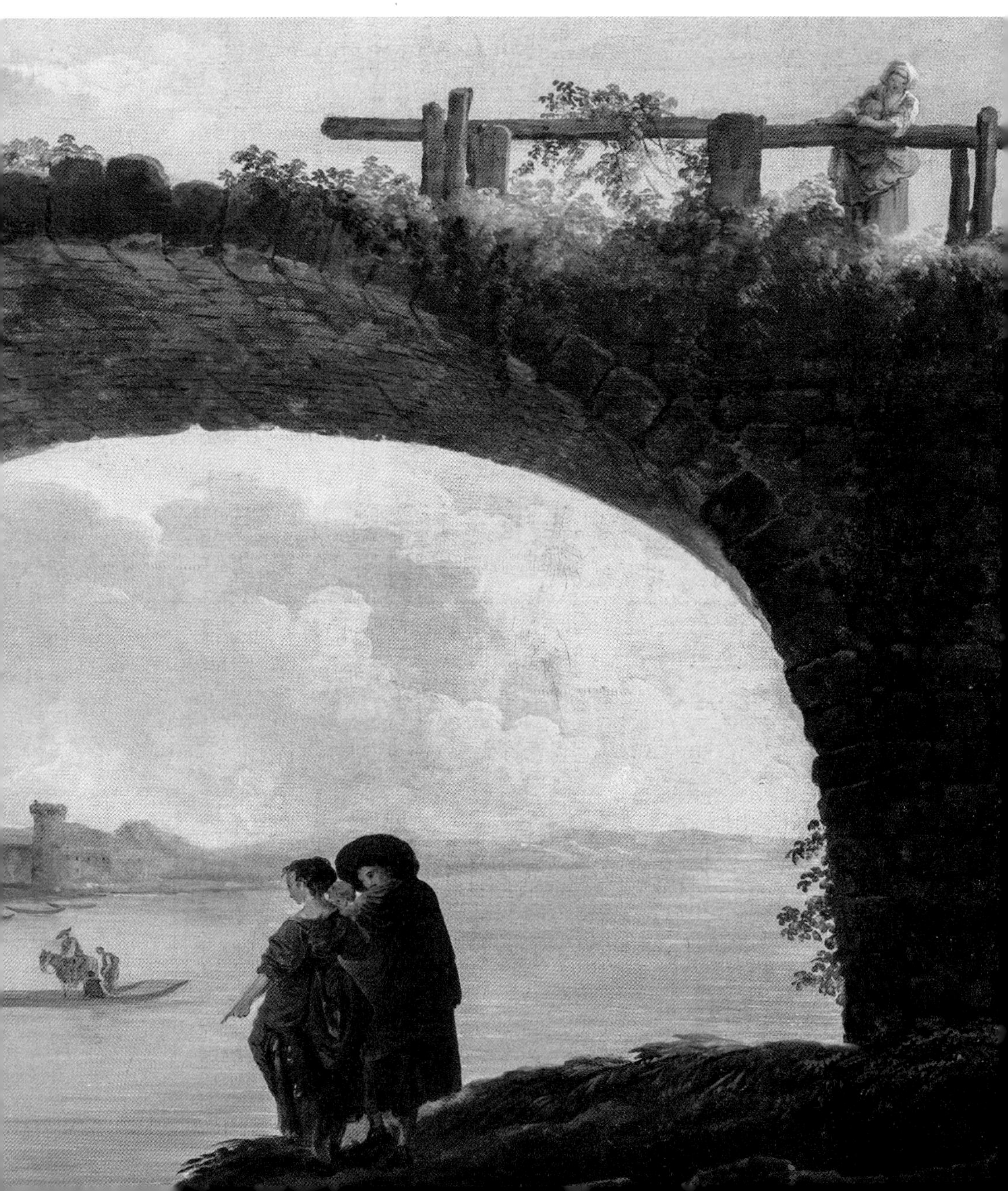

The architectural ensemble of the mansion is relatively well preserved today, and known thanks to the early publishing of postcards (see fig. 7) that the countess often used for her correspondence[1] (pl. 12). The interior layout, of which only a part remains, can be reconstructed by studying various documents that allow us to envisage the contributions of the decorator Hoentschel with regard to Second Empire elements and the arrangement of part of the collections amassed by the Countess von Hohenfelsen and the Grand Duke Paul, acquired in Paris or brought from Russia. In 1911, in a notebook,[2] Olga took care to list, room by room, the main works in Boulogne, a place she called "*notre* home."[3]

The mansion's main entrance remained mostly the same as in the Yusupov era, although it had been enlarged by Hoentschel, who had removed a partition separating the vestibule from a first corridor-like antechamber. Covered in stone and punctuated with pilasters, in the manner of vestibules inspired by eighteenth-century models, it is still embellished today with overdoors in relief depicting allegories of Spring and Summer, while on the wall, the crowned monogram of the grand duke stands out from a sculpted medallion (pl. 13). Olga (fig. 15) and her daughter posed in this entranceway, next to furnishings from 1900 consisting of a Louis XVI – style umbrella stand in lacquered, caned wood and an Art Nouveau – style coat rack.

To the right of the entrance, a hallway leads to a service staircase down to the basement kitchens, ingeniously placed beneath the rather undersized dining room, as Grand Duchess Maria noted: "The room was small and could hardly hold anyone but the family. When my father and stepmother gave big dinner parties, the table was set in the next room."[4]

In this dining room, Louis XVI – style woodwork is punctuated by draped Doric pilasters separating the panels. The Louis XVI medallion overdoors, decorated with vases, complete the decor. The trumeau around the fireplace, surmounted by a cartouche with the Cyrillic coat of arms of the grand duke and countess (П Г), now features a mirror but was intended to enclose the Aubusson tapestry from Laurent, chosen with Hitrov. The countess considered it "very pretty." The rest of the furnishings included a round table and chairs covered in yellow silk, as well as a folding screen purchased with the tapestry. As a rule, the screens were placed in front of the service entrance, making comings and goings with the kitchens and service areas more discreet. As for the marble mantelpiece, it bore "two magnificent

1 Archives départementales de la Haute-Saône, Vesoul, Fonds Dagnan-Bouveret, Correspondance (23) Princesse Paley. Postcard to Dagnan-Bouveret, December 31, 1912.

2 GARF, F. 613, op. 1, D. 615, L. 1-6. Document dated April 5, 1911.

3 Olga von Hohenfelsen (Paley) to Robert de Montesquiou, June 10, 1912, BNF, NAF-15085-FF 122-123.

4 Marie de Russie 1937, 52.

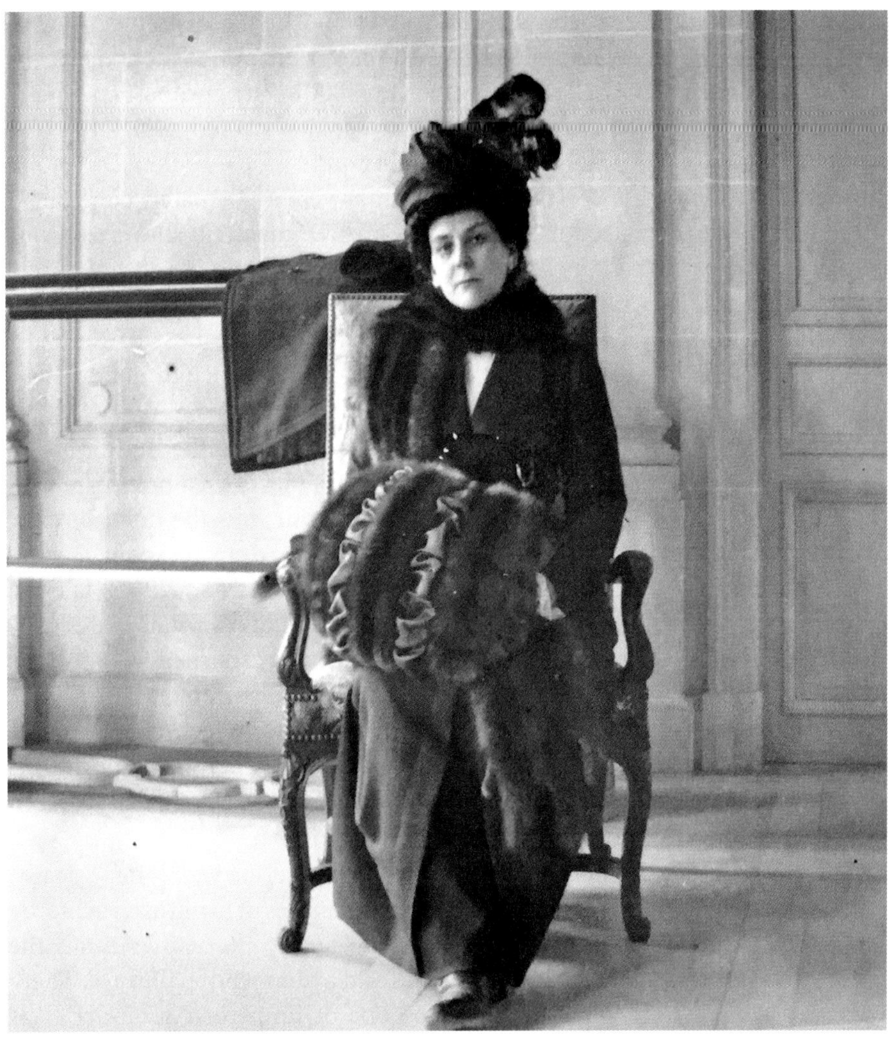

Fig. 15 Countess von Hohenfelsen in the entrance hall of her mansion in Boulogne-Billancourt, ca. 1908. Photograph. Private collection.

Chinese potiches."[5] Today, this room features a large decorative canvas depicting a number of characters animating an immense landscape flanked by a large ruined antique fountain, reminiscent of the art of Hubert Robert. It may be the work by Robert that Olga described as "ideal" and acquired from Larcade in 1907.

Located next door, the *premier salon d'entrée* (first drawing room) served as the couple's dining room when entertaining and was known as the *salon rose* (pink drawing room) in the Yusupov era. Connected by two double

5 *Ibid.*

doors to the dining room, and the first room opposite the vestibule, it forms the central axis of the house, together with the rotunda opposite it at the far side of the garden. Adorned with elegant Louis XVI – style wood paneling, it was furnished with a Regence sofa and six armchairs covered with petit point tapestry[6] (figs. 16, 17), a Regence table with marble top, another Directoire table and an Empire table. In this room, visitors were immediately confronted with the countess's collections, displayed in three thematic showcases, one containing jades and Chinese porcelain, the other two European porcelain. The guests' imperial genealogy was symbolized by Shibanov's portrait of Catherine the Great (see pl. 7) and by a small marble bust of Emperor Alexander I. Also hanging were three pastels of children, including Boucher's *Young Girl with Cat*.

On the other side of the drawing room, opposite the dining room, were two other rooms. One, a blue drawing room in the Yusupov years, was the pink boudoir, behind which, on the vestibule side, was the first staircase. The second, the length of the former *salon d'or* (golden drawing room), served as a library. The countess's boudoir was furnished with a writing table, a delicate drop-front desk, a small ivory-inlaid table,[7] other small tables, and various chairs. The lintel of the marble mantelpiece was adorned with antique trim. The room was also decorated with potiches and other objets d'art. There was a portrait of a young girl in a blue-and-white dress by Jean-Marc Nattier[8] and a portrait of the grand duke by Dagnan-Bouveret. The Nattier portrait is now identified as that of Mademoiselle Marsollier and was probably acquired by the couple from Wildenstein (fig. 18).[9]

The library, which Grand Duchess Maria described as "little,"[10] featured – apart from shelves and books – a number of pieces of furniture, including several seats and armchairs suitable for reading, and works of art. Among the latter, the countess listed Chinese Blue vases and a number of paintings. There were various portraits, including perhaps one of Emperor Alexander II as a child by George Dawe[11] (see pls. 14, 53); an "Empire Lady," a portrait of a young woman by Thomas Lawrence;[12] another depicting Grand Duchess Elena Pavlovna after a model by Stepan Shchukin[13] (fig. 19), and three Hubert Robert works, including *Bridge with Washerwomen*, probably from the Arthur Tooth & Sons gallery (see pl. 10). The other two, depicting imaginary views of

6 Paley sale, Christie's, London, June 6-7, 1929, lot 109, acquired by Stettiner.

7 *Ibid.*, lot 93, acquired by Weiss.

8 Paley sale, Christie's, London, June 21, 1929, lot 37.

9 Wintermute 1996, 97, pl. 13, 51.

10 Marie de Russie 1937, 54.

11 Paley sale, Christie's, London, June 21, 1929, lot 21 or 22.

12 *Ibid.*, lot 34.

13 *Ibid.*, lot 44.

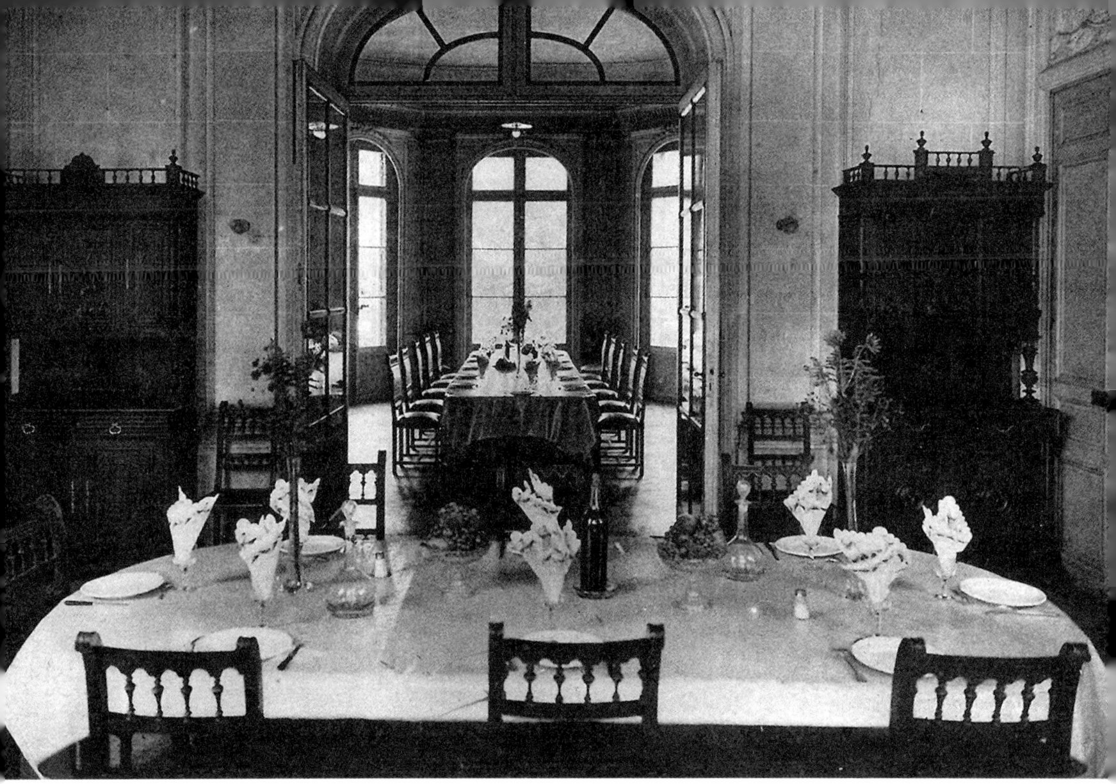

Fig. 16 Cours Dupanloup dining room (former vestibule and first drawing room), former residence of Grand Duke Paul Alexandrovich and Countess von Hohenfelsen (previously the Yusupov mansion) in Boulogne-Billancourt, after 1923. Postcard. Private collection.

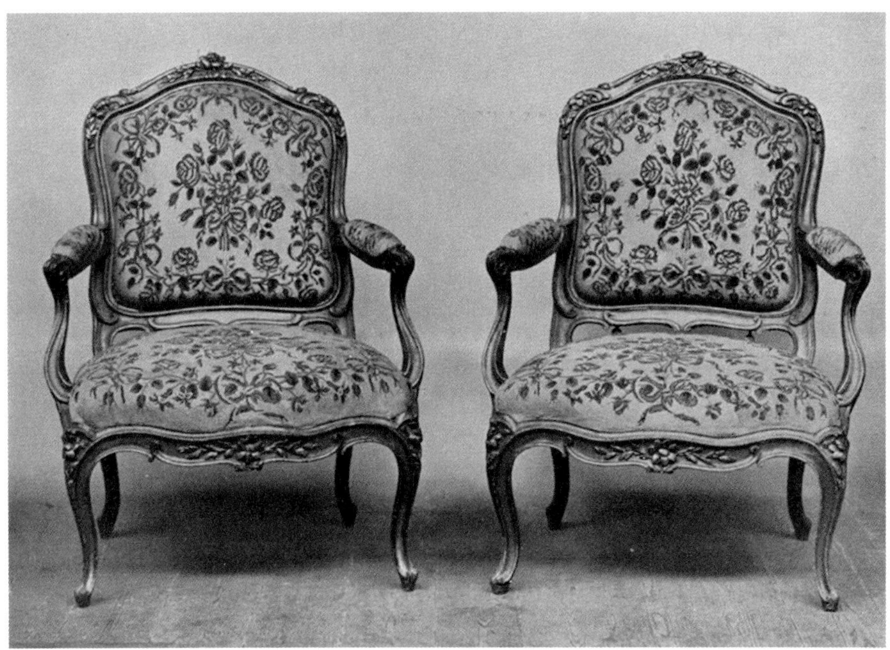

Fig. 17 Armchairs from a suite in gilded wood and covered in petit point, France, Louis XV period. Current location unknown. Hillwood Estate, Museum & Gardens, Archives and Special Collections, Washington, DC.

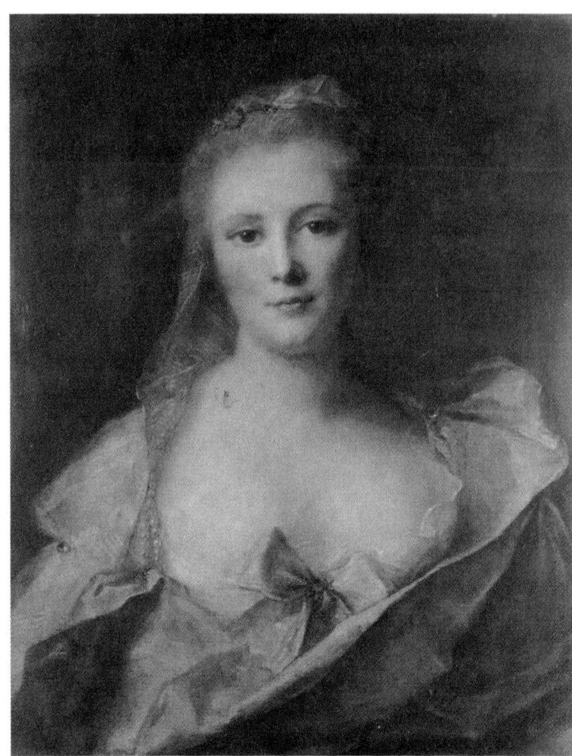

Fig. 18 Jean-Marc Nattier, *Portrait of a Young Girl in a Blue-and-White Dress (Mademoiselle Marsollier, also known as Mlle Lorimier de Chamilly)*, 1757. Oil on canvas. Private collection. Frick Art Reference Library, New York.

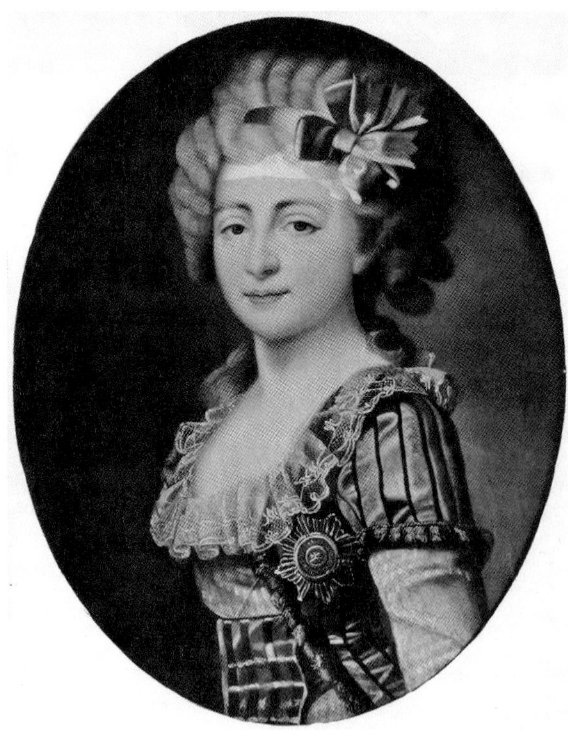

Fig. 19 After Stepan S. Shchukin, *Portrait of Grand Duchess Elena Pavlovna*, ca. 1800. Oil on canvas. Private collection. Frick Art Reference Library, New York.

Rome, came from the Russian collections[14] of Count Lazarev in St. Petersburg, then of Princess Urusov, and are now in the National Museum of Western Art in Tokyo (pls. 15, 16).

The grand duke's study, formerly the Yusupov library, was completely refurbished by Hoentschel in the Adam style, which reminded the owner of his family's palaces. Recently restored and now the office of the Cours Dupanloup management, it was inspired by British-style interiors imported to Russia in the late eighteenth century by artists and architects such as Charles Cameron. Bas-reliefs set in cartouches showing antique subjects, reminiscent of Wedgwood motifs, stand out against green painted panels framed in gold and adorned with palmettes and other garlands (pl. 17). The marble mantel in the corner is also inspired by some Russian interiors, notably the Anichkov Palace. Grand Duchess Maria left a faithful and moving description of the study as she found it after her father's death:

> It was a narrow room with three large windows along one wall. His desk was placed at an angle next to the first window. Near the second was his favorite armchair and a small leather sofa. The armchair had not been covered. An indentation remained in the backrest, where he used to rest his head. I could see my father again, a book in his slender fingers, peering over his dark-rimmed glasses to answer a question. This was where he would take tea when we were alone.[15]

In this somewhat nostalgic interior, the grand duke was surrounded by several portraits, including that of his wife by Dagnan-Bouveret (pl. 11; fig. 20). The art of Dimitri Levitzky, one of the greatest Russian portraitists of the eighteenth century, about whom Diaghilev had published a seminal monograph in 1902,[16] was represented by a portrait in dark blue uniform of Platon Zubov, the last favorite of Empress Catherine II (fig. 21).[17] Emperor Alexander I, the grand duke's great-uncle, was depicted in a canvas, dated 1825, by the British portraitist George Dawe,[18] whose composition showing him in the dark uniform of the Preobrazhensky regiment exists in several copies (fig. 22). There was also a portrait of Empress Maria Alexandrovna, the grand duke's mother, by the Austro-Hungarian Heinrich von Angeli, a fashionable

14 *Ibid.*, lot 40. An early copy of one of these is in the Yekaterinburg Museum of Fine Arts. It entered the museum's collections in 1949 from the Hermitage Museum, where the work had been transferred from the Antikvariat in 1932. Historically, it came from the Durnovo collection. Information provided by Ludmila Budrina, curator at the Yekaterinburg Museum of Fine Arts.

15 Marie de Russie 1937, 54.

16 Sergei Diaghilev, *Dimitri Levitsky* (St. Petersburg, 1902) (in Russian).

17 Paley sale, Christie's, London, June 21, 1929, lot 35.

18 *Ibid.*, lot 23.

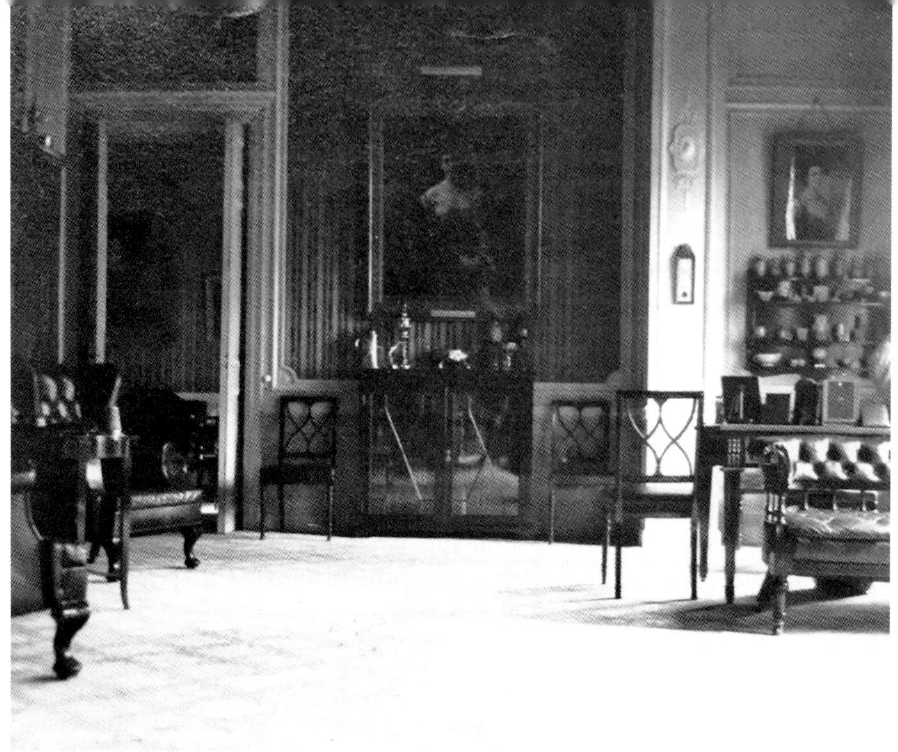

Fig. 20 The residence at Boulogne with the portrait of Countess von Hohenfelsen, ca. 1909. Photograph. Private collection.

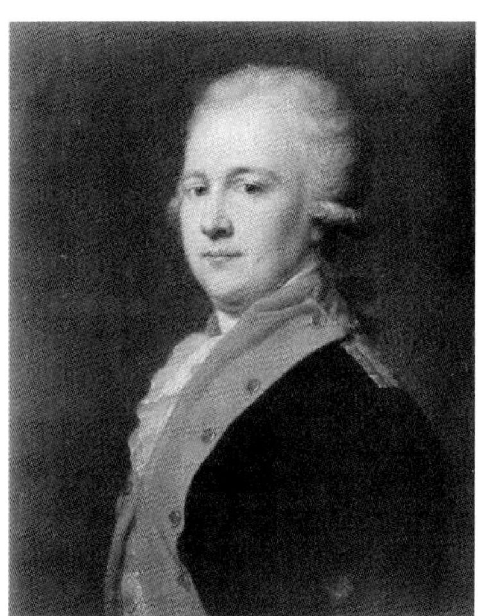

Fig. 21 (above) Dimitri Levitsky, *Portrait of Platon Zubov in Dark-blue Uniform with Red Edging*. Oil on canvas. Current location unknown. Frick Art Reference Library, New York.

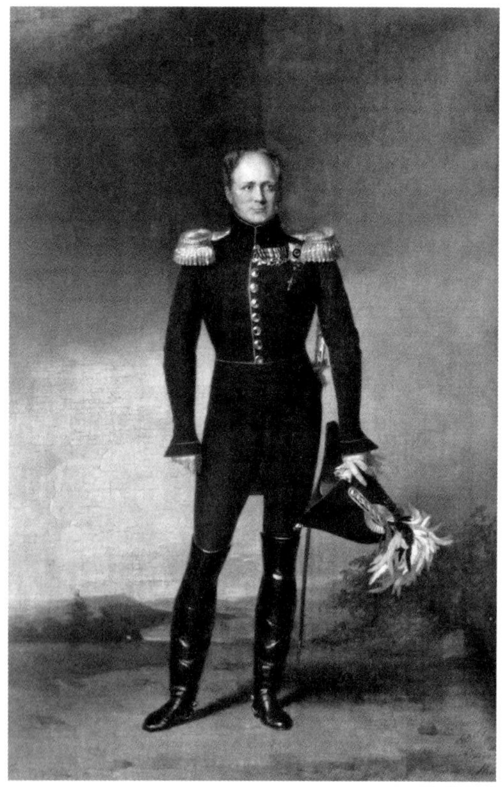

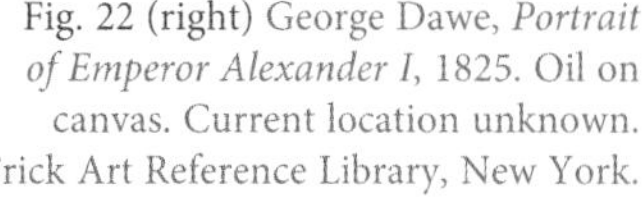

Fig. 22 (right) George Dawe, *Portrait of Emperor Alexander I*, 1825. Oil on canvas. Current location unknown. Frick Art Reference Library, New York.

Victorian portraitist. But the masterpiece of the room was Bellotto's *View of the Church of San Giovanni and Paolo* in Venice (see pl. 8). Given the strong Neoclassical character of this space, the grand duke may also have chosen to display here his artwork by François Flameng in praise of Napoleon, notably his *Isola Bella* (see pl. 5).

The grand duke's study provided a link between the reception areas of the main building and the large room in the wing, formerly the Yusupovs' Henri II gallery. The main reception room of the mansion, it had been completely remodeled by Hoentschel. Originally designed in the Renaissance style, with columns and a gallery, and decorated with large antique tapestries, the room, which had its own entrance, was served by a double-flight staircase, which was redesigned in the style of the eighteenth century, with a wrought-iron banister. A Louis XVI – period desk and a Brussels tapestry from the same period were displayed in the room's entrance.[19] Produced by the van der Borcht family workshop, the tapestry depicts a mythological scene combining the goddess Amphitrite, other marine divinities, and mermaids.

This main reception room, which the countess called the "Louis XVI salon," had lost its gallery to make space for more bedrooms upstairs. Hoentschel is credited with the rich white and gold woodwork, still in place, with pilaster decorations reminiscent of the Versailles fittings of the Louis XV period, and rich cornices with cartouches alternating with musical trophies and groups of putti in relief. "The salon was only used when there were guests,"[20] and especially when the countess was entertaining on Sundays (pl. 18; fig. 23). The floor was covered with a thick Aubusson carpet and the windows decorated with heavy curtains.[21] A piano, Louis XVI furniture – a sofa and eight armchairs – in gilded wood, covered with tapestry decorated with children after Aesop's *Fables* on a pink background[22] (fig. 24), and various antique chairs[23] welcomed visitors, who could admire three Louis XV commodes,[24] small tables, two screens,[25] and other works from the family collection. Those works, notably porcelain, were arranged on several display tables or on the furniture and mantelpiece and included an antique clock and Chinese porcelain (particularly, two Famille rose vases, and two birds). On the picture rails hung a pastel depicting one of the couple's daughters, as

19 Tapestry: Paley sale, Christie's, London, June 6-7, 1929, lot 150, acquired by Feibes (?).

20 Marie de Russie 1937, 57.

21 *Ibid.*, 57.

22 Paley sale, Christie's, London, June 6-7, 1929, lot 90, acquired by Polovtsov.

23 In particular, two gilded wood bergères: Paley sale, Christie's, London, June 6-7, 1929, lot 113, acquired by Fabre.

24 In particular, a pair of commodes with floral marquetry and gilt bronze decor: Paley sale, Christie's, London, June 6-7, 1929, lot 89, acquired by E. Phillips.

25 Including an antique Louis XVI petit point: Paley sale, Christie's, London, June 6-7, 1929, lot 110, acquired by Sticks.

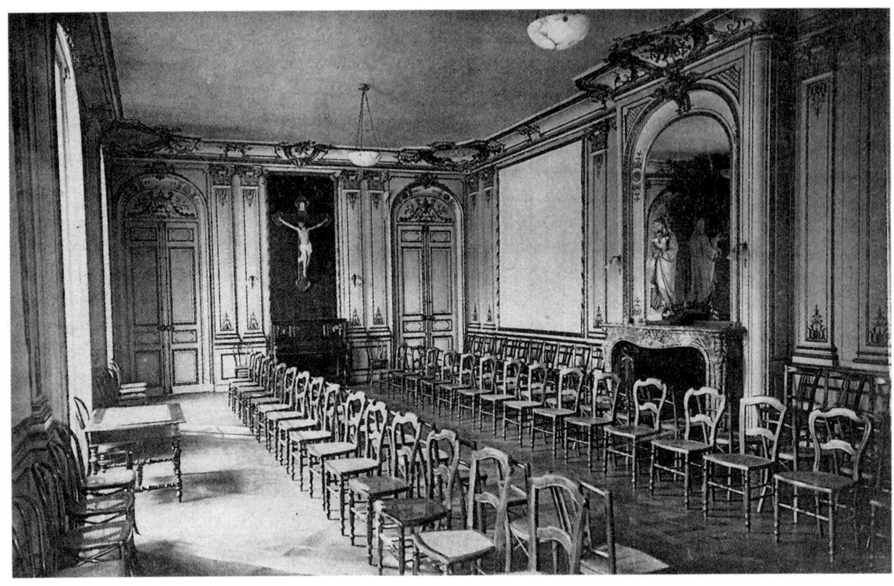

Fig. 23 Cours Dupanloup (former grand salon), former residence of Grand Duke Paul Alexandrovich and Countess von Hohenfelsen (previously the Yusupov mansion), Boulogne-Billancourt, after 1923. Postcard. Private collection.

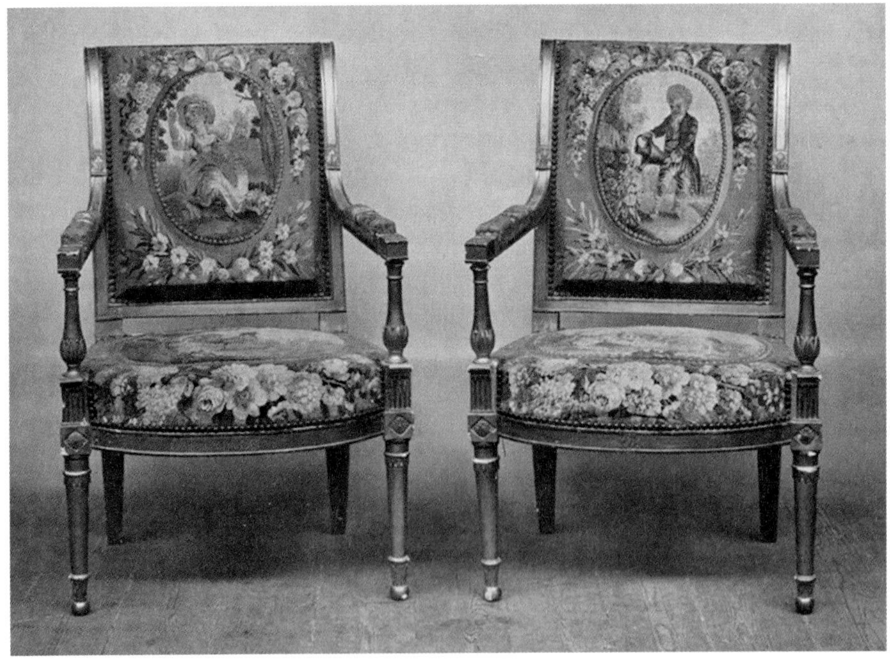

Fig. 24 Armchairs from a suite in gilded wood, covered with Aubusson tapestry depicting Aesop's *Fables*, France, Louis XVI period. Current location unknown. Hillwood Estate, Museum & Gardens, Archives and Special Collections, Washington, DC.

well as the Perronneau from the antique dealer Larcade (see pl. 9) and a van Dyck painting called *The Blue Boy*,[26] now identified as a portrait of Charles Stanley, Lord Strange (pl. 19).

A smoking room adjoined the drawing room, but we know little about its decor. The same holds true of the family's personal spaces, which were distributed over the second floor of the mansion and must have been furnished in a more functional manner, in particular as regards what appears to have been the children's study room. Presumably located upstairs, it featured numerous storage spaces along the walls and a large table in the center of the room, accompanied by bentwood chairs. A family photograph shows several objects used for the children's entertainment and education, including a phonograph and a miniature theater stage, reflecting their parents' interest in the arts.

It was in the aristocratic setting of their transformed and enlarged mansion, which was both a reflection of the eighteenth century and of their own times, that Grand Duke Paul and Countess von Hohenfelsen entertained the best of Parisian society.

26 Paley sale, Christie's, London, June 21, 1929, lot 47.

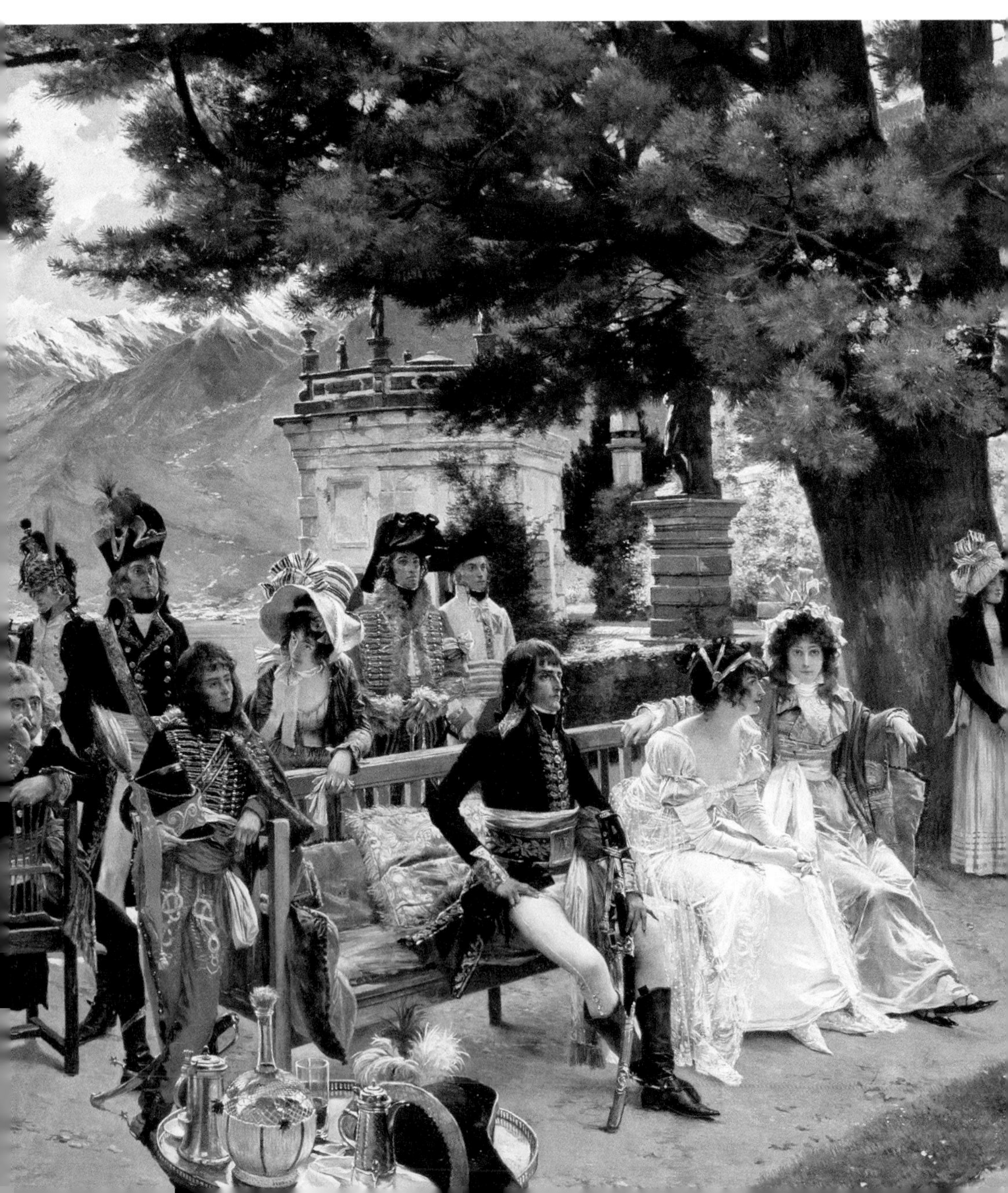

HIGH SOCIETY IN BOULOGNE: A MIX OF DAILY LIFE AND CEREMONY

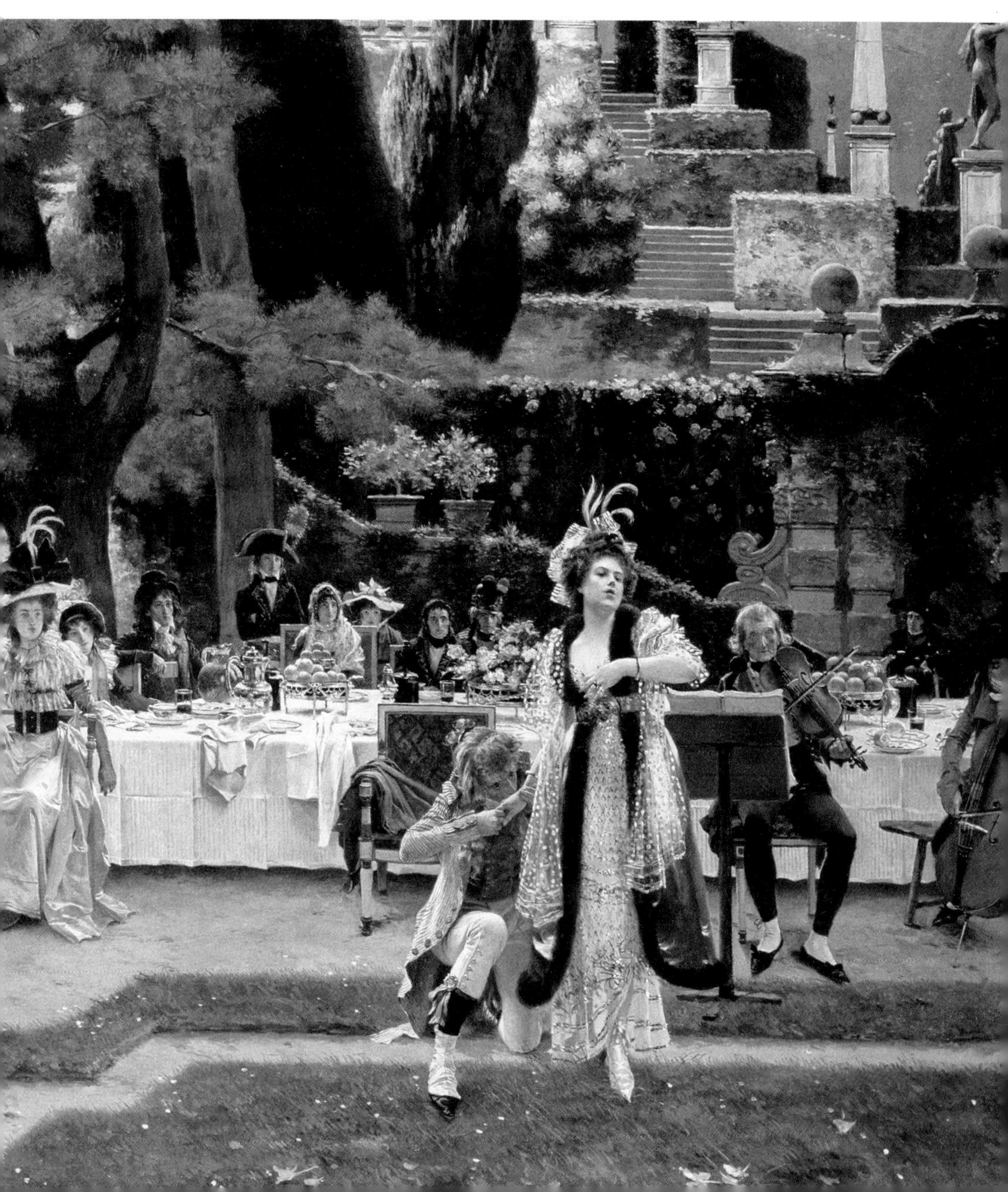

> Whether at large dinner parties or intimate gatherings, Princess Paley was always the soul of this hospitable house, which had become the rendezvous of so many distinguished people.
>
> Countess Kleinmichel

Grand Duke Paul of Russia and Countess von Hohenfelsen were a couple who met all the criteria for belonging to the Parisian and cosmopolitan *grand monde* as defined by Alice Bravard.[1] The couple, the countess in particular, were regularly mentioned in the society columns of numerous newspapers and magazines, such as *Le Figaro* and *Le Gaulois*, one of the criteria for belonging to this fashionable set, as were their networks. In every respect, the countess belonged to the select group of high society women who led an

> idle life filled with obligations. […] First of all, they dedicate a part of their time to keeping house. Furnishing the domestic space, supervising the staff, and bringing up the children are her main duties within the household. This gives them real power in the private sphere. However, these activities keep them only partially occupied, since the high society ladies generally devote only mornings to them. In the afternoons, they give priority to their external relationships: they go out shopping at the outlets of their suppliers, pay visits or invite friends. One afternoon a week or two, they entertain at home on their "Day."[2]

Countess von Hohenfelsen's "Day" was from 4:00 to 7:00 p.m. on Sundays, which *Le Figaro* and other newspapers frequently announced had been canceled or postponed, or resumed following her return from some travels.[3]

A large part of the countess's domestic duties was devoted to furnishing her successive Parisian houses, which were, indeed, places in which to receive guests, but were above all the couple's home, where they lived with their three children and regularly entertained their respective stepchildren. According to the recollections of the grand duke's daughter Irina, he "essentially loved family life"[4] (figs. 25-27). Every morning, he would go for a walk with his daughters in the Bois de Boulogne, as Irina affirmed: "We had a wonderful childhood, because our parents were an exceptionally close couple."[5]

The rare personal photographs showing the family in their intimacy do not lie. The daughters posing with their father in the winter garden or playing

1 Bravard 2013.

2 *Ibid.*, 90.

3 See, for example, *Le Figaro*, March 1st, 1908; March 23 and December 17, 1912; June 12, 1913.

4 Ferrand 1993, 13.

5 *Ibid.*, 15.

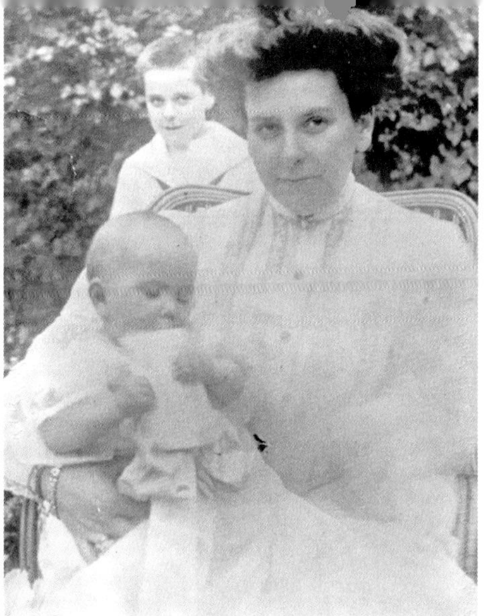

Fig. 25 Countess von Hohenfelsen, Prince Vladimir, and Countess Irina. Boulogne, ca. 1904. Private collection.

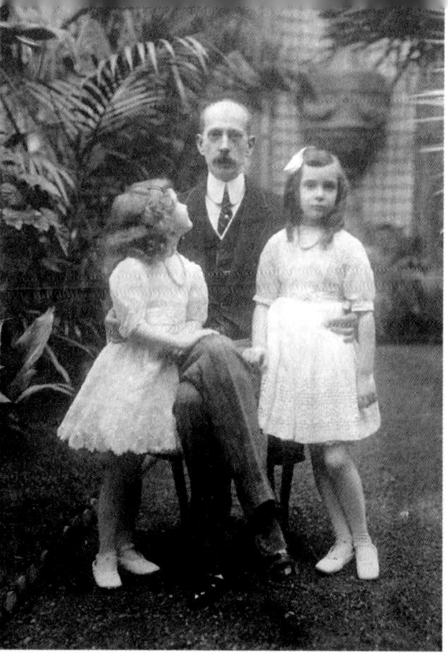

Fig. 26 Grand Duke Paul Alexandrovich and his two younger daughters. Boulogne, ca. 1911. Photograph. Private collection.

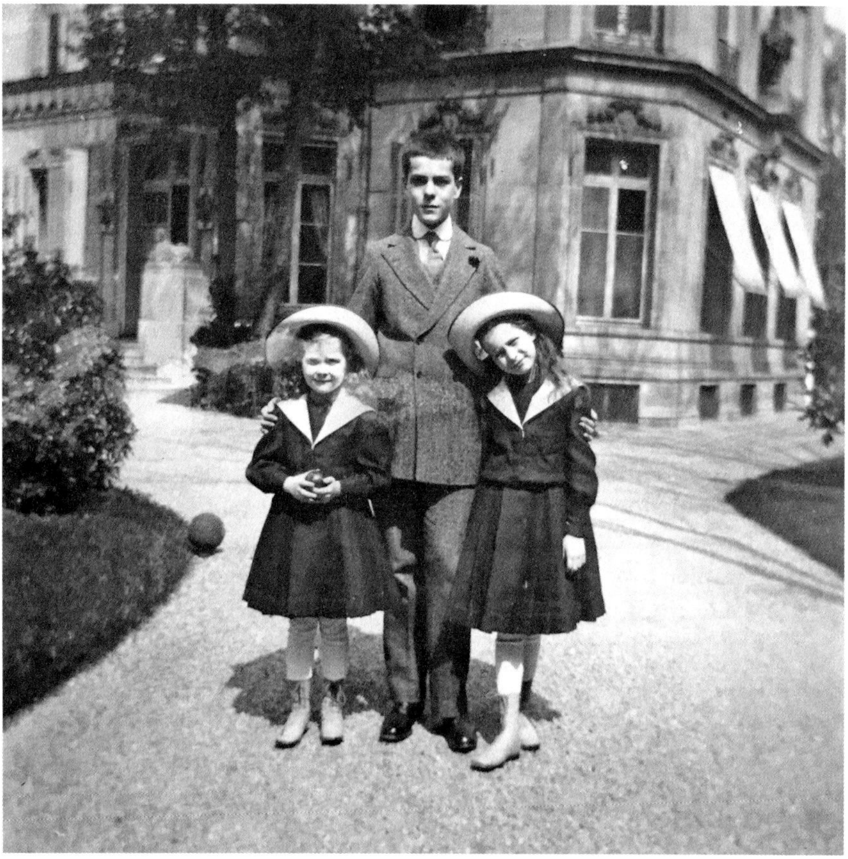

Fig. 27 Prince Vladimir and his two sisters. Boulogne, ca. 1911. Photograph. Private collection.

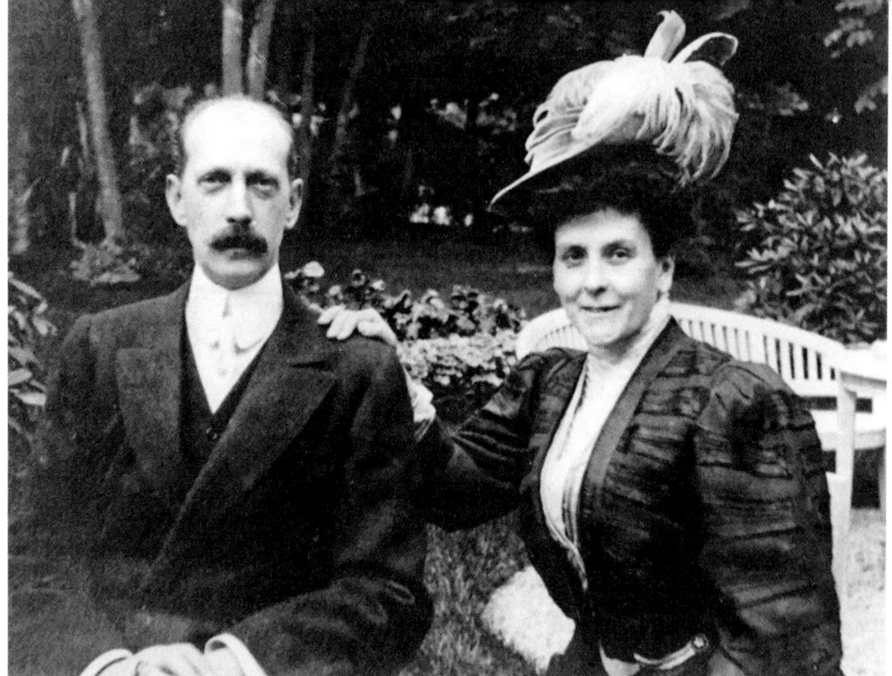

Fig. 28 Grand Duke Paul Alexandrovich and Countess von Hohenfelsen, ca. 1913. Photograph. Private collection.

in the park elegantly dressed as little Parisian girls, the grand duke and countess out for a stroll together – all are true to life (fig. 28). Countess Kleinmichel carefully describes this close relationship: "when his beloved companion was beside him, looking at him with tenderness, he needed nothing else: for him, the cherished eyes contained the universe."[6]

To ensure the family's upbringing and the running of the house, Olga was surrounded by a relatively large staff. A mansion at this level required more than fifteen employees, some of whom worked within the walls and others outside. By cross-checking various sources, we can learn more about these servants, whose roles were essential to the smooth running of the house. Among the staff for whom the countess was responsible were the children's governess, Miss White,[7] and a teacher, notably the tutor Hortense Judlin, who was present at the registration of the two girls' birth certificates. Another was the loyal Jacqueline Theureau, originally from Burgundy.[8] The teaching was perhaps completed by Aline Châtelain, listed in 1914 for a fee of 75 francs for lessons given to two pupils during the first fortnight of May.[9] She had a close relationship with her pupils, as shown by this reference from the correspondence of Dupré, presented as the private secretary of the grand duke, who remained in France during the war while the family was in Russia:

6 Kleinmichel 1927, 245.

7 Paley 1923, 263.

8 *Ibid.*

9 GARF, F. 644, op. 1, D. 270, L. 40.

> Mademoiselle Châtelain came this week to see if I had received any news; she was tormented at not having had any letters from Mesdemoiselles Irina and Natalie, and she asked me to pass on her fond memory to the Demoiselles.[10]

During this same period, the couple also hired Olga Lubimov, who was paid 100 francs and was probably able to give Russian lessons.[11] Letters exchanged between Dupré and the grand duke's aide-de-camp, Efimovitch, provide further details on the staff of the Boulogne household. We learn that the secretary, housed in an apartment in the outbuildings, not only was responsible for maintaining the accounts, but also kept the keys to the wine cellar, traditionally in the hands of the *maître d'hôtel*, or majordomo, a function that may in fact have been Dupré's, unless he was the steward.[12] Also part of the indoor staff, the concierge Gustave and his wife, Joséphine, occupied the lodge. The house also employed a chef, a landscaper (Étienne Berthier), a gardener and two chauffeurs for the cars, a sign of great luxury in the Belle Époque. In 1908, for example, the couple acquired a Lorraine-Dietrich through the luxury coach builder Mühlbacher, a family business founded under the ancien régime[13] and established at 63, avenue des Champs-Élysées in 1863.[14]

These letters also list the names of some whose functions in the household are unknown: Léon Michel, Alfred Magny, Charles Cratère, Émile Drouot, and his two assistants, Madeleine Delahaye and Berthe Marchand.[15] Some of them, in particular nannies and governesses, appear occasionally in family photographs, although they cannot be identified with certainty (fig. 29). In addition to their wages, staff received other remuneration. The countess regularly mentions in her diary, in January, what appear to be Christmas gifts. On January 11, 1904, she lists the following: "Mme Mailly received a brooch[16] and 1,000 francs; Mlle Madaubon, the nanny 50 [francs?] and Rosalie 20 francs."

At Christmastime, Olga had something for everyone, and "Mademoiselle," certainly referring to the governess or teacher, was never forgotten, including at Easter. In 1906, she received a small Gallé vase that had been bought for 200 francs. Gifts for staff were generally selected from department stores, but sometimes they came from luxury shops such as Kendall and *L'Escalier de Cristal*, or the fan maker Kees.

10 *Ibid.*, L. 56-57.

11 *Ibid.*, L. 42.

12 *Ibid.*, L. 50.

13 Arch. Nat. LH 1962/52.

14 *La Ville lumière* 1909, 408.

15 GARF, F. 644, op. 1, D. 270, L. 61.

16 Brooch purchased on January 5 from Morgan.

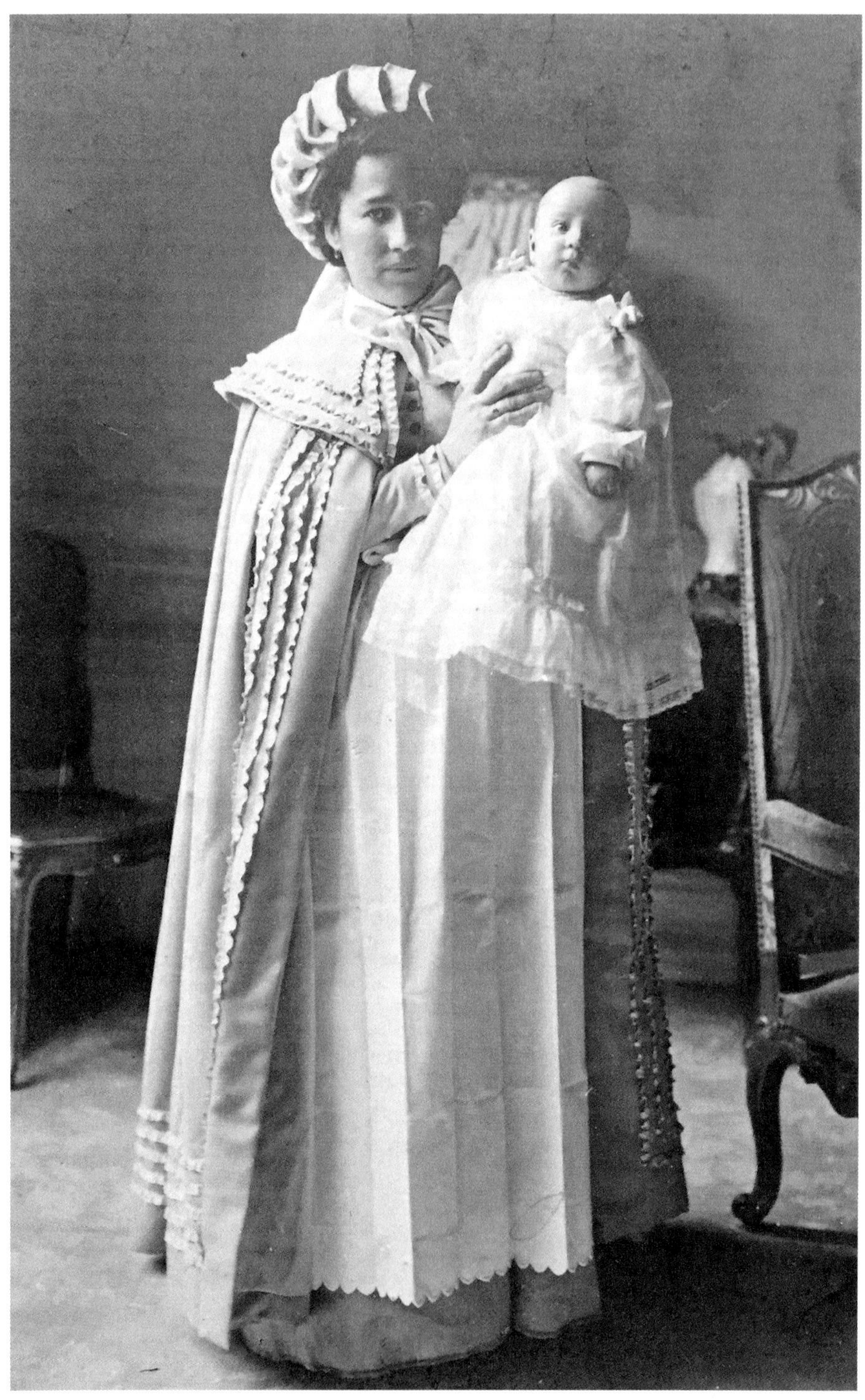

Fig. 29 Baby Irina in the arms of her nurse Madeleine Pochetat, ca. 1903. Photograph. Private collection.

We can imagine the rhythm of the days in Boulogne, divided between housekeeping and family life, punctuated by lessons, reading, walks, meals, and evening prayer. When the couple had no guests, lunch was the main time for sharing news. This meal invariably took place at half past noon. The grand duke, who prized punctuality, went so far as to sit alone at the table without waiting for the rest of the family, especially his wife, who "could never be punctual,"[17] reports his daughter. At dinnertime, the children ate separately, but they met up afterward with their parents, who would read to them when Vladimir and his sisters weren't improvising a staged play in the large drawing room.[18]

Life in Boulogne was also full of the society events typical of the life in their class, from which children were generally excluded. In this respect, Olga was a perfectly accomplished society woman. In *Souvenirs d'un monde englouti*, Countess Kleinmichel lists some of the great names of the Belle Époque who frequented the mansion: the comtesse de Pourtalès, Véra de Talleyrand-Périgord, duchesse de Camastra, duchesse de Rohan, princesse Marie Murat, Lady de Grey, M. and Mme Jean de Reszke, M. and Mme Paul Bourget, the Vigiers, and Reynaldo Hahn (1874-1947).[19] The latter was a famous musician from Venezuela with whom the countess corresponded between 1907 and 1916.[20] He was a key figure of the Belle Époque, "this '*parisianissime*' Parisian, right down to the spirit,"[21] and a close friend of Marcel Proust. While the main figures in *La Recherche* were inspired by Parisians, the foreigners Proust mentions are sometimes real people whose names he did not bother to change. Such is the case with Grand Duke Vladimir, or Countess von Hohenfelsen, who appears in the final volume, *Le Temps retrouvé*, as a close friend of Madame de Guermantes. She is mentioned when Proust describes the way in which the duchess behaved with representatives of the imperial family before the war: "a freedom amounting to social tactlessness," whereas, on the contrary, the duchess is described one of the few to remain loyal to them after the Revolution. The case of the countess is used to illustrate how Madame de Guermantes could indeed displease the wife of Grand Duke Vladimir:

> The very year which preceded the war, she had annoyed the Grande-Duchesse Vladimir by calling comtesse of Hohenfelsen, the morganatic wife of Grand-Duc Paul, the "Grande-Duchesse Paul."[22]

17 Marie de Russie 1937, 53.

18 *Ibid.*, 58.

19 Kleinmichel 1927, 244.

20 GARF, F. 613, op. 1, D. 127.

21 Pierre-Emmanuel Prouvost d'Agostino, "Reynaldo Hahn," in Centorame and Andia 2005, 210-11.

22 Translated from Proust 1999, 2251.

The embodiment of the Parisian world in Proust's work, the figure of the duchesse de Guermantes has been likened to several personalities of the time, in particular the comtesses Laure de Chevigné[23] (1859-1936) and Élisabeth Greffulhe (1860-1952), who were about the same age. Countess von Hohenfelsen met the latter in 1904. Although she chanced upon Greffulhe on a regular basis, the two women do not seem to have been particularly intimate. However, Olga was closer to Laure de Chevigné, great-granddaughter of the famous marquis de Sade, and one of the capital's most popular hostesses.[24] The countess frequented her regularly after she moved to Boulogne. Greffulhe and Chevigné, who embodied the spirit of the Belle Époque in Paris, were not the only acquaintances of Olga whom Proust used in shaping his characters. Robert de Montesquiou, a man of letters and a leading socialite, a friend of artists and high society, was often likened to the aesthete Baron de Charlus.[25] Olga kept up a friendly correspondence with Montesquiou, who repeatedly invited her and the grand duke to receptions at his various residences. Olga wrote to him in 1909:

> It is with the greatest pleasure that the grand duke and I will come to your splendid party on June 18th. We shall be enchanted to see you again and to see you at home, in this setting created by your imagination, more brilliant and richer than all the imaginations in the world. Thank you for thinking of us.[26]

Known for his extravagance, his great taste, and his collections, he was one of the new key figures in the Paris of the 1900s with whom Countess von Hohenfelsen was acquainted. She used to read with interest the works Montesquiou sent her. In 1909, she wrote to him:

> I have just received your book, and I have already been leafing through it before cutting it! But I shall start again from the first page, and read it from cover to cover with the interest I take in reading any work by you![27]

Among the worldly and artistic figures to whom the author offers a poetic dedication in *Les Paroles diaprées,* published in 1910, is Countess von Hohenfelsen, whom he describes as follows:

23 Bibesco 1950.

24 Éric Mension-Rigau, "La comtesse Adhéaume de Chevigné," in Centorame and Andia 2005, 198.

25 Gendre 2003, 51-63.

26 Olga von Hohenfelsen (Paley) to Robert de Montesquiou, June 7, 1909, BNF, NAF-15076-FF24R-26V.

27 Olga von Hohenfelsen (Paley) to Robert de Montesquiou, June 18, 1909, BNF, NAF-15155-FF 29-30, 35.

Beneath your diamond tiara, Madame,
You know that eyes have a softer glow,
And that the proud gem draws less a soul
Than a smiling welcome we receive from you.
Of course, a Crown is still something,
When the brow it surrounds adds to its clarity
That of thought, and when it surrounds it
With a charm that mingles with other royalty.
And the pearls on the collar of the noblest Highness
Would lack orient, iris and sweetness.
If she who wears them with delicacy
Did not know how to weep over heartache.

This description, which lays bare Olga's taste for jewelry, seems to stem from an earlier complicity with the poet, to whom she wrote on a postcard sent from Bad Kissingen on an unspecified date: "The Lady with the diadem sends you her friendship and best memories from a hidden hole in Bavaria."[28]

Montesquiou was not the only literary figure around Olga, who befriended the writer Paul Bourget, an outspoken anti-Dreyfusard. One of the sources sometimes mentioned for the character of the writer Bergotte in Proust's work, he was an intimate of the Boulogne mansion, notably on the occasion of the countess's "Sundays," recalled Grand Duchess Maria:

> One day I was sitting next to Paul Bourget, and we were talking about Leonardo da Vinci, whose life I was particularly interested in at the time. Paul Bourget offered to send me some books on the subject. He kept his promise, and the next morning I received some beautiful volumes. But, of course, he soon regretted his gesture. Doubtless fearing that I might be taken with such valuable books, he asked for them back that very evening, and I barely had time to look at them.[29]

In addition to his love of collecting, Bourget shared Olga's deep attachment to the monarchical system and the idea of nationhood.

"I can hear Paul Bourget's impetuous tongue lashing out against the Republic, for he tolerated only the republic of letters," recalls Charles de Chambrun of his evenings at the house in Boulogne.[30] Bourget, who kept up a correspondence with the countess, wrote the preface to her *Souvenirs de Russie,* published in Paris in 1923, which he begins with these words:

28 BNF, NAF-15155-FF 29-30, 35. Undated postcard.

29 Marie de Russie 1937, 56.

30 Chambrun 1941, 223.

> Here is a document of the first order on the monstrous social phenomenon of the Russian Revolution: the memories of the morganatic wife [...] [of] that heroic and charming Grand Duke Paul Alexandrovich whom we all knew in Paris before the war, so courteous, so noble, so generous. His wife, Mme la princesse Paley, did the honors of the beautiful house they lived in at Boulogne with such grace!

In the preface, Bourget clearly stated his position with regard to the phenomenon of revolution, whether Russian or French, which he described as the result of "a madness, or better still, and to use scientific language, a collective psychosis."

Many other Proustian figures were part of the entourage of Countess von Hohenfelsen and Grand Duke Paul, including Madeleine Lemaire (1845-1928), an artist who specialized in painting flowers and illustrated works by Proust and Montesquiou. Known for her salon, held in her mansion on rue de Monceau, which brought together people of all origins, she is sometimes likened to Madame Verdurin, whose clan was very close to Princess Shcherbatov, another Russian figure in *La Recherche*, showing just how much Russia counted in Parisian society during the Belle Époque. In *Le Figaro* in 1903, Proust described Madeleine Lemaire's salon

> as famous beyond the seas as in Paris itself, whose name signed at the bottom of a watercolor, as if printed on an invitation card, makes the watercolor more sought-after than that of any other painter and the invitation more precious than that of any other mistress of the house [...]. But as soon as an evening is about to take place, each friend of the mistress of the house comes as an embassy to obtain an invitation for one of her friends. For Mme Lemaire assures that every Tuesday in May, the traffic is almost at a standstill in les rues Monceau, Rembrandt, and Courcelles, and, moreover, a certain number of her guests inevitably remain in the garden, under the blossoming lilacs, unable to fit into the vast studio where the evening has just begun [...]. Little by little, the less intimate leave. Those more closely associated with Mme Lemaire prolong the evening, which is more delightful for being less crowded, and in the half-empty room, closer to the piano, one can, in a more attentive, more concentrated manner, listen to Reynaldo Hahn.[31]

There were artists such as Jean Béraud, Puvis de Chavannes, Édouard Detaille, Léon Bonnat, and Georges Clairin, as well as representatives of the political and diplomatic worlds; foreign personalities, notably Russians

31 Proust 2009, 36-51.

such as Grand Duchess Vladimir; the Parisian aristocracy, embodied by comtesse Greffulhe, the comtesse de Chevigné; and many others, most of whom are quoted in the documents Countess von Hohenfelsen left to us. On May 31, 1910, for example, she wrote in her diary: "In the evening, I went to Madeleine Lemaire's where it's always cheerful and beautiful [...] but there are too many people."

Their relationship does not seem to have gone beyond the worldly, as her diary of July 1912 suggests. Olga prefaces the name "Madeleine Lemaire" with a "Mme," implying a certain distance, while she calls the accompanying comtesse de Chevigné by her first name, "Laure," when the small group, including the grand duke, visits Albert Kahn (1860-1940), also based in Boulogne, to admire his Japanese garden.

It may come as a surprise to see how quickly Olga integrated into the Parisian world, but that would be to overlook the cosmopolitan background from which she came and to which she was tied. Her life and activities opened all the doors of Parisian society to her. Even while still a Pistohlkors, she had been introduced to the best of society through the position of her husband, aide-de-camp to Grand Duke Vladimir, a long-standing habitué of European society. And Count Alfred de Gramont, a friend and close associate of the duc d'Orléans, noted:

> I knew the husband Pistohlkors in Marienbad, [...] while his wife was with the Grand Duke Paul. Incidentally, these grand dukes are extraordinary; there are some in Biarritz, Cannes, Nice, Monte-Carlo, just about everywhere.[32]

As early as 1902, the countess's diary succinctly but clearly depicts an intense social life, including receptions, parties, theaters, and other social activities. Among the people most frequently mentioned are those who might be considered her closest friends, often from the French aristocracy or the Russian colony in Paris. One such figure who played a key role in Olga's introduction to Parisian society was the Russian-born comtesse Véra de Talleyrand-Périgord (1842-1919), née Bénardaky, described by Boni de Castellane as follows:

> The countess was a charming, witty woman [...] with a delightfully oriental character, mitigated by French habits. Her husband had once been a brilliant ambassador to St. Petersburg. My aunt, who loved music, was a mediocre singer. She was very sophisticated in her toilette, often adorned with enormous jewels, and dressed in a showy manner. But she was benevolent and charitable, which I am not.[33]

32 Mension-Rigau 2011, 340.

33 Castellane 1986, 69.

Her niece, Marie de Bénardaky (1845-1928), was Marcel Proust's great childhood sweetheart and a friend of Madeleine Lemaire's.[34] The comtesse de Talleyrand-Périgord ran a renowned salon in her Parisian mansion on l'avenue Montaigne, whose atmosphere and spirit can be felt in the writings she left us. Her *Pensées nouvelles, souvenirs anciens* is a kind of collection of reflections and bon mots that must have made her language a success: "There are people who know everything and know nothing."[35] "Often the most interesting thing is what we don't say."[36] Véra de Talleyrand-Périgord's name appears in the very first Parisian pages of Olga's diary. The social chronicles also bear witness to this. The grand duke and countess were received by her at "a very elegant dinner" in November 1906. Among the guests were the marquise Lise Paolucci and Count Albert Vandal (1853-1910).[37] The latter, a doctor of law and professor of diplomatic history at "Sciences Po," founded in 1872, had distinguished himself through his publications on Franco-Russian diplomatic relations, having written a work in 1882 about Louis XV and Empress Elizabeth[38] and a second between 1891 and 1896 on Napoleon I and Alexander I.[39] This guest, whose specialization could not fail to interest the guests of honor, once again demonstrates the place of Russia in France during the Belle Époque, whether in terms of the consequences of the fresh alliance between the two nations, the expression of a new Russophilia in France, or research in the humanities exploring the history of this reciprocal friendship.

An initial circle of social, intellectual, and friendly contacts was formed around Countess von Hohenfelsen, while from 1904 on, another leading figure in Paris of the period welcomed her to her very popular dinner parties: comtesse Robert de Fitz-James (1862-1923), née Rosalie Gutman. Her hand-picked guests included names that would later fill the pages of Olga's diary, such as Paul Bourget, the comte and comtesse d'Haussonville, and Arthur de Vogüé (1838-1924). The comtesse d'Haussonville (1846-1922), née Pauline d'Harcourt, also had a famous salon, described by Proust in *Le Figaro* in 1904:

> Everyone admires the comtesse d'Haussonville, the marvelous rise of an incomparable bearing, surmounted, crowned, "crested" as it were, by an admirable head, haughty and gentle, with brown eyes of intelligence and kindness.[40]

34 Michaël Vottero, "Le Salon de Madeleine Lemaire," in *Femmes peintres et salons au temps de Proust* (Paris: Musée Marmottan Monet, 2010), 76.

35 Talleyrand-Périgord 1912, 9.

36 *Ibid.*, 17.

37 *Gil Blas*, November 27, 1906.

38 *Louis XV et Élisabeth de Russie, étude sur les relations de la France et de la Russie au XVIIIe siècle, d'après les archives du ministère des Affaires étrangères.*

39 *Napoléon et Alexandre Ier: L'Alliance russe sous le Premier Empire.*

40 Proust 2009, 64-75.

Her husband, comte Paul-Gabriel d'Haussonville (1843-1924), was a politician and man of letters, close to the comte de Paris and Paul Bourget.

From salon to salon, Countess von Hohenfelsen's address book expanded, and other great names of Parisian life made their appearance in her diary, such as Madame Édouard André, who passionately devoted herself to her collection of Renaissance and eighteenth-century art, assembled in her mansion on le boulevard Haussmann, the present-day Musée Jacquemart-André, and in her Chaalis estate; she was a possible source of inspiration for Olga. Finally, another *grande dame* of Parisian society became a close friend: comtesse Mélanie de Pourtalès (1836-1914), whom Boni de Castellane, in his *Mémoires*, includes in what he calls "true society."[41] Further on, he describes her as follows:

> The countess [...] of enduring beauty, one of the most brilliant women of her time, truly ruled Paris. She had been very prominent during the Empire. [...] The whims of her life exuded an atmosphere of affection that added to the admiration she inspired. Kings and emperors, billionaires and statesmen, artists, and scholars, all formed an art circle around her, where people kept quiet to hear her tell witty and delightful stories.[42]

The countess's son, Jacques de Pourtalès (1858-1919), is often mentioned in Olga's diary and correspondence, along with other names from the Parisian world – primarily aristocratic, as Alice Bravard[43] has shown – such as Béarn, Broglie, Castellane, Ganay, Gontaut-Biron, Murat, Polignac, and Rohan.

The interactions of the network formed around Countess von Hohenfelsen and Grand Duke Paul are evident in the many and frequent rituals that brought together the members of this social group. The most important social events were the weddings the couple attended on a regular basis. Here, too, the society columns of the press list their presence and the prestigious gifts presented by the distinguished guests. In 1906, the couple presented a liqueur table at the wedding of Marguerite de Rohan-Chabot (1887-1976) to prince Josselin de Léon (1879-1916),[44] then a pink enamel clock to comte Charles de Vogüé (1882-1914) and Diane de Pastré (1888-1971),[45] and finally a marquetry tea table presented at the evening given in honor of the marriage of Anne de Talhouët-Roy (1893-1964) and vicomte Jean de Rohan-Chabot (1884-1968).[46]

41 Castellane 1986, 57.

42 *Ibid.*, 58.

43 Bravard 2013, 37.

44 *Les Modes*, no. 67 (July 1906): 8.

45 *Les Modes*, no. 68 (August 1906): 6.

46 *Les Modes*, no. 72 (December 1906): 12.

That same year, Olga noted on May 23: "At 11 a.m., I went with Paul to Aucoc, Cartier and Taburet to get the gift for the Rohan wedding." In 1910, the wedding festivities between Jean de Broglie (1886-1918) and Marguerite Decazes (1890-1962) provided an opportunity to describe the gifts received, displayed in the salons on the second floor of the Decazes mansion, rue Constantine. Among the latter, the press pointed to the clock presented by Grand Duke Paul, prominently displayed among the "princely gifts."[47]

If the exchange of gifts is a sign of sociability, it is also a means of expressing attachment. The couple frequently gave each other gifts to commemorate a birthday or anniversary; Olga regularly distributed gifts to her friends, as evidenced by the pages of her diary, such as an enamel box from Boin-Taburet presented to the comtesse d'Haussonville in 1910, or, in 1912, jades acquired from Langweil given to the comtesse de Pourtalès and a watch for Marguerite Murat.

Funerals are also among the events that brought the best of society together, to commemorate the memory of one of its members. The press thus mentioned the couple paying tribute to their departed friends, notably compatriots such as Prince Alexander Vladimirovich Baryatinsky (1848-1909), whose funeral ceremony was celebrated in the Orthodox splendor of Paris's most famous Russian colony, the cathedral on rue Daru. The couple, who were present, had sent a silver palm, mounted on a black velvet frame and bearing the dedication "To our dear friend Prince Baryatinsky, in the devoted memory of Grand Duke Paul and Countess von Hohenfelsen," as well as a wreath of flowers. "Princess Anna Baryatinsky attended her husband's funeral, flanked by her daughter and son-in-law, comte and comtesse Raoul de Leusse, Prince and Princess A. Baryatinsky."[48]

Grand Duke Paul and Countess von Hohenfelsen were present at many other funerals, notably in 1912, at the funeral of Duke Georgy of Leuchtenberg (1852-1912),[49] and in 1914, at that of the duc de Rohan.[50]

Other activities, such as philanthropic and cultural events, punctuated the life of the best society and occupied the afternoons. Charity events were an opportunity to demonstrate generosity. Grand Duke Paul and the countess were among the personalities "recognized"[51] at the gala organized by a Boulogne regular, comte Arthur de Gabriac (1867-1948), a famous music lover and patron of the arts.[52] The much-appreciated musical program raised 6,000 francs for the victims of the French naval battleship *Liberté*,

47 *Le Gaulois*, May 8, 1910, quoted in Ferrand 1993, 209.

48 *Le Gaulois* (March 23, 1909), quoted in Ferrand 1993, 207.

49 *Le Figaro*, May 9, 1912.

50 *Le Figaro*, January 11, 1914.

51 *Le Figaro*, November 23, 1911, quoted in Ferrand 1993, 210.

52 He was one of the guests at a reception held in June 1907. *Le Figaro*, June 6, 1907.

whose accidental explosion had killed more than three hundred people on September 25, 1911. Olga was also among the first to sign up to support an evening under the patronage of the comtesse d'Haussonville and Maurice Barrès (1862-1923). Following riots in Fez in April 1912, this reception in aid of the French Red Cross was intended to raise funds to send nurses to Morocco, as part of the campaign to "pacify" the country, then under the newly established French protectorate.[53]

As for cultural pursuits, they abounded in Belle Époque Paris and were conducive to new encounters. Olga attended art and historical exhibitions, which reflected her taste for art and collecting, and many other events, alone or with family or friends. For example, in 1904, she wrote in her diary that while she was having breakfast, Jacques de Pourtalès arrived and took her to see the exhibition *Les Primitifs*, which had just opened. Organized at the Pavillon de Marsan and the Bibliothèque nationale by Henri Bouchot (1849-1906), curator of the Department of Prints at the national library, the exhibition – to which Proust was also a visitor – was devoted to painting in France under the Valois, as illustrated by the subtitle of the catalog.[54] Conceived as a response to the *Flemish Primitives* exhibition held in Bruges in 1902, the event marked a new interest in the early French school. In the context of the times, the event was even described as "a real turning point in the process of building a "national art."[55] Illustrating the Belle Époque's interest in older art, the countess favorably judged the exhibition, finding it "very interesting."

Olga visited the Louvre regularly, especially the paintings department, along with the Musée Carnavalet and the Union centrale des arts décoratifs, and she also went to the Bibliothèque nationale, where she visited the historical exhibitions. Her interest in history led her to attend lectures, notably in 1911, when the marquis Pierre de Ségur (1853-1916) gave a talk on the last of the Condé family, the subject of his book published in 1899,[56] whose love story fascinated Olga, having probably identified her own journey with it.

Olga also visited thematic exhibitions or on contemporary creations. In May 1906, she admired *Les Arts de la femme*, an event organized at the Palais de Glace in the tradition of one held in 1892 and reflecting the activities organized by the Comité des dames within the Union centrale, designed to encourage the artistic training of women.[57] Olga noted that she spent little time there,

53 *Le Figaro*, April 26, 1912.

54 Henri Bouchot, *L'Exposition des primitifs français: La Peinture en France sous les Valois* (Paris, Librairie centrale des beaux-arts, 1904).

55 Dard, Leymarie, and McWilliam 2010, 215.

56 *La Dernière des Condé: Louise-Adélaïde de Condé; Marie-Catherine de Brignole, princesse de Monaco.*

57 Guillemette Delaporte, *Le Comité des dames* (Paris: Bibliothèque des arts décoratifs, 2012).

but she supported the event by buying a cushion in the Calabrian embroidery section. *Le Figaro* also noted that the queen of the Two Sicilies, Marie-Sophie of Bavaria (1841-1925), when visiting the exhibition, lingered in the embroidery section and asked to "see the objects sold, in particular the cushion purchased by the Countess von Hohenfelsen."[58] Olga herself practiced this art, traditionally mastered by aristocratic women, as her step daughter noted:

> I loved these visits to Boulogne [...]. We went out into the world and to the theater, but more often than not, we spent our evenings at home; my father would read aloud, while my stepmother and I embroidered.[59]

The countess also supported her artistic relations. In March 1914, her friend Boni de Castellane, who had become accustomed to taking her to museums, including the Jacquemart-André,[60] and to various cultural events, decided to accompany her to a preview, where she acquired six "Directoire" gouaches by Lemaire.

A typical day in the life of a member of the countess and grand duke's milieu included many different places and occasions for interaction. Around the countess and the grand duke, a network of receptions and festive activities reflects the intensity and diversity of the pleasures offered by Paris at the beginning of the twentieth century.

58 *Le Figaro*, June 2, 1906.

59 Marie de Russie 1938, 158.

60 Mension-Rigau 2016 (Kindle ed.), loc. 2708.

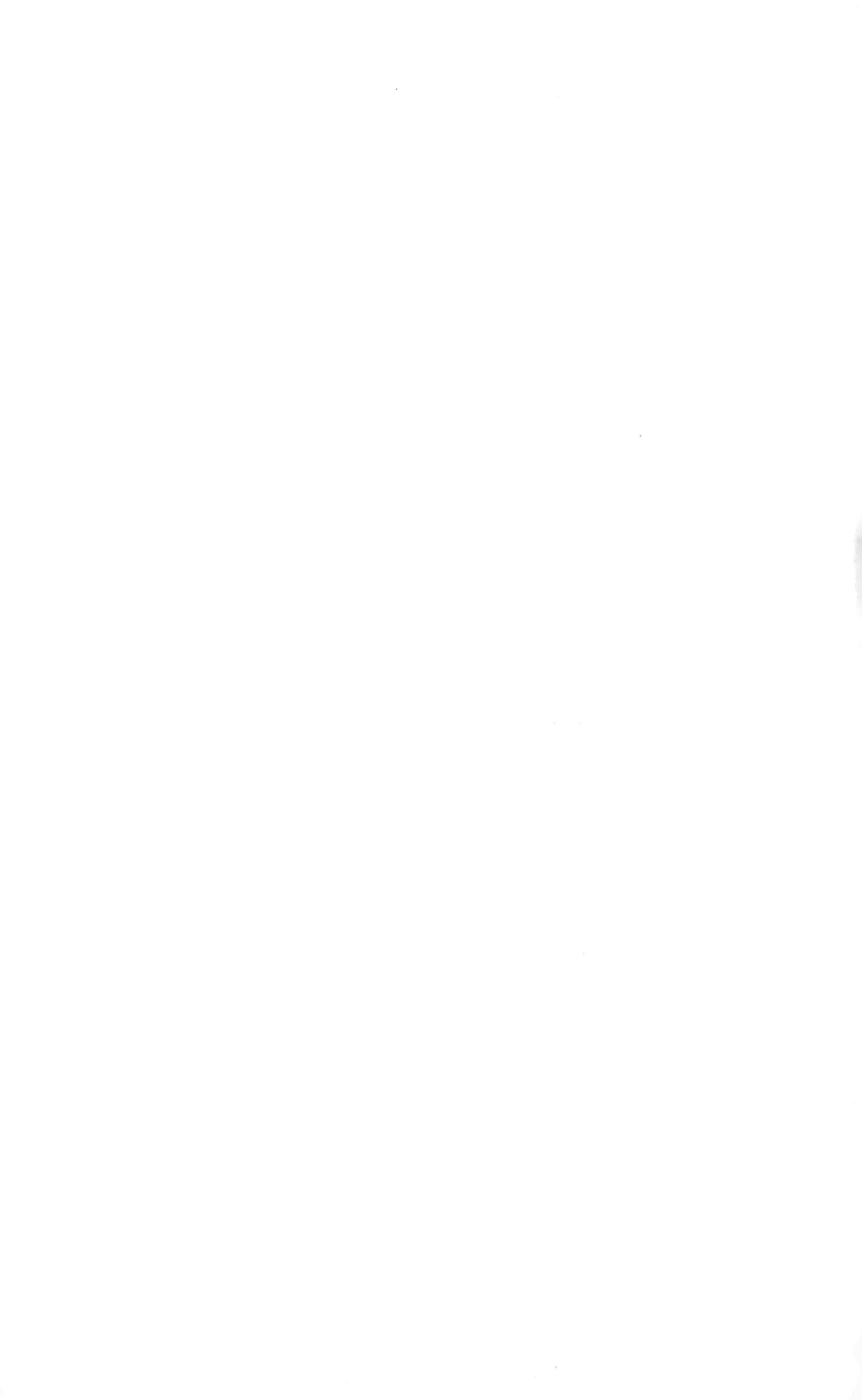

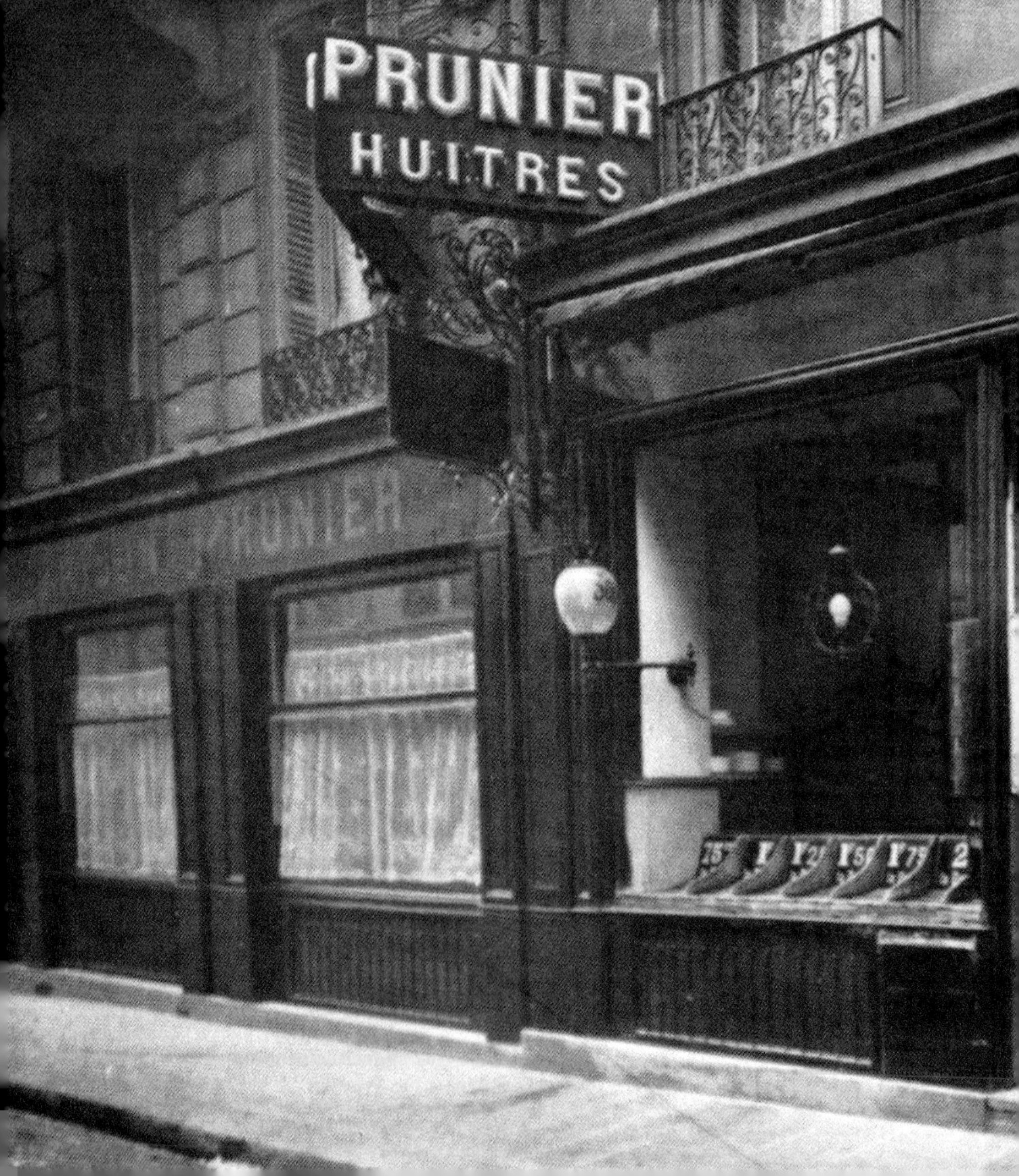
PRUNIER
HUITRES
PRUNIER

FROM ONE PLACE TO ANOTHER: RECEIVING, APPEARING, AND BEING SEEN

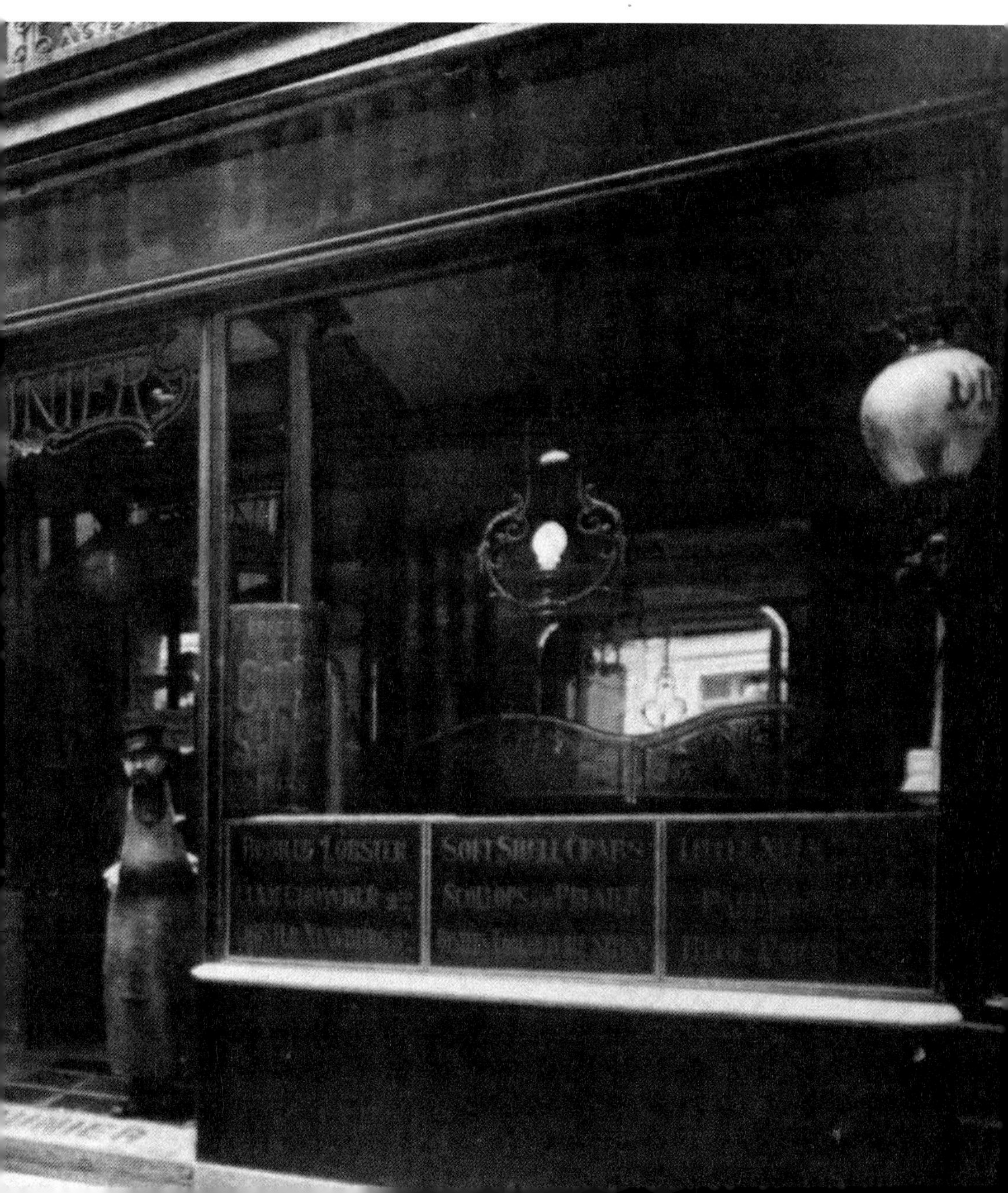

> Grand Duke Paul and the countess are a continuous ornament to the most varied parties: christenings, weddings, garden parties, tennis, boule, archery, aerostation, yachting, fishing and the rest. It's all very beautiful.
>
> Frédéric Masson to Grand Duke Nicholas Mikhailovich

The couple's lives were punctuated by receptions and other social activities, including numerous seasonal trips. This nomadic existence, which Alice Bravard describes as "aristocratic itinerancy,"[1] manifested itself for Grand Duke Paul and Countess von Hohenfelsen in regular stays in French spa towns such as Vichy or Aix-les-Bain, abroad, in Germany and in Italy; and in holiday resorts, in the countryside or by the sea, notably in Biarritz, all of which were reported and commented on in the press. While the couple's social activities took place mainly in Paris, members of their networks sometimes crossed paths on their travels. For example, they met in Venice in 1907, as *Le Figaro* reported:

> The Venice season was particularly brilliant this year. Many "five o'clocks" and extremely elegant and select dinners at the home of Grand Duke Paul of Russia and Countess von Hohenfelsen, princesse de Polignac [...]. We sang in the gondolas as we crossed the lagoon. Great success especially for the songs of the comtesse de Guerne and M. Reynaldo Hahn.[2]

In the capital, in addition to the countess's Sunday receptions, dinners and parties were held on a less regular basis. Here are a few examples: "received for tea at the Yturbes'" (1902), "dinner at Rosa Fitz-James's" (1904), "went to the vicomtesse d'Harcourt's and the duchesse de Mouchy's" (1914). In Olga's accounts, the statements give more information on their frequency: "Murat dinner" (May 16, 1909), "Pracomtal dinner" (May 31, 1909), "Vigier dinner - Murat ball" (June 2, 1909). Sometimes she confided her impressions. In 1907, on her return from an evening at Clara de Pastré's, she noted that the meal had been marvelous and later added in French, as she often did when expressing appreciations or feelings, "c'était très élégant et très bien."[3] The society columns are an inexhaustible source of information on the course of these receptions and their success, often synonymous with good attendance. In 1912, for example, *Le Figaro* reported that Grand Duke Paul and the countess "did not attend the dinner given last Tuesday by the comte and comtesse du Bourg de Bozas,"[4] proof if any were needed that Grand Duke Paul and the

1 Bravard 2013, 149.

2 *Le Figaro*, October 8, 1907.

3 "It was most elegant and very fine." *Le Figaro*, February 1st and 14, 1907.

4 *Le Figaro*, January 12, 1912.

countess were part of the fashionable set, worth a mention whether present or absent.

A few days later, Robert de Montesquiou came back to this snippet, which he felt illustrated new practices in vogue on the "world stage," in particular what he describes as "rectification" or "fine-tuning."[5] He continued: "Following these negations without comment, brief as a salon pistol shot, dry as a door closing, pinching a finger, 'silence fills the obscure pause,' as Shelley eloquently put it."[6]

These chronicles, which the countess cut out, collected, and kept, list the receptions the couple gave and attended. It would be pointless to list them all, but the details of some of them shed light on the couple's daily life and provide details of their network, establishing Paris as "the social capital of the Belle Époque."[7]

The first important evenings that Olga organized are referenced more regularly with the acquisition of the mansion in Boulogne, which was well suited for entertaining. In 1906, the grand duke and countess hosted a "dinner followed by an intimate reception"[8] for a set formed mainly around the Russian colony in Paris, of which the grand duke became the most important figure. As *Le Gaulois* noted in 1911:

> Is he not one of the most refined Parisians, the Grand Duke Paul, who resides here almost all year round, surrounded by respectful tributes, as well as the Countess von Hohenfelsen, his wife, one of the most beautiful people in Paris, a *grande dame* by spirit and heart as much as by situation, affable with all and admired by all?[9]

The Russian colony was represented at the dinner in 1906 by members of the diplomatic corps and the aristocracy, including Ambassador Alexander Nelidov (1835-1910) and his wife; Anna Schebeko (1871-1958), née Princess Kourakina, wife of the embassy's first secretary, Nicholas Schebeko (1863-1953); Countess Kleinmichel; and Prince Alexander Vladimirovich Baryatinsky, most likely the husband of Princess Catherine Yurievskaya (1878-1959), half-sister of Grand Duke Paul. The Baryatinsky couple owned a mansion on place des États-Unis where they received the grand duke and countess for a dinner in their honor in 1908.[10] Also attending the Boulogne reception were Baron de Berckheim, former French military attaché in St. Petersburg,

5 *Gil Blas*, February 28, 1912.

6 Probably the British poet Percy Bysshe Shelley.

7 Bravard 2013, 33.

8 *Le Figaro*, March 15, 1906.

9 *Le Gaulois*, April 23, 1911.

10 *Le Gaulois*, February 29, 1908.

and diplomat Maurice Paléologue (1859-1944), future ambassador to Russia. Among the other European diplomats and aristocrats were Prince Wilhelm zu Wied (1876-1945), future and short-lived king of Albania; the vicomte and vicomtesse Henri de Vaufreland (1874-1954); and the marquis Alfred du Lau d'Allemans (1833-1919), a member of the famous Cercle de la rue Royale, featured in James Tissot's painting of the same name (now in the Musée d'Orsay).

In 1907, a similarly cosmopolitan Mardi Gras dinner was held in Boulogne, as described in *Le Figaro.*[11] Among the guests were the marquise Lise Paolucci, whom Olga met a few months earlier at a dinner at the home of the comtesse de Talleyrand-Périgord, who was also present; the comte and comtesse d'Aramon; diplomat Reginald Lister (1865-1912); and comte Henri de Vogüé. Henri was a son of Eugène-Melchior de Vogüé (1848-1910), a good friend of Paul Bourget and a diplomat who had been stationed in St. Petersburg. Henri's mother, née Alexandra Annenkov, was Russian and related to the Galitzine, Nelidov, and Struve families.

A few months later, the Austrian-Hungarian ambassador, Count Benckendorff, presumably Alexander (1849-1917); the then Russian ambassador to London; the couple's loyal friend Alexis de Hitrov; and Countess Tyszkiewicz attended a dinner in Boulogne, which was described as "very elegant."[12] The guest list also included some of the best of Parisian society, Paul Bourget and his wife, prince and princesse de La Tour d'Auvergne, comte and comtesse André de Ganay, comte Arthur de Gabriac, and comtesse Joachim Murat, whose family was related to the prominent aristocratic Dadiani family of Georgia.

The receptions at Boulogne were also an opportunity to honor members of the imperial family visiting Paris, notably Grand Duke and Grand Duchess Vladimir, who were regulars at the mansion on each of their visits,[13] and the grand duke's niece, the future Queen Maria of Romania.[14] These soirees were also an occasion to bring the Russian community together for special events such as Orthodox Easter, Christmas, and New Year, all of which occur several days later than in France due to the difference between the Gregorian and Julian calendars.[15] In addition to the list of the leading members of the Russian colony and the "regulars," friends, and representatives of the cosmopolitan aristocracy, in 1913 we note the presence of the wife of Arthur Meyer (1844-1924), director of *Le Gaulois.*

11 *Le Figaro*, February 15, 1907.

12 *Le Figaro*, June 6, 1907.

13 See, for example, the dinner given in their honor in 1906, *Le Figaro*, December 4, 1906; or the 1908 luncheon, *New York Herald*, May 18 and 31, 1908.

14 *Le Figaro*, June 8, 1913.

15 *Le Figaro*, January 15, 1913.

Famous for her portrait by Antonio de La Gandara presented at the 1911 Salon (SNBA, the Société nationale des beaux-arts), Mrs. Meyer (1880-1945), née Marguerite Turenne d'Aynac, came from the French nobility and found her fortune by marrying a much older but wealthy and influential man. And so it was that the world of the press and the cream of Paris society mingled, their legend being forged through columns and glowing commentaries in newspapers read by representatives of the international elite. Gaston Calmette (1858-1914), director of *Le Figaro* since 1902, met many of them at elegant receptions organized by the newspaper, notably in 1908. Among them were Grand Duke and Grand Duchess Vladimir, Grand Duke Cyril and his sister-in-law Princess Beatrice of Saxe-Coburg-Gotha, and Grand Duke Paul and Countess von Hohenfelsen. The newspaper noted that the audience was "more numerous and brilliant than ever."[16]

The grand duke and countess's receptions were highly reputed, especially the dinners. Winnaretta Singer, in her *Souvenirs*, recalled these evenings in Boulogne: "I often dined there; everything was perfect; their cuisine was renowned."[17] And Charles de Chambrun added:

> During their sumptuous dinners, over the epergne, porcelains and flowers, a secret correspondence united the spouses; they did not direct the conversation, but smiled to see it come alive little by little in this rhythm that heats up artificially. Elegance was the rule, etiquette banished although not deliberately so, and then the spirits fused.[18]

Gabriel-Louis Pringué (1885-1965) noted the importance of dinners in social life:

> The charm of Parisian dinners, apart from the refined elegance of the atmosphere and the luxury of the decor, was to bring you, along with the excellence of the food and the quality of the wine, the attraction of pretty, intelligent, witty neighbors who knew what was going on. In addition, there was usually an unexpected surprise in the form of a distinguished guest, an important person, a great traveler, a statesman, an eminent literary figure, a new acquaintance who smiled at your desires, an admirable storyteller [...], a philosopher diplomat who knew how to draw the most seductive picture of European and world imbroglios, a high-profile minister with a political showcase, a glorious soldier or some star of sport, art, theater or science. The hostess was the mainstay of these dinner parties.[19]

16 *Le Figaro*, May 28, 1908.

17 Singer 2000, 48.

18 Chambrun 1941, 223.

19 Pringué 1948, 61.

A number of menus embossed with the grand ducal coat of arms, monogrammed tableware and linen bear witness to the culinary refinement of Countess von Hohenfelsen[20] (pls. 20-25; see pl. 4).

Charles de Chambrun summed up the spirit of the Boulogne salons in a long paragraph, addressed to Marie de Rohan-Chabot:

> The grand duke triumphed to see his wife occupying a prominent place in this society enamored of original and thorny situations, a sparkling, brilliant society, which paraded itself with glee before privileged strangers, just as learned dogs prefer to show off their science and perform tricks right under the noses of strangers. The less fortunate, for want of wit, would scrape together that of their forebears, but whatever the case, it was a refined elite, where the desire to please through the exchange of ideas became a charming coquetry in which novices practiced. It was a place where gourmandise was the key to apprenticeship. Various famous guests met there: Jean de Reszke, a prodigious tenor, whose beauty had made the hearts of countless Marguerites and Juliets beat faster all over the world. At these dinners, he remained silent between courses; there was also the duchesse de Camastra, your parents, Véra de Talleyrand[-Périgord], who rolled her *r*'s as she cooed, flaunting her opulent bosom covered with worn pearls, which her sighs shook. Chatty, she talked to her neighbors with a touching frenzy about her adventures and about God, whom she had only recently discovered. The comtesse de Pourtalès was still as beautiful as a well-kept and even better-repaired painting; there was also Reynaldo Hahn, a pampered composer who executed his enemies with brio; the glorious Lady de Grey, taller than a maypole, still won royal favors and protected Russian dancers. Olivier Taigny was teasing André Tardieu, whose self-confidence at the end of the table was cutting through the academics; and comte d'Haussonville, mounted on small horses, was shining his impertinent monocle without indulgence on those young chatterboxes, escaped from their ministries, who dared not listen to him. All these memories were lost in the mists of the Seine. Ah! How good it would be to live again in Boulogne.[21]

The grand duke and countess were in turn invited to the capital's finest homes, which were honored by their august presence. The couple became the pride of the evening at the mansion of princesse Edmond de Polignac, avenue Henri-Martin (now avenue Georges-Mandel), and at the mansion of the duc and duchesse de Rohan in le boulevard des Invalides. Winnaretta Singer, heiress to

20 Ferrand 1993, 205.

21 Chambrun 1941, 223-24.

an American fortune built on the sewing machine industry, had married Prince Edmond de Polignac (1834-1901) in 1893, a marriage orchestrated by comtesse Greffulhe and her cousin Robert de Montesquiou. "He was a musician, she was a musician, and both were sensitive to all forms of intelligence," wrote Proust in his 1903 chronicle of the princess's salon.[22] The Polignac-Singer union testifies to the cosmopolitanism of the Parisian *grand monde*, unlike the Rohan couple, which reflects the endogamy that persisted in this milieu. In 1872, duc Alain de Rohan[23] (1844-1914) had married Herminie de La Brousse de Verteillac, known until 1893 as the princesse de Léon (1853-1926). Boni de Castellane considered her salon to be one of the most famous in Paris:

> By virtue of her high social status, her authority, her virtues, and her talents, this lady is one of the queens of Paris. The doors of her house open generously to those who wish to enter [...]. Her mischievous gaze is combined with a benevolence tinged with indifference. A great kindness makes her indulgent to all and encouraging to those who seek her support.[24]

A poetry enthusiast and author herself, she counted Robert de Montesquiou among her regulars, and had allied her children with the Caraman, Murat, and Talleyrand-Périgord families, belonging to the circles of Countess von Hohenfelsen.

The grand duke and countess sometimes came across members of the imperial family visiting Paris in the Rohan home, when they were not receiving them at their own. In December 1906, Grand Duke Alexei, Grand Duchess Vladimir, and her son Boris gathered on le boulevard des Invalides.[25] The same group met there again in 1907.[26]

The Russian world also crossed paths at Boni de Castellane's home, where he enjoyed the fortune of his wife, Anna Gould (1875-1961), heiress to the American railroad magnate. He recounted several amusing anecdotes about the protocol embarrassment that could result from the presence of members of the imperial family at these soirees:

> On another occasion, I invited the Grand Duchess Vladimir, the Grand Duke Paul and his wife, the Countess von Hohenfelsen, [...] and a few other people to dinner. My *maître d'hôtel* had been instructed to announce dinner by saying, "Their Imperial Highnesses are

22 Proust 2009, 58.

23 See, for example, the dinner described in *Gil Blas*, March 1st, 1906.

24 Castellane 1986, 386.

25 *Gil Blas*, December 9, 1906.

26 *Les Modes*, no. 74 (February 1907): 4.

> served." He got confused and exclaimed, "His Royal Highnesses are served." That didn't stop me from feeling cheerful and content. But this was the day of blunders. I had my best champagne served. My cupbearer loudly told each guest the name of the vintage he was to taste. He served Grand Duchess Vladimir first, and shouted into her ear, loud enough for the whole room to hear: "Brut impérial 1890." The grand duchess gasped. So did Grand Duke Paul. All my guests burst out laughing. The blunder had come out as an attack. To add insult to injury that evening, I had ordered some rice *à l'impératrice* for dessert, and the grand duchess jokingly said to me, "I hope at least this one isn't poisoned."[27]

Gabriel-Louis Pringué recounted with admiration one of these dinners in honor of august Russian visitors. He places it at the home of princesse de La Tour d'Auvergne (1885-1960), née Élisabeth-Marguerite de Wagram, in "her palace on l'avenue de la Motte-Picquet":[28]

> Panther skins were thrown over the marble of the hall, where flowers in profusion lit up the pedestals of the high colonnades. On the steps stood the army of powdered-haired footmen, motionless and almost statuesque [...]. At the top of the grand staircase of honor stood the princess, adorned in her rivers of diamonds, wielding a fan of ostrich feathers like a welcome caress, knowing how to say to each the welcoming word that made the heart blossom.[29]

He added:

> I felt a striking impression of beauty when one evening, [...] I saw the entrance of [...] the Grand Duke Paul of Russia; Princess Paley, then Countess von Hohenfelsen; Grand Duchess Maria Pavlovna, then Princess Royal of Sweden, and Grand Duke Dimitri in the glow of adolescence. This quartet of race and grandeur sang the glory of a civilization that has since disappeared.[30]

The Russian network was frequently brought together for receptions in the sumptuous premises of the embassy on rue de Grenelle, known for its splendor. Chronicler Gabriel-Louis Pringué noted, probably with exaggeration,

> It was all very theatrical, especially at the Russian embassy, where oriental luxury had become very fashionable since the arrival of

27 Castellane 1986, 321-22.

28 Pringué 1948, 88.

29 *Ibid.*, 88-89.

30 Pringué 1948, 91. The last two mentioned were Grand Duke Paul's children by his first wife.

> the northern sovereigns in Paris. At la rue de Grenelle gate, two great giants from the Urals acted as Swiss guards, wearing tasseled bicorn hats and large white coats with gold braiding. They struck the flagstones with their halberds as the carriages entered. The livery was powdered, in white and gold, with aiguillettes, short breeches, silk stockings, and pumps. They were particularly numerous. The ceremonial dinners were served in gold crockery, with precious orchids and purple lilies arriving in suitcases from the imperial greenhouses at Livadia in the Crimea. A special train brought caviar, Baltic fish, and Norwegian grouse from Archangelsk. Rarely have I seen, except perhaps at the Court balls in London and Madrid, similar tides of tiaras. The grand duchesses of Moscow and the princesses of Georgia and the Caucasus sparkled with gems.[31]

This was perhaps the tone of the glittering evening given to celebrate Ambassador Nelidov's twenty-fifth anniversary of service in May 1908.[32] In addition to the grand duke and countess, the ceremony, followed by a thirty-six-guest dinner, was graced by the presence of the Vladimir couple; their children Cyril, Andre, and Elena, the latter accompanied by her husband, Prince Nicholas of Greece; Grand Duchess Maria of Saxe-Coburg-Gotha and her daughter Beatrice; Dukes Alexander and Georgy of Leuchtenberg; prince and princesse Murat, prince Louis Murat, the Baryatinsky couple, Prince Yusupov, Prince Trubetskoy, the comtesse de Talleyrand-Périgord, the faithful Hitrov, and many others. The reception was such that the menu was reproduced in the press:

Consommé Chavigny
Small Montmorency croustades
Lobster Parisian style
Demidov saddle of veal
Pojarsky chops à la Clamart Punch romaine
Roast duckling à la Valencienne
Mimosa salad
Chaudfroids of larks à la strasbourgeoise
Asparagus with mousseline sauce
Marie-Louise iced timbale
Little mille-feuilles
Chester cakes

31 *Ibid.*, 46.

32 *Le Figaro*, May 16 and 29, 1908.

Held at a time when Mussorgsky's opera *Boris Godunov* was triumphant on the Parisian stage, the evening benefited from performances by the opera's singers. "These wonderful melodies were the object of indescribable enthusiasm," concludes the article in *Le Figaro*. It is perhaps this or a similar event that Boni de Castellane recounts in his memoirs, revealing once again the lineage rivalries that could exist between Grand Duchess Vladimir, from one of Europe's oldest reigning dynasties, and "Grand Duchess Paul" when they appeared together in the Parisian world:

> I attended a party at the Russian Embassy, where all the grand dukes were present. Among them was Princess Paley, then Countess von Hohenfelsen [...], who wore royal jewels; Grand Duchess Vladimir took umbrage and scowled at her.[33]

Parisian receptions during the Belle Époque were not just about chatting over fine food; they were also an opportunity to get to know young talents or leading exponents of a given field, and to promote the arts, especially music. Musicologist Myriam Chimènes, in her monumental work on the capital's musical salons of the period, noted:

> The musical activities of Madame Verdurin's salon reflect a reality admirably perceived by Marcel Proust. Whether a simple pleasure of intimacy or a necessity for society receptions, music occupies a place of choice in the salons.[34]

Many of the personalities who played a leading role in the musical life of the Belle Époque belonged to the circles surrounding Countess von Hohenfelsen, who, in addition to French art of the eighteenth century, Chinese jades, and porcelain, showed a genuine interest in music. This sensitivity is clearly and enthusiastically expressed from the very first pages of her exile diary, particularly with regard to Wagner's work. The role played by comtesse Greffulhe in Parisian musical life is well-known,[35] and she was resolutely committed to promoting and appreciating Wagner's work, which had been violently rejected in France since the defeat of 1870 and Germany's annexation of Alsace-Lorraine. The revelation of this music came for the countess at Bayreuth in 1891, and for Olga von Hohenfelsen in Munich in 1903. In August, as the grand duke and countess continued their European tour, the couple visited Bavaria, including its cultural treasures in Munich: the Nationalmuseum, the Schatzkammer, the English Garden, and more.

33 Castellane 1986, 334-35.

34 Chimènes 2004, 13.

35 Hillerin 2014, 142-43.

The couple also took the opportunity to visit the theater, in particular the Prince Regent Theater, where the Wagner Festival, a rival to the Bayreuth Festival, was held. Olga prepared for her experience by reading *Lohengrin* and *Tristan und Isolde*. She attended *Tannhäuser* first, which she enjoyed, especially the staging, which she deemed "extraordinary." The next day, Olga went to see *Die Meistersinger von Nürnberg*, which overwhelmed her: "The *Meistersinger* are a real revelation for me. What *ideal* music, what poetry!"

She then saw *Das Rheingold*: "2 3/4 hours without intermission," she explained, "effective and beautiful." Then came *Die Walküre*, *Siegfried*, and *Götterdämmerung*, before they returned to Paris on the Orient Express. There, the countess confirmed her taste for Wagner's music, gracing the opera house with her presence at performances of *Lohengrin* in 1907 and *Tristan und Isolde* in March 1908, with Russian-born soprano Félia Litvinne and Belgian tenor Ernest van Dyck, who specialized in the Wagnerian repertoire.

Her interest, and that of the grand duke ("I know of His Highness's enlightened taste for fine music,"[36] said Madeleine Lemaire), was evident in the evenings the couple attended or gave in Boulogne. The family library also contained hundreds of librettos of musical compositions and notes.

The grand duke and the countess's acquaintances included one of the leading figures in the world of music, princesse Edmond de Polignac, a passionate patron of the arts. Her salon was a formidable springboard for the young performers and composers she supported,[37] a place "where high society people, artists and true amateurs meet."[38] In honor of Grand Duke Paul, she regularly entertained the celebrities of the day. On February 5, 1905, the composer Gabriel Fauré (1845-1924), who was also the critic for *Le Figaro* and director of the prestigious Paris Conservatoire, performed his works there.[39] In May 1905, *Les Modes* reported on the success of one of these evenings, organized in Fauré's honor and attended by the couple. The program also included works by composer Vincent d'Indy (1851-1931), Mozart, Camille Saint-Saëns, and Reynaldo Hahn.[40] A similar event was repeated in 1908, and *Le Figaro* reported its success:

> Princesse Edmond de Polignac gave a musical soiree yesterday in honor of Grand Duke Paul Alexandrovich. The program featured nothing but works by Gabriel Fauré, wonderfully sung by Mme Jane

36 Madeleine Lemaire to Olga von Hohenfelsen (Paley), undated, GARF, F. 613, op. 1, D. 286, L. 1.

37 Chimènes 2004, 84-114.

38 *Ibid.*, 110.

39 *Ibid.*, 96.

40 *Les Modes,* no. 77 (May 1905): 3.

> Bathori. The composer, who played the piano, and his admirable interpreter were enthusiastically acclaimed.[41]

At one of these musical evenings, on May 11, 1907, Countess von Hohenfelsen listened to the world-famous tenor Enrico Caruso (1873-1921), then at the height of his career, in the company of the comtesse de Chevigné and the princesse de La Tour d'Auvergne.

In the salons of the Belle Époque, "by becoming part of an ostentatious social ritual, music penetrated the most exclusive Parisian salons"[42] and played an important role in the social life of the grand duke and countess. They attended numerous musical evenings, such as a student audition organized at the home of Jean de Reszke (1850-1925), a famous tenor and teacher, in his mansion on rue de la Faisanderie, in the presence of comte and comtesse Adhéaume de Chevigné, the marquis and marquise de Ganay, the marquise and Mlle Montagliari, Mme Maurice Bischoffsheim, the marquis de Breteuil, the comte de Gabriac, the comte de Gontaut, Mme Madeleine Lemaire and Mlle Lemaire, M. de Radwann, M. Nicolopoulo, and M. Roufflard.[43] The phenomenon affected all circles in which the grand duke and the countess mingled in the name of art. They were invited to the musical soirees of Princess Dominique Radziwill,[44] comte and comtesse Jean de Castellane,[45] and Clotilde Lebaudy, wife of industrialist and politician Paul Lebaudy (1858-1937).[46] The phenomenon spread to Olga's salon, as evidenced by a note from Princess Joachim Murat's secretariat addressed to Gabriel Astruc (1864-1938), who acted as impresario for the princess's musical receptions. She specified, with regard to the artists to be placed, "that people with gardens like the Rothschilds in Boulogne and Paris, His Imperial Highness the Grand Duke Paul would be happy to let their guests hear them."[47]

It wasn't long before the countess's and grand duke's evenings were distinguished by their musical appeal. Winnaretta Singer noted that "conversation was often enlivened by delightful pieces, quartets or melodies, performed by Reynaldo Hahn or Jean de Reszke."[48]

In May 1907, guests had the privilege of meeting and listening to singer Feodor Chaliapin (1873-1938), an event announced by *Le Figaro*.[49] During the

41 *Le Figaro*, April 6, 1908.

42 Chimènes 2004, 395.

43 *La Revue illustrée*, December 20, 1906.

44 *Le Figaro*, May 17, 1908.

45 *Le Figaro*, January 18, 1911.

46 *Le Figaro*, June 24, 1910.

47 Letter dated July 1st, 1910, quoted in Chimènes 2004, 400.

48 Singer 2000, 48.

49 *Le Figaro*, May 24, 1907.

same period, the artist triumphed at the Paris Opéra in an aria from Borodin's *Prince Igor* as part of the "Russian historical concerts"[50] organized by Diaghilev. Later that year, Reynaldo Hahn was the guest of honor: "after dinner, [he] held everyone under the spell of his marvelous talent,"[51] noted *Le Figaro*. The reception had been organized for Grand Duke and Grand Duchess Vladimir, in the presence of many of the mansion's regulars, including the comtesse de Béarn, also known for her brilliant musical evenings;[52] the comtesse de Chevigné; Reginald Lister; Maurice Paléologue; and the Russians Hitrov and Benckendorff. These Russian connections in Paris, and in particular his meeting with Diaghilev, encouraged Hahn to travel to Russia in March 1911, to St. Petersburg, where he presented the composition of his ballet *Dieu bleu*. The Parisian star, now enjoying the best introductions, was feted by high society, including Grand Duchess Vladimir, who invited him to her palace.[53]

The evenings in Boulogne went on and on... For the record, *Gil Blas* opened on April 16, 1912, with a story about the sinking of the *Titanic*: "The gigantic liner breaks up on an iceberg: the passengers and crew are safe and sound"; in its social chronicles, the newspaper reported: "The Grand Duke Paul and the Countess von Hohenfelsen gave a grand dinner the day before yesterday, after which several excellent artists, including the singer Léoni, were much applauded."[54]

The grand duke's and countess's musical sensitivity, coupled with their Slavic origins, made them perfect spectators of the effervescence generated in Paris by the Russian seasons, be these concerts or ballets organized under Diaghilev's direction. The couple attended the sumptuous 1908 opera presentation of *Boris Godunov*.[55] The event thrilled the Parisian public, who had had the opportunity to appreciate the talents of Chaliapin the previous year, when he had played *Prince Igor* and performed at the countess's home, and who here played the title role. The work, directed by Alexander Sanin of the Moscow Art Theatre, involved the collaboration of several artists from the Russian Art World Association (*Mir Iskusstva*), including Ivan Bilibin (costumes) and Alexander Golovin and Alexander Benois (sets). A fine illustration of the fusion of the arts, the show was a success, heralding the forthcoming triumph of the Ballets Russes. The day after the performance, on May 20, *New York Herald* critic Pierre Veber echoed the success, praising Chaliapin, "who is superb in the role of Boris; an excellent singer, gifted with

50 Pojarskaïa and Volodina 1990, 9.

51 *Le Figaro*, October 27, 1907.

52 Chimènes 2004, 128-37.

53 *Le Figaro*, March 17, 1911. See also Marcel Proust *Lettres à Reynaldo Hahn* X-121, http://www.reynaldo-Hahn.net/lettres/10_121.htm#3.

54 *Gil Blas*, April 16, 1912.

55 Vadim Gaevsky, "Sergei Diaghilev et sa troupe," in Bowlt, Tregulova, and Rosticher Giordano 2009, 64.

a unique voice, he is also an extraordinary actor. You must see him, in the act of hallucinations and in the act of death; it's superior art,"[56] and Diaghilev: "Messrs De Diaghiloff [*sic*] and Sanine have just given the opera management a fine lesson in the art of performing a fine work."[57]

The show was a total success, both artistically and socially, as revealed by the list of spectators who, following the most prestigious, the president of the Republic and Madame Fallières, included Grand Duke Paul and Countess von Hohenfelsen, "the latter wearing a magnificent diamond tiara," Grand Duke Michael and Countess Torby, [...] Grand Duke Cyril, the Duchess of Coburg, the Russian ambassador and Madame Nelidov, comtesse Greffulhe, Prince and Princess Baryatinsky, Countess Kleinmichel... the whole Parisian set and the couple's regulars... The latter met again for the triumph of the ballets presented by Diaghilev the following year at the Théâtre du Châtelet. On May 19, the countess, in the company of the grand duke, the Vigiers, Berthe and Jean de Ganay, attended the *Pavillon d'Armide*, *Prince Igor*, and *Le Festin*. The event was supported by comtesse Greffulhe, and the hall was packed with the best society, as Olga noted in her diary. She had an excellent evening and found that "everything was superb." The program flattered both her taste for the ancien régime, the source of inspiration for the *Pavillon d'Armide* with its sets and costumes by Alexander Benois, champion of the Versailles Revival, and her Russian roots with the brilliant arias of *Prince Igor* and the Polovtsian dances whose sets and costumes were the work of Nicholas Roerich, the painter who reinvented early Russia. As for *Le Festin*, the audience was treated to the polychrome richness of Léon Bakst's costumes. The crowd that evening admired the modernity of the choreography masterfully performed by Tamara Karsavina, Anna Pavlova, and Vaslav Nijinsky. The society columns rejoiced at the event, and the august international audience confirmed the survival, if not the rebirth, of the splendors of the ancien régime in the heart of a Third Republic that was asserting itself as its heir.

"What an evening, what a theater, what an audience! Will I ever have enough epithets to describe such a spectacle, from the breathless hubbub of cars in endless rows to the shimmering brilliance of the diamonds glittering even up there, in the last rows of the amphitheater?!"[58] exclaimed reviewer Raoul Brévannes.

On the occasion of the third show of the Russian season, the press notes: "Grand Duke Paul occupied a front box with the Countess von Hohenfelsen, she in black satin, tiara of brilliants, and the marquis and marquise de Pracomtal."[59] Hitrov was also present; the countess and her

56 *New York Herald*, May 20, 1908, quoted in Ferrand 1993, 202.

57 *Ibid.*

58 *Le Figaro*, May 19, 1909, quoted in Huesca 2001, 9.

59 *New York Herald*, June 1909, quoted in Ferrand 1993, 206.

entourage unknowingly witnessed the birth of the Ballets Russes legend.[60] The fascination they elicited, apart from artistic causes, was undoubtedly intertwined with that of imperial Russia embodied by these personalities of the Belle Époque, who as a group were soon to be extinct, but whose spirit would live on for a few more years through the revolutionary productions of Diaghilev and his acolytes.

The Ballets Russes episode propelled Paris to the summit of the world's major performing arts capitals,[61] of which Countess von Hohenfelsen and the grand duke were great fans. The couple's attraction to this art form went beyond the traditional occupations of people in their milieu and manifested itself in a sincere interest. The grand duke, a connoisseur and amateur actor himself in his youth, was known for his enthusiasm. George Painter reports that the manifestations of his admiring élan at the theater are said to have inspired an anecdote that Proust associates with Grand Duke Vladimir in *La Recherche.*[62] He is said to have applauded the performances of Mademoiselle Julia Bartet, the star of the Parisian stage, shouting "Bravo la vieille!" (Bravo, old woman!) But the grand duke's interest was serious. As early as 1882, he offered his support to the Moscow Society of Musical and Dramatic Art; the grand duke, a subscriber to specialized newspapers and magazines such as *Le Théâtre,*[63] is remembered by scholars for his enthusiasm in amassing a library of over twenty thousand volumes inherited from his ancestors and added to by himself, with the assistance of a librarian, including thirty-five hundred volumes devoted to the performing arts.[64] Miraculously preserved, the latter collection has been housed at the St. Petersburg Theatrical Library since 1927, and it forms one of the most complete collections on Russian dramatic art from the eighteenth to the nineteenth century, bringing together texts, programs, and documents, sometimes unique, often autographed, relating to the subject. Originally, there were many more works dedicated to this field: nearly six thousand volumes, of which a portion, probably the most contemporary, was lost during the Revolution. The collection was intended to bear witness to the many shows the couple attended during their years in Paris. The offering was immense, with the public able to choose between some thirty establishments, divided between official venues run by the state or the city and private spaces with varied programming, to which were added café-concerts and cabarets. Testifying to the vitality of the Parisian scene, as a sign of a

60 Pojarskaïa and Volodina 1990.

61 Jean-Claude Yon, "Les Spectacles à Paris autour de 1900," in Leribault 2014, 39-42.

62 Painter 2008, 718.

63 GARF, F. 644, op. 1, D. 301.

64 S. P. Sobolevskaya published a study in Russian in 2006 concerning Grand Duke Paul Alexandrovich's book collection from the Paley Palace in Tsarskoye Selo.

show's success, the press reported the presence of prestigious spectators in the audience, including the grand duke and countess.[65] But the document that provides the most information on the couple's choices, reflecting the Parisian scene, is Olga's diary, which, with great regularity, lists the shows and celebrities she went to applaud. An analysis of the evenings the couple attended gives an idea of their taste at a time when theater was one of the most popular forms of entertainment. The couple's choices were mainly concentrated on the biggest theaters on the boulevards. The countess and the grand duke attended a few revivals, which sometimes received mixed reviews in the press. *Petite mère*, by the inseparable Henri Meilhac and Ludovic Halévy, which Olga saw at the Théâtre des Variétés in 1903, had already been reviewed when it was revived in 1880:

> The old is made new again, the antique rejuvenated, the Rococo restored to the fashion of the day. In this way, we have the play of forty years ago and, at the same time, the play of today, if not tomorrow. Critics have judged this new work severely, but I must admit that I took great pleasure in it.[66]

Generally speaking, however, the couple attended shows in the year of their creation, often appearing at the premieres of fashionable playwrights or of their entourage. The works they saw also reflected the couple's interest in music. In addition to her admiration for Wagner, the musical evenings in Boulogne, at the Opéra and the Théâtre du Châtelet, the countess mentions Hector Berlioz's *Damnation de Faust*, revived in 1903 at the Théâtre Sarah-Bernhardt (now Théâtre de la Ville). The couple's taste for romantic subjects inspired by Goethe was again evident when Olga went to the Opéra-Comique in 1912 to hear a revival of Jules Massenet's *Werther*, an opera she had already seen in the same theater in 1906 and which the countess had judged "very beautiful." That same year, she had also seen Édouard Lalo's *Le Roi d'Ys*. The libretto, inspired by the famous Breton legend, was by Édouard Blau, who, along with Paul Milliet and Georges Hartmann, had adapted *The Sorrows of Young Werther* for Massenet. Beyond these productions, the countess appreciated the lighter musical entertainments exemplified by the success of opéras bouffes on Parisian stages. In 1903, for example, she listed Charles Lecoq's *Giroflé-Girofla,* revived at the Théâtre de la Gaîté; and *Le Sire de Vergy*, inspired by the medieval legend of Gabrielle de Vergy and written by Claude Terrasse, considered one of Offenbach's best successors, premiered at the Théâtre des Variétés. In a slightly different register, no doubt attracted by the subject matter that nourished her nostalgia for Russia, Olga attended

65 See, for example, *Le Figaro*, November 2 and 22, 1911.

66 *La Revue politique et littéraire* 18 (1880): 882.

Michel Strogoff at the Châtelet in 1903, a production in sixteen tableaux based on Jules Verne's bestseller. The 1880 premiere was a triumph, requiring the collaboration of the best decorators of the day. The music was by Alexandre Artus and Georges Guilhaud. One of the theater's most successful productions, *Strogoff* was in its thousandth performance in 1900.[67]

The countess also attended the production of the Viennese operetta composed by Léo Fall to a libretto by Austro-Hungarian Viktor Léon, which premiered at the Apollo in 1911. Its title, *La Divorcée*, says a great deal about the subjects explored in the theater around 1900, and about Olga's choices, directly concerned by this social phenomenon widely dealt with by contemporary authors. In her diary, she lists numerous plays written on the theme of adultery, divorce, and remarriage. In 1903, she went to the Théâtre de la Renaissance to see *L'Adversaire*, "the great success of the season,"[68] as *Le Théâtre,* to which the grand duke was a subscriber, put it. The comedy by Alfred Capus, journalist, novelist, playwright, and columnist for *Le Figaro*, and writer Emmanuel Arène, starred Lucien Guitry, a former celebrity at the Théâtre Michel in St. Petersburg, where he triumphed from 1882 to 1891, and Marthe Brandès, known for her roles as great lover and femme fatale. All of Paris's fashionable set flocked to the theater:

> The press was unanimous in celebrating him. The dining rooms and salons are full of talk of *L'Adversaire*, and the high society people, who are on their guard against the complacency and confraternal indulgence of dramatic critics, ask you in your ear: is it really a masterpiece? Yes, it certainly is a masterpiece.[69]

Presenting opposing points of view through different family members confronted with divorce, certain passages in the play could not help but appeal to Olga's own experience. One line from the husband's mother-in-law certainly did not leave her indifferent:

> Ah! when it's the wife who's guilty, it's a different matter: she's the guardian of the honor of the home, she carries it within herself, she must not fail, since her fall can introduce a foreign child into the marital home. For her, there's no forgiveness. She has only one thing to do: go back to her lover and live happily ever after with him, if she can! She has condemned herself to exile.[70]

67 Robert Pourvoyeur, "Michel Strogoff au théâtre," in Piero Gondolo della Riva and Bernard Sinoquet, eds., *Jules Verne: Michel Strogoff* (Amiens: Centre international Jules Verne, 2004), 20.

68 *Le Théâtre*, no. 117 (November 1903): 6.

69 *Ibid.*

70 Quoted in *ibid.*, 4.

A few years later, in 1908, Olga attended the production of *Le Divorce*, adapted by André Cury from the work by Paul Bourget. In other words, the subject was very topical. Shown at the Théâtre du Vaudeville, the play explores the issues of civil versus religious marriage and divorce. It glorifies the sacrament over the contract, and bears witness to the author's Catholic commitment. It raises questions about Bourget's judgment of his friend's situation. *L'Opinion*, taking part in the debate sparked by the play, judged it boring and its subject "retrograde."[71] Olga didn't seem to hold Bourget's opinion against him and followed his career, attending the *Tribun* in 1911, which, inspired by contemporary political life, features a father and renowned politician using his position to save his son from a political and financial scandal. The theme of divorce did not escape the Comédie-Française, where, in 1904, Olga applauded Paul Hervieu's *Le Dédale*. A novelist and playwright, Hervieu frequented the same salons as Paul Bourget and Marcel Proust. His play has a dramatic ending, with adultery, divorce, and remarriage punctuating it, leading to the disappearance of both husband and lover.

The theme was also explored in the context of the extreme anti-Semitism surrounding the Dreyfus affair, which divided French public opinion into two camps. *Le Retour de Jérusalem* by Maurice Donnay, presented at the Théâtre du Gymnase in 1903, focuses on the subject of adultery, divorce, and free union between an "Aryan" man, Michel, driven away by his wife after being deceived, and a Jewish woman called Judith.[72] The play caused a scandal and was clearly perceived as anti-Semitic by audiences of the time. Olga attended the show in 1904, but it is not clear whether she was attracted by the subject matter, the scandal surrounding the play, or its anti-Semitism; most likely for all three reasons.

Notes from Olga's diary show that, in addition to Bourget's productions, she supported those of her close friends. She marked with her presence *Le Cœur dispose*, a play performed at the Théâtre de l'Athénée in 1912 by her friend Laure de Chevigné's son-in-law, Francis de Croisset. The play tells the story of a dowry hunter, a young, handsome secretary, who attempts to win over his employer's daughter.

Olga also followed the progress of celebrities of the time, such as playwright Henri Bernstein. He took his first steps on the Parisian stage with *Le Détour*, which she saw at the Théâtre du Gymnase in 1902. Witnessing its success, he became its director between the wars. In 1906, Olga went to the Théâtre de la Renaissance for *La Griffe*, a play for which Bernstein drew inspiration from the political and amorous scandals of Parisian life. The same year, he triumphed in the same theater with *Le Voleur*, whose success made him a fixture on the Parisian stage. The play, starring Lucien Guitry

71 *L'Opinion*, February 1st, 1908, 22.

72 Meyer-Plantureux 2005, 203.

and Simone Lebargu, depicts a young woman willing to steal extravagant dresses to please her husband. The countess wrote in her diary about the lead actors that "they performed divinely." Although her diary is relatively silent on her assessments, a few brief mentions betray her enthusiasm. In 1904, for example, she wrote of Marcelle Lender's performance in *Les Sentiers de la vertu*, a comedy by Robert de Flers at the Théâtre des Nouveautés, noting that she was "in great form."

Vaudevilles and comedies on the theme of husbands, wives, and lovers entangled in multiple misunderstandings were among the plays that charmed the couple, including several works by Georges Feydeau, a master of the genre, such as *La Main passe* performed at the Théâtre des Nouveautés in 1904 or *La Puce à l'oreille* at the Théâtre des Variétés in 1907. While some of these plays are still in the repertory today, others are less well-known and not always critically acclaimed, such as Sacha Guitry's *Le Scandale de Monte Carlo*, presented at the Théâtre du Gymnase in 1908, which was not praised by *Théâtre & Littérature*:

> Here, with *Le Scandale de Monte-Carlo*, which is of an acute Parisianism containing a hodgepodge in which anything may be encountered, and where, without bothering to order his ideas but determined to take everything in jest and try to baffle his audience, M. Sacha Guitry passes from vaudeville to comedy and from comedy to drama, from extreme sentimentality to the most audacious sauciness, from the subtlest wit to the most execrable puns.[73]

In addition to the trials and tribulations of married life and political and financial scandals, the world of fashion for which Paris was so famous was a perfect breeding ground for drama. This theme, dear to Olga's heart, certainly prompted her to attend Louis Artus's play *Les Midinettes*, starring the famous Mistinguett, at the Théâtre des Variétés in 1911. In this play, the lives of the seamstresses who make the reputation of French design take the spectator behind the scenes of the fashion world.

In another register, historical subjects – often revivals – were also part of the repertoire that attracted the countess and the grand duke. As early as 1902, Olga mentioned *La Maison du baigneur* at the Porte-Saint-Martin theater, with Constant Coquelin, the great actor of the boulevards, in the role of Pontis. This historical drama set during the reign of Louis XIII is the work of Auguste Maquet, known for his collaboration with Alexandre Dumas, champion of historical literature. The French seventeenth century was also the setting for Victor Hugo's play *Marion de Lorme* at the Comédie-Française in 1907, with Julia Bartet in the title role and Mounet-Sully as Louis XIII.

73 *Théâtre & littérature* 1, nos. 1-8 (1908): 258.

The same year saw the premiere of *Adrienne Lecouvreur* by Eugène Scribe and Ernest Legouvé. This drama, inspired by the life of the eponymous actress of the eighteenth century, celebrated by Voltaire, was performed by Sarah Bernhardt in her own theater. Olga followed this parade of French history onstage. In 1908, at the Théâtre Réjane, she attended the revival of Victorien Sardou's *Madame Sans-Gêne*, which, at the time of its premiere in 1893, participated in the vogue for themes inspired by the revolutionary era, which was given pride of place by the Third Republic, and in particular for the Reign of Terror and the Directoire.

Some foreign shows also attracted the countess, including, in 1911, *L'Oiseau bleu*, an initiation tale written in 1908 by Belgian Symbolist author Maurice Maeterlinck, produced by the Théâtre Réjane. In 1912, at the Théâtre des Arts, she attended the premiere of Bernard Shaw's scandalous play *La Profession de Madame Warren* (*Mrs. Warren's Profession*), about the relationship between a former prostitute and successful owner of several brothels, and her unaware daughter. At the Théâtre des Bouffes-parisiens, she also saw *Mon bébé*, Maurice Hennequin's adaptation of *Baby Mine*, produced on Broadway in 1910.

Going to the theater was one of the main distractions offered to Parisian society, which took advantage of the opportunity to frequent the upper echelons of the Parisian restaurant and nightlife scene, often after the show. Elegant audiences and Countess von Hohenfelsen often rubbed shoulders at Prunier or at the Café de Paris.

Prunier, on rue Duphot, is an oyster and seafood institution founded in 1872.[74] An embodiment of French gastronomy, the establishment owes its success to the adaptation of recipes from the United States for preparing seafood, particularly oysters. Open to innovation, the company developed a home delivery service using refrigerated cars and dozens of deliverymen who crisscrossed Paris. At the end of the nineteenth century, Prunier's success with Russian customers led it to specialize in caviar too. At the time, Grand Duke Paul's brothers, the Grand Dukes Vladimir and Alexei, were among Prunier's regulars. In 1899, for example, Grand Duke Vladimir and his guests ordered one hundred Colchester oysters[75] (fig. 30).

The Café de Paris, founded in 1822, was a popular address for foreign visitors, especially for lunches, as was the Café Anglais on le boulevard des Italiens, which disappeared in 1913. The first floor of the latter had three rooms, complemented upstairs by salons reserved for VIPs, about which Gabriel-Louis Pringué, who considered the establishment to be the most renowned in Paris, gave details:

74 Prunier, http://www.prunier.com/histoire/24 septembre 2016. See also *La Ville lumière* 1909, 54.

75 RGIA, F. 528, op. 1, D. 1684, L. 46, 51, 52, 189.

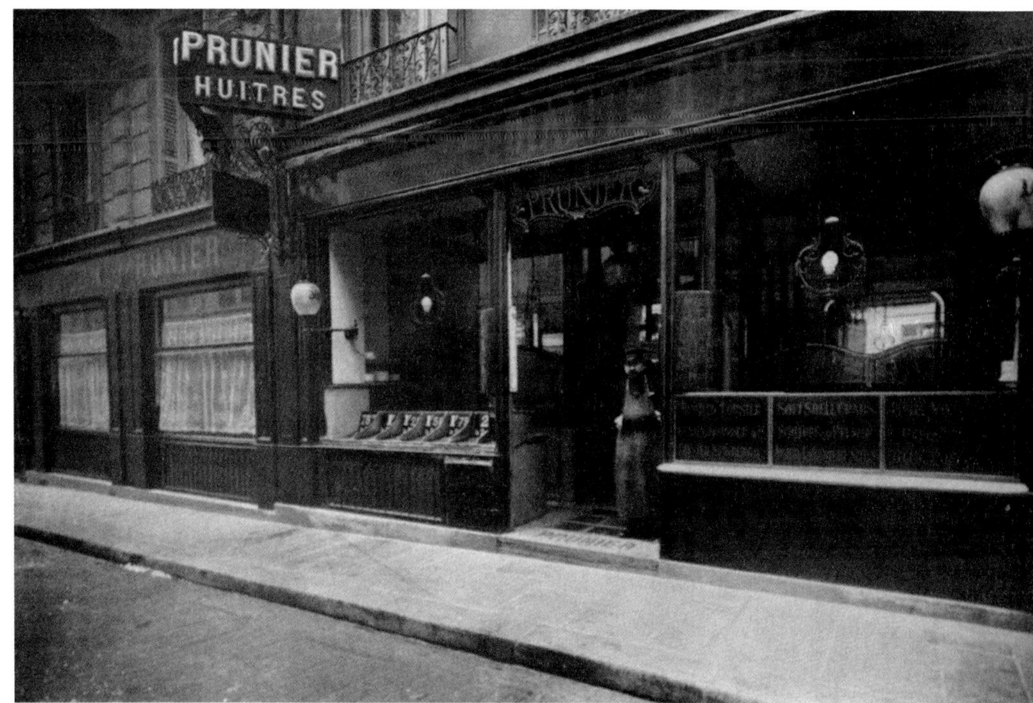

Fig. 30 The Prunier restaurant in Paris. *La Ville lumière* 1909, 57. Private collection.

> The famous salon known as "Le Grand 16" overlooked the Opéra-Comique and the boulevard. [...] It was in this salon that King Edward VII, then Prince of Wales, King Alfonso XII, King George I of Greece, King Leopold II of Belgium held their banquets with beautiful people, and where men of culinary refinement gave their weekly dinners.[76]

From her diary, we know that Olga often frequented the famous Café Voisin on rue Saint-Honoré and the Durand restaurant on place de la Madeleine.

> On Mondays and Fridays at the Opéra, it [Durand] became the evening of tiaras. Everyone greeted each other, everyone knew each other, the big press was represented by the regulars. The swanky sycophants did cartwheels, much ogled by the women of high society.[77]

In 1899, Grand Duke Vladimir occupied two salons at Durand's with his guests, and seemed to find it difficult to enjoy anything other than Russian cuisine: for 122.55 francs, he ordered Russian brandy, smoked salmon,

76 Pringué 1948, 74.
77 *Ibid.*, 74.

anchovies, Russian-style soles and a cigar. Like Olga, the grand duke also enjoyed the restaurants of the Champs-Élysées district, such as Chevillart, at *le rond-point*, or Paillard, on the avenue. The success of the latter enabled its owner to build the current Pavillon Élysée around 1900, a Belle Époque extravaganza that was just as popular with other members of the imperial family. In 1899, Grand Duke Vladimir was treated to a caviar meal, complete with coffee, liqueur, and cigar, for 320.50 francs, 15 of which went to the coachmen's supper. Paillard was also awarded the Pré-Catelan concession, built in 1905 in the Bois de Boulogne and finally taken over in 1908 by restaurateur Léopold Mourier. Built in the spirit of the garden pavilions of the eighteenth century, this place became one of the incarnations of Paris Belle Époque, notably through Henri Gervex's painting of it, exhibited at the 1909 Salon (SNBA – Musée Carnavalet).[78] This elegant and fashionable place was one of the venues appreciated by Countess von Hohenfelsen, especially as it was close to her home. Much more rarely, she writes about an outing to the emblematic Parisian nightspots. In 1903, she mentions the Folies Bergère, and on January 31, 1908, she confides to her diary: "went to the Moulin Rouge and then had supper at the Café de Paris."

The most elegant Parisian evenings are embodied by balls and parties, rare and sought-after social events. In 1908, *Le Figaro* reported on one of these nights, "one of the most brilliant parties of the season,"[79] the Bachelor's Ball held at the Pavillon de l'Élysée. The evening had a garden theme, and costumes and hairstyles had to pay homage to flowers. To make the evening even more appealing, the area around the pavilion was "enchantingly illuminated with electric light."[80] In addition to the grand duke and the countess, the guests listed in the press included the maharaja of Kapurthala, the duchesse de Guise in pink hydrangea, and the duchesse de Morny in buttercup. The ball, at which the Boldi orchestra performed, was opened by Prince William of Sweden (1884-1965) and his young bride, Maria Pavlovna, daughter of Grand Duke Paul; they had married on May 3 in Russia. The festivities ended at dawn with a dinner, the menu of which was reproduced in the press: "Consommé froid à la d'Orléans / Beef à la Moscovite / Chaudfroid of poultry à la Scandinave / Glace Bragance / Desserts / Clicquot doux et brut / Café – liqueurs."

Another grand celebration attended by the grand duke and countess, among other Parisian personalities, was given by comtesse Edmond de Pourtalès on June 19, 1910. It took place at the Washington Palace, a reception hall that once stood on rue Magellan. Preceded by dances and skits, "the evening ended with a waltz round followed by a cotillion led with gusto by

78 Bruson and Leribault 2002, 92.

79 *Le Figaro*, June 11, 1908.

80 *Ibid.*

M. André de Fouquières and baroness de Watteville, and Prince Charles de La Tour d'Auvergne with Mlle de Pourtalès."[81]

However, the most documented and probably the most sumptuous ball attended by the grand duke and countess was undoubtedly that given by the Yturbe family in 1912. As early as 1902, the Yturbes, a Mexican family of Basque origin, had counted among the Parisian personalities close to the countess and grand duke. Manuel de Yturbe y del Villar (1844-1904) had been Mexico's ambassador to St. Petersburg, before pursuing his career in Vienna, Paris, and Madrid. From 1882 on, he built a sumptuous mansion with a facade almost 76 meters (250 feet) long on l'avenue Foch in Paris, a major work by architect Ferdinand Gaillard.[82] His wife, María de la Trinidad von Scholtz-Hermensdorff y Caravaca, Marquesa de Belvís de las Navas, was behind the ball held in the family mansion. The event was heralded as an example of the return of costume balls to high society, with the invitation specifying "Hungarian costume or as close to it as possible."[83] This Eastern European extravaganza, in terms of both dress and attendance, was enthusiastically described by numerous newspapers: "What a stream of gems, what a wealth of costumes glittering with sequins, multicolored to infinity!"[84]

Madame de Yturbe welcomed her guests, flanked by her daughter and sister. Grand Duke Paul made his entrance on the arm of the Infanta Eulalie of Spain "in a magnificent gown of old rose satin, brocaded in gold, with an all-diamond bodice, wearing a gold kokoshnik, with diamonds and pink topaz," followed by Princess Stéphanie of Belgium, "in a pearl-gray toilette covered in point de gaze with necklace and tiara of brilliants," accompanied by Prince Heinrich of Bavaria "in old Montenegrin costume." Next came Infante Louis Fernando "in Hungarian national costume," as well as Countess von Hohenfelsen, princesse Murat, representatives of the diplomatic corps, and many others: among the greatest names in the Parisian world.

"Amidst this Gotha of aristocracy, elegance, foreign society, clubmen, how do you choose names?"

The evening was punctuated by Hungarian dances performed by Berkes' orchestra and his "Gypsies,"[85] followed by a supper served on small tables. Countess von Hohenfelsen recorded in her diary her visit to the Worth couturier on April 11 to settle the bill for her costume, one of the most talked about of the evening: "The Countess von Hohenfelsen in a magnificent Slavic costume, diamond pendant and pearls in her hair," noted *Les Modes*, which published a photograph of the ball with the most prominent guests. On

81 *Le Figaro*, June 20, 1910.

82 Rousset-Charny 1990, 226-33. The mansion was demolished in the 1920s.

83 *Le Gaulois du dimanche*, 1913.

84 *Les Modes*, no. 138 (June 1912): 6.

85 *Le Figaro*, April 22, 1912.

April 20, the day of the ball, Olga explained: "My Lord, what a success. [...] I got home at three in the morning, Pucia half an hour earlier."

It was on this occasion that one of the most emblematic photographs was taken of the countess, who, dressed in her costume by Worth and covered in her jewels by Cartier, is a fine embodiment of the Parisian of the Belle Époque (see fig. 52). This image would be an allegory if it weren't real. This shot by the fashion photographers of the Boissonnas & Taponier studio bears witness to the luxury of Belle Époque parties, where appearances imposed a perfect allure for which couturiers and designers worked. It is no coincidence that Jean-Philippe Worth reproduced this image in his 1928 book, *A Century of Fashion*.[86] In many ways, Olga belonged to the set of women who shaped the myth of the elegant, well-groomed Parisian woman, who went to the best suppliers and stores in and around la rue de la Paix.

86 Worth 1928, 213.

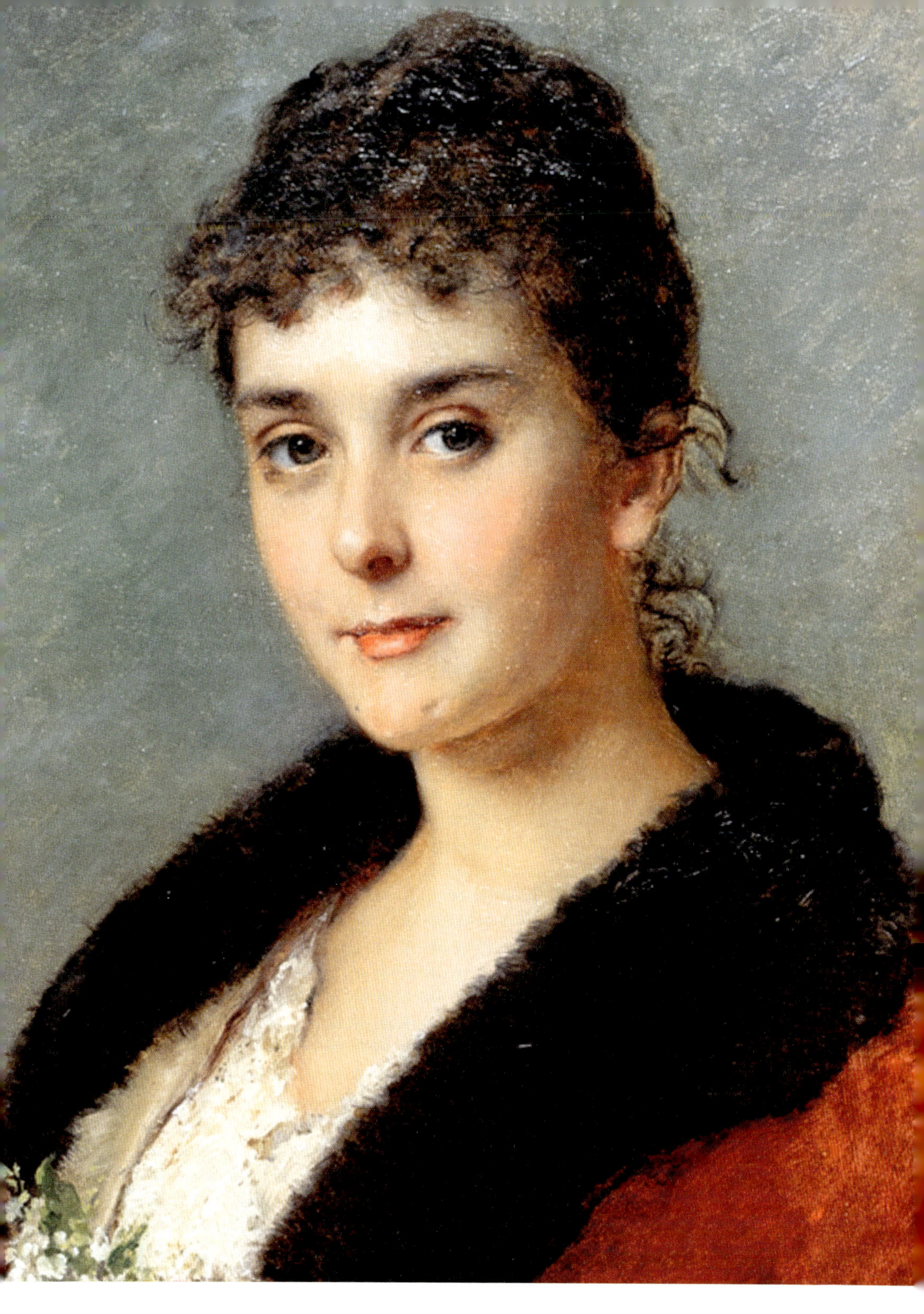

pl. 1 Konstantin Makovsky, *Portrait of Olga von Pistohlkors*, 1886. Oil on canvas. Hillwood Estate, Museum & Gardens, Washington, DC, inv. 2022.2.1.

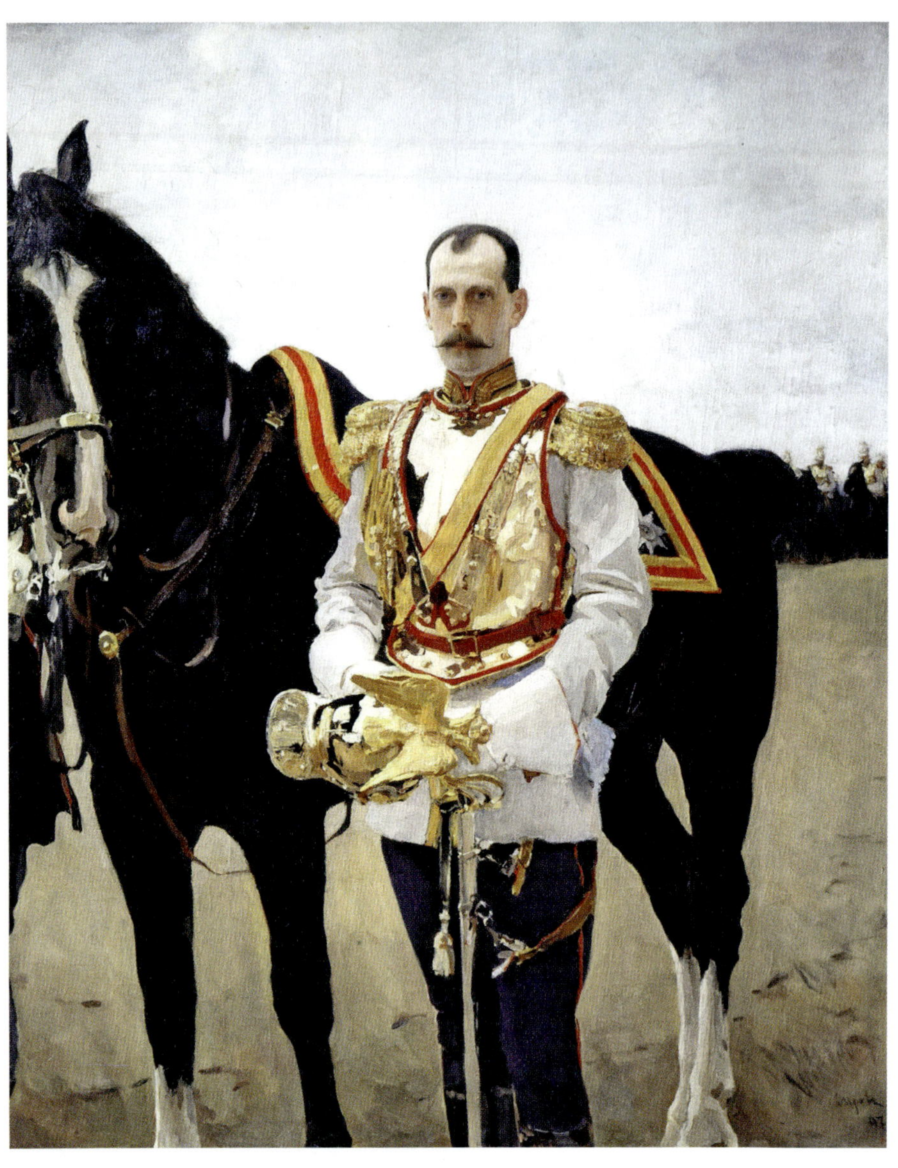

pl. 2 Valentin Serov, *Portrait of Grand Duke Paul Alexandrovich*, 1897. Oil on canvas. Tretyakov Gallery, Moscow, inv. 15697.

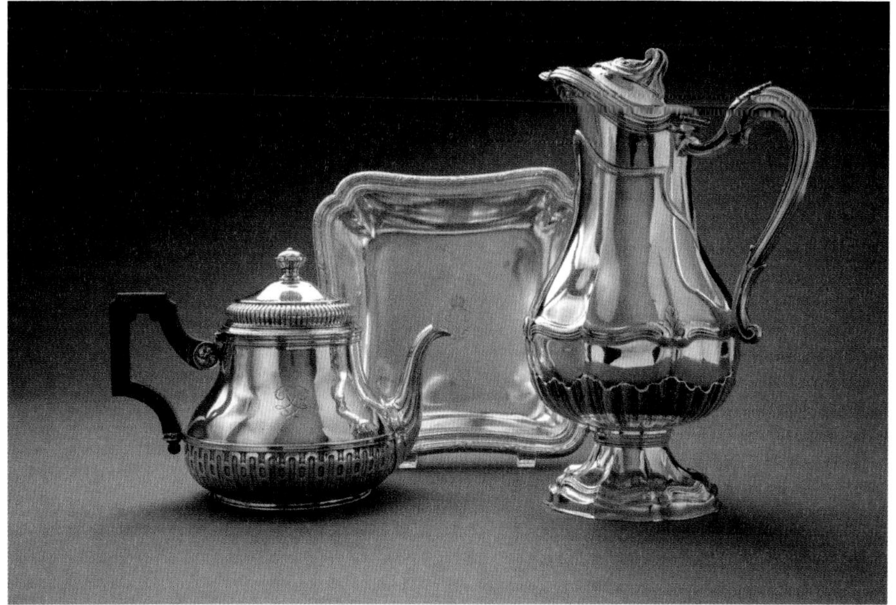

pl. 3 Risler & Carré and André Aucoc, Tea pot and dish (Risler & Carré) and pitcher (André Aucoc) from Grand Duke Paul's collection, Paris, 1903-1907. Hillwood Estate, Museum & Gardens, Washington DC, inv. 2022.2.8.1-3 and 2022.2.84.

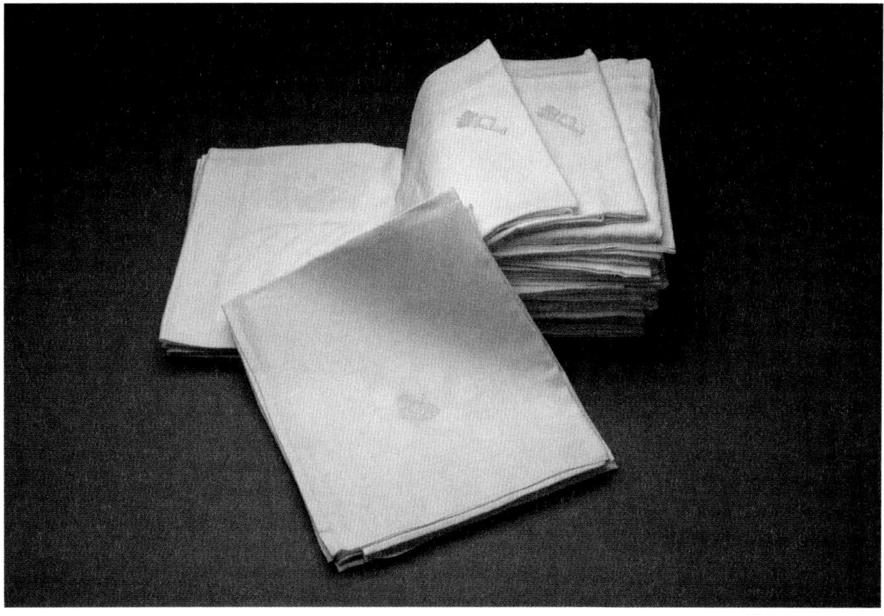

pl. 4 Linen with Grand Duke Paul's cipher and imperial crown, France and Russia, 1889-1914. Hillwood Estate, Museum & Gardens, Washington DC, inv. 2022.2.31.1-12, 2022.2.34.1-33, and 2022.2.37.1-10.

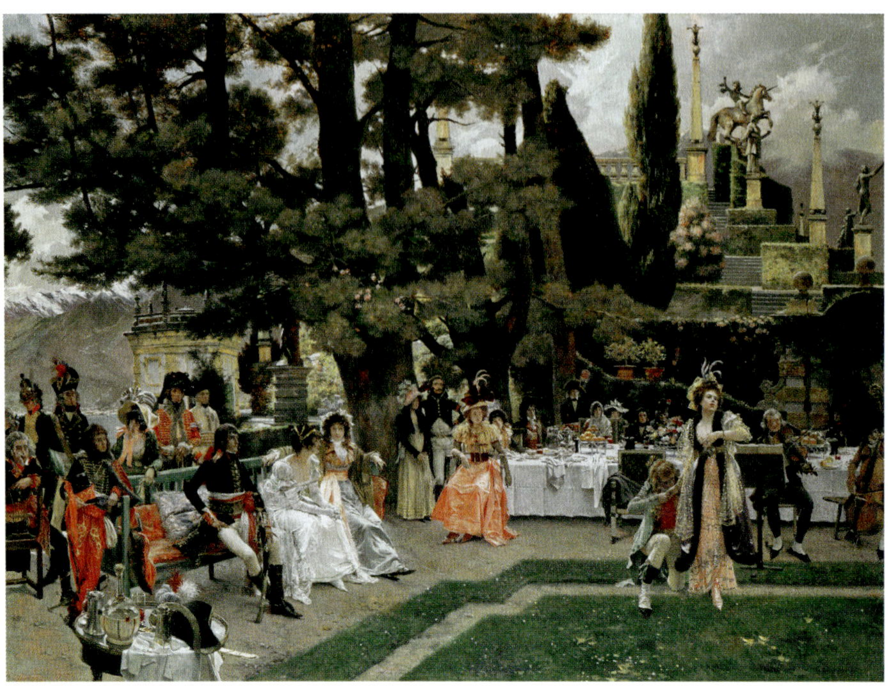

pl. 5 François Flameng, *The Reception for Napoleon I on the Isola Bella in the 5th Year of His Reign*, 1892. Oil on canvas. Private Collection.

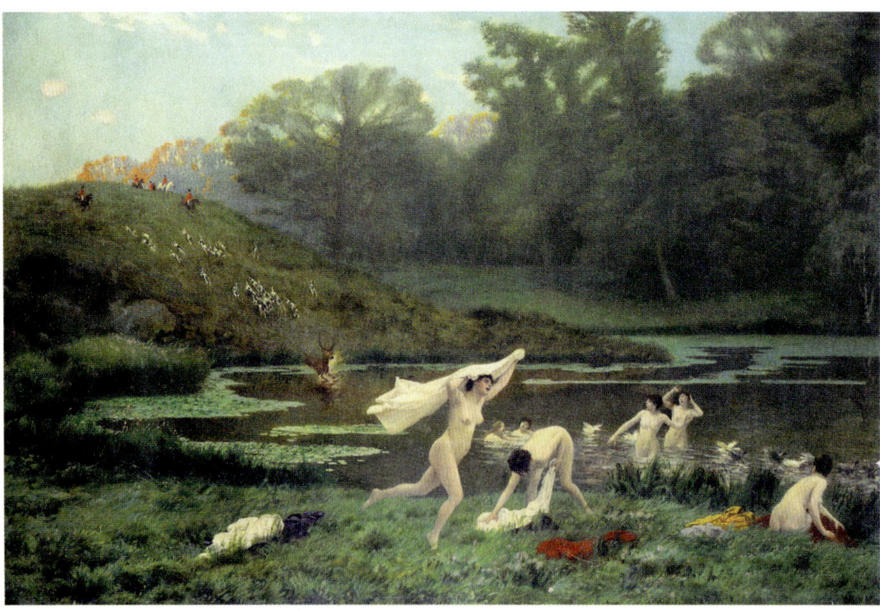

pl. 6 Jean-Léon Gérôme, *Diana and Actaeon*, 1895. Oil on canvas. Private Collection.

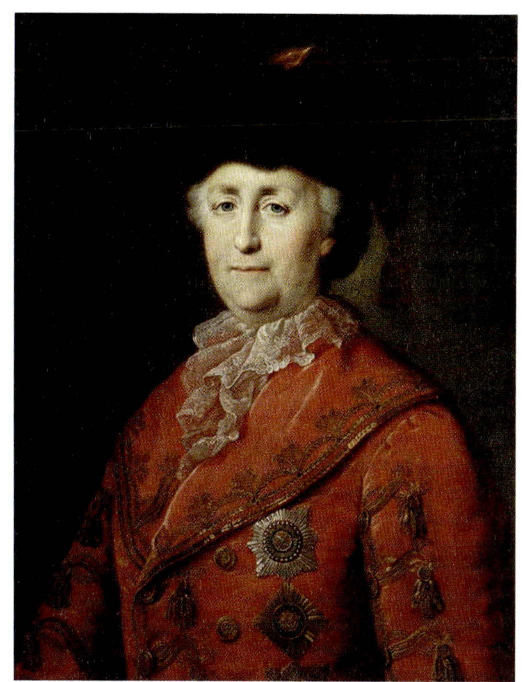

pl. 7 Mikhail Shibanov, *Portrait of Empress Catherine II*, 1787-89. Oil on canvas. Royal Collection, London, inv. RCIN 400964.

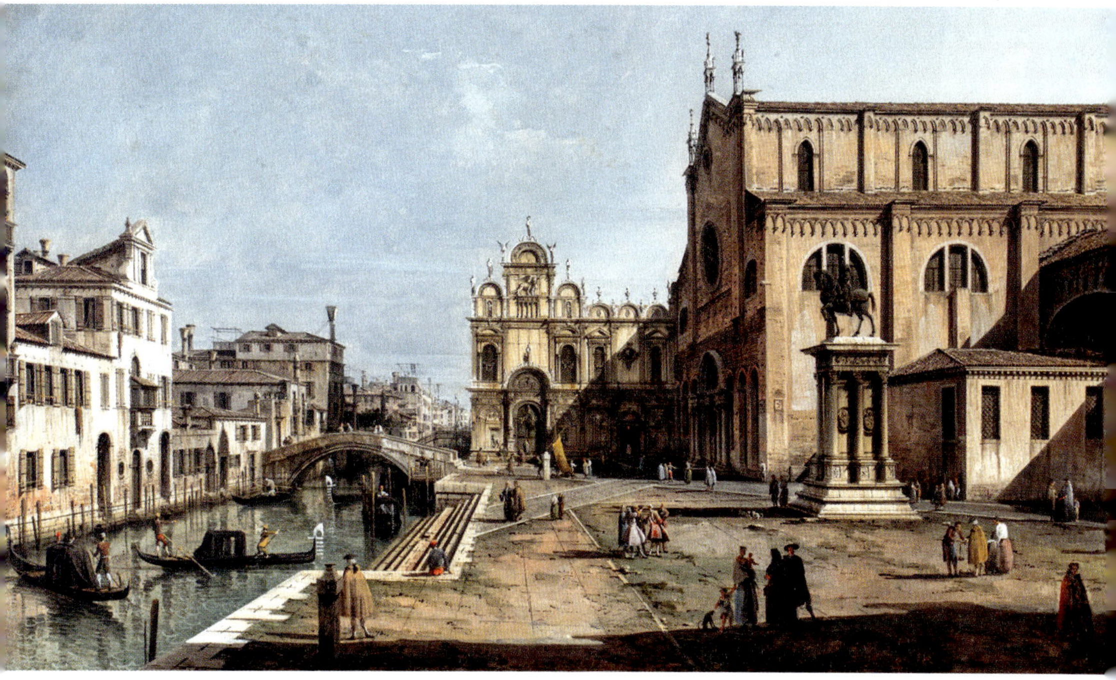

pl. 8 Bernardo Bellotto, *View of the Church of San Giovanni and Paolo*, ca. 1741. Oil on canvas. Michele and Donald D'Amour Museum of Fine Arts, Springfield, Massachusetts / The James Philip Gray Collection.

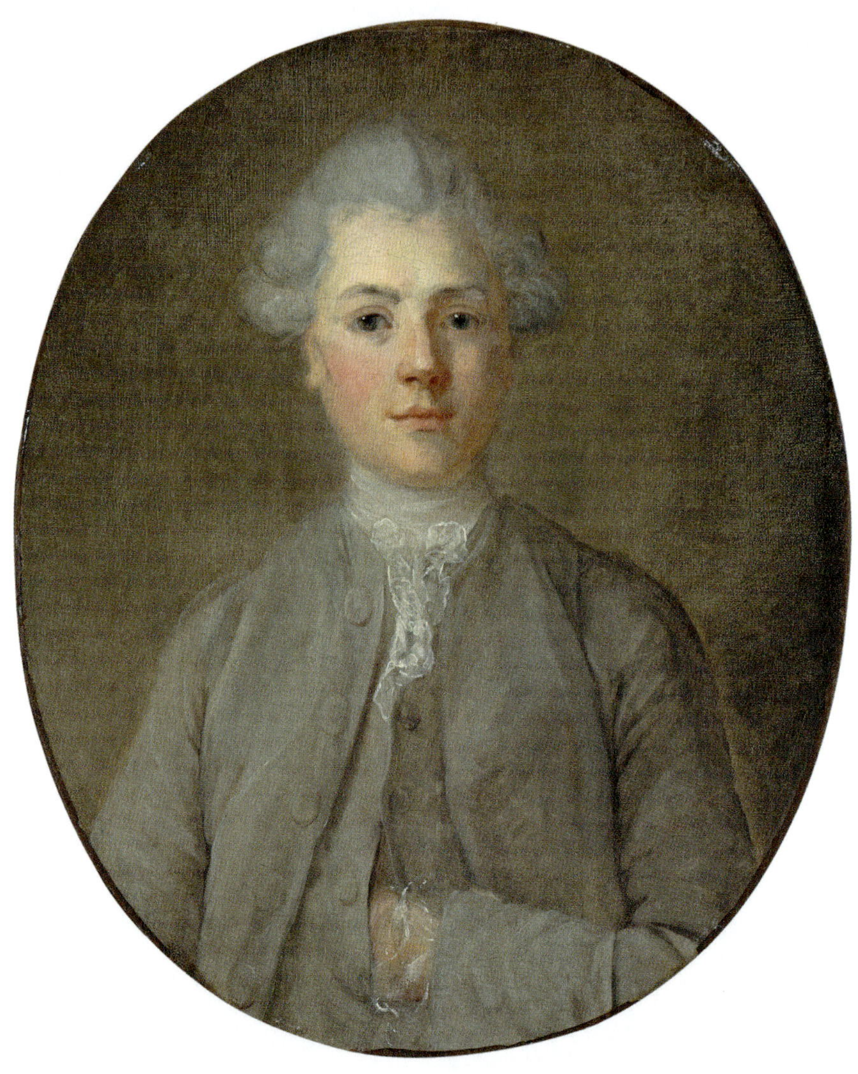

pl. 9 Jean-Baptiste Perronneau, *Portrait of a Young Man in Gray Suit and Jacket*. Oil on canvas. Private Collection.

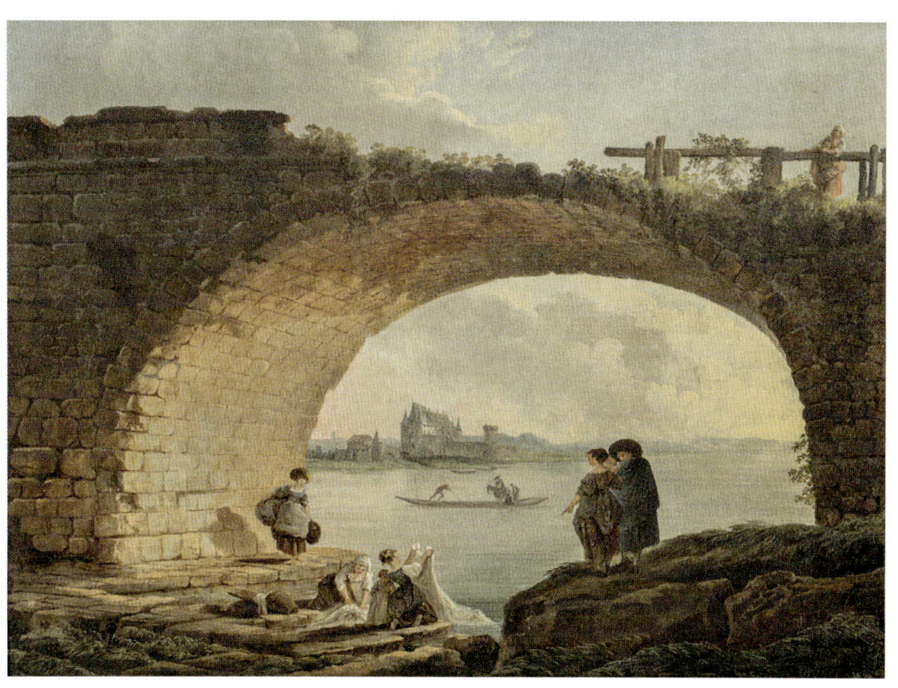

pl. 10 Hubert Robert, *Bridge with Washerwomen*. Oil on canvas. Palazzo Barberini, Galleria nazionale d'arte antica, Rome, inv. 2479.

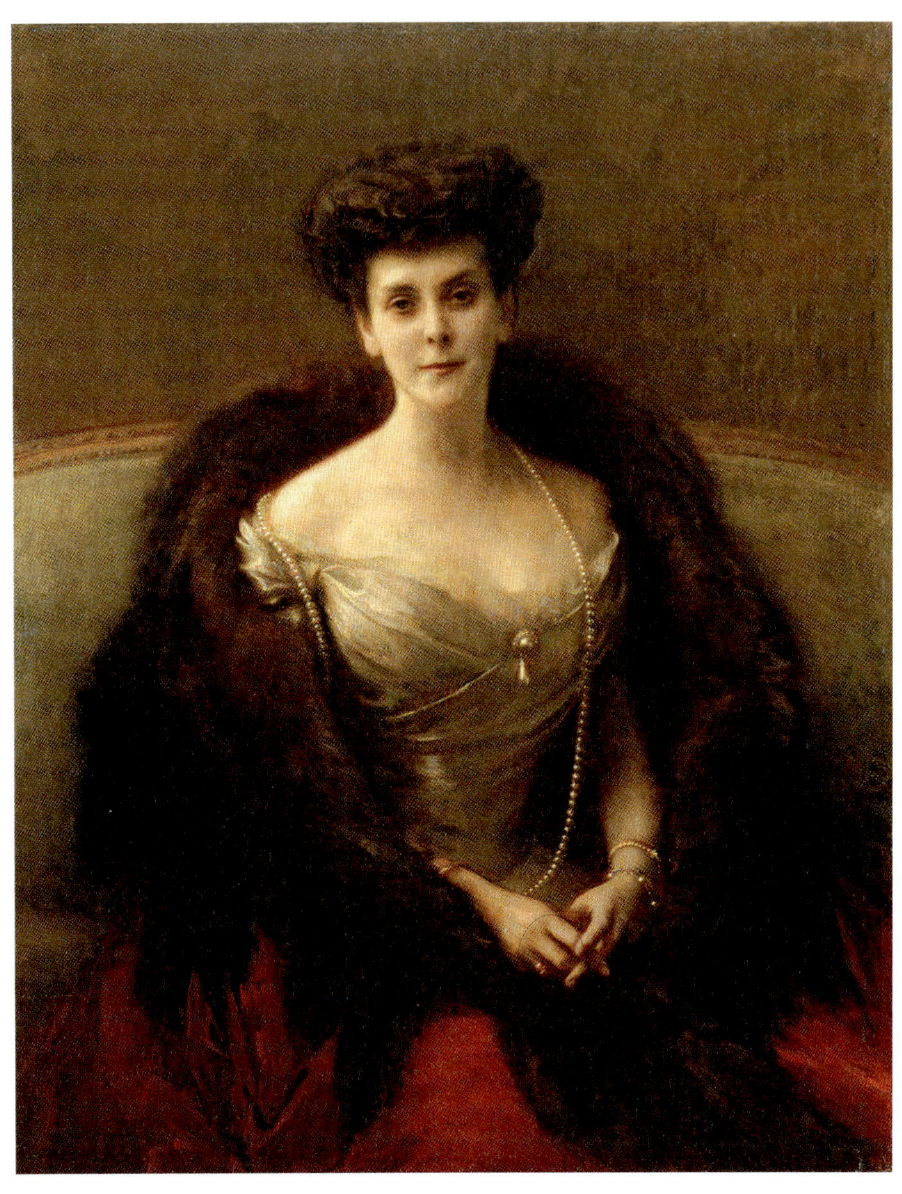

pl. 11 Pascal Dagnan-Bouveret, *Portrait of Countess von Hohenfelsen*, 1907-8. Oil on canvas. St. Petersburg, State Hermitage Museum, St. Petersburg, inv. ГЭ-9474.

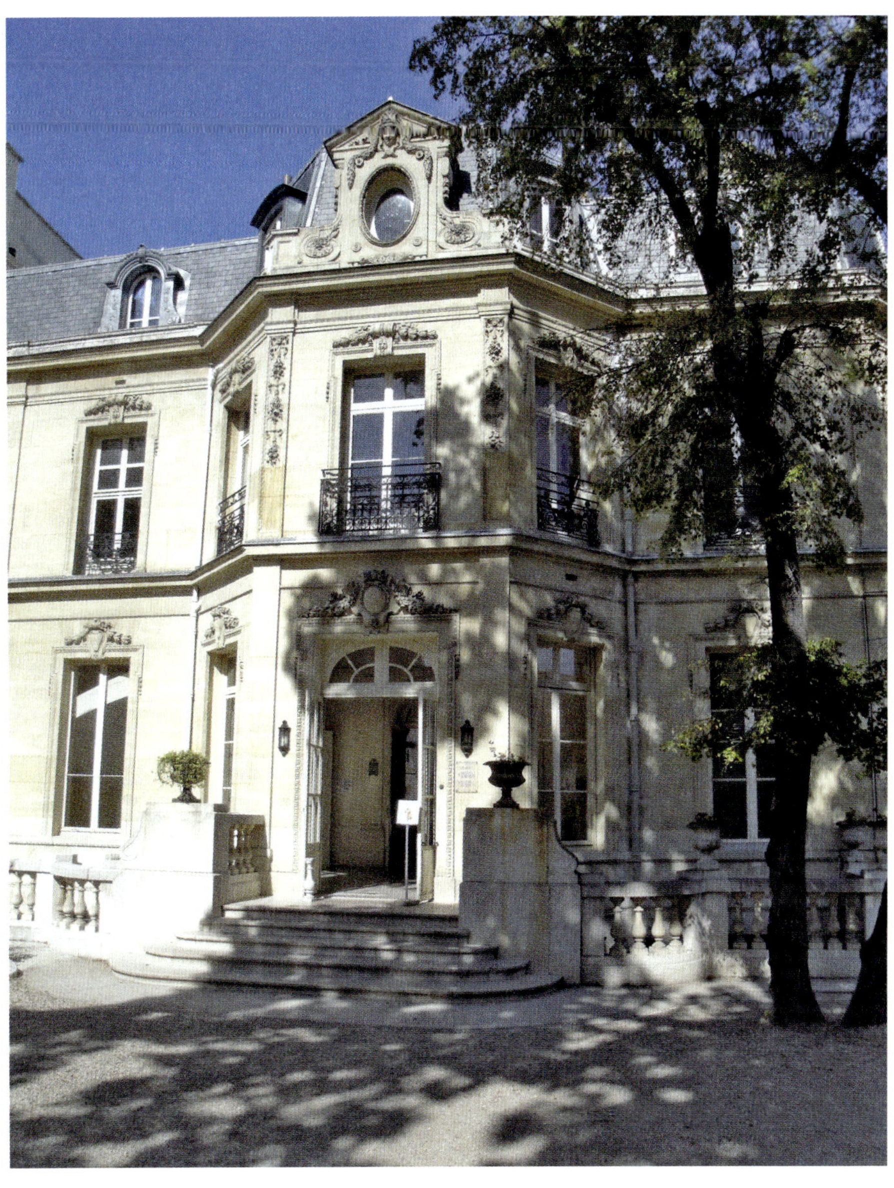

pl. 12 Detail of the facade of the Cours Dupanloup, former residence of Grand Duke Paul Alexandrovich and Countess von Hohenfelsen (previously the Yusupov mansion) in Boulogne-Billancourt, September 15, 2012.

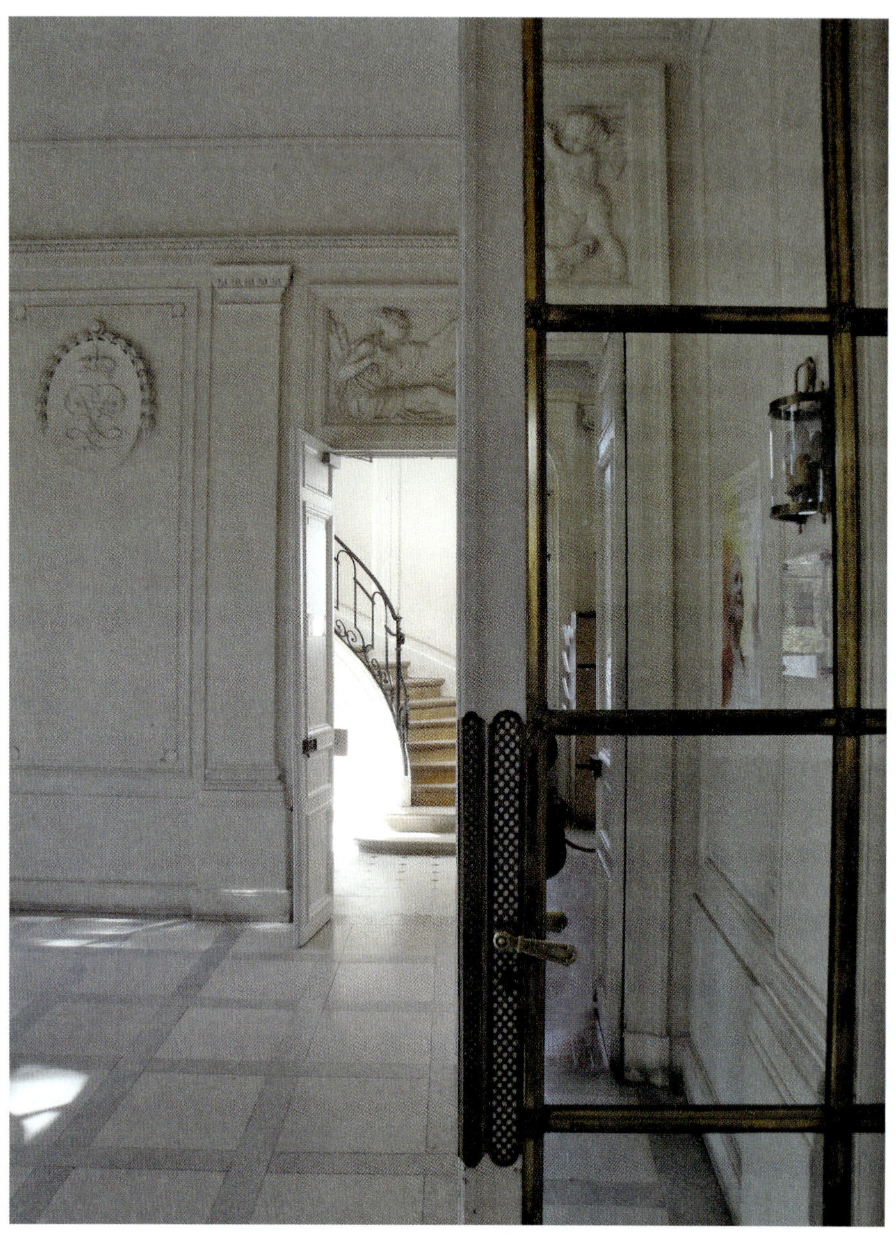

pl. 13 Vestibule of the Cours Dupanloup, former residence of Grand Duke Paul Alexandrovich and Countess von Hohenfelsen (previously the Yusupov mansion) in Boulogne-Billancourt, September 15, 2012.

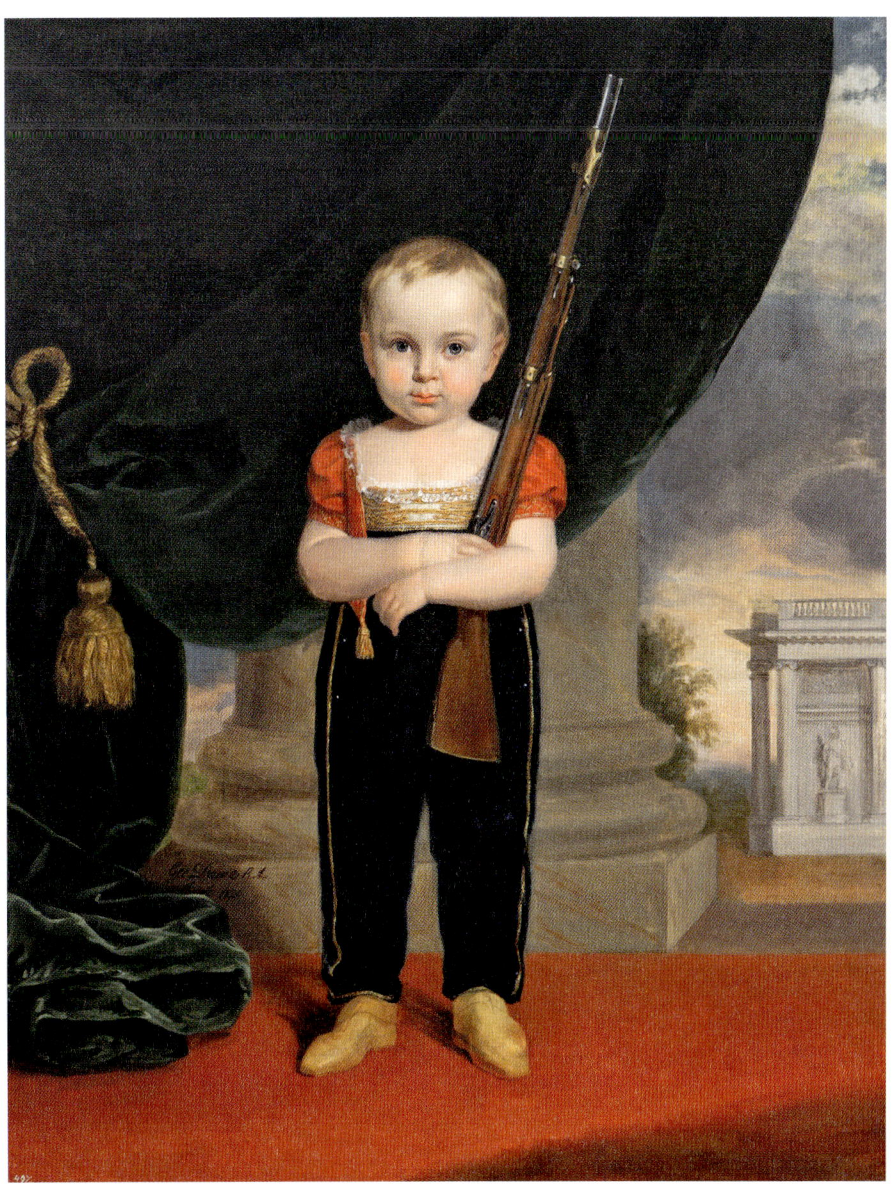

pl. 14 George Dawe, *Portrait of Emperor Alexander II as a Child, on a Terrace Holding a Pistol*, 1820. Oil on canvas. Hillwood Estate, Museum & Gardens, Washington, DC, inv. 2022.2.2.

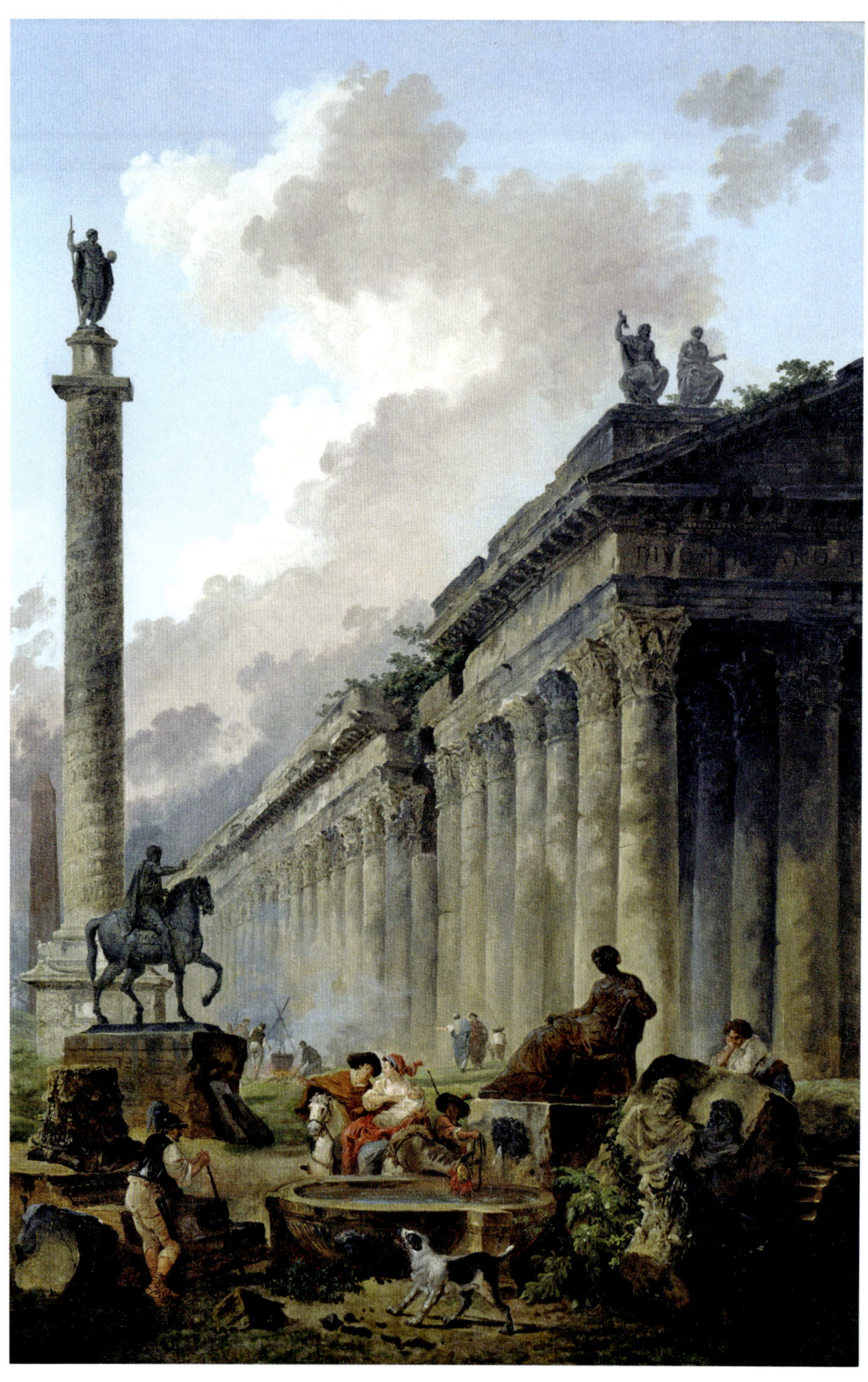

pl. 15 Hubert Robert, *Imaginary View of Rome with Equestrian Statue*, 1786. Oil on canvas. The National Museum of Western Art, Tokyo, inv. P. 1976-0002.

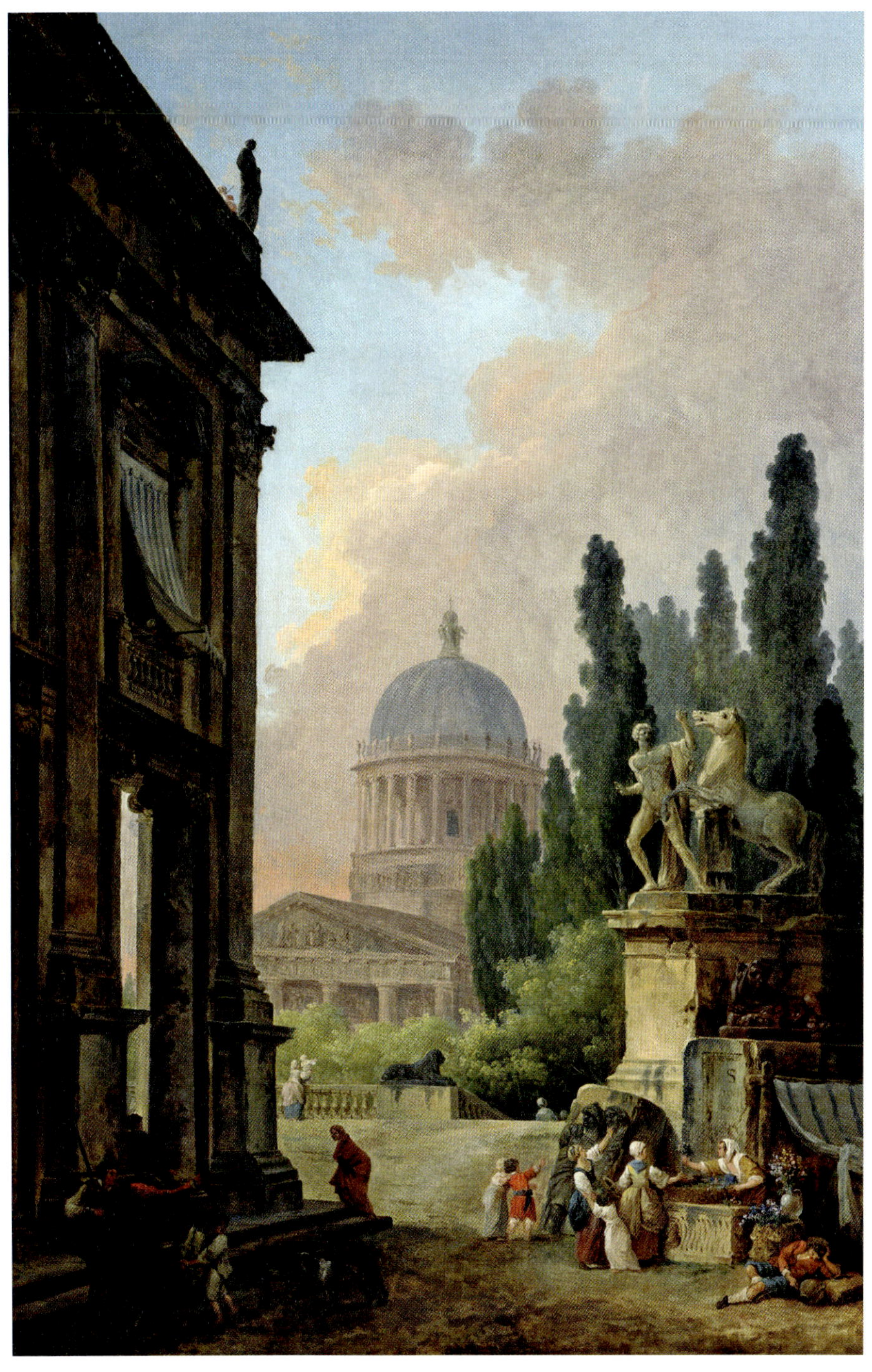

pl. 16 Hubert Robert, *Imaginary View of Rome with the Horse-Tamer of the Monte Cavallo and a Church*, 1786. Oil on canvas. The National Museum of Western Art, Tokyo, inv. P. 1977-0002.

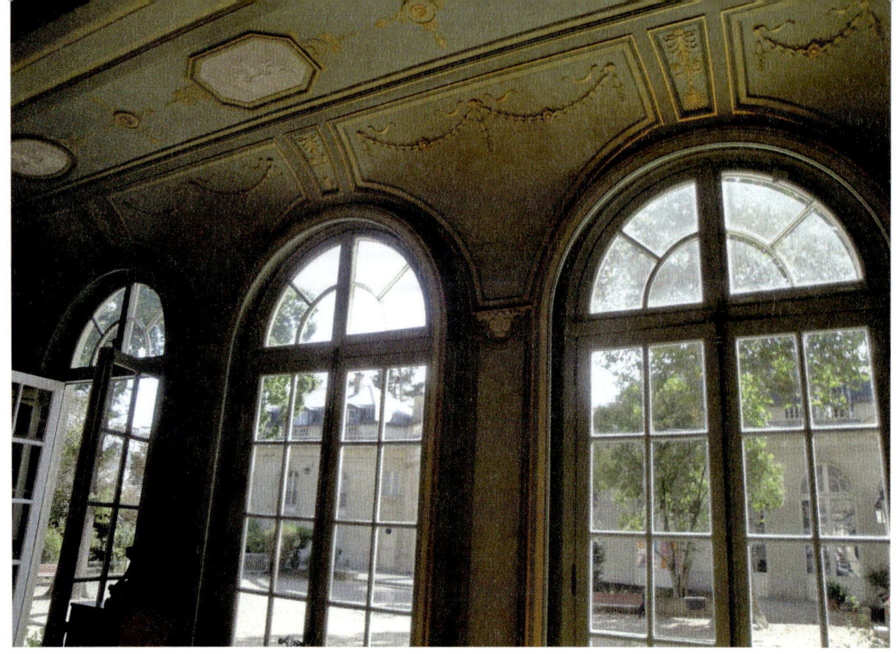

pl. 17 Former study of Grand Duke Paul, Cours Dupanloup, former residence of Grand Duke Paul Alexandrovich and Countess von Hohenfelsen (previously the Yusupov mansion) in Boulogne-Billancourt, September 15, 2012.

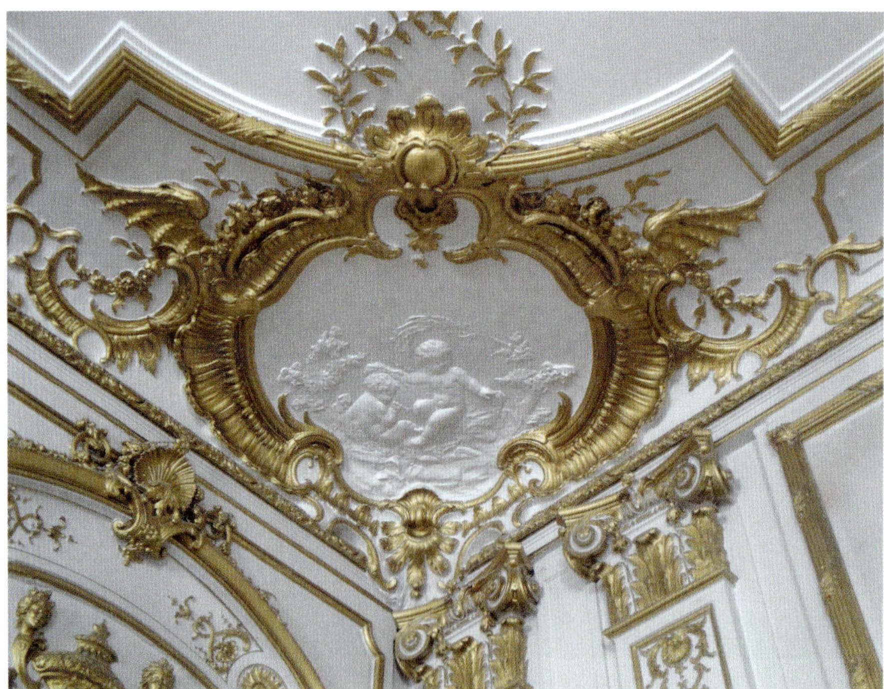

pl. 18 Detail of the wood paneling and moldings in the Cours Dupanloup library (former grand salon), former residence of Grand Duke Paul Alexandrovich and Countess von Hohenfelsen (previously the Yusupov mansion) in Boulogne-Billancourt, September 15, 2012.

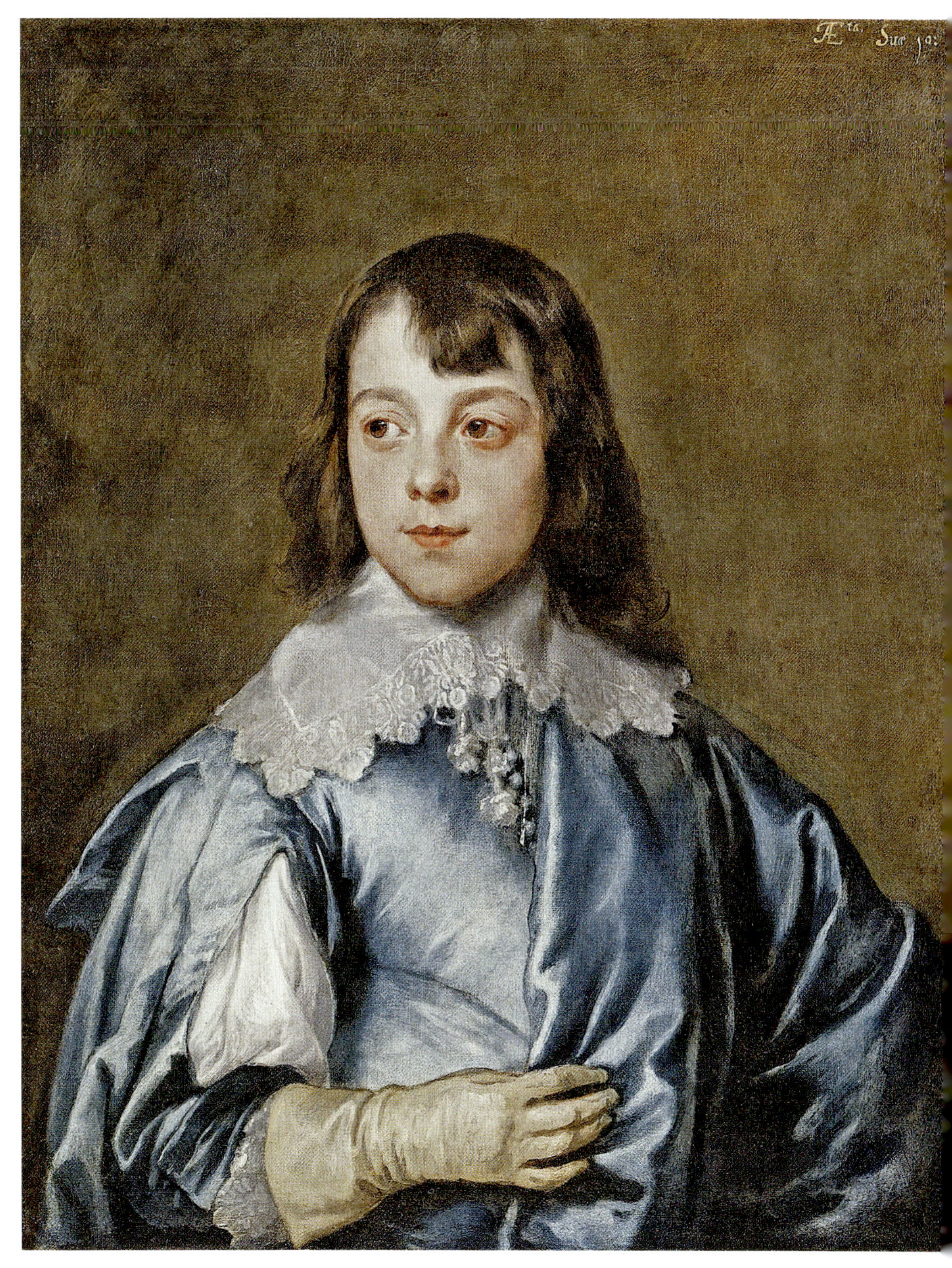

pl. 19 Anthony van Dyck, *The Blue Boy*, ca. 1638. Oil on canvas. Private collection.

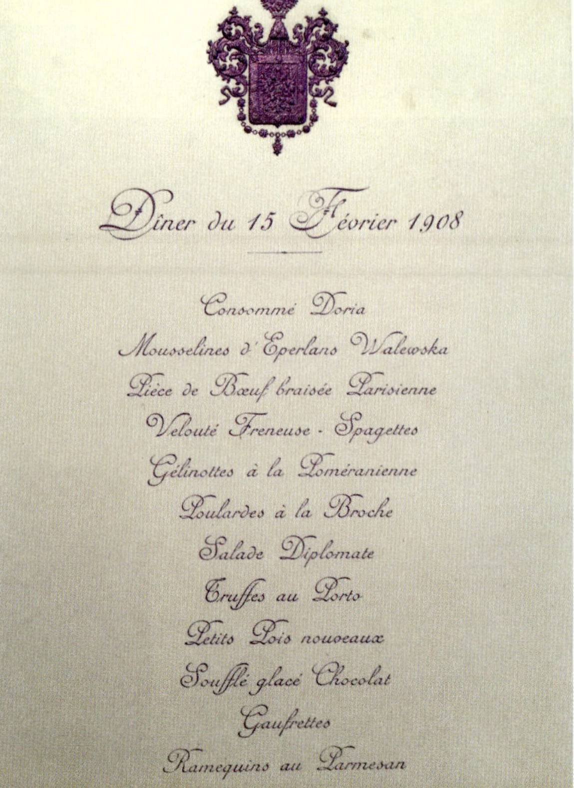
Dîner du 15 Février 1908

Consommé Doria
Mousselines d'Eperlans Walewska
Pièce de Bœuf braisée Parisienne
Velouté Freneuse - Spagettes
Gélinottes à la Poméranienne
Poulardes à la Broche
Salade Diplomate
Truffes au Porto
Petits Pois nouveaux
Soufflé glacé Chocolat
Gaufrettes
Ramequins au Parmesan

pl. 20 Menu with the grand ducal coat of arms for the dinner given in Boulogne on February 15, 1908. Private collection.

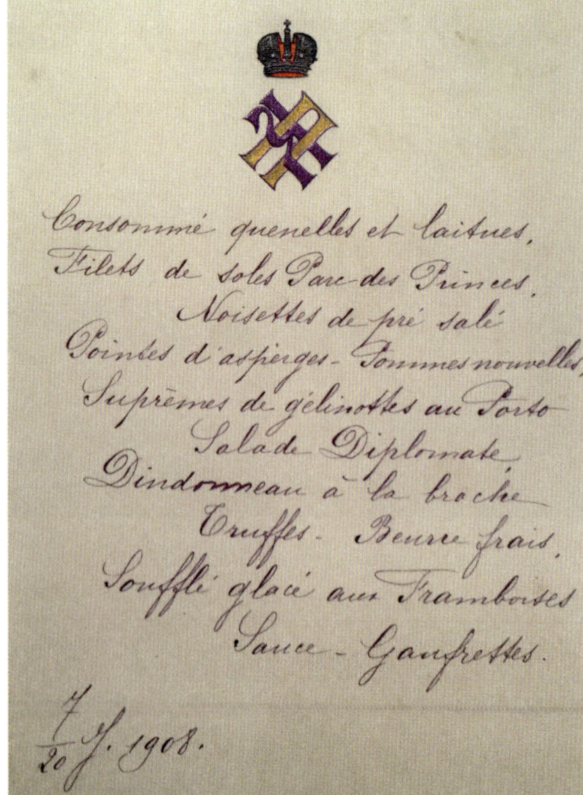
Consommé quenelles et laitues,
Filets de soles Parc des Princes,
Noisettes de pré salé
Pointes d'asperges - Pommes nouvelles,
Suprêmes de gélinottes au Porto
Salade Diplomate
Dindonneau à la broche
Truffes - Beurre frais,
Soufflé glacé aux Framboises
Sauce - Gaufrettes.

7/20 F. 1908.

pl. 21 Menu with Grand Duke Paul's monogram, 1908. Private collection.

Dîner du 13 Novembre 1912

Consommé aux ailerons

Petites croustades bressanes

Barbue sauce Genevoise

Agneau de Pauillac Fermière

Bécassines glacées Zingara

Salade Demidoff

Poulardes à la broche

Petits pois Bonne-Dame

Biscuit glacé Tosca

Pâtisseries

Profitrolles au chester

pl. 22 Menu with Grand Duke Paul's monogram for the dinner given in Boulogne on November 13, 1912. Private collection.

Dîner du 17 Décembre 1912.

Consommé Florentin

Petits Soufflés St Hubert

Filets de Soles à la Mentonnaise

Agneau de Pauillac Bouquetière

Parfait de foie Gras

Salade Bignon

Poulardes truffées à la Broche

Asperges en branches

Biscuit Glacé Cardinal

Pâtisseries

Profitrolles au Chester

pl. 23 Menu with the grand ducal coat of arms for the dinner given in Boulogne on December 17, 1912. Private collection.

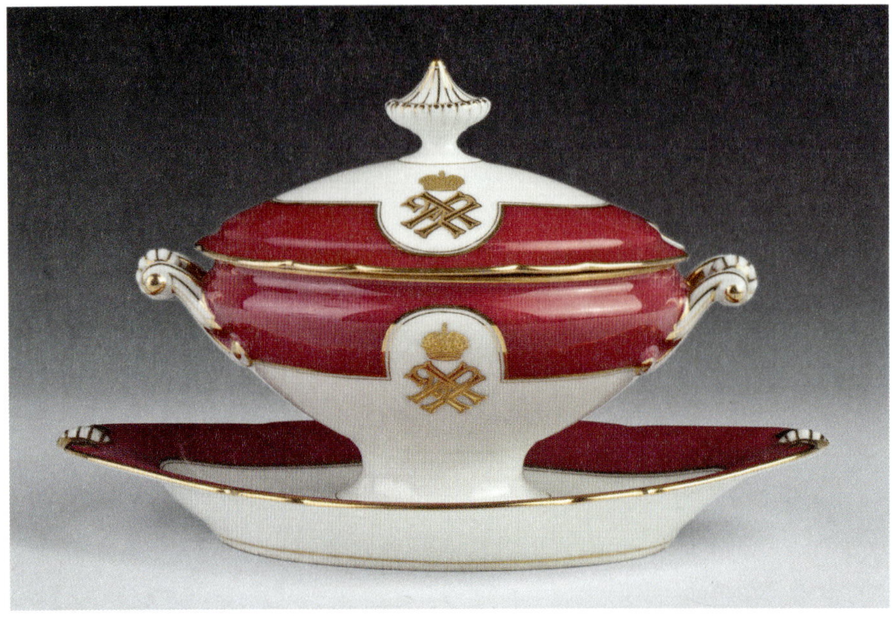

pl. 24 French manufacture. Sauce boat from a service made for Grand Duke Paul Alexandrovich, ca. 1885. Porcelain. Hillwood Estate, Museum & Gardens, Washington, DC, inv. 24.174.1-2.

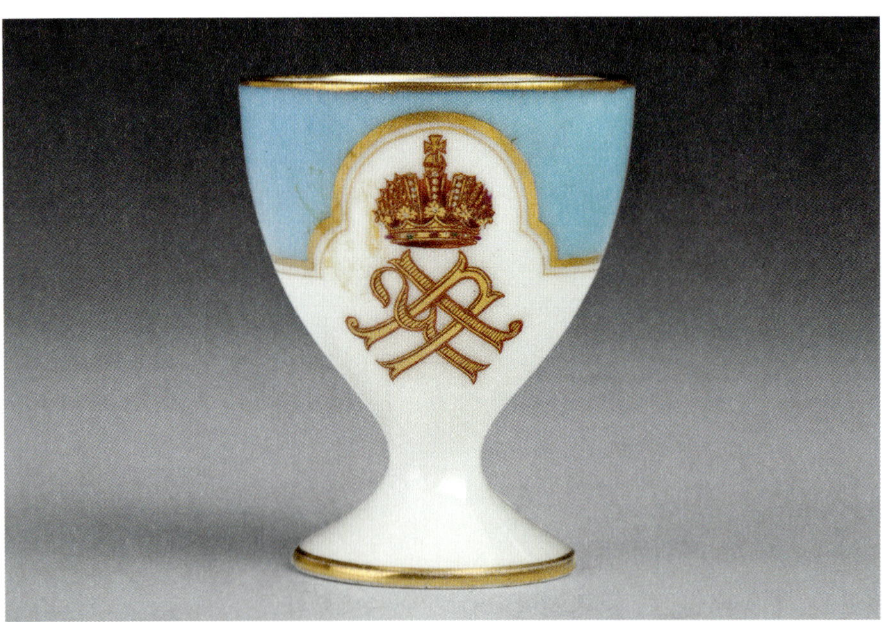

pl. 25 Le Rosey (?), porcelain decorator. Egg cup from a service made for Grand Duke Paul Alexandrovich, ca. 1885. Porcelain. Hillwood Estate, Museum & Gardens, Washington, DC, inv. 24.175.

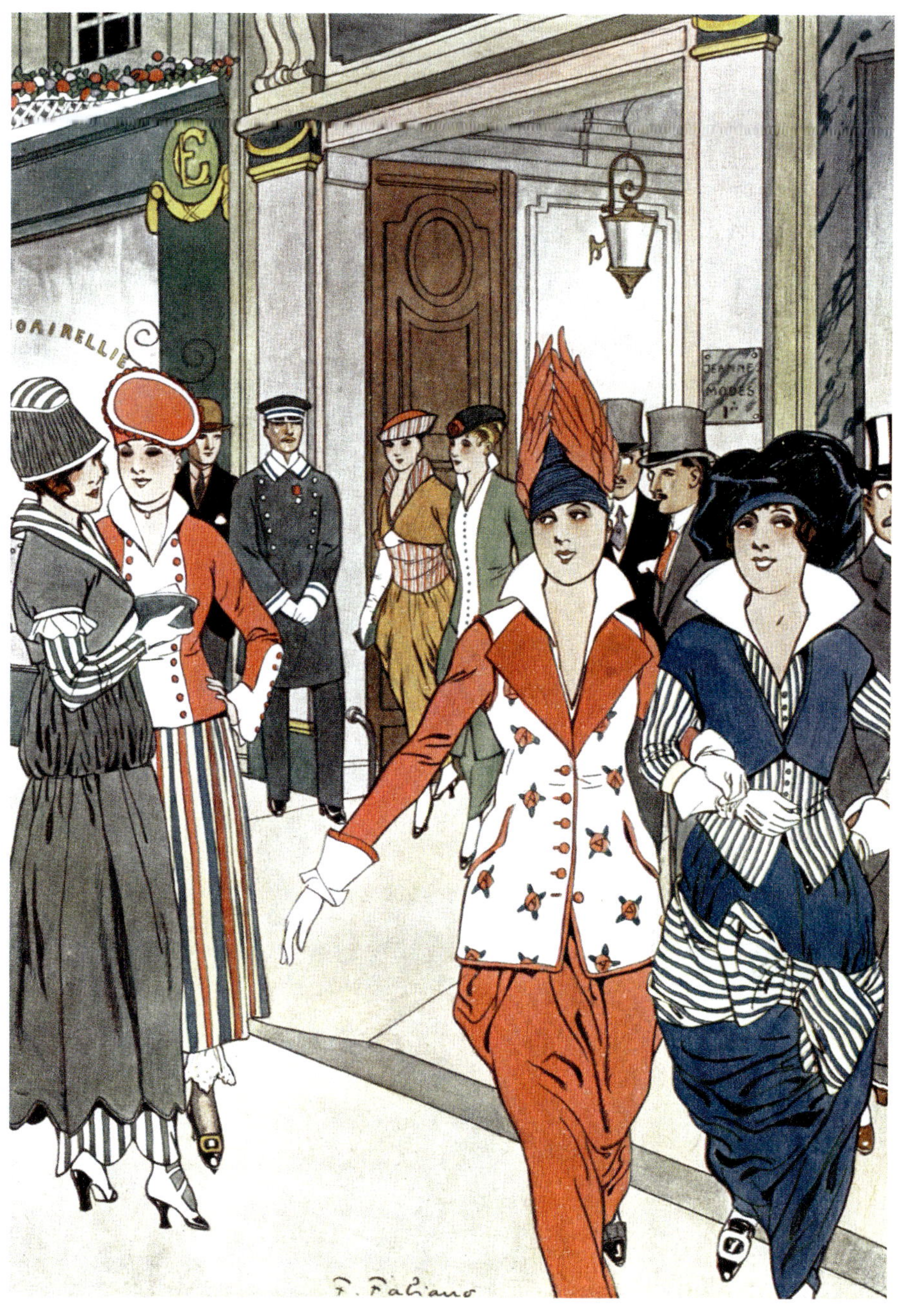

pl. 26 La rue de la Paix after F. Fabiano, ca. 1914. *Stolitsa i Usadba*, nos. 12-13 (July 1, 1914): 33. Hillwood Estate, Museum & Gardens Archives and Special Collections, Washington, DC.

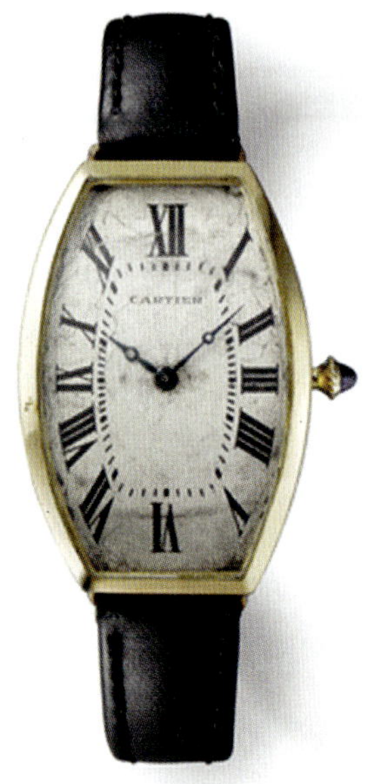

pl. 27 Tonneau wristwatch by Cartier, Paris, 1908. Gold, sapphire cabochon, leather strap. Sold to Countess von Hohenfelsen. Box: 3.8 × 2.6 cm (1 1/2 × 1 in.). Cartier Collection, inv. WCL 122 A08. Vincent Wulveryck, Collection Cartier © Cartier.

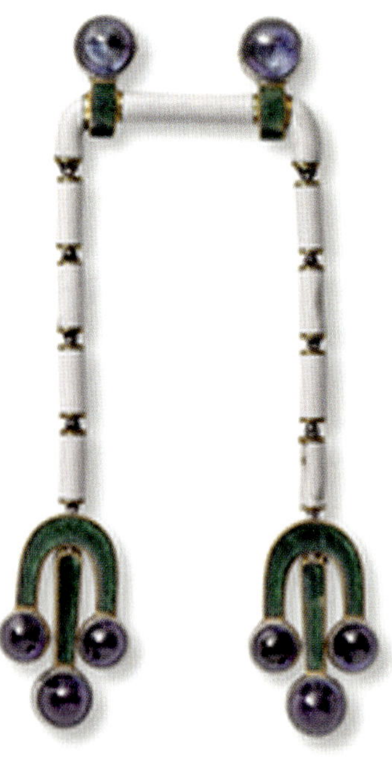

pl. 28 Brooch by Cartier, Paris, 1913. Gold, platinum, sapphire cabochons, enamel. Acquired by Countess von Hohenfelsen in 1914. Cartier Collection, inv. CL 121 A 13. Vincent Wulveryck, Cartier Collection © Cartier.

pl. 29 Order placed by Captain von Pistohlkors with Tassinari & Chatel in 1892. Tassinari & Chatel Archives, Paris.

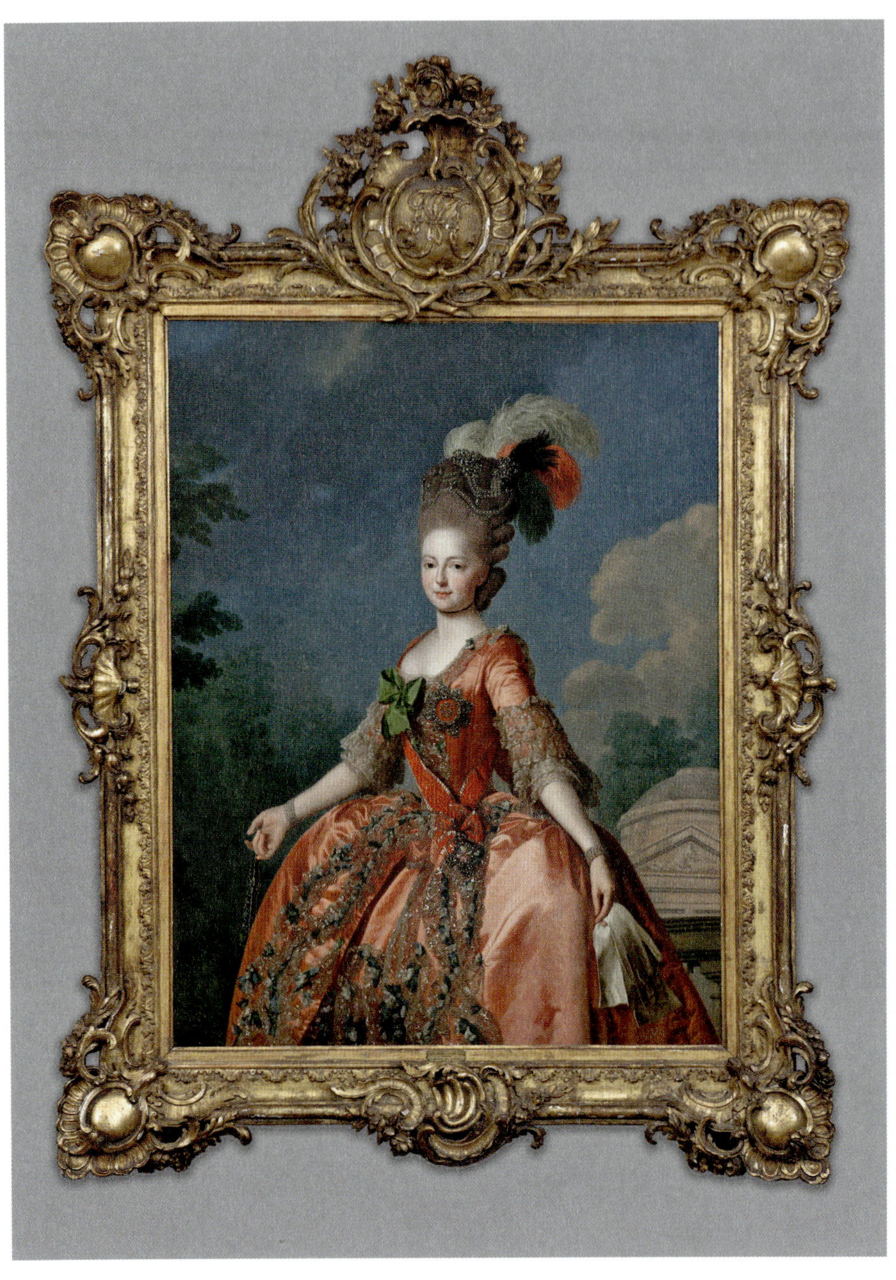

pl. 30 Alexander Roslin, *Portrait of Empress Maria Feodorovna*, 1777.
Oil on canvas. Fondation Zoubov, Geneva, inv. FZ 113.

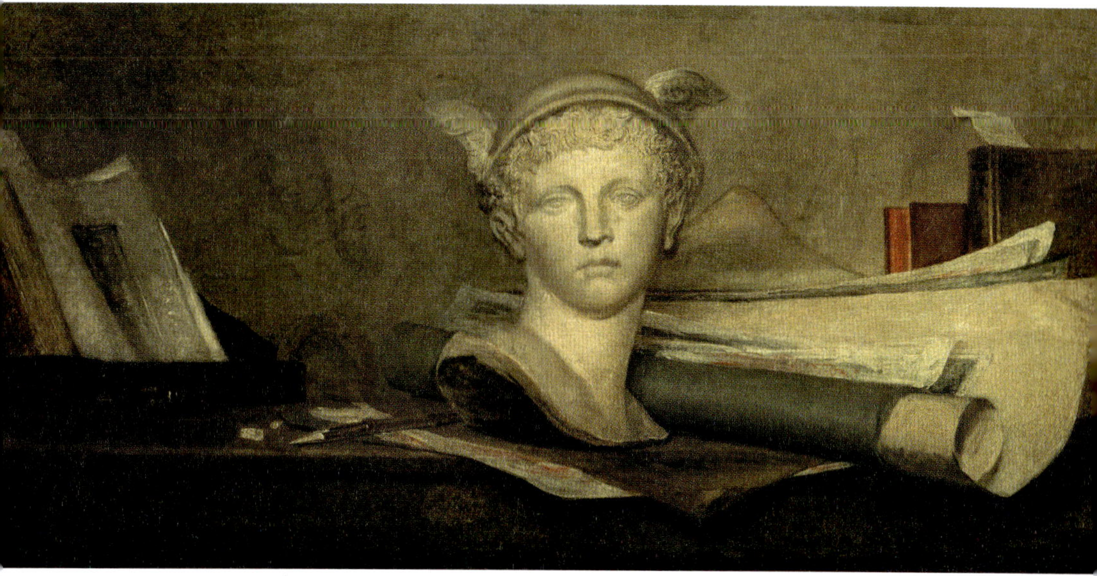

pl. 31 Jean-Baptiste-Siméon Chardin, *The Attributes of the Arts with a Bust of Mercury*, before 1728. Oil on canvas. Pushkin State Museum of Fine Arts, Moscow, inv. 1140.

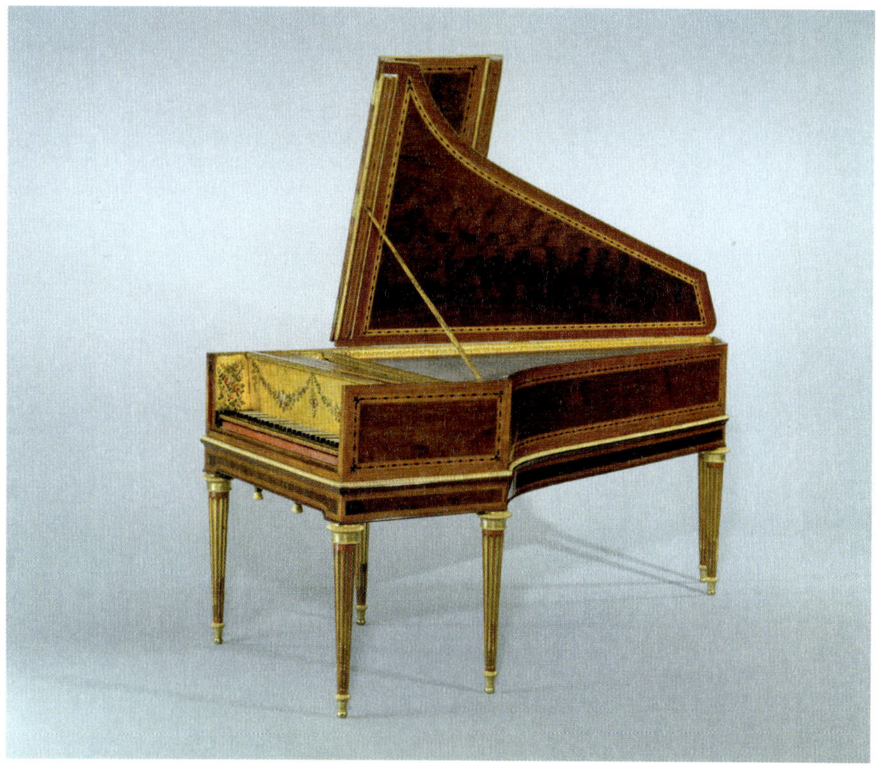

pl. 32 Pascal Taskin, fortepiano, 1788, reputed to have belonged to Marie-Antoinette. On loan to the Musée de la musique from the Musée du Louvre, Paris, inv. D.OA.10298.

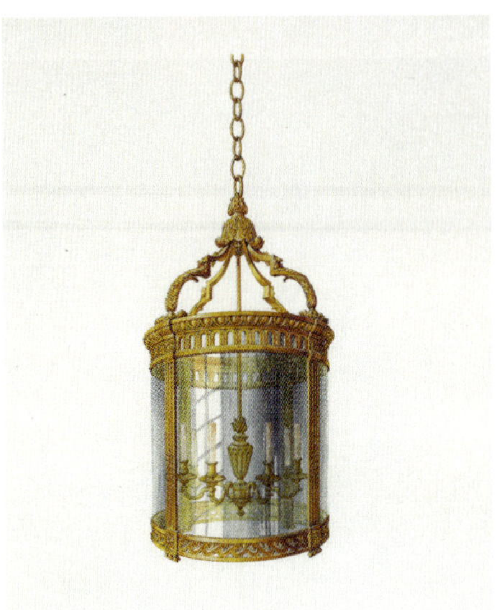

pl. 33 Maison Delisle. Project for a lantern for the entrance hall to the palace of Countess von Hohenfelsen and Grand Duke Paul, Tsarskoye Selo, ca. 1913. Delisle Archives, Paris.

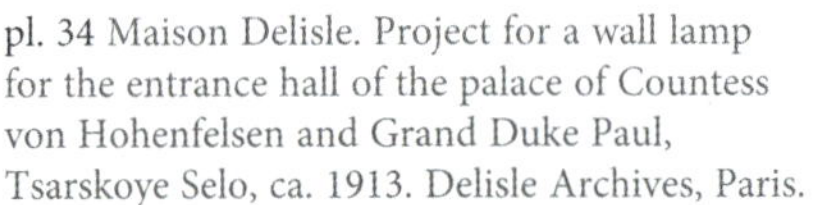

pl. 34 Maison Delisle. Project for a wall lamp for the entrance hall of the palace of Countess von Hohenfelsen and Grand Duke Paul, Tsarskoye Selo, ca. 1913. Delisle Archives, Paris.

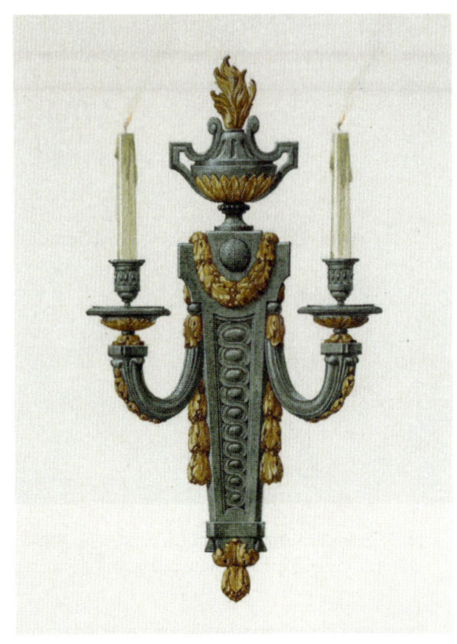

Palais de TSARSKOE-SELO.

pl. 35 Maison Delisle. Project for a chandelier for the great hall of the palace of Countess von Hohenfelsen and Grand Duke Paul, Tsarskoye Selo, ca. 1913. Delisle Archives, Paris.

pl. 36 Maison Delisle. Project for a wall lamp for the small study in the palace of Countess von Hohenfelsen and Grand Duke Paul, Tsarskoye Selo, ca. 1913. Delisle Archives, Paris.

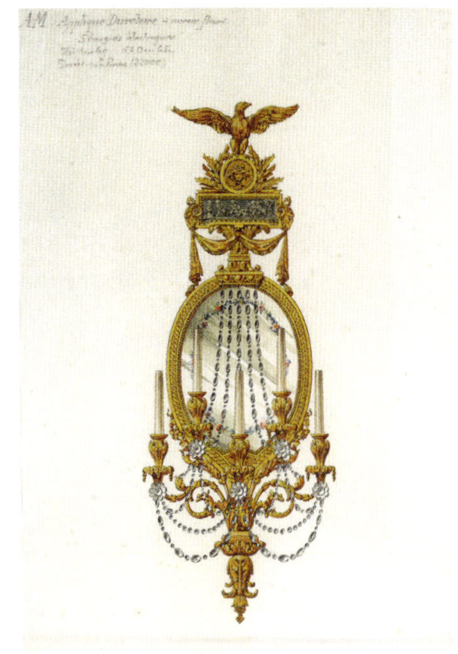

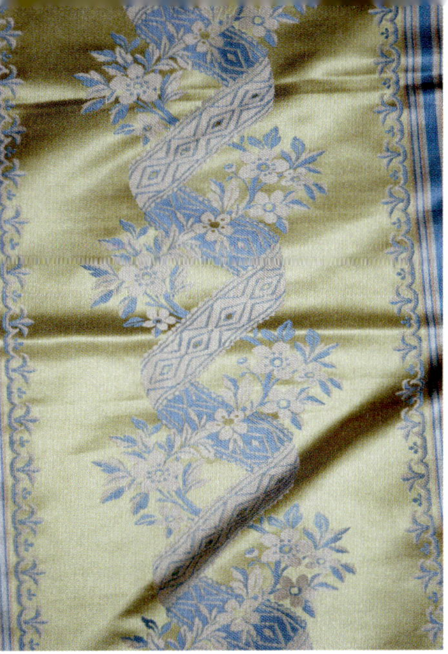

pl. 37 Yellow-blue cream lampas commissioned by Marcel Boulanger for the bedroom of Countess von Hohenfelsen, Tsarskoye Selo, in 1913. Tassinari & Chatel Archives, Paris.

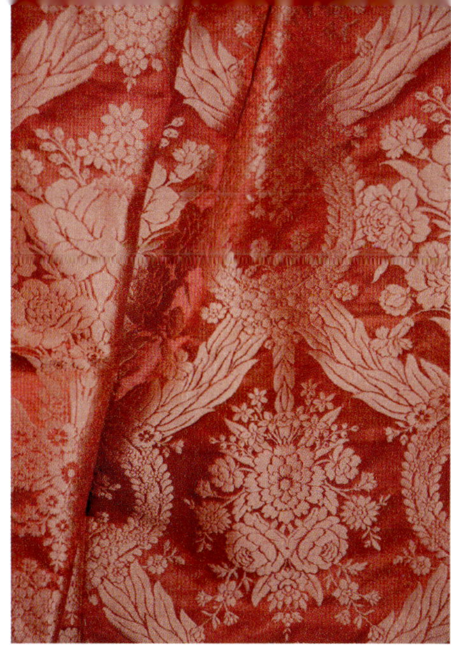

pl. 38 Cherry damask commissioned by Marcel Boulanger for the oak salon of the palace of Countess von Hohenfelsen and Grand Duke Paul, Tsarskoye Selo, in 1913. Tassinari & Chatel Archives, Paris.

pl. 39 Pattern for the buttercup and 2 gray lampas commissioned by Marcel Boulanger for the furniture in the grand salon, palace of Countess von Hohenfelsen and Grand Duke Paul, Tsarskoye Selo, in 1911. Tassinari & Chatel Archives, Paris.

pl. 40 Cream cherry lampas commissioned by Marcel Boulanger for Tsarskoye Selo, in 1913. Tassinari & Chatel Archives, Paris.

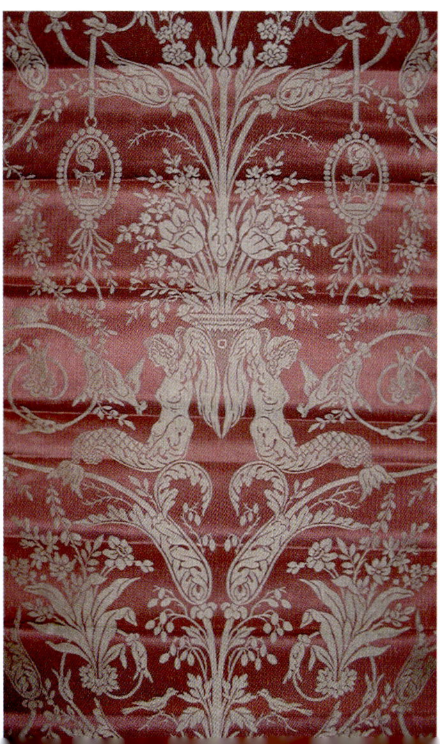

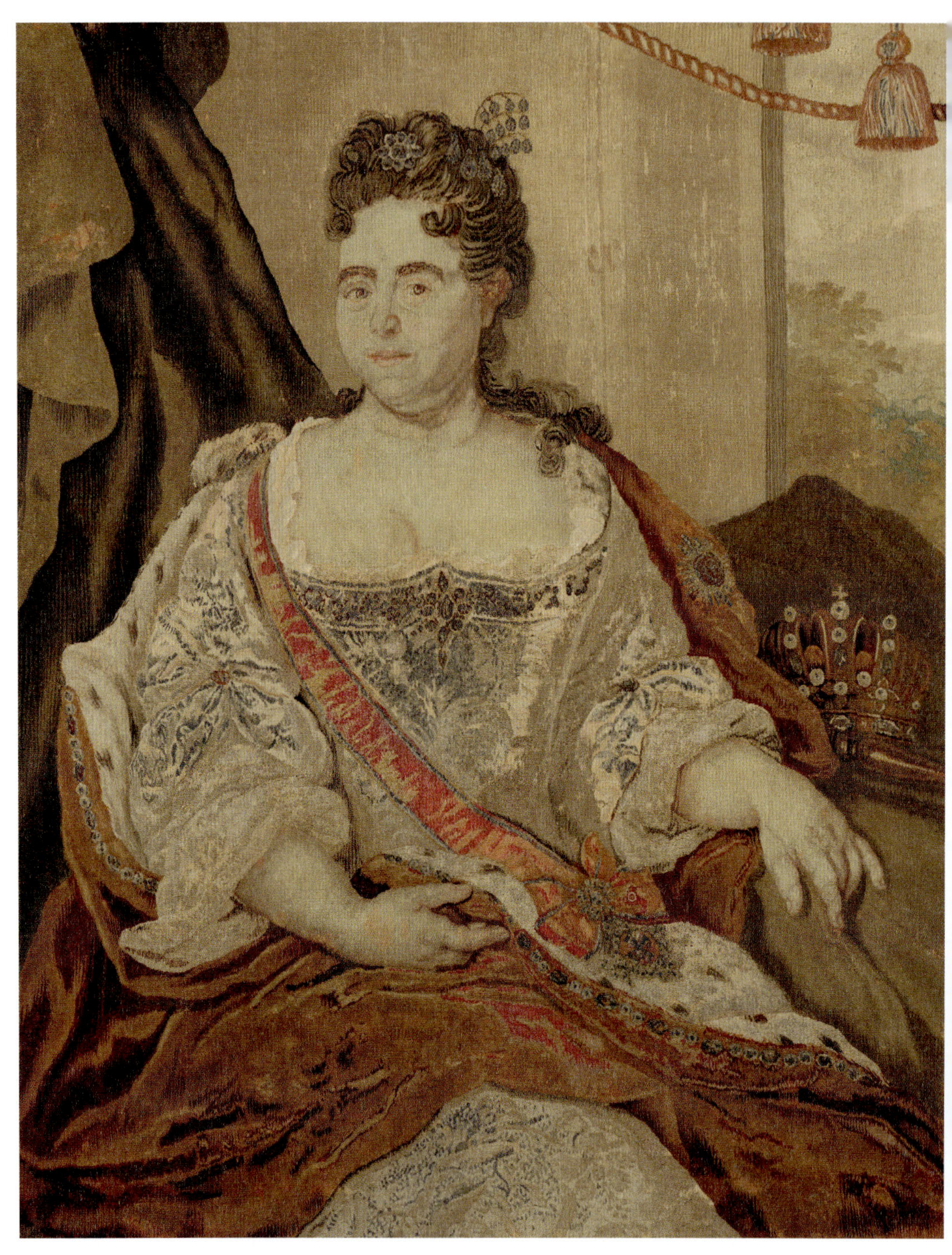

pl. 41 Imperial Tapestry Manufactory. Portrait of Empress Catherine I, after 1717. Silk and silver threads. Walters Art Museum, Baltimore, inv. 82.4.

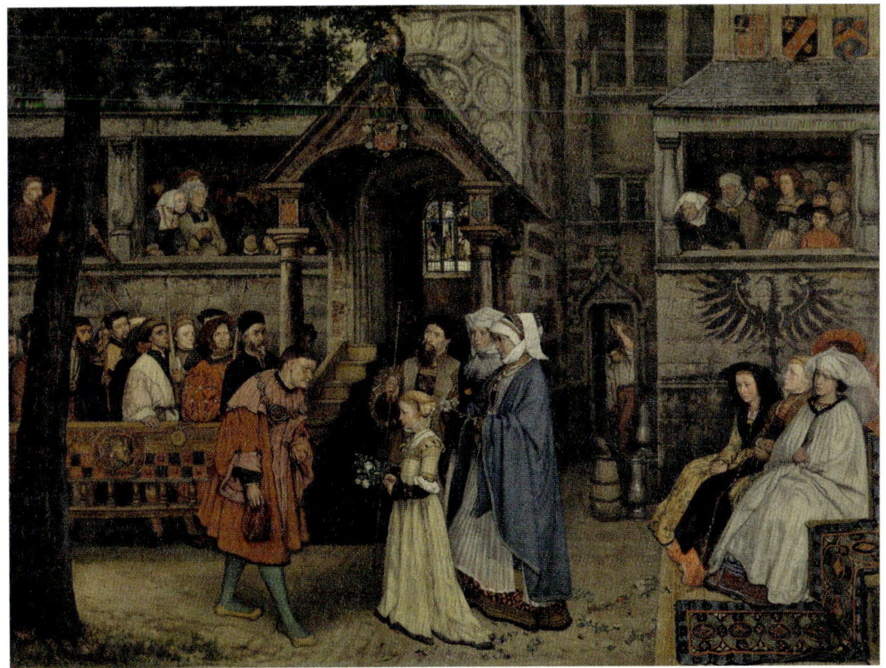

pl. 42 Henri Leys, *The Guild of the Archers Welcomes Margaret of Austria*, 1860. Oil on panel. Royal Museum of Fine Arts, Antwerp, inv. 2111.

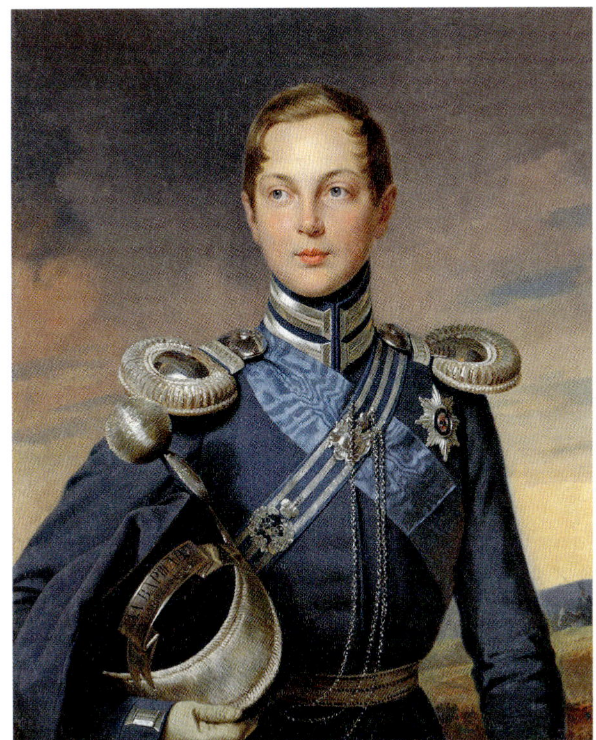

pl. 43 After Franz Krüger (1797-1857). Portrait of Grand Duke Alexander Nikolayevich in Blue Uniform and Silver Epaulets, 1833. Oil on canvas. Private Collection.

pl. 44 Flask. Chelsea Red Anchor, 1754. Soft-paste porcelain, gold. H. 9.5 cm (3 3/4 in.). Givaudan Collection, Paris.

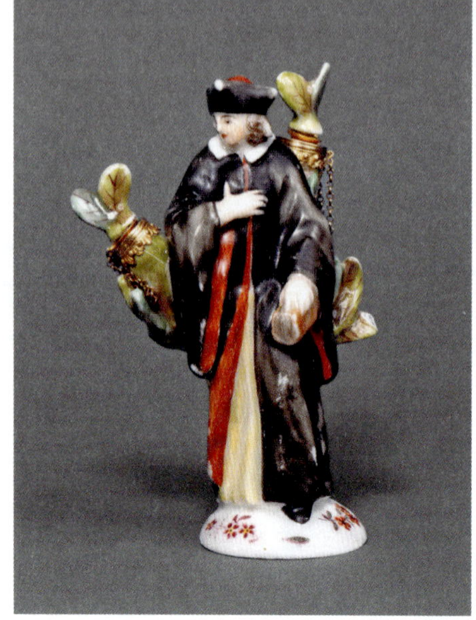

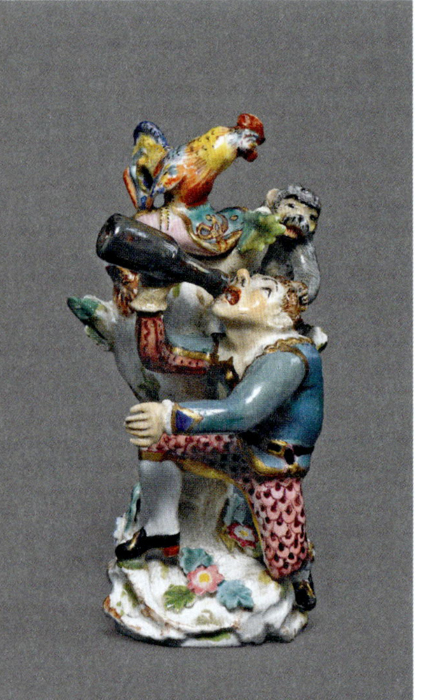

pl. 45 Flask. Chelsea? Soft-paste porcelain. H. 10 cm (4 in.). Givaudan Collection, Paris.

pl. 46 Flask. Chelsea Gold Anchor, 1760. Soft-paste porcelain, gold. H. 7.5 cm (3 in.). Givaudan Collection, Paris.

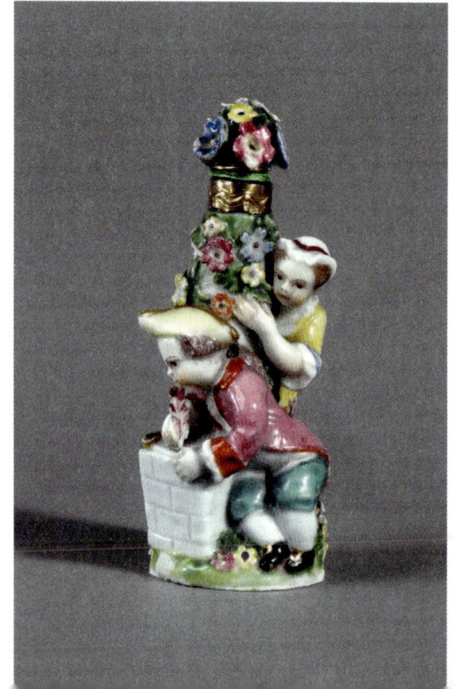

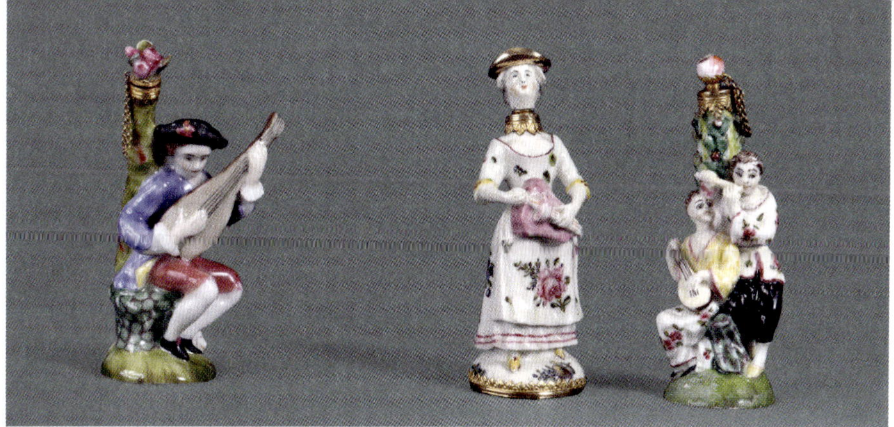

pl. 47 Three flasks. Lute player, 1751-54. Soft-paste porcelain, gilt metal. H. 8.8 cm (3 1/2 in.). Hurdy-gurdy player, 1751-54. Soft-paste porcelain, gold. H. 9.5 cm (3 3/4 in.). Musical duet, 1751-54. Soft-paste porcelain, gold. H. 9 cm (3 1/2 in.). Givaudan Collection, Paris.

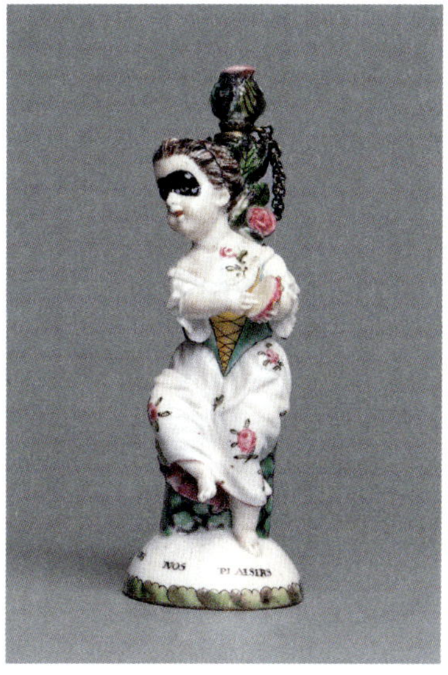

pl. 48 Flask. Girl in a Swing, 1751-54. Soft-paste porcelain. H. 10 cm (4 in.). Givaudan Collection, Paris.

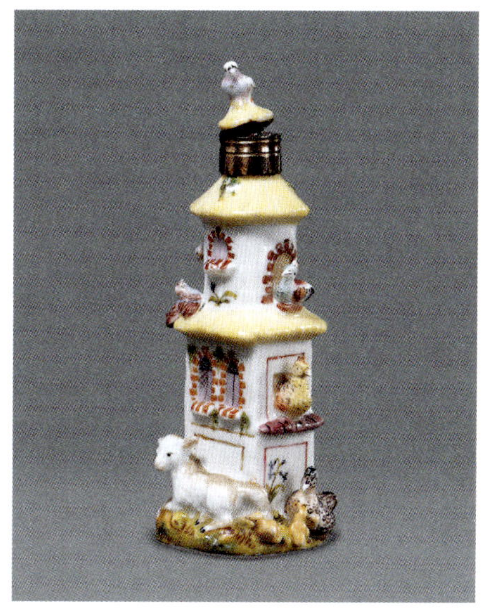

pl. 49 Flask. Chelsea Red Anchor, ca. 1758. Soft-paste porcelain, gold. H. 9.5 cm (3 3/4 in.). Givaudan Collection, Paris.

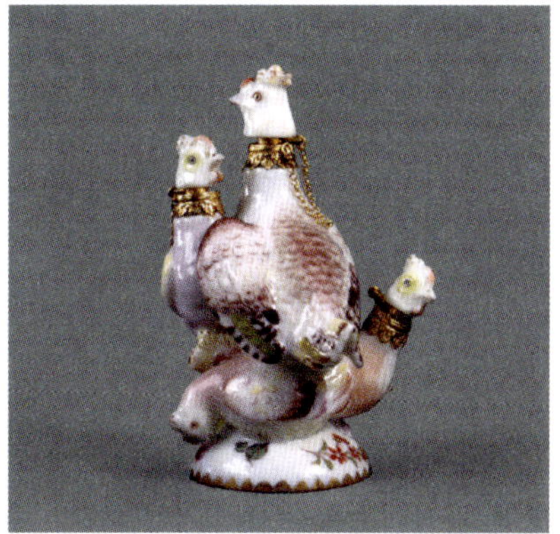

pl. 50 Flask. Chelsea Red Anchor, ca. 1754. Soft-paste porcelain, gold. H. 8 cm (3 1/8 in.). Givaudan Collection, Paris.

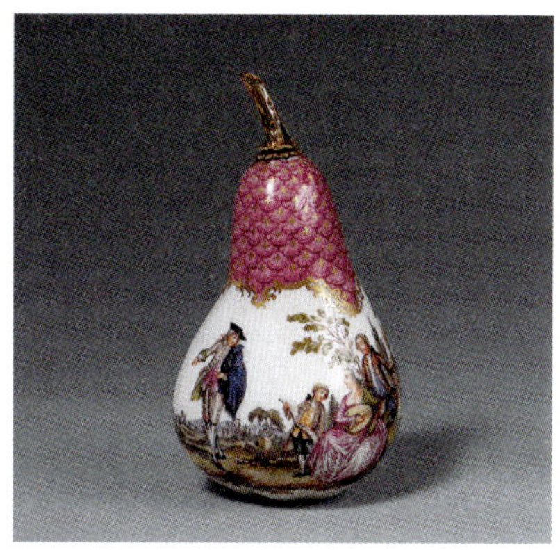

pl. 51 Flask. Meissen, 1750-55. Porcelain, gold. H. 8.6 cm (3 3/8 in.). Givaudan Collection, Paris.

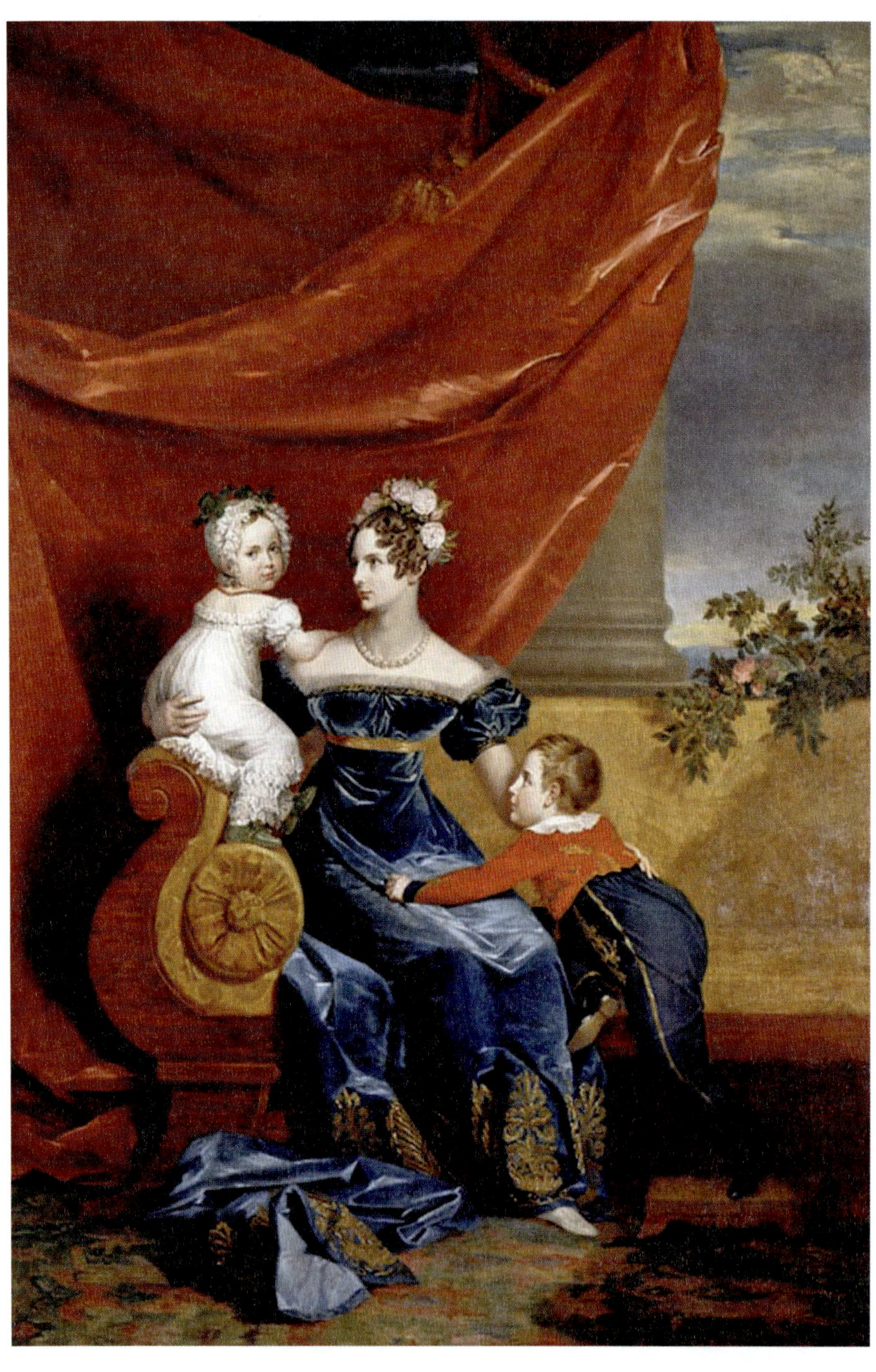

pl. 52 George Dawe, *Charlotte (Alexandra Feodorovna), Empress of Russia, with Her Eldest Children, Alexander and Maria*, ca. 1821. Oil on canvas. Royal Collection, London, inv. RCIN 404608.

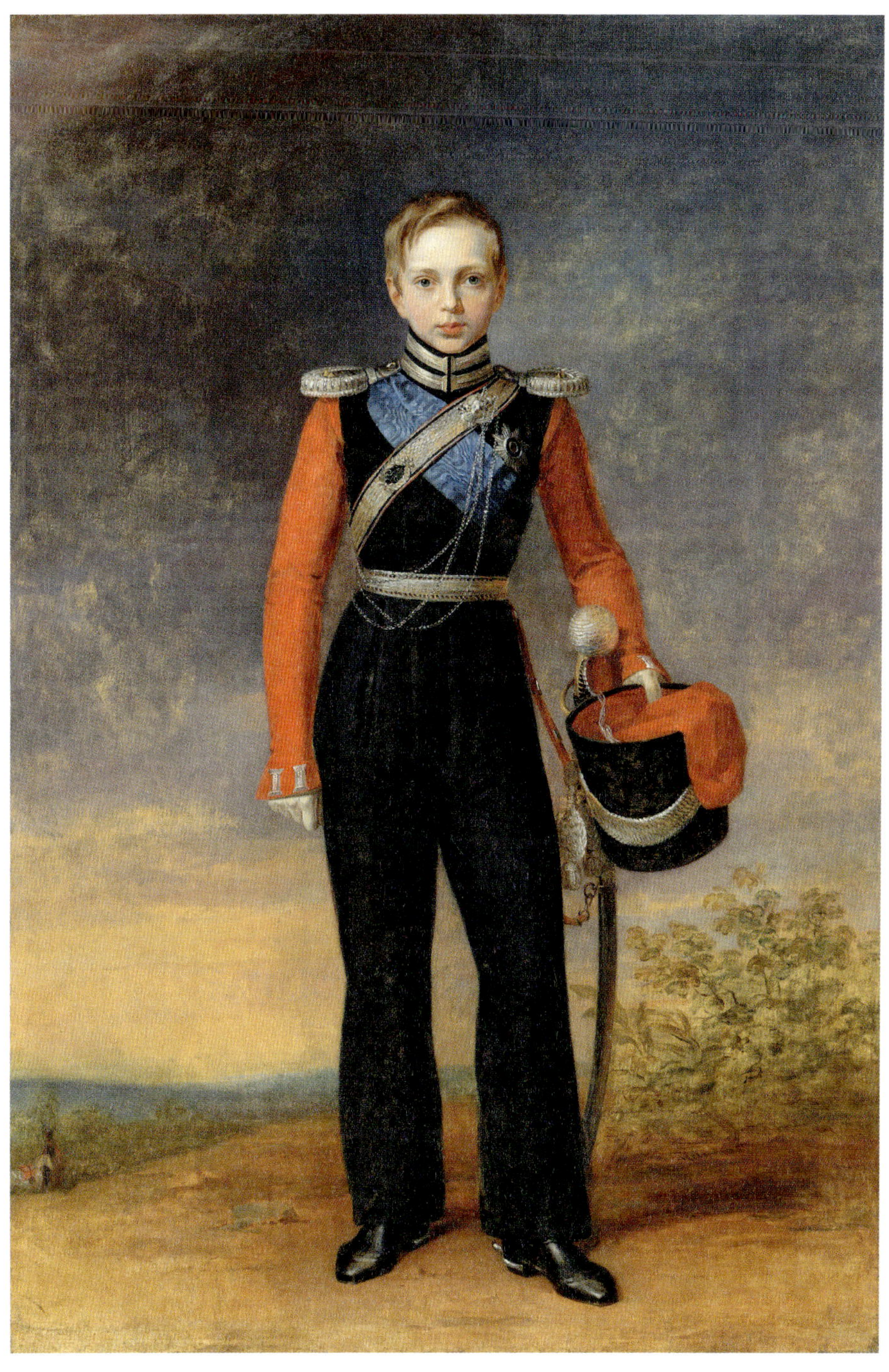

pl. 53 George Dawe. *Portrait of Emperor Alexander II as a Child in Uniform against a Landscape Background*, ca. 1825. Oil on canvas. Private collection.

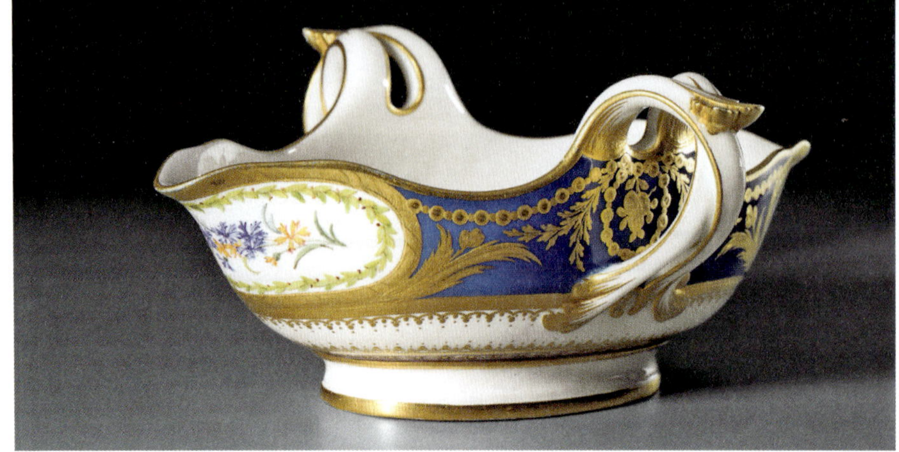

pl. 54 Manufacture de Sèvres, Edmé-Francois Bouillat, decorator. Sauce boat probably from the collection of Countess von Hohenfelsen, 1785 (see Paley sale, Christie's, London, June 6-7, 1929, lot 40). Soft-paste porcelain. Hillwood Estate, Museum & Gardens, Washington, DC, inv. 24.17.

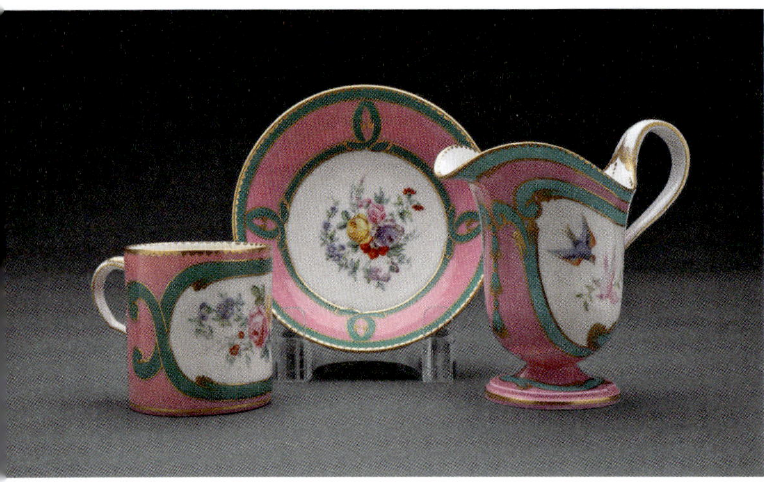

pl. 55 Sèvres Porcelain Manufactory. Creamer, litron cup and saucer from the collection of Countess von Hohenfelsen, 1700s-1800s (see Paley sale, Christie's, London, June 6-7, 1929, lot 224). Soft paste porcelain. Hillwood Estate, Museum & Gardens, Washington DC, inv. 24.96.1-2 and 24.111.

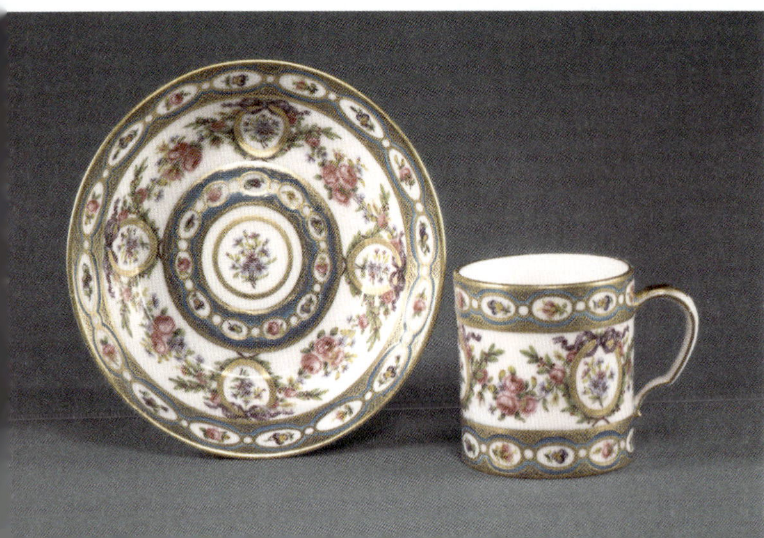

pl. 56 Manufacture de Sèvres, Nicquet, decorator. Litron cup and saucer probably from the collection of Countess von Hohenfelsen, 1780 (see Paley sale, Christie's, London, June 6-7, 1929, lot 13). Soft-paste porcelain. Metropolitan Museum of Art, New York City. Gift of R. Thornton Wilson, in memory of Florence Ellsworth Wilson, 1950.

pl. 57 Manufacture de Sèvres.
Square compotier from a pair
from the collection of Countess
von Hohenfelsen, 1754.
Soft-paste porcelain.
The Fitzwilliam Museum, Cambridge,
L.C.G. Clarke Bequest, 1960.

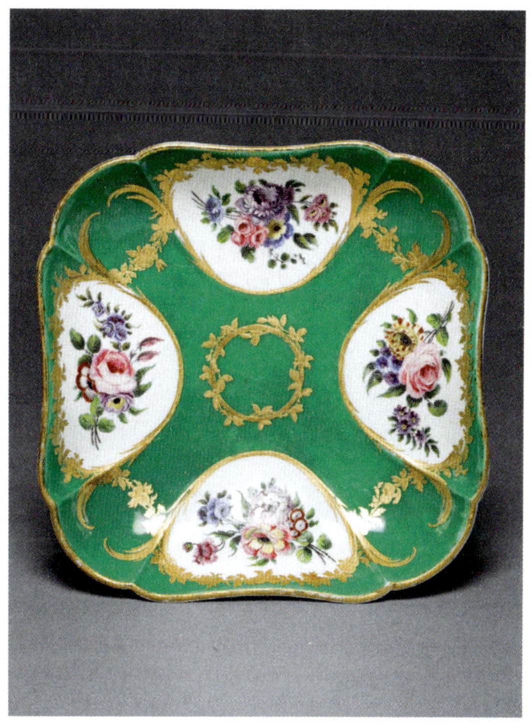

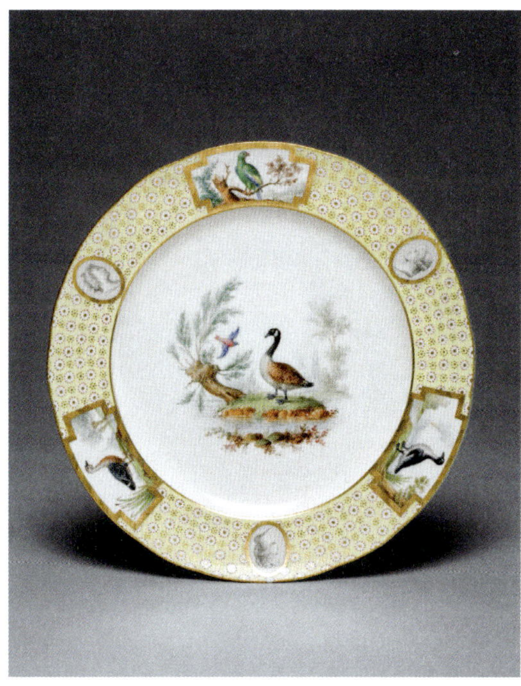

pl. 58 Manufacture de Sèvres.
Plate decorated with birds
after Buffon's *Histoire naturelle*
from the collection of Countess
von Hohenfelsen, 1784.
Soft-paste porcelain. The Fitzwilliam
Museum, Cambridge, L.C.G.
Clarke Bequest, 1960.

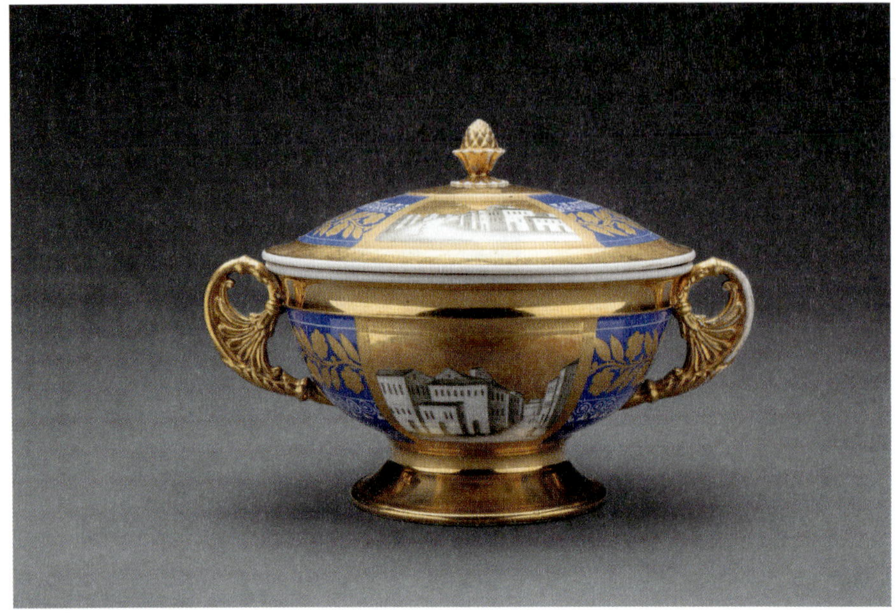

pl. 59 Popov porcelain Factory. Sugar Bowl from the collection of Countess von Hohenfelsen, 1815-1840 (see Paley sale, Christie's, London, June 6-7, 1929, lot 221), Porcelain. Hillwood Estate, Museum & Gardens, Washington, DC, inv. 25.555.1-2.

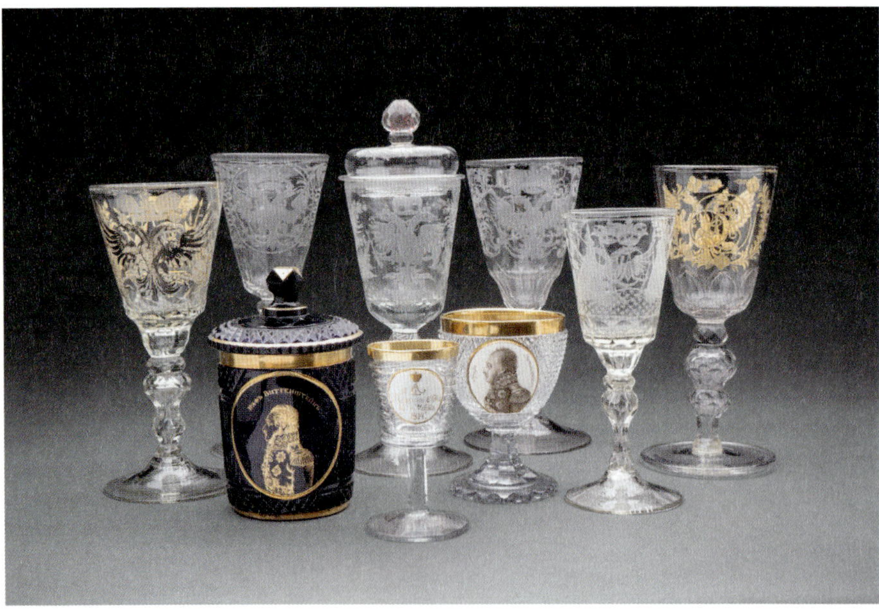

pl. 60 Russian Glassware from Grand Duke Paul's collection, 1700s-1800s, Glass. Hillwood Estate, Museum & Gardens, Washington, DC.

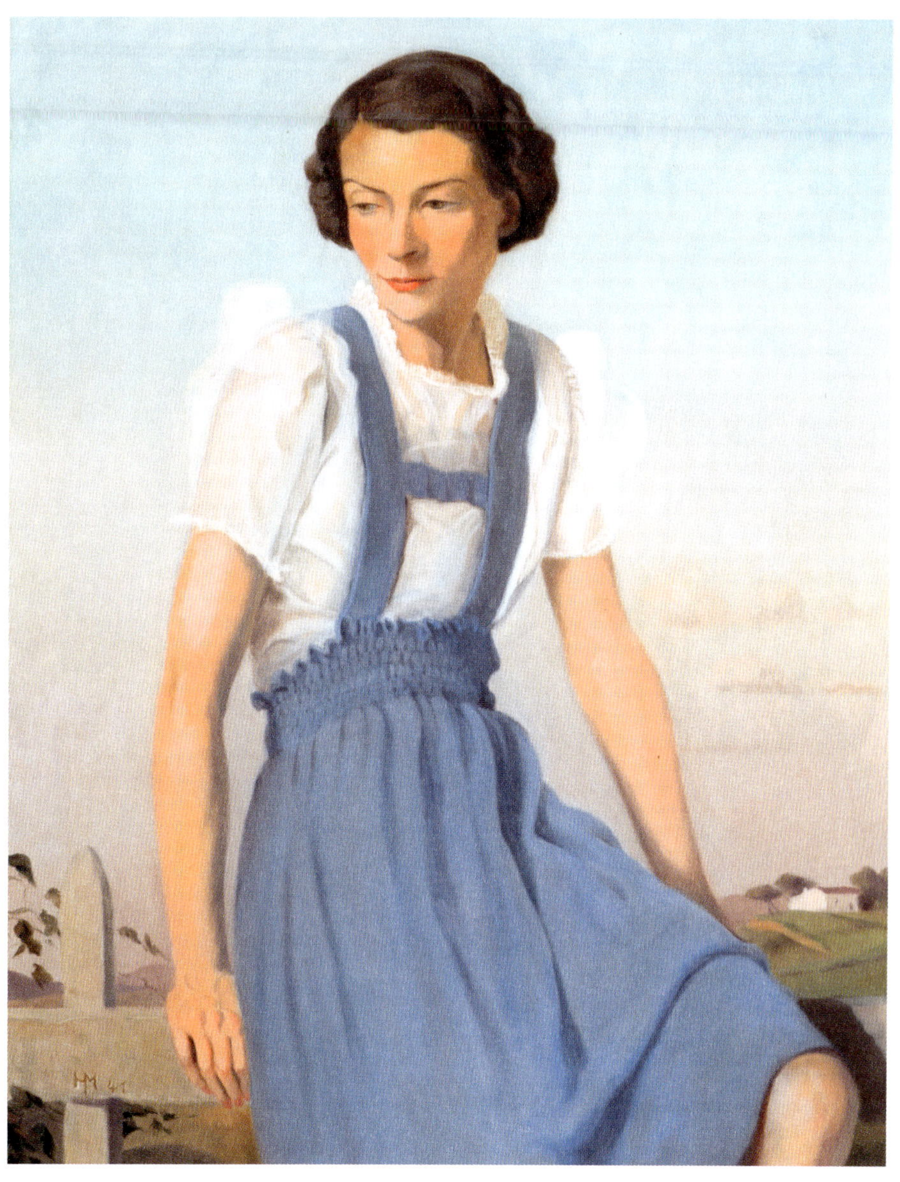

pl. 61 Hubert de Monbrison. Portrait of Princess Irina Paley, 1941. Oil on canvas. Hillwood Estate, Museum & Gardens, Washington, DC, inv. 2002.2.3.

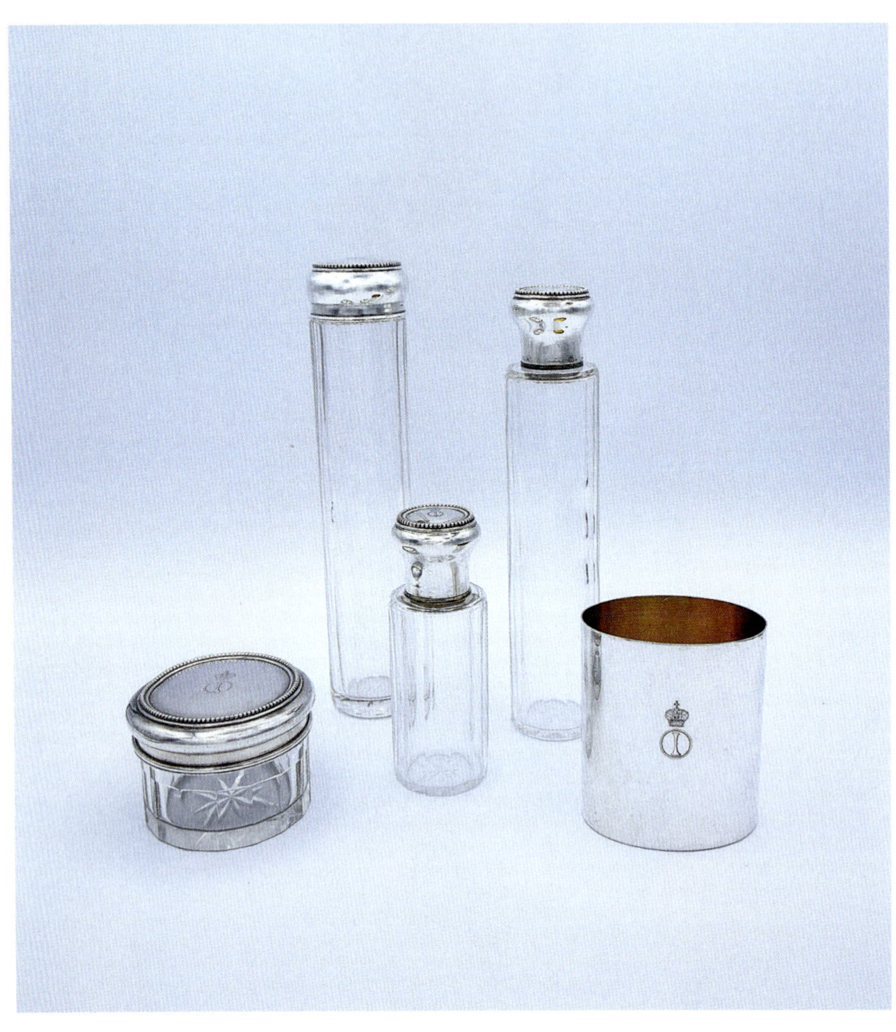

pl. 62 Pinteaux. Princess Irina's traveling dressing table set, ca. 1923. Silver and crystal. Hillwood Estate, Museum & Gardens, Washington DC, inv. 2022.2.7.1-5.

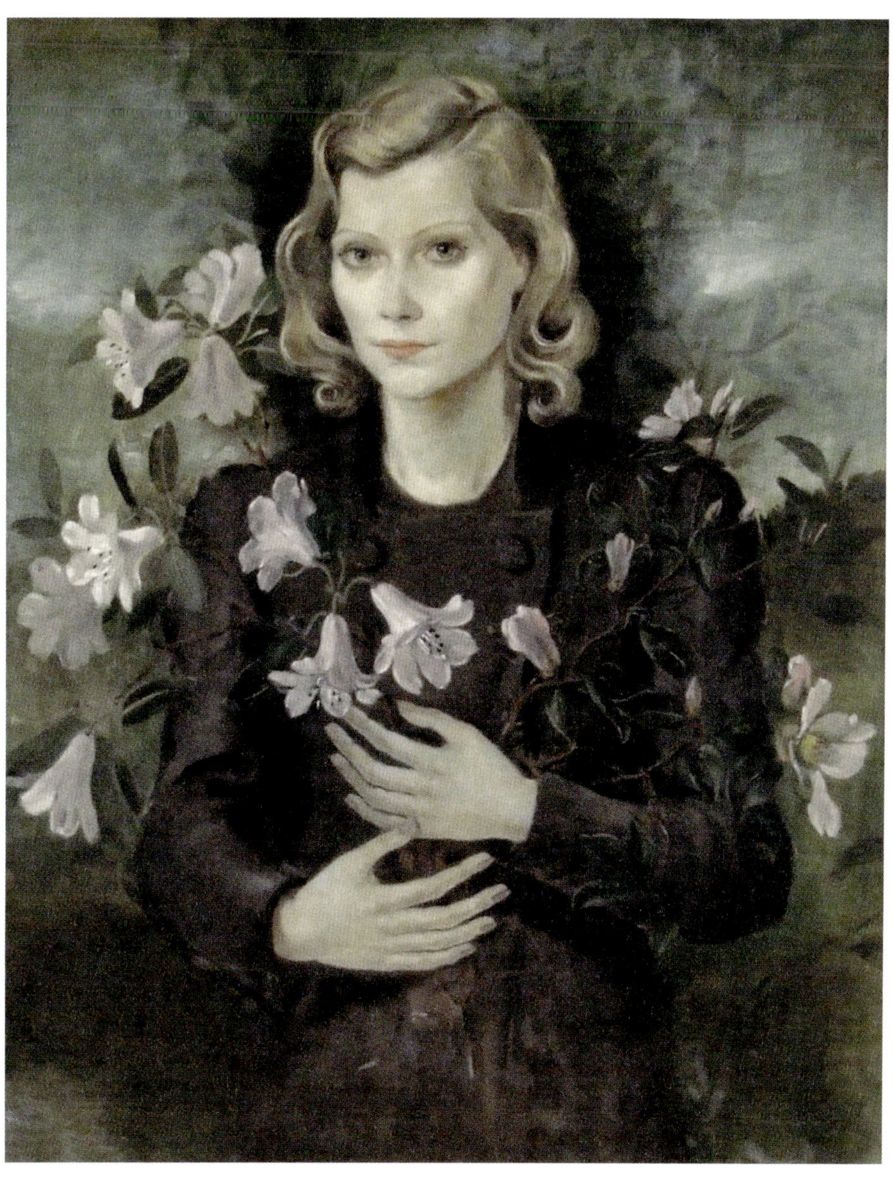

pl. 63 Oliver Messel, *Portrait of Princess Natalie Pavlovna Paley with Lilies*, ca. 1935. Oil on canvas. National Trust, Nymans.

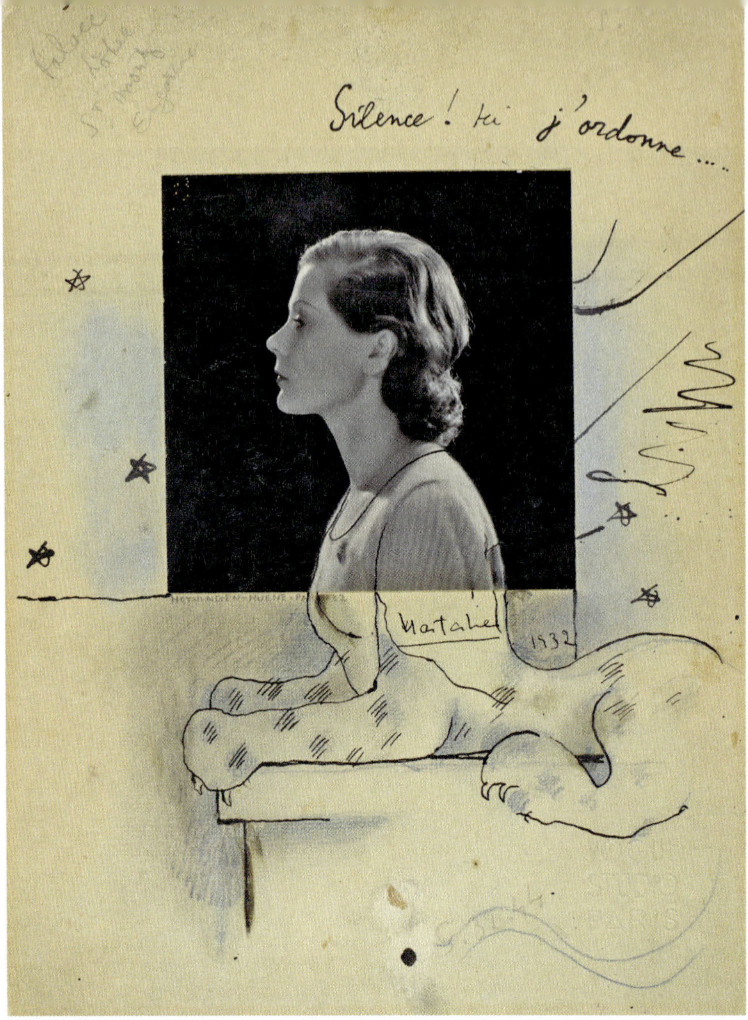

pl. 64 Jean Cocteau, *Nathalie Paley,* ca. 1932. Graphite, colored pencil, ink, photograph, paper. Centre Pompidou, Paris.

pl. 65 Lucien Lelong, N perfume, 1937. Hillwood Estate, Museum & Gardens, Washington, DC, inv. 2024.5.1-3.

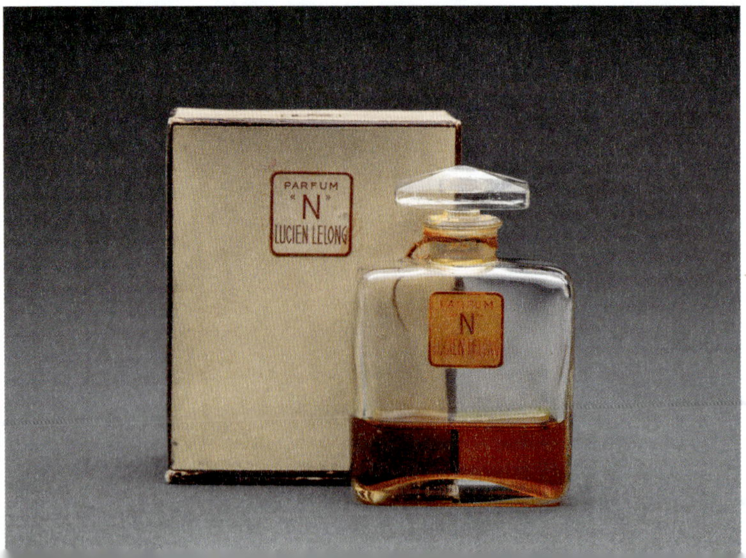

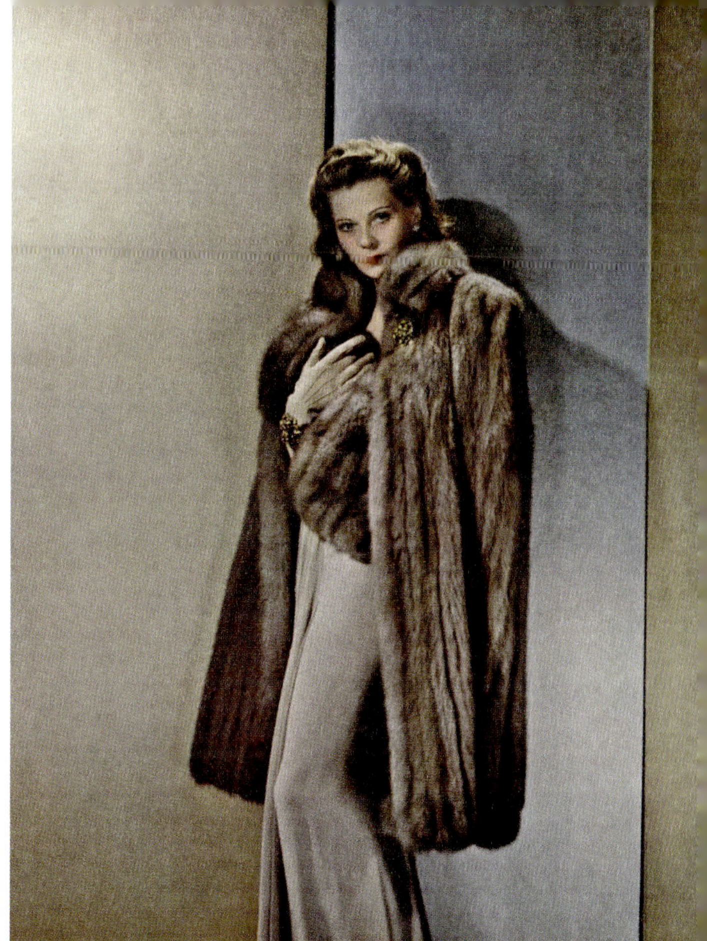

pl. 66 Princess Natalie Paley models a Saks Fifth Avenue fur coat, photographed by her friend George Hoyningen-Huene in Kodachrome for *Harper's Bazaar*, November 1941 issue.

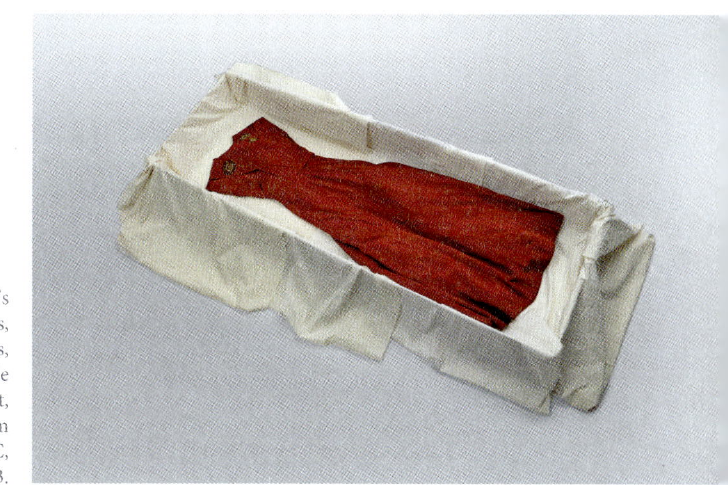

pl. 67 Princess Natalie Paley's Mainbocher evening dress, New York, 1944. Silk taffetta, beads, sequins. Gift of Princess Natalie Paley's biographer, Jean Noël Liaut, 2024, Hillwood, Estate, Museum and Gardens, Washington, DC, inv. 2024.3.

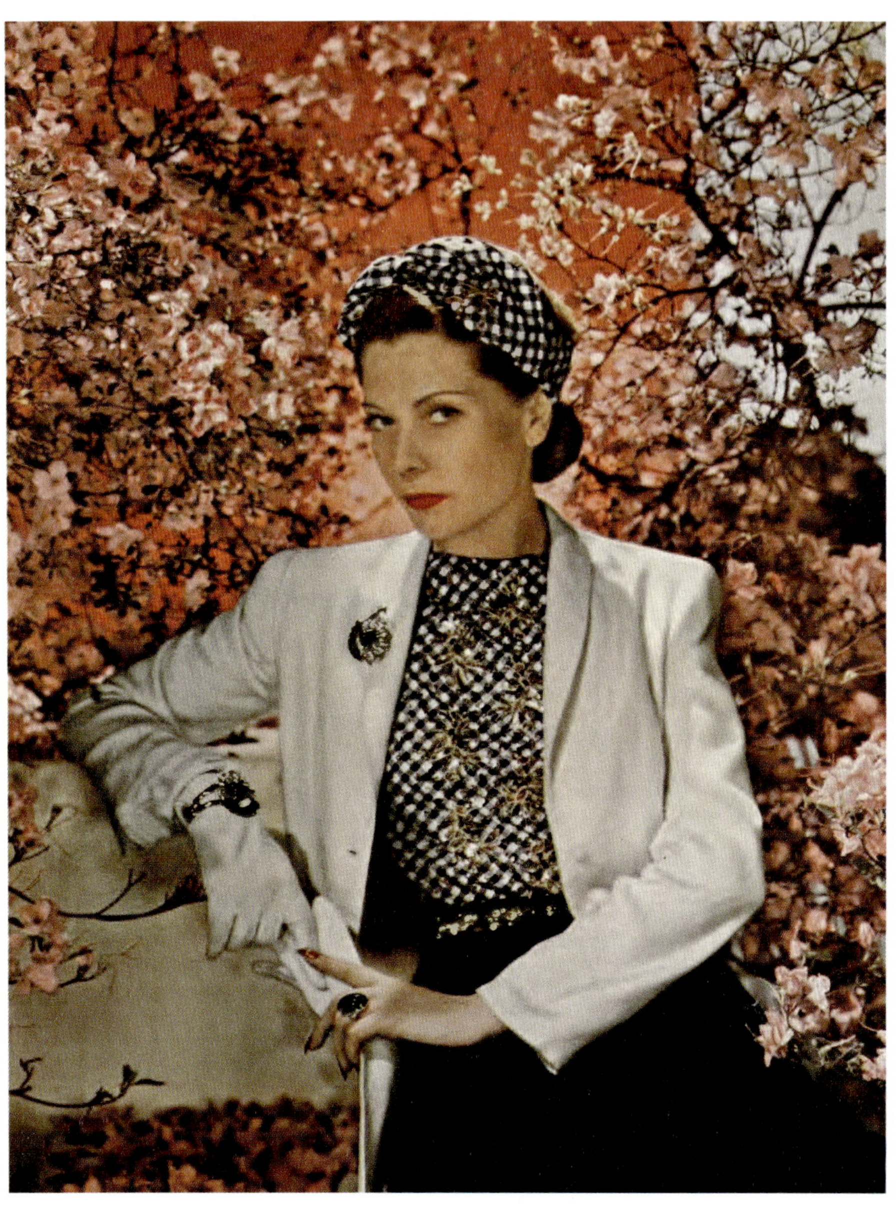

pl. 68 Princess Paley for Mainbocher, photographed by Hoyningen-Huene for *Harper's Bazaar,* May 1943 issue.

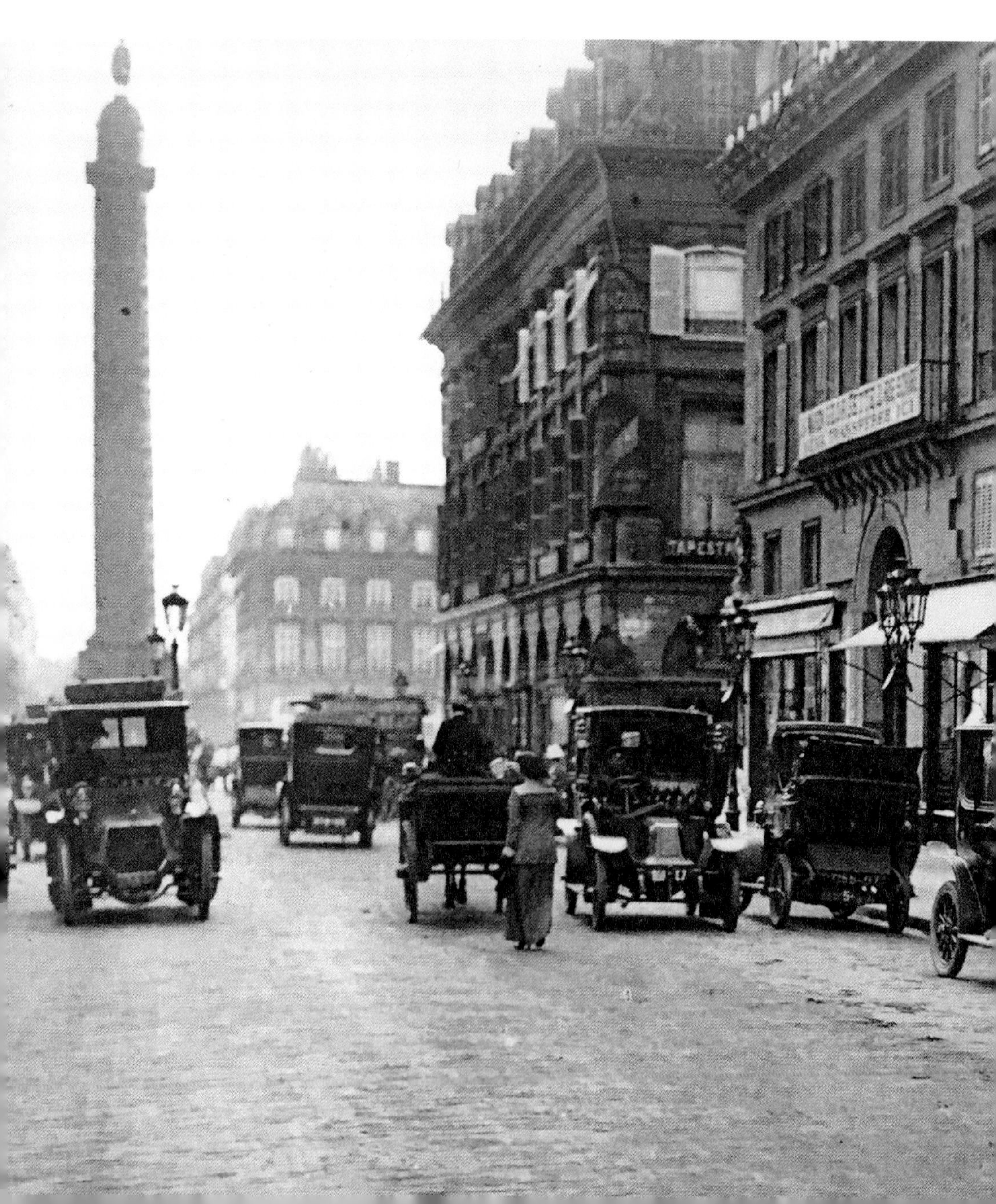

RUE DE LA PAIX SUMMED UP IN OBJECTS: COUNTESS VON HOHENFELSEN'S WARDROBE AND JEWELRY BOX

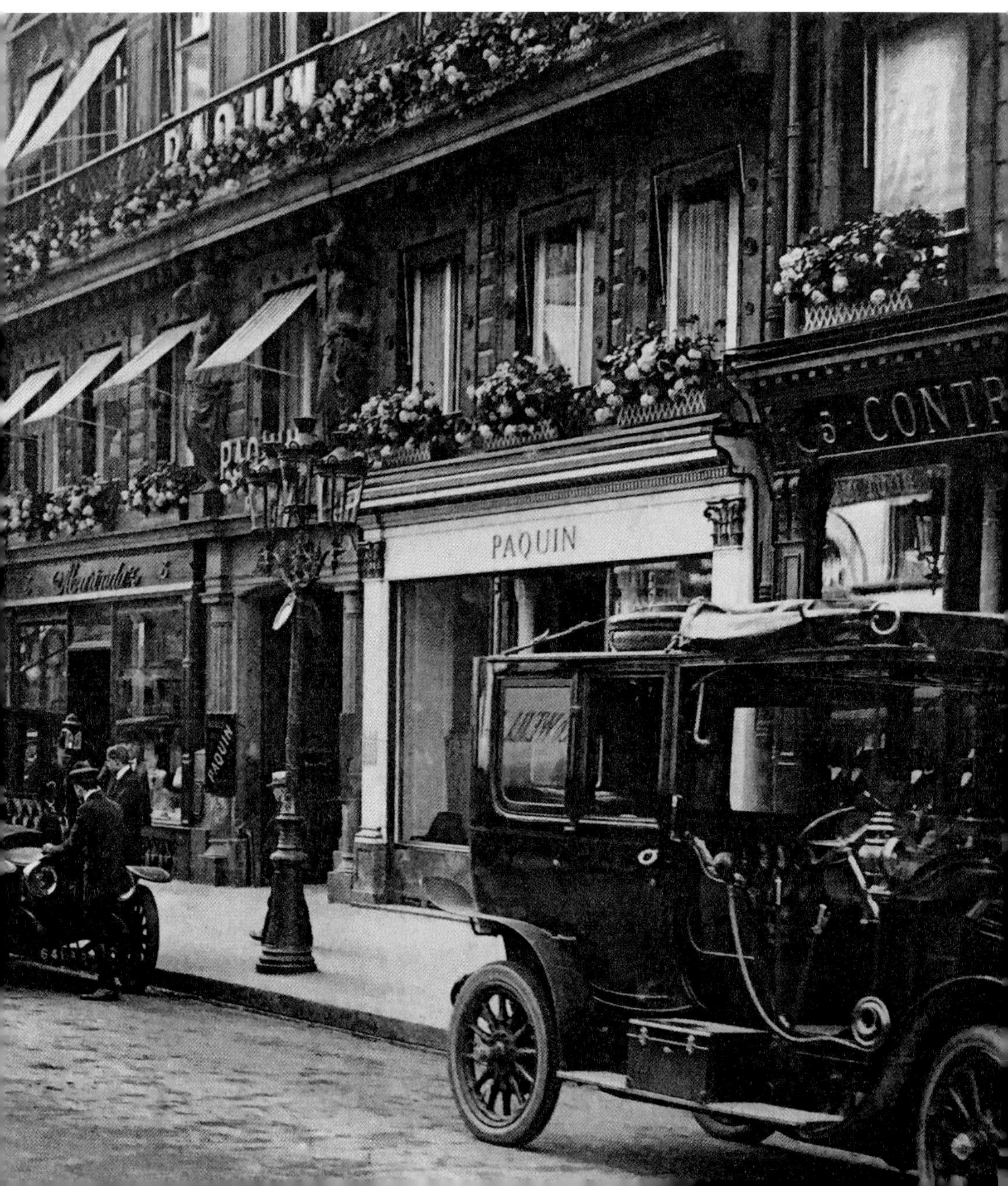

> She was beautiful, very beautiful. An intelligent figure, irregular but fine features, skin of remarkable whiteness, strikingly highlighted by a dress of bishop's purple velvet, trimmed at the neck and sleeves with old lace. I took it all in at first glance and can still see her as she was that day.
>
> Grand Duchess Maria Pavlovna, 1938

Countess von Hohenfelsen's wardrobe, none of which seems to have survived, must have been comparable to that of the greatest ladies of her time, starting with comtesse Greffulhe. Élisabeth Greffulhe "loves and follows fashion, while cultivating originality" and is "not attached to a single couturier; as time goes by, she turns to newcomers."[1] Part of her wardrobe is preserved at the Palais Galliera.[2] These outfits and accessories "tell the story of an exceptional woman."[3] While Countess von Hohenfelsen's wardrobe has disappeared, her daily diary has survived, a rare document that describes her social life and relations with suppliers on a day-to-day basis. Other sources suggest her great interest in Parisian fashion and the attention she paid to her appearance. "She dreaded getting fat, deprived herself of everything at the table, but ate between meals,"[4] recounts her step daughter. This obsession with a slim waistline also manifested itself in her consumption of "anti-obesitin."[5]

Olga was always perfectly dressed and perfumed (figs. 31-36). She frequented her hairdresser, Savary, Alf. Jouot, then Henri, several times a week for her "waves" and even more so before an important social event. Savary is listed in her May-June 1909 accounts as costing between 10 and 15 francs for each appointment: May 15, "charity sale"; May 16, "Murat dinner"; May 25, "grand ondulation"; May 26, "Russian opera"; May 27, "Breteuil dinner"; May 28, "chez nous dinner"; May 29, "Russian opera"; May 31, "Pracomtal dinner"; June 1, "Yurevskaya dinner"; June 2, "Vigier bal Murat dinner"; and June 4, "Russian opera."[6] On the other hand, for the evening at the Yturbe family home in 1912, the bill came to 99.50 francs.[7]

Perfumes and beauty products, including bottles and lotions of various kinds, are abundantly listed in Olga's accounts and came from Guerlain,

1 Catherine Join-Dieterle, "Les Garde-robes aristocratiques," in Centorame and Andia 2005, 222.

2 Saillard 2015.

3 Olivier Saillard, "Des robes souvenirs pour l'inventaire," in Saillard 2015, 11.

4 Marie de Russie 1937, 53.

5 GARF, F. 613, op. 1, D. 613, L. 20.

6 *Ibid.*, L. 6-7.

7 *Ibid.*, L. 43.

Fig. 31 Countess von Hohenfelsen in 1904. *Les Modes*, 1905. Private collection.

Fig. 32 (center) Countess von Hohenfelsen, ca. 1905. Photograph. Private collection.

Fig. 33 (below) Countess von Hohenfelsen, ca. 1911. Photograph. Private collection.

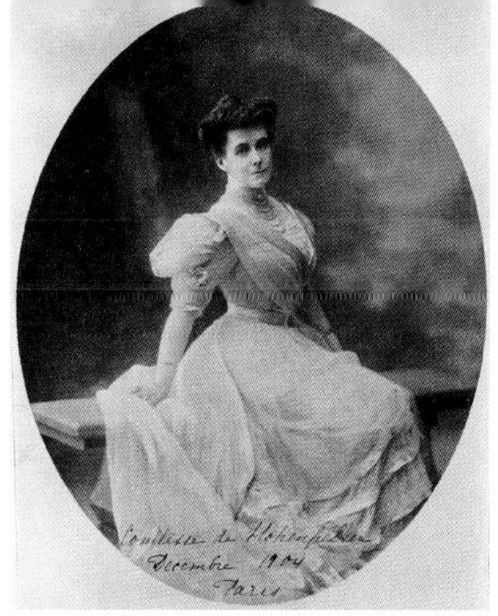

among others, whose Parisian stores she visited regularly, notably at 15, rue de la Paix (fig. 37). Descended from a Picardy family, the Guerlains had established their first store in Paris in 1828, on the first floor of the Hôtel Meurice on rue de Rivoli. The store on rue de la Paix was established in 1841, illustrating the success of the company, which "quickly took its place among the oldest luxury perfumeries in Paris and exported widely abroad."[8]

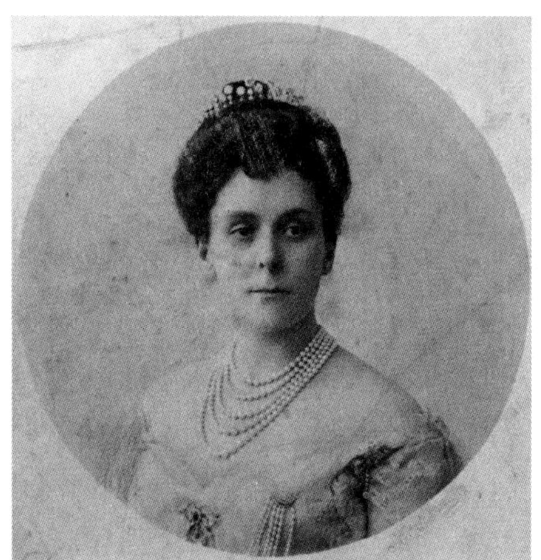

Olga not only frequented Guerlain's elegant salons; she also mentioned Agnel (16, avenue de l'Opéra) and Houbigant (19, rue du Faubourg Saint-Honoré), two institutions of Parisian perfumery. At Roger & Gallé [*sic*], founded in 1862,[9] she bought "bâton pour lèvres," namely, lipstick.

The countess's outfits, like those of the great ladies of the day, were the subject of special mentions in the press at social events, particularly at horse races, and it was often her name that kicked off the list. At

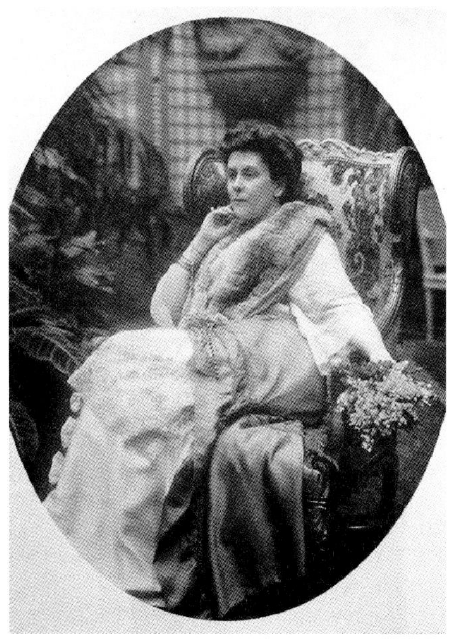

8 Lheureux 2016, 320-21.

9 Roger & Gallet, accessed October 8, 2016, http://www.roger-gallet.com/fr-fr/La-marque/a31.aspx. See also Lheureux 2016, 331-32.

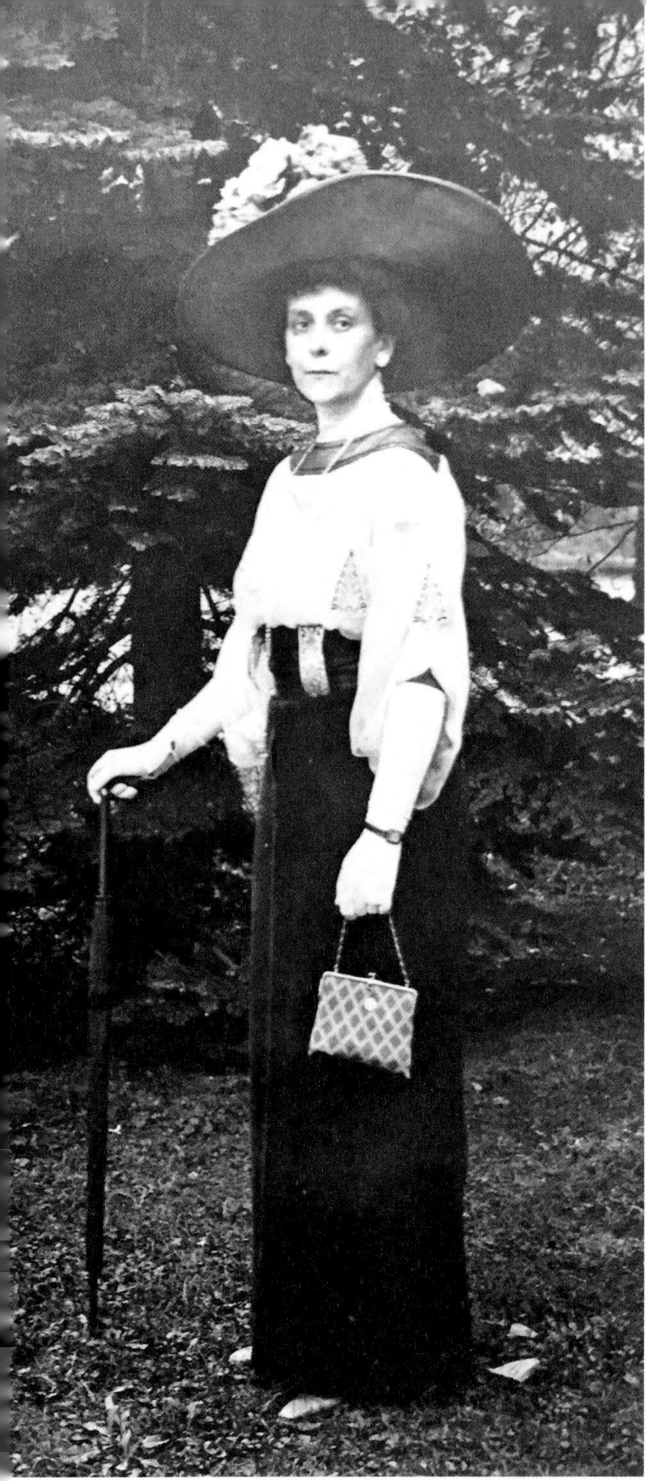

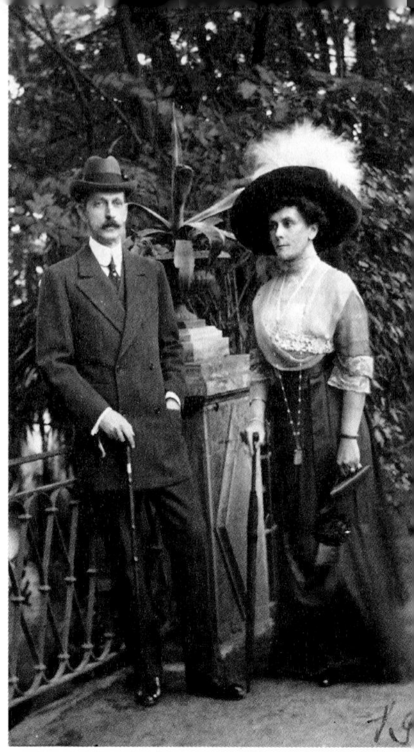

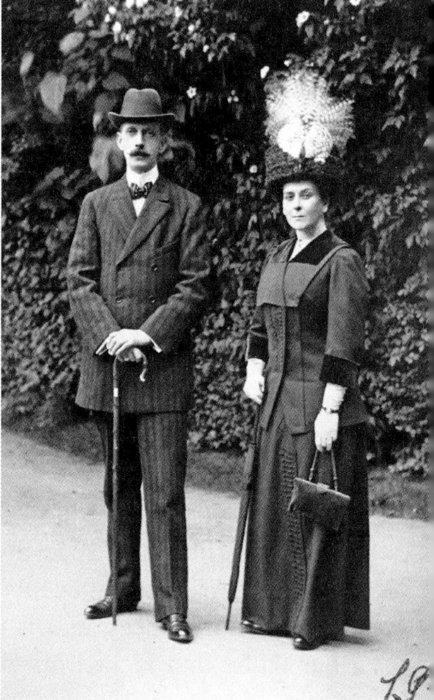

Fig. 34 (right) Countess von Hohenfelsen, ca. 1911. Photograph. Private collection.

Fig. 35 (above left) Countess von Hohenfelsen and Grand Duke Paul, 1911. Photograph. Private collection.

Fig. 36 (above right) Countess von Hohenfelsen and Grand Duke Paul, 1911. Photograph. Private collection.

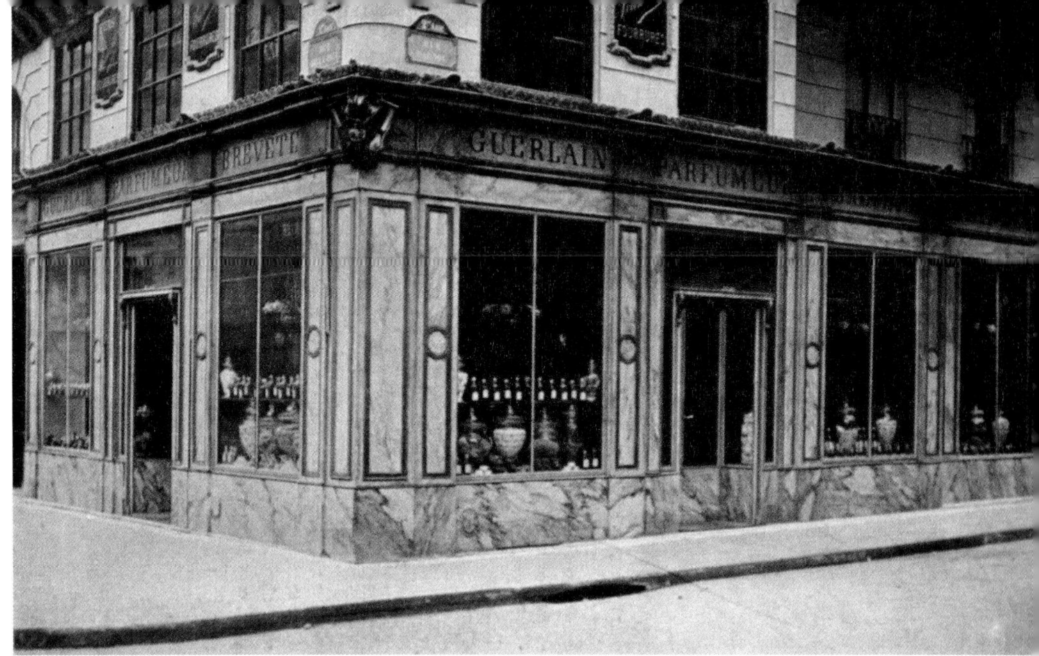

Fig. 37 Maison Guerlain in Paris. *La Ville lumière* 1909, 161. Private collection.

the Grand Prix d'Automne at Longchamp in 1909, despite the rain: "Noticed in the ladies' gallery the Countess von Hohenfelsen, in blue *drap gros*, black soutache, blue plush hat, gray aigrette, princesse Murat, black suit, gray coat, blue hat with blue-green ribbon bow."[10]

Elegance at the horse races in Auteuil in 1913: "Noticed in the reserved stand and at the weigh-in: Countess von Hohenfelsen, in royal blue velvet, chinchilla stole and muff, blue velvet toque with beige aigrette."[11]

It is surprising how quickly the countess became a fashion icon. Indeed, some foreign visitors, such as Grand Duchess Vladimir, sought the advice of Parisians renowned for their great style, foremost among them Laure de Chevigné, to adapt their outfit. "Rue de la Paix, this 'bazaar of the gods,' was her kingdom,"[12] said princesse Bibesco, adding:

> All the secrets of Paris, the choice of suppliers, the good maisons, the finish of the work, the rigors, the precisions and the discipline required by a difficult taste, the importance given to frivolous things which are only frivolous in appearance, because they contain all the more meaning as they appear simpler, found in her [Laure de Chevigné] their supreme expression and their appointed defender.[13]

10 *Le Gaulois*, October 4, 1909.

11 *Le Figaro*, November 17, 1913.

12 Bibesco 1950, 50.

13 *Ibid.*, 48.

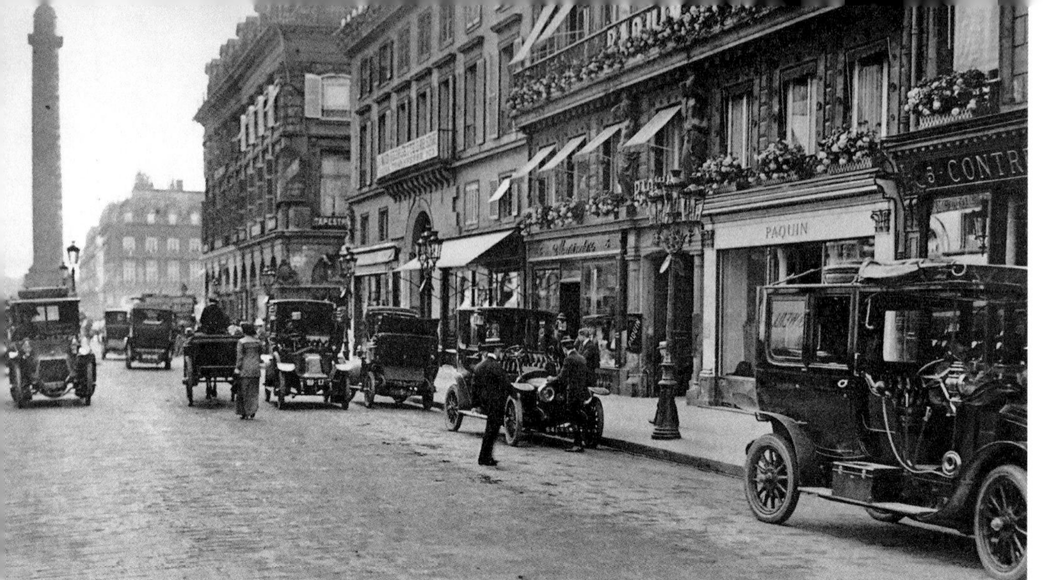

Fig. 38 La rue de la Paix, ca. 1910. Photograph by G. Agié. Léon Roger-Milès, *Les Créateurs de la mode* (Paris: Le Figaro, 1910). Private collection.

According to the unverifiable anecdote recounted by princesse Bibesco,[14] the comtesse de Chevigné found Grand Duchess Vladimir's outfit "impossible" to wear in Paris: "Where did Madame have this made? It looks as though it was made in Ménilmontant." And immediately led her to rue de la Paix to Paquin or Worth to correct the error of taste.

Designed to satisfy Napoleon I's town-planning ambitions, la rue de la Paix, which bore the emperor's name until 1814, was located near traditional luxury districts such as la rue Saint-Honoré and le Palais-Royal. During the nineteenth century, with the proximity of the Gare Saint-Lazare and prestigious hotels, luxury commerce flourished along this road, while gradually colonizing la place Vendôme and surrounding streets. During the Belle Époque, all aspects of this typically Parisian industry were concentrated here: goldsmiths, antiques, fashion, and jewelry. La rue de la Paix was the world center of luxury, and "the address alone was enough for an advertisement in the directories"[15] (pl. 26; fig. 38). It was in this district that the countess and the grand duke had already sought out silver and objets d'art to furnish their residence, from Aucoc, Risler & Carré, and *L'Escalier de Cristal.*

Established on rue de la Paix in 1836, the first was run by goldsmith André Aucoc, grandson of the founder and a famous maker of toiletry bags (*nécessaires*). The couple spent tens of thousands of francs on their ceremonial tableware. Risler & Carré was a more recent firm, founded in 1897 by André Risler and his partner Georges Carré, and located at 16, rue du Faubourg Saint-Honoré.[16] Here, the countess purchased silver tableware and

14 *Ibid.*, 49-50.

15 Lheureux 2016, 78.

16 Zeisler 2014b, 353.

the necessities required to set up a good home. *L'Escalier de Cristal*, which the countess visited regularly, is often referred to in her diary as "*Esc. de Cr.*" "A continual object of admiration for foreigners and Parisians alike,"[17] this luxury establishment had been a well-known address in the capital since 1804. The store's windows were located on the corner of the Grand Hôtel, in the heart of the Parisian luxury district, whose growth was the result of the Second Empire's development around the Grand Opéra and of the commercial vitality of the art industries under the Third Republic. While this district offered a wide variety of goods, it was above all known for its fashion-related industries.

Since the eighteenth century, the Parisian style had been a model for the Russian aristocracy, and many sovereigns and noblewomen were celebrated for their acquisitiveness in this field.[18] Countess von Hohenfelsen had developed her own taste, even before moving to Paris. As the wife of Grand Duke Vladimir's aide-de-camp, she often traveled abroad, particularly to Paris, and knew the suppliers who steadily worked for the grand duchess and members of the Court. A subscriber to fashion journals and magazines reflecting the evolution of Parisian design, long before marrying Grand Duke Paul and settling in Paris, Olga used to frequent Paquin, a house to which she remained extremely loyal. In March-April 1899, her stay at the Ritz in Paris provided an opportunity for her to discover antique shops, go to the theater to see Feydeau's *Un fil à la patte*, and dine at Paillard's, but also to visit Paquin (fig. 39).[19] At the time, the fashion house was still in its infancy, the result of a partnership between businessman Isidore Jacob, known as Paquin, and couturier Jeanne Beckers (1869-1936), who had made her debut at Rouff, 13, boulevard Haussmann.[20] Paquin came from a family of entrepreneurs specializing in menswear. In Paris, he was first associated with J. Lalanne, a clothing house established at 3, rue de la Paix in 1888. Recently engaged, Jeanne Beckers married Paquin in 1891. Open to aesthetic and commercial innovations, collaborating with artists such as Léon Bakst, sending models dressed in the company's latest creations to premieres and races, and supplying costumes for fashionable pieces, Jeanne contributed to Paquin's international reputation, gradually opening stores around the world: London in 1896, Madrid and Buenos Aires in 1914, and New York on Fifth Avenue in 1912. The refined and extremely elegant models created by the company were not for everyone. The dresses commissioned by Olga were an extreme luxury. Such creations from this maison cost an average of 5,000-6,000 francs, while a monthly salary of a model was estimated around 200 francs.[21] In the same vein, Worth points

17 Quoted in *Ibid.*, 341; see also 111-39.

18 *Ibid.*, 97.

19 GARF, F. 644, op. 1, D. 301, L. 22, 24, 26.

20 Garnier 1987, 250; Sirop 1989, 167.

21 Sirop 1989, 10-11.

out that in 1912, a dressmaker was paid 150 francs to make a dress, and a head seamstress 15,000 francs a year.[22] The Paquin house played a key role in the fashion industry, and its economic role was enthusiastically praised in a 1909 promotional campaign for the capital:

> The name is known throughout the world, and women everywhere consider it a great joy to be able to dress at this haute couture house, whose commercial, economic, and financial importance is worth mentioning. If we say that four million francs are spent every year on the fabrics used to make the outfits that emerge from Paquin, that the ribbons used could cover the distance from Paris to Versailles, that the twenty-two million meters of thread that pass through the hands of the seamstresses could link the two poles of the earth, that the try-on girls make use of more than a thousand kilograms of pins every year, that three hundred and sixty kilograms of silk thread, one hundred and fifty kilograms of whalebone, three hundred kilograms of hook and eye fastenings are consumed, we can only give a small idea of the incalculable number of supplies used by Paquin, and we do not have the space to complete this fantastic enumeration.[23]

Perfectly structured, the Paquin company, immortalized in 1906 by painter Henri Gervex, was a fashionable meeting place.[24] The lead saleswomen were responsible for looking after prestigious customers. Grand Duchess Vladimir, whose trousseau had been ordered from Corbay in Paris in 1874, was one of them, and she welcomed a Paquin envoy and a few mannequins from Paris to present models to the Court.[25] Regularly mentioned in Olga's diary, Paquin was one of the Parisian institutions she frequented assiduously to see the latest fashions or to do the numerous fittings required to complete her orders.

At this time, Worth was still the most famous couturier in Paris (fig. 40). Since the beginning of the nineteenth century, la rue de la Paix had been home to several luxury businesses, such as the jeweler Mellerio *dits* Meller, established at this address in 1815, and the perfumer Guerlain in 1841. Charles Frederick Worth's move to number 7 in 1858 paved the way for his competitors and colleagues to flock there, making the street the epitome of French luxury and savoir faire. Of British origin, Worth trained in London in the textile trade. He started out in Paris in 1845 with Gagelin (a textile sales company), which made a name for itself at the Great Exhibition in London (1851) and Paris Exposition (1855). In 1858, he went into business for himself

22 Worth 1928, 186.
23 *La Ville lumière* 1909, 152.
24 Sirop 1989, 18.
25 *Ibid.*, 17.

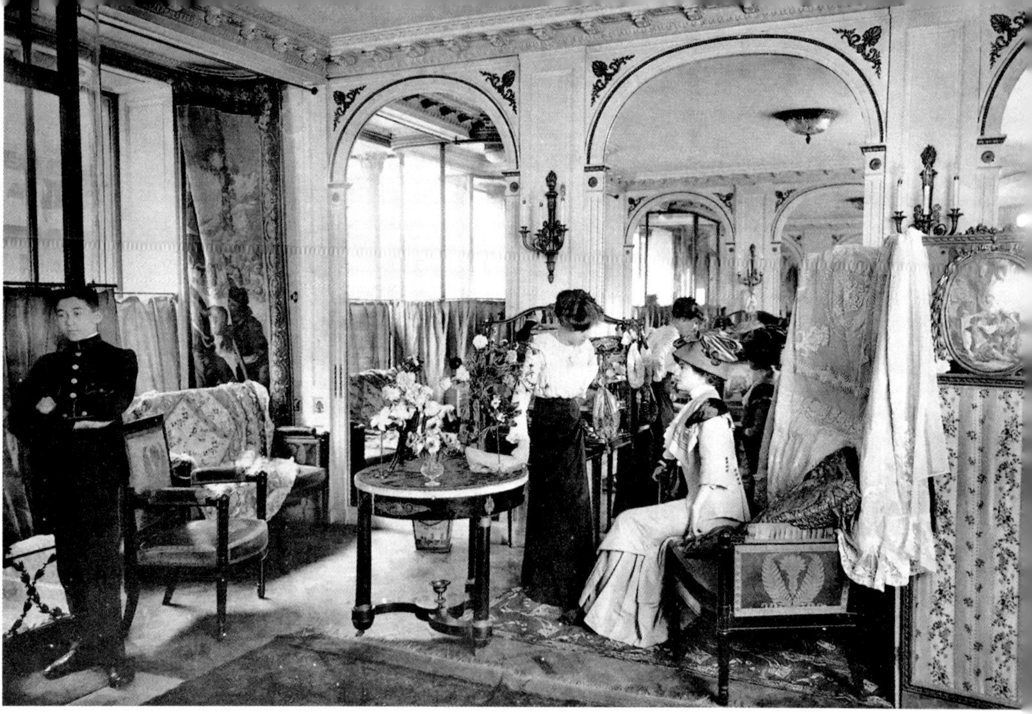

Fig. 39 (above) The salons at Paquin in Paris, ca. 1910. Photograph by G. Agié. Léon Roger-Milès, *Les Créateurs de la mode* (Paris: Le Figaro, 1910). Private collection.

Fig. 40 (opposite) The salons at Worth in Paris, ca. 1910. Photograph by G. Agié. Léon Roger-Milès, *Les Créateurs de la mode* (Paris: Le Figaro, 1910). Private collection.

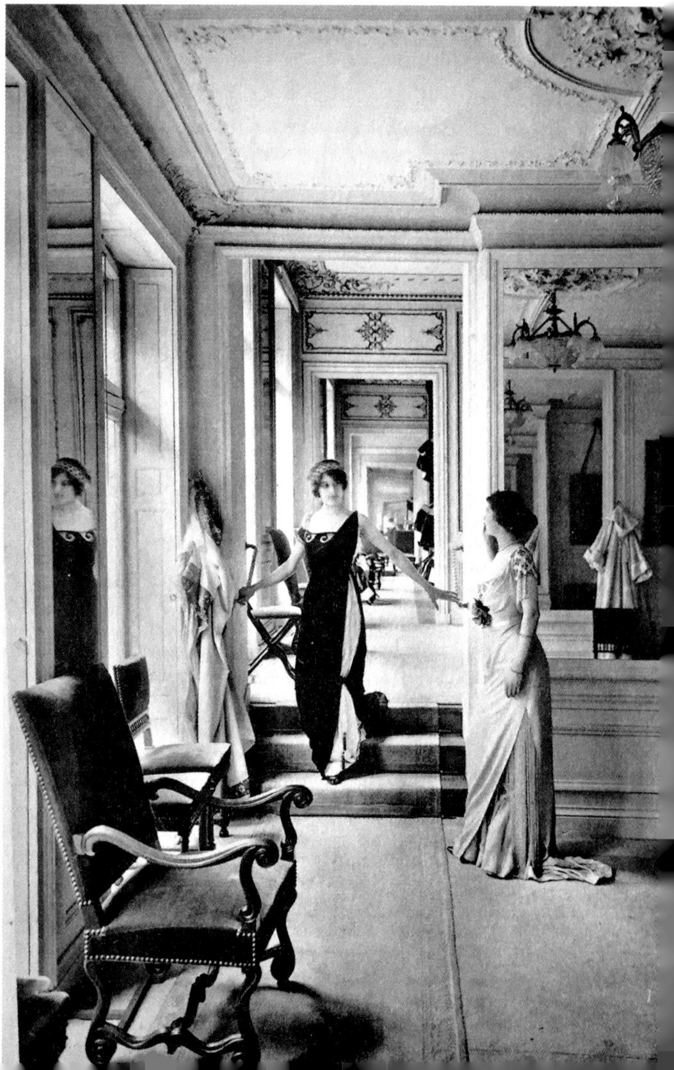

in partnership with the Swedish-born Otto Gustave Bobergh (1821-1882), who had already proven his value in the cloth trade. Worth revolutionized the traditional fashion environment, in which the couturier had to comply with customer demands; with Worth, the couturier invented and created the designs. For the customer, the choice was increasingly limited to colors and materials. He also pioneered the creation of seasonal collections, staging them with the help of "look-alikes" or "mannequins," another innovation. Launched by top society, including the Princess von Metternich, Worth dressed the Second Empire and the world's sovereigns. The company was taken over on the death of its founder by his sons, Jean-Philippe and Gaston-Lucien Worth, the former in charge of design and the latter of the financial management.[26]

By the time Olga arrived in Paris, she was well aware of Worth's long-standing reputation in Russia. "The Russian clientele was beyond doubt exceptional,"[27] reports Worth, whose company had begun its Russian career working for Empress Maria Alexandrovna, wife of Alexander II and mother of Grand Duke Paul. A mannequin in her size served as a model for the dresses that were sent to her without any fitting.[28] The next empress, Maria Feodorovna, and the last sovereign were also customers. Since the death of Alexander III in 1894, Worth had the privilege of supplying both Russian empresses.[29] Empress Alexandra was the only one Worth had the honor of meeting personally.[30] On the other hand, he had the opportunity to see and serve other members of the imperial family in Paris, notably Grand Duchess Vladimir, a loyal customer since the 1870s, whose husband, Worth explains, "took great pleasure in ordering dresses for his wife."[31] Worth's regular customers also included members of the established or seasonal Russian colony, including Countess Alexander Benckendorff (1857-1928), née Sofya Petrovna Shuvalov, wife of the Russian ambassador to London from 1902 to 1916. Her trousseau, ordered from Worth for her wedding in 1879, included thirty coats, fifteen summer and fifteen winter dresses, and a sumptuous court coat.[32] There was also Princess Elizabeth Alexandrovna Baryatinsky (1826-1902), who ordered twelve ball gowns for each of her two daughters, Maria (1851-1937) and Elizabeth Vladimirovna (1855-1938), wife of Count Paul Shuvalov (1847-1902); the gowns were divided into three separate

26 On Worth, see, among others, Haye and Mendes, 2014.

27 Worth 1928, 140.

28 *Ibid.*, 133.

29 On Worth and Russia, see, among others, the exhibition catalog published in Russian, *Russian Empresses: Fashion and Style, Late 18th Century – Early 20th Century* (Moscow: Kutshkovo Pole, 2013), 346-52.

30 Worth 1928, 135.

31 *Ibid.*, 211.

32 *Ibid.*

lots ranging from the simplest to the most luxurious. Worth[33] reports that this order was supplemented by fifteen garments for herself. The couturier then lists several Russian names who "must be mentioned"[34] among the important clients, including Princess Orlov, "the Russian Madame von Metternich,"[35] most likely Olga K. Belosselsky-Belozersky (1874-1924), the wife of Vladimir N. Orlov (1868-1927). The princess had been painted by Valentin Serov and Philippe de Laszlo and ran a popular salon for the aristocracy and the diplomatic world in her family's palace on the banks of the Moyka River in St. Petersburg. She "was beautiful, elegant and, above all, had great self-esteem. Her toilettes were made by the best couturiers in Paris."[36]

Worth also mentions Grand Duchess Elizabeth Feodorovna, sister of the last empress, and the aristocratic names of Davidov, Dournovo, Obolensky, Polovtsov, and Shcherbatov. The couturier concludes this Russian chapter with a paragraph on Countess von Hohenfelsen, whose photograph he reproduces wearing the dress he created for her for Madame Yturbe's ball in 1912[37] (see fig. 52).

All the women in the set revolving around Countess von Hohenfelsen knew Worth, whether they were his Russian clients, Madame Bénardaky,[38] – an intimate of Olga's,[39] – or comtesse Greffulhe.

As early as the first volume of her exile diary in 1902, Olga mentions Worth as one of her favorite shopping destinations. All the best Parisian addresses are listed in this diary, and in addition to Paquin and Worth, there is mention of numerous clothing houses, dressmakers, milliners, and other accessory manufacturers. Some of these companies are more or less documented, such as Linker & Cie, also known as Amy, Linker & Cie, which Olga mentions as early as 1903. Established at 7, rue Auber, the company was active throughout the first half of the twentieth century and, like similar businesses, often advertised its models in trade journals such as *Les Modes*.

Olga was also a customer of the Paris branch of the internationally renowned British fashion house Redfern (242, rue de Rivoli and 8, rue Royale)[40] (fig. 41). A licensed supplier to Grand Duchess Vladimir since 1881,

33 *Ibid.*, 210.

34 *Ibid.*, 211.

35 *Ibid.*

36 M. P. Tseliadt, "Dvorets Beloselskikh-Belozerskikh," in *Dvortsy Nevskogo prospekta* (St. Petersburg: Beloe i Chernoe, 2002), 230-31.

37 Worth 1928, 213-14.

38 *Ibid.*, 114.

39 *Ibid.*

40 David James Cole, "Heritage and Innovation: Charles Frederick Worth, John Redfern or the Birth of Modern Fashion," trans. Dominique Lotti, in *Mode de recherche,* no. 16, *Le luxe* (June 2011): 3-12. See also Saillard 2014, 33-34.

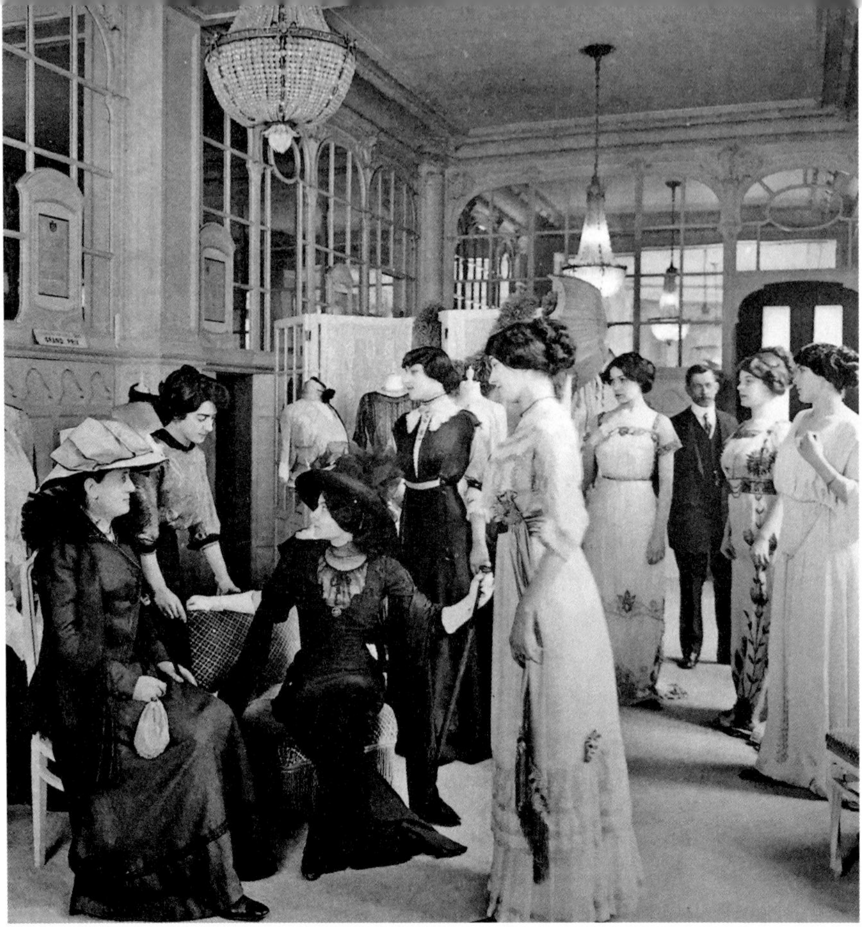

Fig. 41 (above) The salons of Maison Redfern in Paris, ca. 1910. Photograph by G. Agié. Léon Roger-Milès, *Les Créateurs de la mode* (Paris: Le Figaro, 1910). Private collection.

Fig. 42 (below) The salons of Maison Doucet in Paris, ca. 1910. Photograph by G. Agié. Léon Roger-Milès, *Les Créateurs de la mode* (Paris: Le Figaro, 1910). Private collection.

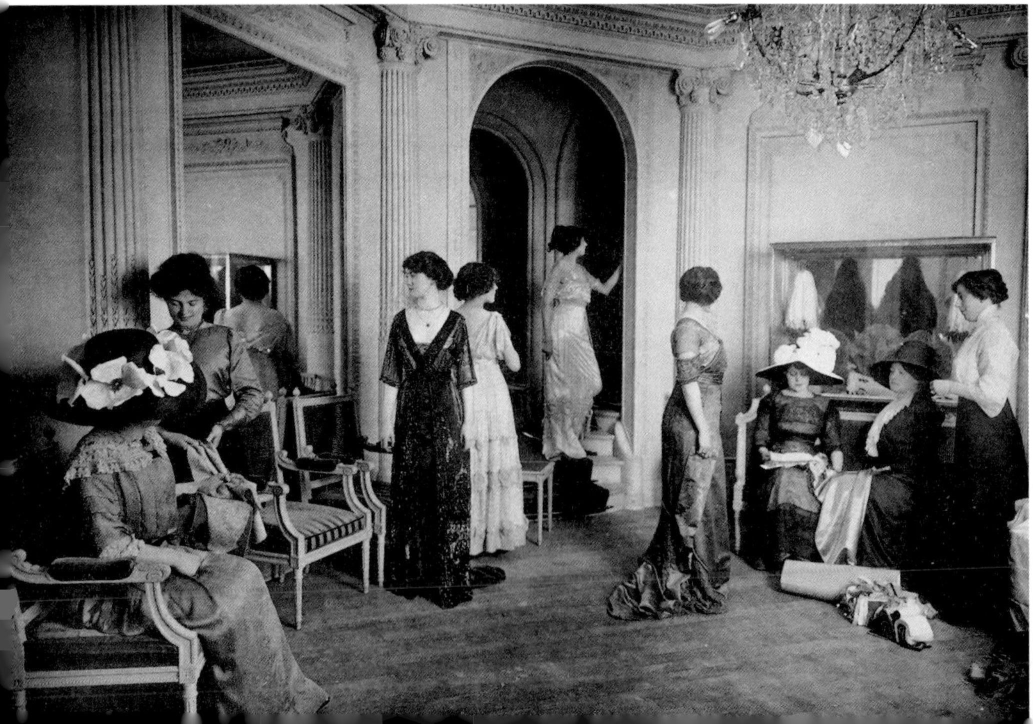

Redfern, which was founded in Cowes, England, in the 1850s, had outlets in London, Paris, Chicago, New York, Nice, and Cannes. This commercial internationalization of luxury was one of the hallmarks of the Belle Époque, when the great houses set up shop where their customers lived and vacationed. John Redfern (1820-1895), who had started out in the textile industry, made a name for himself by designing clothes adapted to the increasingly common playing of sport. The company went on to offer its cosmopolitan clientele the full range of outfits they needed. In Paris, the business was managed by stylist Charles Pennington Poynter (1853-1929), naturalized French in 1908, knighted (1907), and made an officer of the Légion d'honneur (1925).[41] Redfern's career, like those of Worth and many of the great names in French luxury goods, shows the extent to which this industry has been able to attract and make use of the know-how and inventiveness of the many foreigners who, since the seventeenth century, have built the history and reputation of French luxury goods.

In addition to these relatively young houses, la rue de la Paix and the surrounding neighborhood were home to well-known and reputable names that had been around for several generations. At 21, rue de la Paix, Olga was a customer of Doucet (fig. 42), whose invoice headings from around 1900 trumpet the company's reputation based on seniority, awards, and the ruling families for whom it was the official supplier: "Doucet / Shirtmaker / Harson & Pilzer Fils succrs / 21, rue de la Paix / House founded 1816, only prize medal at London Exhibition for shirt cutting."

One of them also features the coats of arms of the Russian court, of the Prince of Wales, the emperor of Brazil, and the Spanish court.[42] Since 1875, the famous Jacques Doucet (1853-1929) had been assisting his father at the head of a lingerie business that gradually diversified its offer and became one of Paris's leading couture houses. Having taken over the management of the maison in 1898, Jacques Doucet also made a name for himself as a great collector of fashionable eighteenth-century art and as a bibliophile. While Olga was building up her collection, Doucet's was sold in 1912. Subsequently, he distinguished himself by his forward-looking taste, becoming a promoter of modern art. At Doucet's, which Olga mentioned as early as 1902, she chose not only clothes for herself, but also shirts and ties for the grand duke.

It was at Doucet that the innovative couturier Paul Poiret (1879-1944) made his debut, from 1896 to 1900, before working for Worth from 1901 to 1903.[43] Later setting up on his own, first on rue Auber, then on rue Pasquier, Poiret dressed celebrities, including the actress Réjane, who furthered his

41 Arch. Nat. LH 2218/10.

42 RGIA, F. 528, op. 1, D. 1679, L. 360, and D. 1692, L. 71.

43 Martine Poulain, "Jacques Doucet," in Centorame and Andia, 2005, 218-19; Garnier 1987, 251.

success. His innovative creations made him a household name, especially as he was one of the first to abandon the corset, which was still imprisoning women's bodies. Famous as far away as Russia, Poiret traveled there in 1911 to present his collections.[44] In her correspondence with the aesthete Alexander Polovtsov (1867-1944) – son of the famous senator and collector who helped organize the museum founded by his father-in-law, Baron von Stieglitz – Olga appears as a connoisseur of Parisian fashion. In 1912, she made some recommendations to his wife Sophia (1871-1957), and Alexander thanked her in the following terms: "Sofica is very interested in everything you have to say about Poiré [*sic*] and I think she will rush there."[45]

When it came to fashion accessories, the choice of shops was enormous. For her headdresses and hats, Olga called on milliner Esther Meyer, mentioned as early as 1902. As for shoes and boots, some of the most refined models came from Hellstern at 23, place Vendôme. Founded in 1846 by German-born Jacob Hellstern (1809-1879), the company, later also established in London and Brussels, was first located at 6, rue du 29-Juillet, then place Vendôme. The family business passed to Jacob's son, Constant-Louis Hellstern (1851-1929),[46] then to his sons, Charles (1884-1959) and Henri (1890-1976). Official supplier to the Prince of Wales and the Russian court, Hellstern & Sons was the shoemaker of the world's greats, including Grand Duke and Grand Duchess Vladimir, Laure de Chevigné,[47] and American high society.

As for fans, an essential part of any elegant woman's panoply during the Belle Époque, the Duvelleroy, Faucon, and Kees brands were the must-haves, supplying all the international celebrities, including Grand Duchess Vladimir. Adapted for each event, and more or less precious, the fans, whose frames could be very costly masterpieces of jewelry, were generally worth between 45 and 240 francs in the 1890s.[48]

Founded by Jean-Pierre Duvelleroy (1802-1889) in 1827, the family business grew steadily and continued to develop under the management of the founder's son, Georges (1856-1930), who took over in 1887.[49] Winner of numerous awards at world's fairs and supplier to most European courts, Duvelleroy stood out for its creations decorated in collaboration with artists such as Louise Abbéma, Maurice Leloir, and Madeleine Lemaire. Having followed the geographic evolution of Parisian luxury, Duvelleroy became the

44 Poiret 1930, 105-6. See also Ameliokhina and Parshina 2011.

45 GARF, F. 613, op. 1, D. 391, L. 8. Pneumatic letter sent to Boulogne, dated September 6 (?), 1912.

46 Arch. Nat. LH 1280/13.

47 Bibesco 1950, 47.

48 Madeleine Delpierre, "L'Éventail, l'élégance et la vie à la Belle Époque," in Falluel 1985, 11.

49 Arch. Nat. LH 885/20.

home of the Belle Époque fan at 11, boulevard de la Madeleine, its address since 1905,[50] as well as its branches in London, Biarritz, and Nice, which enabled it to keep pace with its clientele. The luxurious Parisian store typifies the evolution of commerce at the time, particularly in the neighborhood:

> Women no longer found themselves in the merchant's home, but in their own [...]. The counter was replaced by the boudoir, the merchant by the high society man, ironic and supreme, before whom one trembles a little.[51]

In the Duvelleroy store, designed in the fashionable taste of the Consulate-Empire period, customers were confronted by Louise Abbéma's portrait of the founder's wife, just as those of the master and mistress of the house were admired in the salons of high society.

Not far away, at 38, avenue de l'Opéra, were the premises of E. Faucon, a fan maker whose company was founded around 1869.[52] He had moved to this address around 1895, abandoning le passage des Panoramas, where Duvelleroy also had a historic window display (fig. 43).[53]

Kees,[54] one of the oldest fan makers in Paris, was founded in 1835 by Ernest Kees,[55] an entrepreneur of German origin whose background is in some respects reminiscent of that of the Kellers, who were successful in the Paris goldsmith's trade during the Belle Époque.[56] From its modest beginnings, Kees moved to increasingly prestigious addresses, reflecting its success: first on rue de Crussol, then to rue Neuve-des-Mathurins between 1858 and 1870, and on to rue du Quatre-Septembre (no. 28) and finally to le boulevard des Capucines in 1894 (fig. 44). It was here, at no. 9, that Olga regularly visited, in a store "executed in the purest Louis XV style, and which would merit the title of salon rather than store."[57] Like most of its competitors, the company offered its customers a wide range of accessories, enabling it to diversify its products.

Similarly, fans and many other small items were retailed by specialized boutiques that the countess appreciated. Among these stores, which sold

50 Georgina Letourmy, "Duvelleroy, éventailliste," in Centorame and Andia 2005, 220-21. See also the exhibition catalog by Hélène Alexander, *Duvelleroy. King of Fans: Fan Maker to Kings* (London: Fan Museum, 1995-96).

51 *Paris-vivant: Les Coulisses de la mode*, 1888, 91.

52 *La Ville lumière* 1909, 174.

53 Falluel 1985, 144.

54 Letourmy 2005.

55 *La Ville lumière* 1909, 239.

56 Zeisler 2014b, 19-26.

57 *La Ville lumière* 1909, 239.

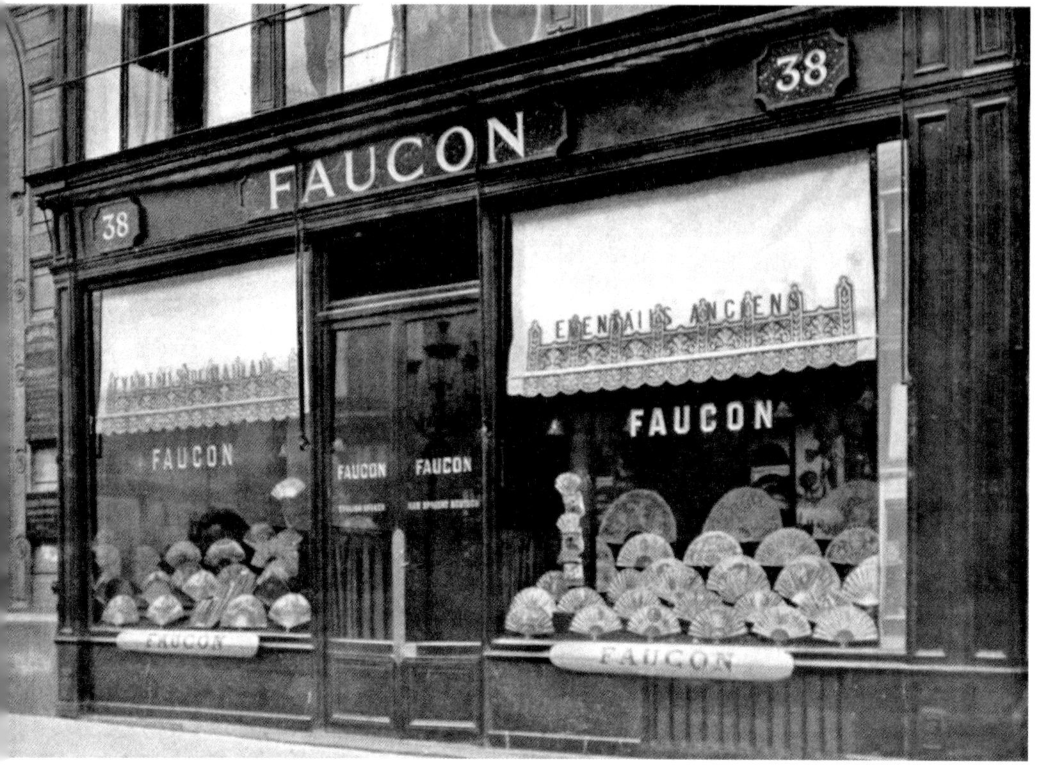

Fig. 43 Maison Faucon in Paris. *La Ville lumière* 1909, 174. Private collection.

luxury stationery, leather goods, accessories, and jewelry, were G. Glasens, Au Carnaval de Venise (3-5, boulevard de la Madeleine); Henry-À la pensée (5, rue du Faubourg Saint-Honoré), founded in 1800; Kendall & Co. (17, rue de la Paix); and Tonnel / P. Leroy successor (12, rue de la Paix).

In the field of leather goods and packaging, Olga mentions Louis Vuitton[58] as early as 1902. Founded in 1854 on rue Neuve des Capucines, then established on rue Scribe and finally on l'avenue des Champs-Élysées, the famous trunk maker began to develop its market among Russian customers in 1858.[59] Like many representatives of French luxury goods, Vuitton soon opened branches in London and Nice. As soon as the grand duke and countess arrived in Paris, they turned to him. The company's trunks and boxes could be adapted to any accessory, meeting the expectations of the great Parisian fashion consumers. In 1912, Olga chose a Vuittonite-covered shoe box with movable dividers.[60] Embellished with her crowned monogram

58 Pasols, 2012.

59 RGADA, F. 1290, op. 9, D. 49, L. 307.

60 Louis Vuitton Collection, Livre Journal, 1912, July 5.

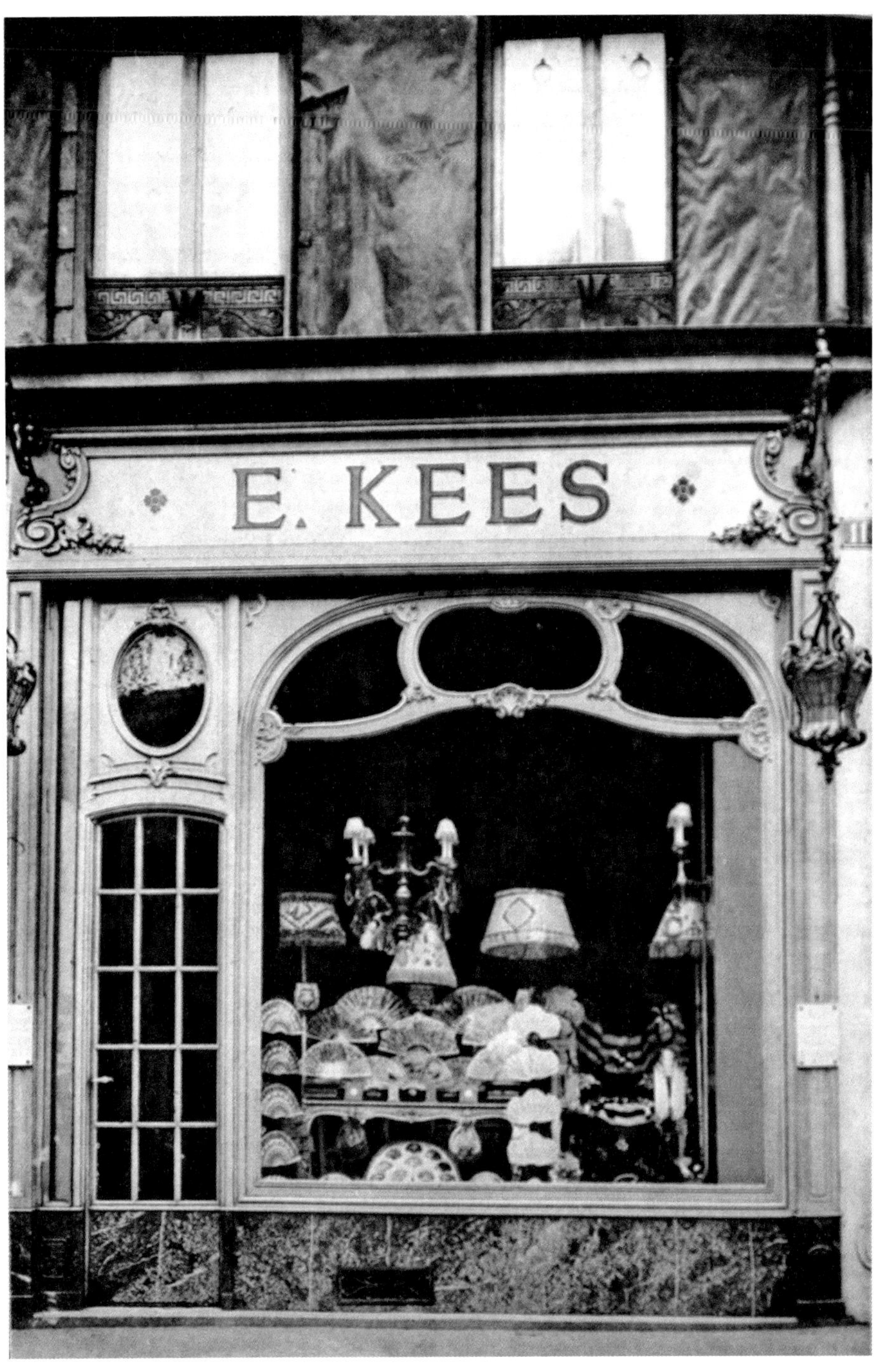

Fig. 44 Maison Kees in Paris. *La Ville lumière* 1909, 240. Private collection.

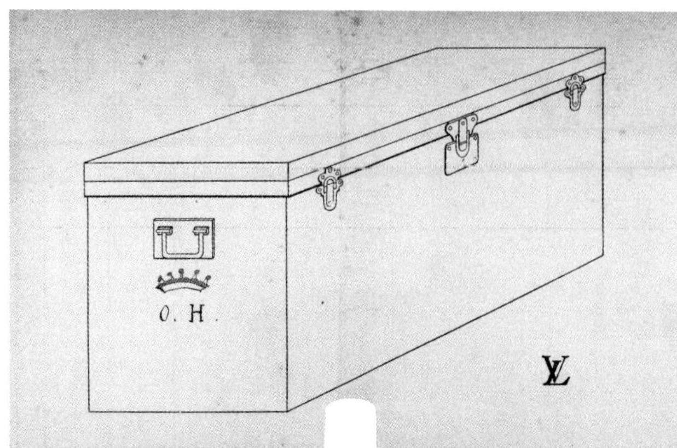

Fig. 45 Countess von Hohenfelsen's customer card, ca. 1912. Louis Vuitton Collection, Paris.

O. H. (fig. 45), it was where she could store her precious shoes, most certainly from the bootmaker Hellstern.

As with the regular furnishings of her mansion, the countess also visited department stores for accessories, lingerie, and simpler garments. She often makes note of Old England, a very French company despite its name, as well as Aux Trois Quartiers, Au Bon Marché, Printemps, Grands Magasins du Louvre, and Les Galeries Lafayette, which she referred to in her diary as "Gal. Laf.," as many Parisians still do today. Members of the imperial family were not averse to these temples to consumerism, witnesses to the commercial revolution of the nineteenth century. Grand Duchess Maria, whose financial means were more limited, recounts: "When I went to Paris, for example, I could not buy my outfits at the grand couturiers. I chose ready-made dresses at Galeries Lafayette and bought my shoes there too."[61]

Grand Duchess Vladimir, on the other hand, only selected sets of handkerchiefs, gloves, or ribbons at such stores.[62] This is probably the type of merchandise that Countess von Hohenfelsen and Grand Duke Paul bought during their regular shopping trips, which Olga particularly enjoyed.

A perusal of her diary reveals just how much time the high-society women devoted to shopping. In 1947, journalist Maurice de Waleffe (1874-1946) recounts his experience with a Countess Tolstoy, who gave up visiting the Louvre with him, justifying her decision in the following words: "Dressmakers, fittings, so many errands to do!," referring to the Paris of the 1900s, "where you can find Russian countesses on every corner!"[63]

61 Marie de Russie 1938, 156.

62 Zeisler 2014b, 98.

63 Waleffe 1947, 23.

Indeed, if contemporary literature is anything to go by, this activity was almost an obligation:

> For a truly elegant woman, a visit to the grand couturier is an obligation she cannot shirk. She must, of necessity, go to these salons, not only to find out what the latest fashions will be, but also to be seen there, and to see the good friends! – and good enemies – with whom it is always fun to compete for elegance. Having established this principle, it will surprise no one to learn that most ladies do not know what they have come to order when they enter a couturier's shop: will it be an evening gown, a traveling coat, a trotteur outfit, a matinee, or all these at once?[64]

Olga is one of these elegant women. Grand Duchess Maria reports on her step mother's repeated lateness, especially at lunchtime:

> She'd be in her room, getting dressed, or out on the town running errands. After a shopping expedition, she'd come home laden with neatly tied packages and cardboard boxes, which she'd throw on a chair by the windows.[65]

With curiosity, the young woman would try to learn more about the contents of the packages. To get an idea of this daily routine, let us follow some of Olga's expeditions through Paris. These outings were an almost daily occurrence, often on her own, to meet up with friends, or with Grand Duke Paul. They were made by automobile or cab, more rarely by public transport.

> November 26, 1903:
> This morning, we walked with Pucia – To À la Pensée Henry – To Doucet […] and along la rue de la Paix.
> January 30, 1904:
> This morning Paul and I went to Linker's, where we chose a beautiful blue dress, and from there to Worth's, where we also ordered a ball gown, an evening gown, and another.
> We're back home; I'm terribly tired.
> May 21, 1904:
> This morning, we went to Falize to see Princess Mathilde's jewelry, then to Cartier, where we looked at various objects, bought […]. After lunch I ordered a hat from Est. Meyer, went to Rumpelmayer, and again to Cartier.

64 Roger-Milès, 1910, 41.

65 Marie de Russie 1937, 53.

From May 26 to June 4, the jewels of Princess Mathilde, a cousin of Emperor Napoleon III who had died in January, were sold in Paris. Jeweler André Falize, the expert for the sale, took the opportunity to present them to the public. This event was bound to arouse the interest of the countess, a great lover of jewelry. Such a sale represented an opportunity for jewelers to acquire gems. Falize, Louis Aucoc (brother of goldsmith André Aucoc), and Lacloche were among the buyers.

Anton Rumpelmayer, meanwhile, was a famous confectioner of Austrian origin, established on the Côte d'Azur, among other places. Number 226, rue de Rivoli had been his Paris address since 1903, and it was succeeded by the famous Café Angelina. This last mention shows that these outings also provided opportunities for gourmet breaks or tea with friends and family. The countess's walks were interspersed with necessary stops at public lavatories, at a cost of 20 centimes, which Olga dutifully added to her accounts.

These shopping trips continue unabated and are described in varying degrees of detail.

On September 30, 1904, having just arrived in Paris from Germany, Olga's train pulled into the station at 8:45 a.m., and by 2:00 p.m. she was already at Paquin's, the starting point for a long afternoon of shopping, including at Linker's store.

> September 8, 1905:
> took the metro to [Magasin(s) du] Louvre where I went shopping, from there to Bon Marché, Doucet, ordered ties for Ef.[imovich] and then came home.
> January 17, 1908:
> In the morning, I went to Paquin, paid my bill, then Worth…
> April 11, 1912:
> went to Worth, for the bill for the headdress for the Yturbe ball – went to Printemps – to Guerlain, again to Worth, to Cartier and to Paquin, where I ordered a tailor dress – tea, lunch, and evening at home.
> March 28, 1914:
> After lunch, at 2:30 p.m. I went to Paquin's, leaving at 6 p.m. Terribly tiring!

In addition to her choices, the diary sheds light on the relationship between the customer and her suppliers. Olga makes regular visits to her two main designers, Paquin and Worth, to view models, place orders, and do fittings. During her visits, which can last several hours, she never fails to tip the Paquin or Worth "girl" an average of 1 franc. Olga maintains a special relationship with certain saleswomen, with whom she corresponds. At Worth, she is in contact with Mme Louise or Alice, while at Paquin, Olga deals with

Mlle Claire.[66] On a regular basis, the saleswomen would ask how their orders have been received, and how they are appreciated by their customers. Such is the nature of a missive Louise sent from Worth in 1914:

> I hope you like the little pink crepe de chine dress we have made for you to wear under your damask coat and that you are completely satisfied with it. If it were otherwise, let me remind you, Madame la comtesse, that we are at your complete disposal to arrange it and even to take it all back. Mr. Worth asks me to tell you in this respect that far from being upset, he would be very happy to have the opportunity to prove to you once again how much he wishes to please you.[67]

These rarely documented exchanges between saleswomen and customers are reminiscent of those maintained by sisters Hortense and Alice, who worked at Worth and Chéruit in the early twentieth century.[68] They are similar to those maintained by Olga, whom Géza von Habsburg described as a "jewelry fanatic,"[69] with her main jewelers.

Cartier was the supplier she appreciated most. Founded in 1847, Cartier enjoyed tremendous growth at the end of the nineteenth century, culminating in its move to 13, rue de la Paix in 1899.[70] The company's growing reputation attracted an international clientele. As early as 1899, Grand Duke Alexei was one of the maison's customers,[71] which also supplied some of Grand Duchess Vladimir's most prestigious jewels. In addition, an alliance through double marriage could only play in favor of two luxury brands on rue de la Paix: Louis Cartier (1875-1942) – associated with his father, Alfred Cartier (1841-1925), in the family business since 1898 – and his sister Suzanne (1885-1960) married, respectively, children of the heads of the couture house Worth, Andrée (1881-1939), daughter of Jean-Philippe Worth, and Jacques (1882-1941), son of Gaston-Lucien Worth. The names Cartier and Worth are constantly mentioned in the countess's diary, in which the family union is even mentioned in 1907: "went to Worth where Louis Cartier came by." The maison became a destination to be taken in during a stroll, where Olga sometimes met up with friends such as Boni de Castellane, who became her

66 Olga is probably referring here to Claudine Seurre, also known as "Claire," who was an important employee at Maison Paquin. I am grateful to Barry Shifman for helping me identify her. See also Sirop 1989, 18, 167.

67 GARF, F. 613, op. 1, D. 117. L. 1-2.

68 Léri and Saillard 2013.

69 Habsburg 2003, 83.

70 Concerning Cartier, see, among others, Nadelhoffer 1984 and Salomé and Dalon 2013. See also Gautier 1980. Thanks also to the Cartier maison for its invaluable help in finalizing this research.

71 Nadelhoffer 1984, 305.

constant companion. The place was a fashionable rendezvous for worldly personalities, as suggested by an anecdote Louis Cartier recounted in his notebook:

> During my career, I often had the honor of being in contact with royal families, and many sovereigns or members of their families came to la rue de la Paix to see the fashions we were launching. They were amused by the new ideas that were gradually spreading throughout the world. The Grand Duke [Paul] and his wife were sitting in my office one day, studying an order for a large tiara [...]. I saw the grand duke, seated on my left by the glass door, lean over and call "Arthur!" The other customer turned and came over to us. It was His Royal Highness the Prince of Connaught, brother of His Majesty Edward VII, and both princes were delighted to meet up here.[72]

Even before his exile to Paris, Grand Duke Paul had been a customer, and he appears in the company's accounts for the purchase of "opera binoculars by Wedgwood"[73] in 1901. At the time of her marriage and move abroad, between 1902 and 1903, the countess needed jewelry in keeping with her new position, a set of pieces that can be considered to have been her wedding gift, consisting of two necklaces, one of which had nine drop diamonds with a double ruby and diamond surround, as well as a long bodice front and a gold-and-silver-mounted meandering tiara. It is difficult to keep precise track of the couple's purchases from Cartier, in whose accounts the grand duke is mentioned as having bought or ordered around a hundred items between 1903 and 1906.[74] Again according to Géza de Habsburg's records, 44 purchases were made in the countess's name during the same period, with a further 23 between 1908 and 1914. The total number of purchases was approximately 170, including jewels, accessories, and small decorative objects. Other sources confirm the frequency of her purchases and give some sums that enable us to estimate the budget the countess devoted to her jewels. In her personal account books between 1909 and 1915, the countess indicates all her expenses and income, 5,500 francs per month.[75] Her largest bills were often paid in several installments. During this period, she spent nearly 56,000 francs at Cartier. These were the couple's minor expenditures with the jeweler, mainly for small items, often gifts for festive occasions, such as tiepins acquired in 1907, or animals and other stone items. The countess had a penchant for the latter, and in 1904 she chose "a reddish carnelian hen with 2 shining eyes."[76] Occasionally,

72 Gautier 1980, 145.

73 Nadelhoffer 1984, 114.

74 Habsburg 2003, 83.

75 GARF, F. 613, op. 1, D. 613, L. 1-95.

76 Habsburg 2003, 447.

she would treat herself to a few pieces of jewelry, such as the two bracelets she chose on July 12, 1907. However, major expenses were most often the responsibility of the grand duke, who sometimes selected items for himself, like a shagreen set with the motto "Je suis couleur d'espérance" (I am the color of hope), acquired in 1904. Sometimes, they were joint purchases, conducive to discussion in front of Cartier's showcases. On June 16, 1907, Olga wrote in her diary: "This morning, Paul and I spent a long time at Cartier, where I chose three objects for him, and then to Doucet."

The countess's Cartier collection thus consisted of the 1902-3 set, to which should be added a diamond ribbon bow that she mentions in her diary in 1903. The following year, she listed a necklace of round solitaire diamonds on a platinum wire and a corsage front with rubies and diamonds with a Louis XVI motif in a supple platinum setting, referenced in 1905 in the Cartier archives. In the same year, the grand duke presented her with a bracelet of diamonds and emeralds. The best-documented order is that of 1908, as it is a double one. On January 22, the grand duke spent 420,000 francs on a new seven-diamond pear-shaped tiara for the countess[77] (fig. 46), and a further 100,000 francs on April 13 on a diamond and sapphire tiara for Grand Duchess Maria, whose wedding to Prince William of Sweden was scheduled for April 20 (fig. 47). In December 1907, the Cartier brothers presented a design for this piece to the grand duke, who welcomed them to Boulogne. Once approved, Pierre Cartier (1878-1974), Alfred Cartier's second son, took the model to Moscow to present it to Grand Duchess Elizabeth Feodorovna, Maria Pavlovna's official guardian. "He hoped to receive large orders," added Olga in her diary of December 31. Grand Duke Konstantin, cousin of Grand Duke Paul, noted in his diary that the tiara matched the bow brooch presented by the dowager empress on behalf of the family, as it was fashioned from the same stones.[78]

Also in 1908, Olga purchased a wristwatch from Cartier (pl. 27); in addition, she chose a cascading brooch front made of pearls and diamonds she had supplied, including two 285-grain pearls, one 145-grain ovoid pearl, and three 247-grain button pearls (fig. 48). The couple were always on the lookout for novelties, and it was not uncommon for them to bring their stones to Cartier to have them reassembled in the form of an updated jewel. In 1909, the grand duke had a number of pieces of jewelry dismantled in order to reuse turquoise stones on a pendant in platinum and diamonds that could also be worn as a brooch (fig. 49). The following year, he had diamonds mounted in platinum to create a headband with a star motif, a Christmas gift that Olga mentions in her diary along with its value of 47,000 francs (fig. 50). In 1910, the countess purchased a necklace of emeralds and diamonds set in platinum. During this period, she also referred to pearls acquired from Cartier.

77 Munn 2001, ill. 276, 305; Habsburg 2003, 83.

78 Efimov and Kovalskaya 2009, 801.

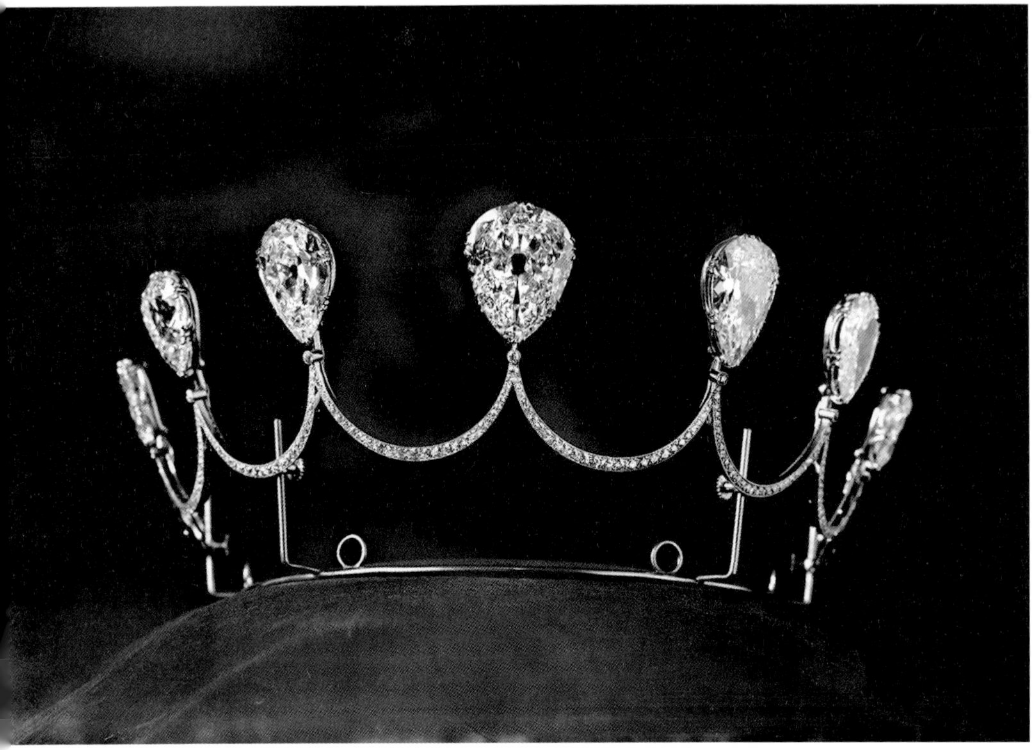

Fig. 46 Tiara by Cartier, Paris, 1908. Made of platinum and diamonds, it was sold to Grand Duke Paul in 1908. Photograph from the original gelatin silver bromide negative on glass. 18 × 24 cm (7 1/8 × 9 1/2 in.). Cartier Archives, Paris © Cartier.

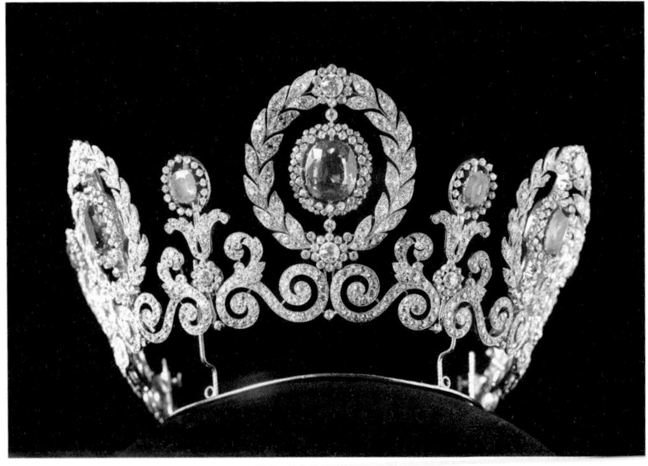

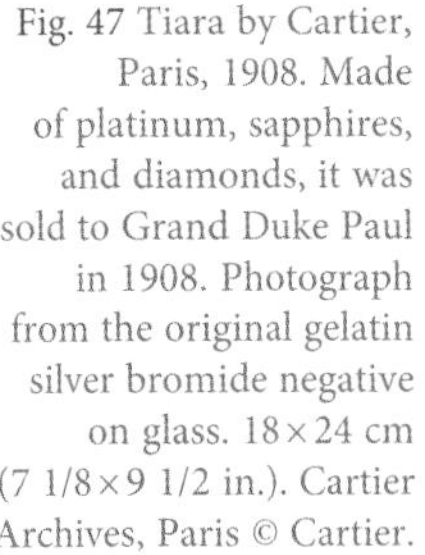

Fig. 47 Tiara by Cartier, Paris, 1908. Made of platinum, sapphires, and diamonds, it was sold to Grand Duke Paul in 1908. Photograph from the original gelatin silver bromide negative on glass. 18 × 24 cm (7 1/8 × 9 1/2 in.). Cartier Archives, Paris © Cartier.

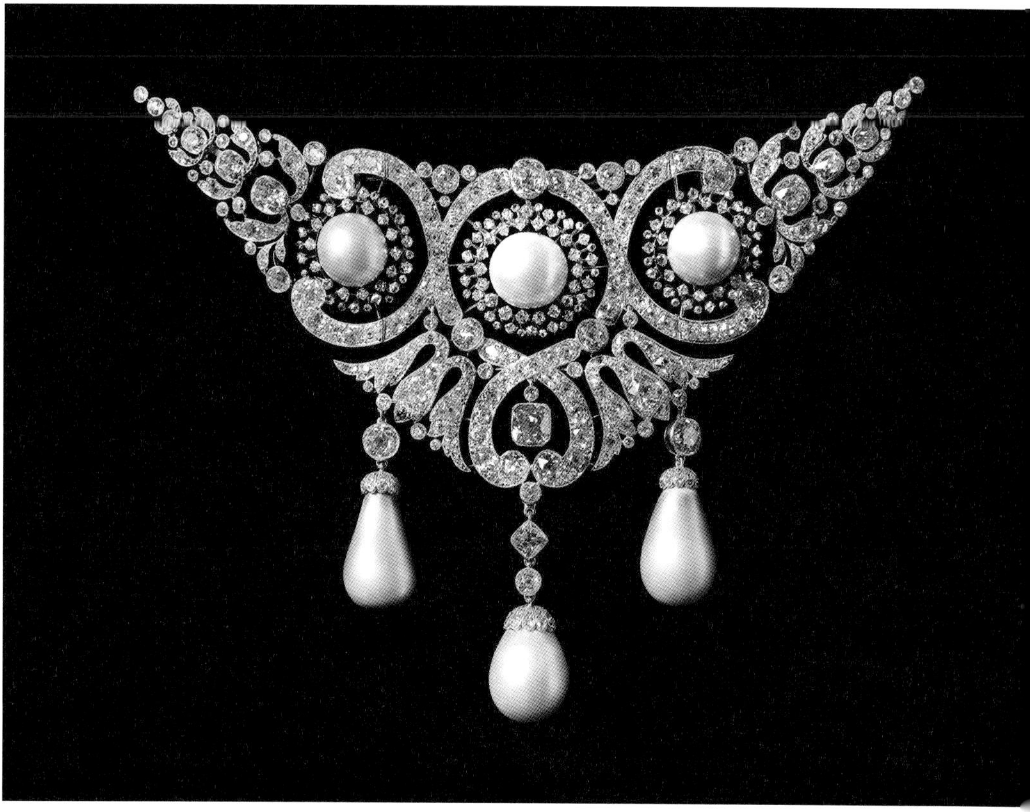

Fig. 48 (above) Pearl and diamond devant de corsage (or stomacher) by Cartier, 1908. Commissioned by Countess von Hohenfelsen. Photograph from the original gelatin silver bromide negative on glass. 30 × 40 cm (11 7/8 × 15 3/4 in.). Cartier Archives, Paris © Cartier.

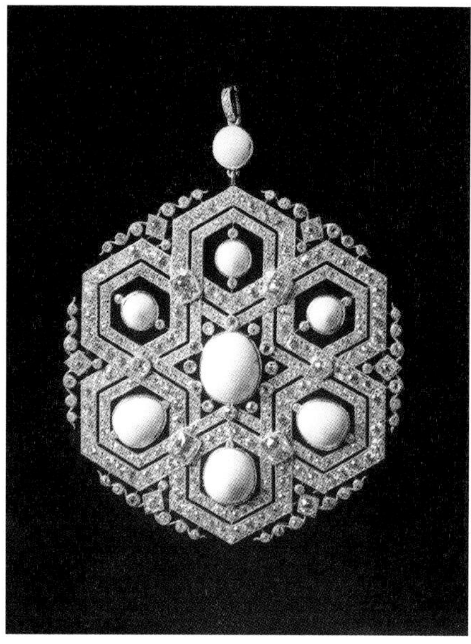

Fig. 49 (opposite) Pendant by Cartier, Paris, 1909. Made of platinum, turquoise, and diamonds, it was sold to Grand Duke Paul in 1909. Photograph from the original gelatin silver bromide negative on glass. 24 × 30 cm (9 1/2 × 11 7/8 in.). Cartier Archives, Paris © Cartier.

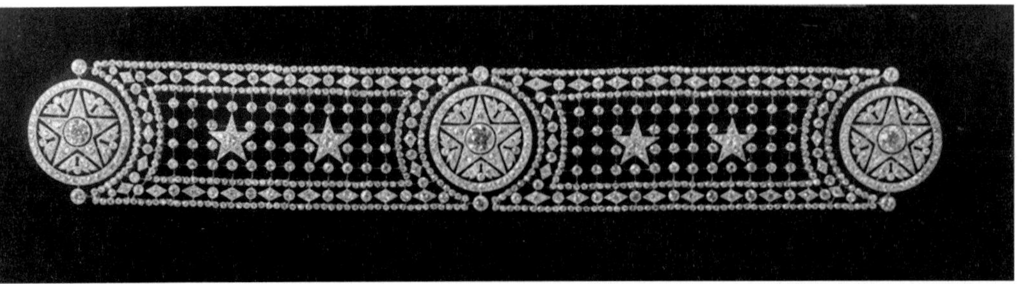

Fig. 50 Headband by Cartier, Paris, 1910. Made of platinum and diamonds, it was sold to Grand Duke Paul in 1910. Photograph from the original gelatin silver bromide negative on glass. 30 × 40 cm (11 7/8 × 15 3/4 in.). Cartier Archives, Paris © Cartier.

In 1911, she had her 1908 tiara updated as a diamond tiara with intertwined ring motifs on a flexible platinum setting that could also be used as a devant de corsage. The central diamond weighed 27 carats and the other seven stones together 121.42 carats (fig. 51). In 1913, Grand Duke Paul bought her a *rivière de diamants* necklace. In the same year, Olga selected a brooch with particularly modern lines that heralded Art Deco (pl. 28). It was in most of these pieces that the countess appeared at the Yturbe Ball in 1912 (fig. 52). There is also a set that appeared on the art market in 2009. Made of aquamarines and diamonds, it comprises a tiara, necklace, and devant de corsage by Cartier and is dated 1912 when it was acquired by the countess.[79]

While Cartier was the main supplier of jewelry and precious objects to the countess and Grand Duke Paul, the couple also occasionally called on other suppliers, most of whom were based in the same neighborhood. As early as 1889, Countess Lunzi – most likely Marie Sechiari (1854-1922),[80] of Romanian origin – had ordered a "Greek missal specially printed by Lahure"[81] from Boucheron for 14,500 francs to mark the union of Grand Duke Paul and his first wife, Princess Alexandra of Greece. The precious white Morocco binding was decorated with monograms and coats of arms in emeralds, rubies, sapphires, and diamonds. The object remained in the grand duke's collection until its dispersal in 1929.[82] The house founded by Frédéric Boucheron in 1858 was then located under the luxurious arcade of the Palais-Royal. As the store followed the general migration of luxury institutions toward the west of Paris,

79 Sotheby's, Geneva, May 12, 2009, lots 281-283.

80 Wife since 1872 of Count Dimitrio Lunzi (1848-1915) of Greece.

81 AB, MC 18, f. 142. Delivered to the countess on May 5, 1889. Lahure is the name of a printing house founded by Charles Lahure, a letterpress printer, and taken over by his son Alexis Lahure after 1879.

82 Paley sale, Christie's, London, July 1st-2, 1929, lot 103: "A book-binding, of white velum, set with a monogram, spray of foliage, & ca., in brilliants, rubies, emeralds and sapphires." The binding was acquired by Polovstov.

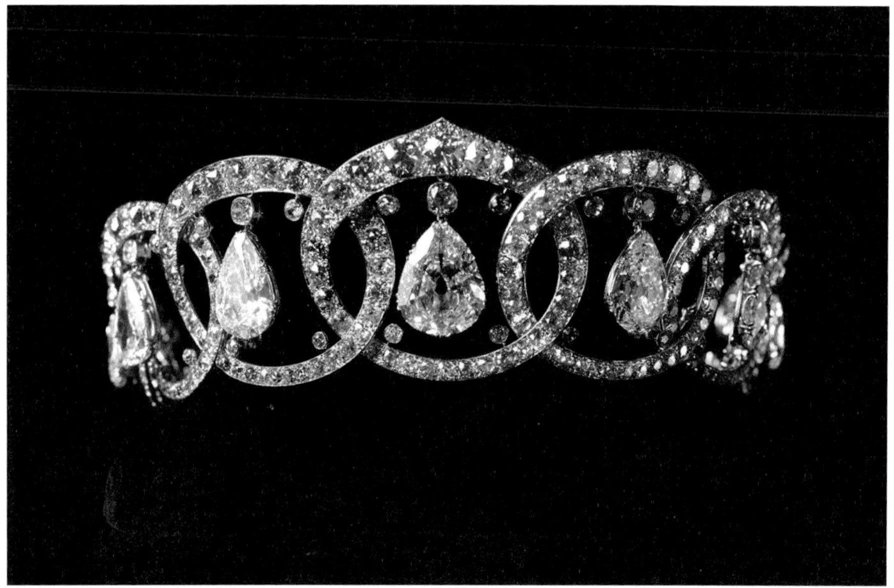

Fig. 51 Tiara by Cartier, Paris, 1911. Made of platinum and diamonds, it was sold to Countess von Hohenfelsen in 1911. Photograph from the original gelatin silver bromide negative on glass. 18 × 24 cm (7 1/8 × 9 1/2 in.). Cartier Archives, Paris © Cartier.

moving to the corner of la place Vendôme and la rue de la Paix in 1893, Grand Duke Paul was listed among its customers. On October 31, he is mentioned for a belt buckle adorned with two matte gold snakes for 500 francs, perhaps one of his first gifts to his new love that year, the future Countess von Hohenfelsen. Although described only summarily, this accessory suggests a work of Art Nouveau decoration and corroborates the grand duke's taste for contemporary creations, confirmed a few years later when he bought a blue-green stoneware signed Auguste Delaherche, mounted in gilded silver[83] for 1,200 francs. In 1913, the grand duke is mentioned for the last time in Boucheron's accounts. He brought the clocks that Grand Duke Nicholas Mikhailovich[84] had given to his daughters, "to make them work."[85]

With his taste for contemporary creativity, the grand duke had no hesitation in turning to René Lalique, champion of Art Nouveau jewelry. Lalique, whose international reputation was growing, triumphed at the Salon, which, having opened a section dedicated to objets d'art in the early 1890s, elevated the decorative arts to the rank of works of art, thus fostering the development of artistic luxury. Always eager for novelties, the Russian court,

83 AB, MC 27, f. 352.

84 AB, MC 51, f. 107. A round tortoiseshell clock (lot 2193), paid 425 frs, and an agate and enamel clock (lot 2191), paid 545 frs.

85 AB, MC 51, f. 431.

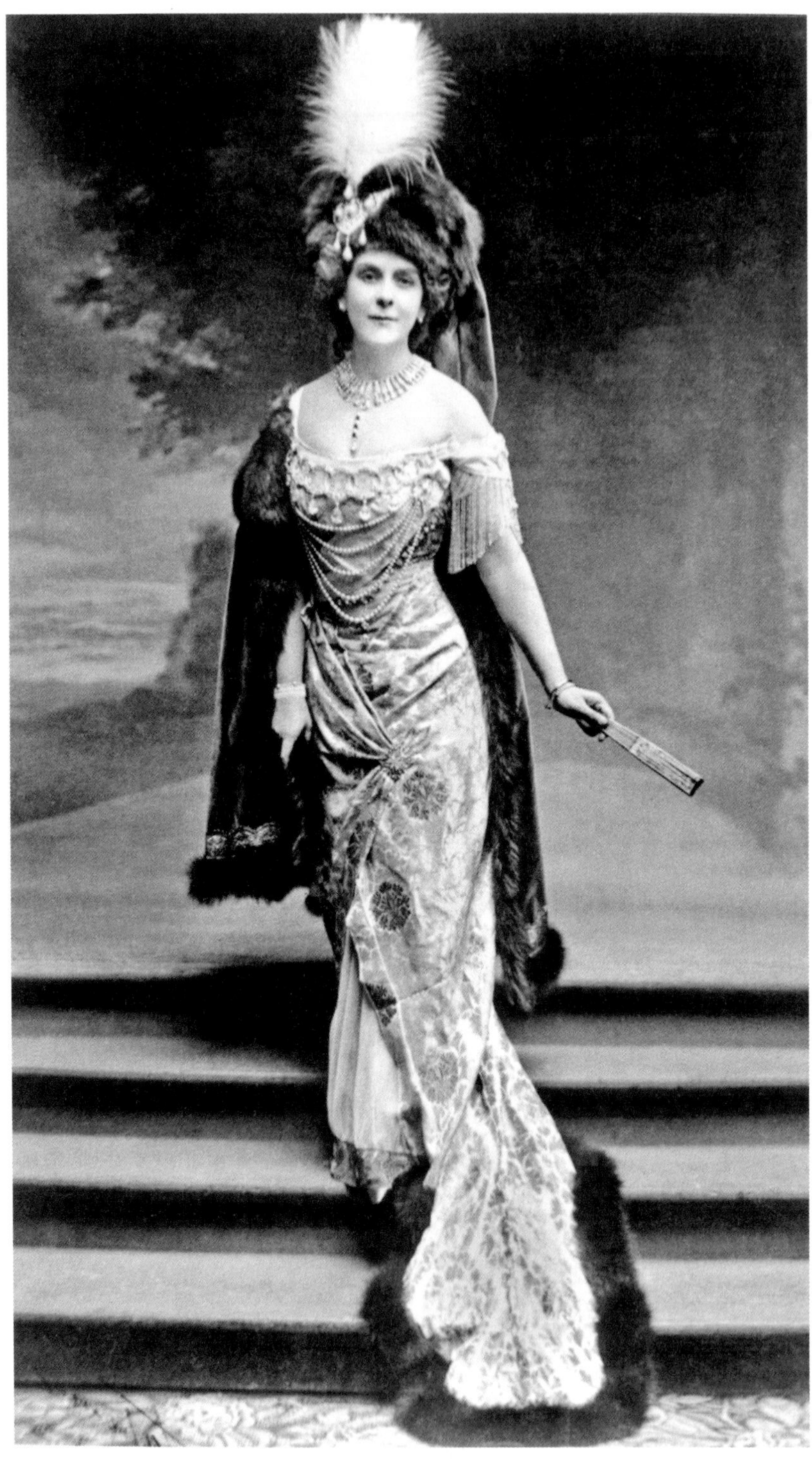

Fig. 52 Studio Boissonnas & Taponier. Countess von Hohenfelsen, 1912. Photograph. Cartier, Paris, Documentation.

preceded by the emperor, flocked to the Salon or rue Thérèse, the jeweler's address, to find a "Lalique" that would cause a sensation in St. Petersburg.[86] In 1898, in *Le Journal* under the pseudonym of Raitif de la Bretonne, Jean Lorrain remarked on the "marvelous Lalique exhibition" at the Champ-de-Mars Salon: "Nine enormous combs, unreasonable in size and which are unlikely to fit in a lady's bedroom, but which all the enthusiasts in London and St. Petersburg will be fighting over tomorrow."[87]

One of the pieces presented was probably the one that would later go to the Russian emperor, while other chroniclers noted the masterpiece destined for Grand Duke Paul: "The gold devant de corsage made for the Grand Duke Paul of Russia"[88] was admired.

Henri Vever gave more details about this jewel:

> a glass bodice ornament with a large brooch representing Winter, with crystallizations on snowy trees of great finesse of coloring; the invention was truly original. This ornament had been commissioned for Russia.[89]

An example of Lalique's inventive use of enamels, this jewel explored the theme of winter, an appropriate image for Russia, symbolized by snowy branches whose colorful effects made use of diamonds to form the decoration centered on a "very clear sapphire or opal," as suggested by a drawing with indications that could correspond to the front of a bodice, of which several designs with variations are known.[90]

Sadly no longer in existence, this magnificent example of Parisian Art Nouveau jewelry can reasonably be considered to have been a gift specially chosen by the grand duke for Olga, who, during her stay in Paris in 1899, visited Lalique's shop accompanied by a certain "Eugène." He urged her to spend 3,700 francs on an ornament that had just been completed. If the grand duke didn't like it, he could always return it, but Eugène added: "I know Monseigneur, he'll keep it."[91] This anecdote shows once again the grand duke's pronounced taste for the creations of his time, which Olga initially reproached him for. After the wedding, she developed her interest in antique art and designs inspired by models from the past. Indeed, Lalique does not seem to appear in any documents linked to the couple from this date on, especially as he gradually devoted his activities to the art of glass.

86 Zeisler 2014b, 298-99.

87 *Le Journal*, May 22, 1898.

88 *Le Temps*, May 1st, 1898.

89 Vever 1906-8, 3:714.

90 Peshekhonova 2010, no. 35, 120. See also Barten 1989, no. 935-1-3, 385, ill. 45.

91 Olga von Pistohlkors to the grand duke, April 3/15, 1899, GARF, F. 644, op. 1, D. 141, L. 31.

As soon as they settled in Paris, the countess and the grand duke turned almost exclusively to the big names on rue de la Paix, in particular Cartier, known for its creations inspired by the Neoclassical forms and motifs of the reign of Louis XVI, a period that Olga cherished and of which her jewelry collection is a reflection. During this time, her shopping trips sometimes took her to Tiffany, of which there was a branch on l'avenue de l'Opéra, and to Lacloche[92] or Morgan, neighbors on rue de la Paix, at numbers 15 and 17 respectively. Both houses had branches in Nice and Biarritz, and had long attracted Russian customers, including Grand Duke Alexei. Lacloche had opened on rue de la Paix in 1896, while Morgan, whose salons had remained unchanged since 1862, was an institution. Vever provides the entrepreneurial genealogy of this address, originally occupied by jeweler Eugène Jacta, named a supplier by appointment to the Russian court in 1865.[93] In 1868, Léon Bassot, whose jewelry shop had been mentioned in Palais-Royal in 1835, took over, before Edgar Morgan in 1886. Olga made small purchases from these jewelers or called on them for various jobs and repairs. She took her bracelets to Morgan for cleaning in 1903 and a watch to Lacloche for repair in 1904. She chose several pairs of Lacloche cuff links for the grand duke, including a 400 francs pair and a 140 francs pair in 1909. She also bought him a watch for Christmas that year, at a cost of 1,160 francs.

When it came to acquiring major pieces, Olga turned mainly to Cartier. She did, however, sometimes turn to the competition. In October 1905, she was looking for emeralds, and on the 6th, after a walk in the Bois de Boulogne, she went to Cartier "about the emerald necklace!" Olga returned on the 11th to discuss the same subject at length. It was then that Cartier's serious competitor Joseph Chaumet, established at 62, rue de Richelieu before moving to 12, place Vendôme in 1907, came into the picture. On October 15, after breakfast, he visited the countess to tell her about the "emeralds"; she later noted: "nothing decided." Chaumet paid her another visit on October 26, but nothing seemed to come of it. The question of emeralds came up again in 1907, when Cartier presented her with a set that Olga described as "ideal." Seduced, Olga hesitated, as it was an ensemble, whereas she wanted only a necklace. The jeweler insisted. A few days later, on February 23, as Olga passed by on rue de la Paix, Cartier came out and told her about the emeralds… He presented himself again to the countess on February 28 with the stones. Hitrov, always a good adviser, suggested taking only the necklace for 256,000 francs. Negotiations were unsuccessful. Olga finally received her emerald and diamond necklace in 1910.

Chaumet supplied Olga in 1906. On May 14, the jeweler presented her with pearls. Olga chose one for the grand duke's pin, and on May 25, she went to Chaumet to pay 8,000 francs of the total bill.

92 Zeisler 2014b, 348.

93 Vever 1906-8, 3:546.

Many of Olga's purchases were, in fact, intended as gifts. The act of giving was a fundamental element of sociability, especially for the Russians, whose monarchy had elevated the reward, symbolized by a gift, to the rank of a system of government. Shopping was an opportunity to find the perfect gift for any occasion. On the eve of the major holidays, Olga's tours intensified. November 1903 is a fine example. Out for a walk on the 14th with her stepson, Grand Duke Dimitri Pavlovich, she went to Lacloche and Cartier for gifts. She returned the next day and the day after that; she decided on Cartier, but also visited Morgan, Risler, Houbigant and Aux Trois Quartiers on the 17th. On the 18th, Olga went to Paradis des Enfants, Doucet, Galeries Lafayette, l'Escalier de Cristal… A similar program continued on the following days. Finally, on the 24th, she noted: "This morning with Pucia, we bought a lamp for DM.[itri] PAVL.[ovich] from Gagneau. Then to Bréguet and Cartier."

Watches and other chronometers often constituted a handsome present. The countess presented Efimovitch with a Bréguet watch in 1905, while the grand duke received at least two watches from Leroy & Cie, one for 1,000 francs in 1909 and the second for 350 francs in 1913. Bréguet, founded in Paris in the eighteenth century by the Swiss Abraham Bréguet, is still one of the world's leading representatives of luxury watchmaking. The family business was located at 39, quai de l'Horloge.[94] Watchmakers to sovereigns, Bréguet worked for all the courts of Europe. The windows of Leroy at 7, boulevard de la Madeleine, were also a must-see in this field (fig. 53). This Parisian institution of luxury watchmaking had set up shop in the Palais-Royal as early as 1785.[95]

> There isn't a sovereign passing through Paris who doesn't visit Messrs. Leroy, and bring back a fashionable watch or clock. Their stores on le boulevard de la Madeleine are in perfect taste. And the setting reflects the finery within. Everything is meticulous and artistic.[96]

The luxury items intended as gifts also came from stores frequently mentioned by Olga, including Kendall or Tonnel / P. Leroy at numbers 17 and 12, rue de la Paix, respectively; both specialized in luxury stationery and leather goods.

Children's gifts were often chosen at the famous Nain Bleu at 27, boulevard des Capucines, a temple to luxury toys founded in 1836, which supplied some of the industry's finest games for the children of Emperor Nicholas II[97]: "La maison du Nain Bleu has become, at present, the store where

94 Arch. Nat. LH 355/95; LH 355/96; LH 355/98.

95 Champier and Sandoz 1900, 189-90.

96 *La Ville lumière* 1909, 58-60.

97 *Ibid.*, 245-46.

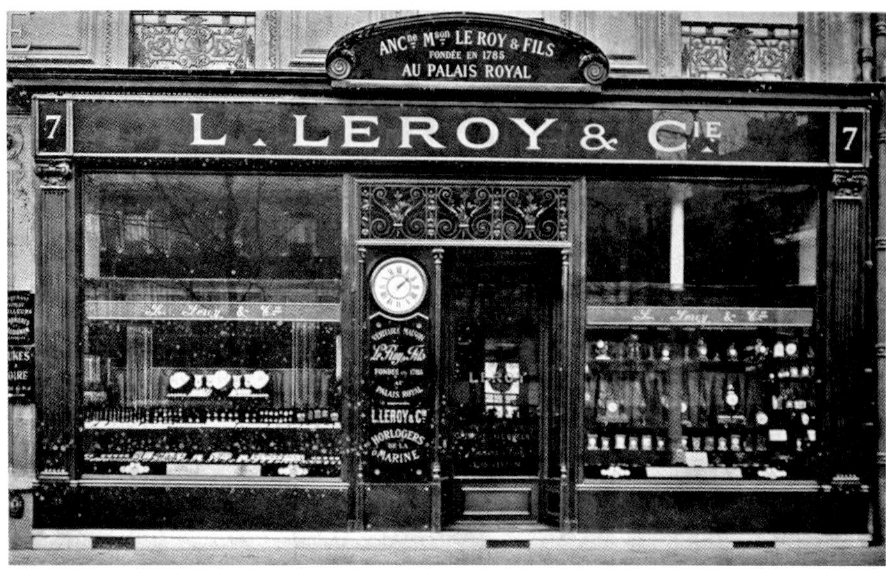

Fig. 53 The Leroy & Cie shop in Paris. *La Ville lumière* 1909, 59. Private collection.

you can find the most beautiful and luxurious toys, the prettiest living room games, and the most sought-after garden games."[98]

Gifts between the spouses were particularly generous, a sign of their affection for each other. Those for Christmas 1907 are representative. Olga gave "Pucia" a pair of gold, sapphire, ruby, and diamond cuff links by Cartier, which the grand duke lost at the Théâtre Réjane in 1911, a second pair by Fabergé, two blue trinkets by Langweil, a nephrite bird by Fabergé, a wallet, two white handkerchiefs. Their children gave him six ties. For her part, she received from the grand duke a platinum wristwatch, various precious objects including some made of nephrite, a bonbonnière, a lace scarf, and small Chinese objects.

In addition to the end-of-year festivities, Easter was also a time for exchanging gifts. In her diary, Olga noted on March 20, 1906: "went [...] then to Cartier where I chose various objects to make gifts." Grand Duke Paul is listed in the Cartier archives as early as April 1904 for the purchase of various egg-shaped charms, a form of gift appreciated in Russia and testifying to the influence that Russian clientele had on the productions of many Parisian houses during the Belle Époque. These acquisitions were to be repeated regularly. In March 1905, the countess bought a series of crosses, and in April small eggs. Olga and the grand duke made similar choices in 1907, 1908, and again in 1910.

Birthdays – the grand duke's on September 20 and the countess's on December 14 – were also the occasion for important gifts that made the

98 *Ibid.*, 246.

fortune of the Parisian luxury goods industry. In 1905, Olga listed the presents she gave to the grand duke:

> After tea, gave Paul my gifts: from Cartier (1) […] a watch, (2) an emerald and diamond runner, (3) a gold "Levan's pen," (4) 12 ties from Doucet, (5) an amber pipe from Sommer, (6) […] a Freezia bottle, (7) […] a cigar holder from Tonnel, (8) […] from Le Bon Marché, (9) a briefcase and pen from Brigg.

The grand duke was an inveterate smoker, like most members of the imperial family, and so smoking accessories made ideal gifts. From simple leather goods to the most elegant goldsmith's and jeweler's accessories, these lighters, cigarette holders, snuffboxes, and other smoker's utensils could be found in most of the capital's luxury or jewelry stores. Nevertheless, some of them specialized in various fields, such as amber or meerschaum pipes from Sommer, founded in 1855.[99] Its sign "Aux carrières d'écume" had been located since 1860 at 11-15, passage des Princes. All the elite and most members of the imperial family were supplied there. Some of the most original models chosen by this exceptional clientele are still preserved in the Hermitage collections in St. Petersburg.[100]

Another heavy smoker was Grand Duke Alexei, who had lived in Paris almost permanently since 1905, following the Tsushima disaster for which he was held responsible as grand admiral of the Russian fleet during the Russo-Japanese War. Olga, with whom he became very close, also spoiled him. On April 25, 1908, she wrote in her diary: "With P.[ucia] we spent the morning at Girbal and Cartier. I sought something for A.[lexis] A.[lexandrovich]; we found nothing, but we did find a Celadon ashtray at l'Escalier de Cristal."

The grand duke took a liking to Olga and became the couple's advocate to the emperor, of whom he was the favorite uncle. After all, he too had a love life that went against the prevailing principles of the imperial family, with a number of mistresses, forming a "ménage à trois" with his great love, Zinaida of Leuchtenberg, and her husband, and at last remaining at least officially celibate.

99 *Ibid.*, 231.
100 Kostiuk 2010, 135-47.

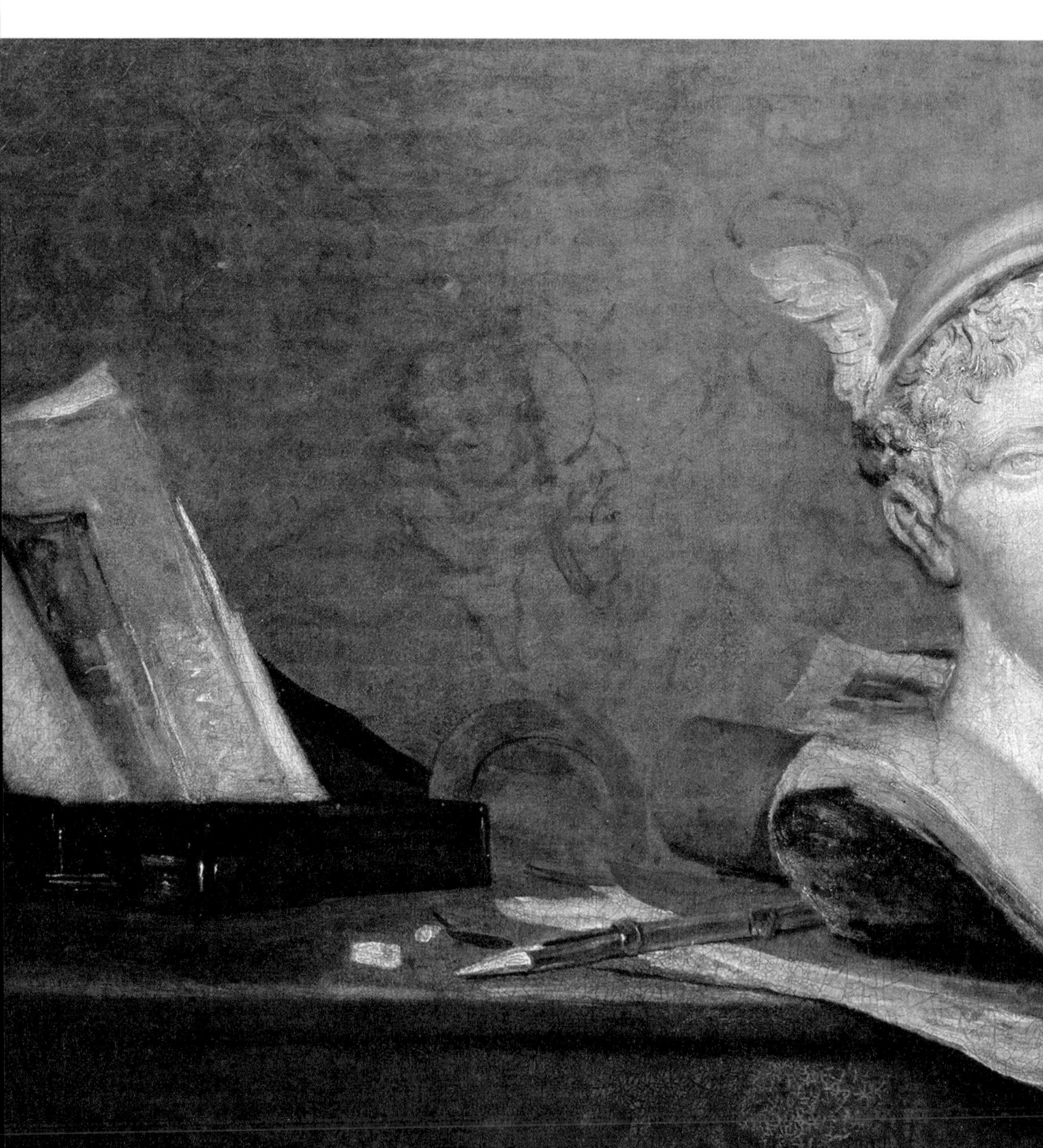

RETURN TO GRACE

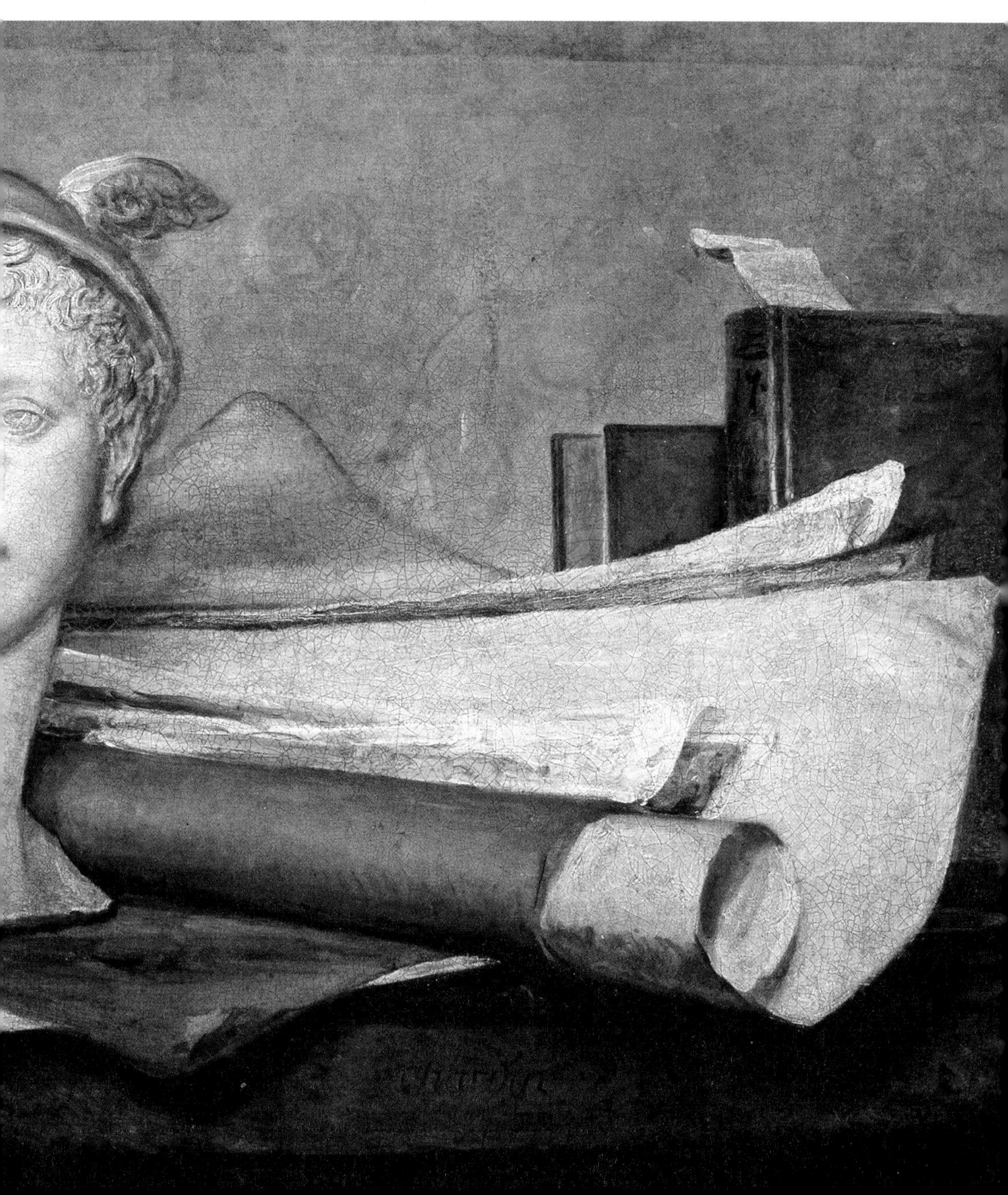

The years 1907 and 1908 were pivotal in the life of the couple. Consumed by nostalgia for his homeland, the grand duke did everything in his power to obtain permission for his wife to accompany him to Russia. The countess, who was also suffering from homesickness, wanted to travel to St. Petersburg to take care of her eldest daughter, Olga, who was expecting a child. The planned marriage of the grand duke's daughter, Maria Pavlovna, to Prince William of Sweden offered the perfect opportunity. However, the grand duke's request was turned down by the emperor, to whom he responded angrily on May 12, 1907:

> I am replying to your second telegram by letter. Your words that a conversation on a subject that affects me personally will only take place "following Maria's wedding," oblige me to reply immediately that I cannot come. Let everyone know why the father shall not be attending either the engagement or the wedding of his daughter. I was prepared to be understanding at first and endure everything patiently, but after five years of exemplary family life, I feel I have the right to expect a different attitude toward us both. Did you really think I would leave my wife alone, whom everyone here appreciates and respects [...]. I did not [...] sacrifice everything to let her be humiliated and insulted for no reason. If she cannot take her rightful place by virtue of our morganatic marriage, a marriage recognized by you through decrees in the Senate and the Ministry of the Court, then, I cannot be present – This is my irrevocable decision.[1]

In the same letter, Paul expressed his bitterness at having been excluded from all conversations concerning his daughter's wedding and the choice of a fiancé, whom he had not met. Grand Duchess Xenia, the emperor's sister, wrote in her diary on June 2:

> Uncle Paul [...] sent an official reply to the fiancé's letter, asking for his daughter's hand in marriage, saying that as she had a guardian (appointed without his knowledge or consent), he was in no position to say anything, and he signed it Grand Duke Paul! What an incredible lack of heart! I feel sorry for poor Maria – he has ruined everything for her![2]

Despite fierce opposition from Grand Duchess Elizabeth Feodorovna, guardian of Grand Duchess Maria, but with Grand Duke Alexei's support, the emperor finally authorized Paul and Olga to travel to Russia together. Paul

1 Maylunas and Mironenko 1996, 294.

2 *Ibid.*, 296.

officially thanked Nicholas II in a letter dated October 27, 1907.[3] Maria Pavlovna spoke movingly of her reunion with her father and first meeting with her stepmother in St. Petersburg. These took place in the grand duke's former palace on the English Embankment, under the watchful eye of Grand Duchess Elizabeth: "As my father kissed Aunt Ella's hand and turned to embrace us, I caught a glimpse in a mirror of the profile of the Countess von Hohenfelsen. Her face was pale with emotion."[4]

One can imagine the tension of the moment, with Olga wanting to make a good impression on her stepdaughter, and presumably worried about being confronted by her most fervent detractor, Grand Duchess Elizabeth. Olga was elegantly dressed as a Parisian, wearing a purple velvet gown embellished with antique lace, matching the colors of her amethyst pearl necklace. She behaved like the mistress of the house: "The countess did the honors. Her hands, laden with rings, deftly handled the white cups, edged in red."[5]

The atmosphere remained heavy, however. After the usual conversation, it was decided to study the collection of jewels, furs, and lace, unpacked on the billiard table, of Grand Duchess Alexandra (Grand Duke Paul's first wife), in preparation for their distribution to her children, Maria and Dimitri:

> In silence, my father and aunt bent over the dusty jewelry boxes containing the old-fashioned ornaments and tarnished gems that had been neglected for nearly twenty years. [...] I was not impressed by the lackluster fortune laid out before me, half of which was supposed to be mine. Jewelry was part of our outfits, but for me it was just a regular adornment. I attributed no material value to them.[6]

It was at this point that Olga and Maria began to draw closer, and the latter was able to benefit from her stepmother's advice on fashion and good taste, subjects that were bound to appeal to a seventeen-year-old:

> the countess examined the furs with me. Twenty years of mothballs had not made them more appealing; the countess offered to take them to Paris to be refurbished. We talked about my trousseau and Parisian fashion houses.[7]

Olga's amethyst necklace was to be her gift as a memento of that first meeting. Official relations softened, and even though Maria expressed serious doubts

3 *Ibid.*, 299.
4 Marie de Russie 1938, 123.
5 *Ibid.*
6 *Ibid.*, 124.
7 *Ibid.*

about her feelings, the wedding took place the following year, in the presence of the grand duke but without the countess.[8] The event, which was intended to be a happy one, turned out to be a terrible failure, ending in their separation in 1914:

> My father tried, unsuccessfully, to reason with me. My stepmother, fearing that part of the blame might fall on her, also spoke to me in the same vein. But it was in vain, and as soon as my father understood that my decision was irrevocable, that no influence could change this, he bravely took my side and supported me wholeheartedly. He took charge of all the arrangements and correspondence.[9]

After his daughter's wedding in May 1908, the grand duke was recalled to Russia by a family tragedy. At 6:00 a.m. on November 14, 1908, Grand Duke Alexei, aged fifty-eight, succumbed in Paris to influenza-like bronchopneumonia with myocardial complications.[10] Olga reproduced in her diary the full text of the telegram that her husband sent to the emperor the same day:

> Will accompany Alexei's body to Petersburg. Am broken by grief, unable to travel alone. Beg you, in the name of dear Alexei, so affectionate to my wife; allow her to accompany me. Her moral support is indispensable to me; dear Nicky, beg you not to refuse me! Paul.

The emperor consented. The couple officially took part in the ceremonies organized with great pomp first in Paris, in the Russian church on rue Daru, and then in Russia.[11] The event, which was of interest to both Russia and France, within the framework of the Franco-Russian Alliance, gave "this ceremony the character of a particularly grandiose funeral solemnity," noted *Le Petit Parisien*.[12] A long procession of dignitaries, including the previous French president, Émile Loubet, and envoys from the presidency and the government, marched from l'avenue Gabriel to the church. Representing the imperial family were Grand Duke Paul, Duke Georgy of Leuchtenberg and his son, Prince George of Greece, the Duke of Oldenburg, Grand Duke Cyril, and, among the ladies, Countess von Hohenfelsen. After the ceremony, the coffin was taken to the Gare du Nord for travel to Russia by special train "Along with Grand Duke Paul, his wife [...], Grand Duchess Sergei and Archpriest Smirnoff climbed into the sleeping car."[13]

8 Efimov and Kovalskaya 2009, 801.

9 Marie de Russie 1938, 179.

10 Archives de la Police, Paris, EA 17, grand-duc Alexei.

11 *Le Petit Parisien*, November 17, 1908.

12 *Le Petit Parisien*, November 19, 1908.

13 *Ibid.*

Countess von Hohenfelsen was now officially part of the imperial family. "Things are looking up," noted Grand Duke Konstantin in his diary, the day after the grand duke and countess's first visit to Russia in autumn 1907,[14] followed all too soon by the visit in connection with the death of Grand Duke Alexei. The idea of a partial return to Russia in the form of a holiday residence then germinated in the minds of the grand duke and countess, especially as in 1908 their son, Vladimir von Hohenfelsen, was sent to St. Petersburg to enter the Page School.

While work was in full swing at Boulogne, which was being enlarged at the time, Olga began looking for a home in Russia. She could have settled for the grand duke's palace, but this residence, built between 1859 and 1862 and a manifesto of historicist eclecticism, was not to her taste. Acquired by the crown in 1887 from Nadezhda Polovtsova, the adopted daughter of its builder, Baron von Stieglitz, the palace was also too closely linked to the memory of the grand duke's first marriage. So the countess asked her friends about houses the couple could buy. One of them seemed an ideal choice: it was in Tsarskoye Selo, close to Grand Duchess Vladimir's house and the Alexander Palace, which had become the imperial family's main residence since 1905. This proximity could not fail to appeal to Olga, who had made a much desired and well-deserved comeback. For her, Tsarskoye Selo was also the memory of her first meetings and nights with Grand Duke Paul, thus an ideal place to establish her home. As for the grand duke, who was born in Tsarskoye Selo, he could not but be seduced by the opportunity to return to the places that recalled his childhood.

The loyal Hitrov helped with the search, and the choice fell on the country house of Alexander Polovtsov, who wrote to Olga about it in 1910:

> I was at Tsarskoye the day before yesterday with Hitrov, who seemed delighted with the house; but of that he will communicate his impressions to you himself. It has been a long time since I have been there, and I have never looked at it critically, but having done so now, I think the house would suit you anyway. It is in very good order and solid throughout.[15]

Already in negotiations with another potential buyer, Polovtsov, who enclosed a plan of the land with his letter, urged her to make a decision. It took only a short time for the couple to give a positive answer, especially as the price was very reasonable, 50 rubles a *sajene* for 12,000 *sajenes*.[16] The house, which

14 Efimov and Kovalskaya 2009, 801.

15 GARF, F. 613, op. 1, D. 391, L. 10. Letter dated July 23, 1910.

16 *Ibid.*, L. 17. Letter from Polovstov, dated March 3/16, 1911. The *sajene* (2.134 m or 7 feet) is an old unit of measurement used in Russia before the Revolution.

Polovtsov described as an "old shanty," needed renovation. To this end, he recommended the architect Carl Schmidt (1866-1945), who had just completed some alterations to his villa in Kamenny Ostrov.[17] Trained at the Imperial Academy of Fine Arts in St. Petersburg, the architect is also known for having designed the Petersburg store of court jeweler Carl Fabergé on Bolshaya Morskaya, inaugurated in 1900.

For this new commission, Schmidt was merely an executor, subject to the plans of the Parisian decorator hired for the occasion. Schmidt went to the site to assess the feasibility of the project, which involved raising the height of the former Polovtsov residence. He discovered, and reported back, that the wooden structure could not support an additional floor. The couple was disappointed; Polovtsov, who felt responsible, worried:

> I recommended Schmidt to you thinking he was going to lay heating pipes, raise or knock down partitions and nothing more; now he wants to build a new palace and be promoted to artist at your expense.[18]

This was an unhoped-for opportunity for Schmidt to build a palace in Tsarskoye Selo. He could curry favor with the imperial family and receive further commissions. In the end, everything fell into place, and the couple decided to wipe the slate clean and build a brand-new residence, the one Olga had been dreaming of. Maria Pavlovna noted during a visit to her father in autumn 1912: "I found him and his wife happily making plans to build a house on an estate in Tsarskoye Selo, the imperial residence."[19]

For the third time since settling in Paris, Olga, assisted by the grand duke, became fully involved in the design of a house. In early 1911, the couple had already contacted decorator Marcel Boulanger (1867-1929),[20] who was almost the same age as the countess, just two years younger. Born into a family of ornamental sculptors from Valenciennes, Boulanger, who had lived in Paris since 1887, had begun his career working for the furniture manufacturer and upholsterer Ternisien, before setting up on his own in 1902 (fig. 54). His clients and projects included Marcel Proust's parents on l'avenue Hoche,[21] the Café de la Paix, and the Cartier store in Paris, as well as the Ritz and Claridge's in London. He also worked for couturier Jean-Philippe Worth on his Champ-de-Mars mansion, built around 1909 by architect René Sergent.[22] Olga and the grand duke visited this house on February 10, 1911. They spent

17 Fogt and Kirikov 2011.

18 GARF, F. 613, op. 1, D. 391, L. 17. Letter dated March 3/16, 1911.

19 Marie de Russie 1938, 170.

20 On Boulanger, see Zeisler 2014b, 333.

21 Francis and Gontier 1981, 149.

22 René Bétourné, *René Sergent* (Paris, 1931), 16-19.

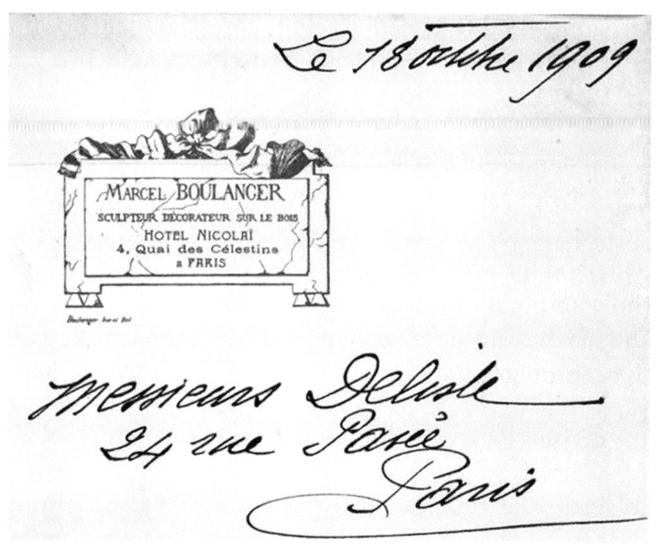

Le 18 octobre 1909

MARCEL BOULANGER
SCULPTEUR DÉCORATEUR SUR LE BOIS
HOTEL NICOLAÏ
4, Quai des Célestins
à PARIS

Messieurs Delisle
24 rue Pavée
Paris

Fig. 54 Letterhead on the correspondence of decorator Marcel Boulanger, ca. 1909. Delisle Archives, Paris.

over an hour observing the fittings, and Olga noted in her diary: "There's some splendid Sèvres at Worth!" The deal done, Boulanger began meeting regularly with the couple, who would pay him over a million francs between 1911 and 1914 for the design of their palace and most of the furniture.[23] The couple regularly visited his studio to see the plans and models of their future home. After one of these many visits, Olga wrote in her diary with, one senses, a certain enthusiasm: "I'm satisfied."

The architect and contractors were Russian,[24] but nothing escaped the vigilance of Boulanger and his team, who followed the construction site, not without conflict, mainly from Paris. Nevertheless, Boulanger and his employees, including foremen Lacroix, Mayer, and Gommerat, laborer Poissy, and upholsterer Gaston Raffy, made several trips to Tsarskoye Selo to check on the progress of construction and interior fittings. Hitrov, who had Olga's trust in matters of taste, often acted as an intermediary on-site until his death in 1912. In a final letter, dated August 18, 1912, he gave her his last words of advice:

> I was so pleased to receive your good long letter explaining everything you desire in relation to the palace. The first thing I find is to finish the stucco work on the palace and start on the communal areas afterward; otherwise, they will drag this work out indefinitely.[25]

23 Boulanger received 40,000 francs for this work in 1911, GARF, F. 613, op. 1, D. 92, L. 3; and 1,260,000 francs between 1912 and 1914, GARF, F. 644, op. 1, D. 326, L. 18.

24 RGIA, F. 526, op. 1, D. 217, L. 1-13, or RGIA, F. 526, op. 1, D. 219, L. 1-8.

25 GARF, F. 613, op. 1, D. 500, L. 3.

Olga validated all decisions, as evidenced by her correspondence with Boulanger. Sometimes at odds with Schmidt, the decorator deferred to the countess:

> he thinks he understands our eighteenth century but I must say that nothing resembles their beautiful proportions; so I write to him that he should make no other study of this facade because you must accept the one I am studying and for which you have given me all the indications both of the whole and of all the small details, I tell him that you are very decided and that having the great knowledge of the French style he must work only according to the studies decided and accepted by you.[26]

The same applied to the architect's planned outbuildings:

> I am sorry to disturb your rest, but yesterday I received a letter from M. Carl Schmidt that baffles me. [...] M. C. Schmidt is keen to do some station architecture; see for yourself Madame la Comtesse, it looks like a railway station's hall.[27]

The archives reflect the countess's exchanges and meetings with Boulanger, or with her suppliers, and her quest for new objets d'art to adorn the future building required a new plunge into the heart of the Paris art market. In 1912, for example, Boulanger presented the couple with models of the house and various rooms. On June 28, Olga wrote in her diary: "In the morning, we were with Paul at Boulanger's. He's preparing wonderful woodwork for us for T.[arskoye] S.[elo]."

Everything was imagined in advance. Olga listed the results of her many meetings and discussions with the decorator and Hitrov, who chose, among other things, the model for the lighting fixtures.[28] Room by room in the Boulogne mansion, she wrote up an inventory of the objects that would go to Tsarskoye Selo, indicating exactly in which room they would be placed. She then added the works of art she had spotted in the grand duke's palace in St. Petersburg, the creations Boulanger was responsible for, and ended with these notes: "We shall also have to decide on the carpets. [...] M. Boulanger will also do the fireplaces (if I can't find any old ones), the volts [*sic*], the lighting etc., etc., etc."[29]

The suppliers included some of the most renowned in the French and Parisian art industries. All the silks and furnishing textiles were carefully

26 Boulanger to Olga von Hohenfelsen (Paley), July 12, 1911, GARF, F. 613, op. 1, D. 92, L. 1.

27 Boulanger to Olga von Hohenfelsen (Paley), August 2, 1912, *ibid.*, L. 10-11.

28 Archives Delisle, invoice dated February 18, 1914. The "Empire" chandeliers in the Salon d'Honneur are said to be "Hitrov."

29 GARF, F. 613, op. 1, D. 615, L. 1-6. Notebook dated March 23/April 5, 1911.

selected, following numerous meetings and visits to the Paris workshops of Tassinari & Chatel, a firm from Lyon that had already worked for the countess in 1892 when she was still married to Pistohlkors (pl. 29).

The bronzes, chandeliers, sconces, and ceiling lights were chosen by special order from Delisle, which had also worked for the countess during the construction of the new Boulogne outbuildings. Faced with the sheer volume of these fixtures, Delisle suggested that Boulanger send at least one experienced worker to the site to supervise the unpacking and electrical installation.[30] The cost of this trip, 1,200 francs, was added to the total bill, which came to nearly 200,000 francs[31] (fig. 55).

Another 150,000 francs went to the company owned by the Hamot brothers, René and Georges[32] (75, rue de Richelieu), which delivered the carpets. Founded in the eighteenth century, Hamot specialized in the cloth trade and made a name for itself with the carpets it produced in Aubusson.[33]

Everything was designed by Boulanger to be of the highest quality, right down to the locks. These were chosen from Bricard for a total of 22,700 francs. Specialists in this field since 1782, Bricard's historic Vimeu factories had won awards at most national and international industrial exhibitions, delivering artistic locks to customers around the world, marked with the famous initials S. T., named after the company's founder Sterlin, which can still be seen on the door and window frames of many Parisian houses, Russian palaces, and the grand mansions built during the Belle Époque in Newport and along the Hudson River in the United States.

The future installation was a pretext for acquiring new works to add to the collection the couple had built up. The usual dealers and antique dealers were approached, notably Laurent-Perdreau, which supplied furniture and objets d'art for around 128,000 francs.[34] At Langweil, Olga chose jades and other masterpieces of lapidary and Far Eastern art. She also found them at Allain's. Little documented, this Parisian dealer is known to have sold eighteenth-century porcelain to the collector Count Moïse de Camondo[35] at the same time.

There were also purchases from unidentified dealers such as Mantorani and Lagrèze, and those made directly from private owners, such

30 Delisle to Marcel Boulanger, February 5, 1913, GARF, F. 613, op. 1, D. 92, L. 11-12.

31 Archives Delisle, Paris. Invoice for 191,794.05 francs sent to Grand Duke Paul on February 18, 1914.

32 GARF, F. 613, op. 1, D. 26, L. 153.

33 "Fonds de la société commerciale Hamot (Tapis, tapisseries, étoffes d'ameublement) (1846-2003): Répertoire numérique détaillé des archives écrites et figurées," compiled by Charline Revardeau, intern studying for a master's degree in history and archival professions at the University of Angers, under the supervision of Gabriel Poisson, conservateur du patrimoine, director of the Archives départementales de la Creuse, Guéret, 2012.

34 GARF, F. 644, op. 1, D. 330, L. 18.

35 Legrand 2016 30.

1

FABRIQUE DE BRONZES
Meubles et Ferronnerie d'Art
Eclairage Décoration
LES FRÈRES DELISLE
Hôtel du Président de LAMOIGNON
24, RUE PAVÉE AU MARAIS
PARIS

Paris, le 5 Février 1913

Palais de S.A.I. Monseigneur
le Grand Duc PAUL de RUSSIE
à Tsarskoe-Selo

Monsieur Boulanger Architecte Décorateur

Devis des Appareils d'éclairage.

Porche. Nitrate Mercure vrai

3 Plafonniers fer galvanisé et peint. Les glaces en opale dépolie. Pour 5 lampes.	à 450 l'un	1350	1350	
Vestibule d'honneur.				
3 Plafonniers bronze vert L XVI, à 4 montants. En opale ou cristal dépoli taillé. Pour 5 lampes	à 700 l'un	2100	2100	
Gd Hall.				
6 Appliques L XVI à 2 fortes bougies électriques décorées au bronze vert.	à 475 l'un	2850	2850	
2 Girandoles L XVI à 3 montants, 6 bougies électriques et 1 ou 2 pyramides lumineuses, garniture gouttes ou roche ou plaquettes id. pr Torchères	à 1150 ou 1300 l'un	2300	2600	
Gde Galerie.				
4 Appliques Delafosse à 3 fortes bougies électr. plaques bronzées et dorées.	à 1050 à 1200 l'un	4200	4800	
3 Vasques albâtre sculpté monture anses et chaînes bronze doré. à 8 ou 9 lampes	à 1450 ou 1550 l'un	4350	4650	
Les Girandoles indiquées au Hall sont transportées ici.				
	à reporter	17150	18350	

Fig. 55 (above and opposite) "Quotation for the lighting systems" submitted to Grand Duke Paul by Delisle, Paris, February 5, 1913. Delisle Archives, Paris.

2

Reports 17150. „ 18350 „

Vestibule circulaire.

8 Appliques LXVI à 2 fortes bougies électriques Modèle gde Wallace. A 875 A 1000 | 7000 „ | 8000 „

Cabinet de travail de Monseigneur.

2 Lustres Régence, à 5 montants, 10 bougies électriques A lampes dans la couronne. Ornements relevés au marteau Peints et dorés, garnis gde roche. A 3200 l'un | 6400 „ | 6400 „

2 Appliques de Ch. A. Boulle, à 3 bougies électriques Mascarons en contrepartie A 750 A 825 l'une | 1500 „ | 1650 „

Bibliothèque.

1 Lanterne LXVI forme cloche à 5 bougies électriques dans un bouquet de tulipes. | 650 „ | 800 „

1 Lanterneau d'accompt à 1 bougie électrique. A placer sous la coupole | 275 „ | 325 „

Boudoir.

4 Appliques LXVI miroir fleuri et amaïen. Aigle de la Reine Marie Antoinette. A 5 bougies électriques Chaînes de cristal taillé guirlandes id. A 3200 A 4000 l'une | 12800 „ | 16000 „

Escalier privé.

1 Lanterne fer peint en vert et or à la feuille. A 4 bougies électriques, cristaux taillés. | 475 „ | 475 „

au Lavatory 1 Plafonnier hublot LXVI métal repoussé | 100 „ | vitr. 100 „

1 Applique au W.C. à 1 lampe électr. Nitraté ou nickelé | 50 „ | 50 „

Salon de réception.

2 Lustres „ Dec d'Aumont „ 4 montants, 20 bougies cire mais avec fils passés en attente, cornets lumineux Coupe réflecteur au pavillon Garniture plaquettes gde ancien A 4500 ou 5200 l'un | 9000 „ | 10400 „

55400 „ 62550 „

as the six Louis XVI – period decorative panels from Baroness Alice von André (1859-1941) in 1912. Born Mary Alice Palmer, she was the wife of Baron Adolf von André (1844-1911), whose death in 1911 may well have been the reason for this sale.

It was at this time that Olga and Paul's collection was enriched by several masterpieces. On November 21, 1913, the grand duke purchased a view of Venice by Francesco Guardi from Thomas Agnew & Sons of London (45,000 francs),[36] joining his Bellotto acquired from the same dealer in 1908 (see pl. 8). Earlier in the year, in March, at the Bacri Frères gallery, established at 141, boulevard Hausmann in the early twentieth century, other important pieces were selected, including a screen and porcelain for 5,400 francs. This internationally renowned house specialized in old art. Aaron Bacri (1880-1958) was listed as an art dealer and co-partner in the family business when he was awarded the Légion d'honneur in 1925.[37] His father, Jacob Bacri (1830–?), was already known in 1880 as a dealer (1, rue de Richelieu). A curiosity dealer, Jh. Bacri, also appears in the 1862 *Almanach du commerce parisien*, at 178, rue de Rivoli. Jacques Bacri (1911-1965) took over the gallery from Aaron and his brother, whose collection was looted during the Second World War.[38] It was also at Bacri that the couple purchased a fine portrait of Empress Maria Feodorovna, based on the famous composition by Alexander Roslin in the Hermitage Museum, which still has its magnificent carved and gilded frame (pl. 30).[39]

Olga was becoming increasingly familiar with the Paris art market and wanted to know more about the objects Grand Duke Paul inherited from his mother, Empress Maria Alexandrovna, which the countess discovered during her now-authorized Russian visits. Documents relating to this inheritance mention in particular a "*Child with Dog* by Greuze,"[40] probably a work in the spirit of the *Fillette au petit chien* in the Musée Cognacq-Jay.[41] On February 25, 1914, Olga noted in her diary that she was talking to Boni de Castellane about "the painting of Paul's mother," which he considered a copy. By this time divorced from Anna Gould, the latter fancied himself an art broker. He had been seeing the countess since 1913 and became her friend and adviser.[42] His role grew all the more important as Olga's faithful mentor in matters of taste, Hitrov, had recently passed away. Boni made her appreciate the eighteenth century even more, and accompanied her on her tours: "I like

36 NGA, NGA27/1/1/10.

37 Arch. Nat. LH 19800035116l4594.

38 *Le Monde*, January 4, 2000.

39 Elsig 2012, no. 37, 128-29.

40 RGIA, F. 526, op. 1, D. 161, L. 20-22, no. 5.

41 Thérèse Burollet, *Les Peintures, les Collections du musée Cognacq-Jay* (Paris: Paris-musées, 2004), no. 45, 140-41.

42 Mension-Rigau 2016 (Kindle ed.), loc. 2705.

to see beautiful things with you, to be influenced by your sure taste, and above all I like to hear you speak," wrote Olga that year, under his charm.[43]

Determined to find out the truth about the picture, Olga presented the work to Wildenstein. Nathan Wildenstein (1851-1954), whose family is still an authority on art history, was a renowned antique dealer and painting expert. He founded his business in Paris in 1881[44] and, after a spell on rue du Faubourg Saint-Honoré, moved to 57, rue de la Boétie in 1905. The expert's verdict was unambiguous: "a copy of Greuze," reported Olga in her diary, adding that "there are some magnificent works at Wildenstein!"

Motivated by what she saw in the galleries on a daily basis, Olga multiplied her new acquisitions. A month later, on March 25, 1914, after tea at the home of the princesse de Vendôme, she had an appointment at Cartier with Boni de Castellane. From there, they moved on to Laurent-Perdreau, Guiraud, and finally Bernard. She spotted a painting by Chardin, a fortepiano signed by Taskin and dated 1788,[45] and a Chantilly porcelain vase with a polychrome porcelain bouquet of flowers.[46] She concluded the day with the words "Everything is tempting." The very next morning, she was back with the grand duke: "we bought the Chardin, and the fortepiano, and the vase!!!" (pls. 31, 32).

The Chardin, a still life with the attributes of the arts, is now in Moscow's Pushkin State Museum of Fine Arts. A work by Jean-Baptiste-Siméon Chardin was a must-have for any lover of eighteenth-century art, a century that had been revived by the Goncourt brothers. By choosing a Chardin, as they had done with Hubert Robert, the couple united in their artistic choice the general history of French art in the eighteenth century with that of Russian collecting and Francophilia at the time; the imperial collections had included several Chardin paintings since the reign of Catherine II. Another version of the attributes of the arts was in a private Russian collection and has since been transferred to the Hermitage. In Paris, the two counterparts of the attributes of the arts and sciences were the pride of the Jacquemart-André mansion.

As for the fortepiano and the Chantilly vase, both were acquired from an unfortunately poorly documented antique dealer,[47] Georges Bernard (1874 – after 1925), whose business was located at 46, rue du Faubourg Saint-Honoré and whose personal address was 1, rue d'Anjou. Pascal Taskin was a famous harpsichord maker, delivering numerous musical instruments to the Court during the reigns of Louis XV and Louis XVI. This extremely rare model was all the dearer to the countess as it was thought to have come from the Trianon at Versailles and to have belonged to Queen Marie-Antoinette.

43 *Ibid.*, loc. 2708.

44 Arch. Nat. LH 27562.

45 Paley sale, Christie's, London, June 6-7, 1929, lot 91, acquired by Weiss.

46 *Ibid.*, lot 227, acquired by Levy.

47 Arch. Nat. LH 19800035128548334.

As for the vase, it was a welcome addition to the porcelain collection, the variety of which was growing steadily during this period. Increasingly recognized for her taste in old porcelain, Olga was sought-after by Parisian dealers, as evidenced by the letter sent to her on June 25, 1913, by Édouard Wollman, based at 84, rue du Faubourg Saint-Honoré:

> Madame la comtesse, I have just bought a very beautiful piece of St. Petersburg porcelain with the mark of Empress Catherine, decorated with figures, as well as a bust in Saxon biscuit, representing Emperor Alexander I. I would be most obliged if you would drop by my home to see these objects, which I believe will be of interest to you. Please accept, Madame la comtesse, the assurance of my highest esteem.[48]

It is not known whether Olga responded favorably to this missive.

At that time, the great antique dealer Hamburger Frères was also one of the couple's suppliers.[49] The Dutch-born Hamburger family's antiques business was listed in Holland in 1896, and set up in Paris at 362, rue Saint-Honoré (near la place Vendôme) at the same time. The Hamburger siblings included ten brothers born in Utrecht between 1858 and 1879, sons of Mozes Alexandre Hamburger, born in the same city in 1836. The art dealer was highly regarded by both French and international clients. In particular, he did business with Count Moïse de Camondo,[50] Polovtsov, and several members of the imperial family. Grand Duke Alexei purchased antique furniture from his gallery in 1898,[51] while Emperor Nicholas II bought Meissen porcelain from him in 1908.[52]

The collection grew, plans progressed, the new house was completed, and the return to favor was confirmed by a new visit to Russia in early 1913.[53] *Gil Blas* added:

> The Grand Duke Paul of Russia and the Countess von Hohenfelsen, who left for St. Petersburg on January 18 for a few weeks, will supervise the installation of the beautiful palace they have just had built in Tsarskoye Selo, and whose fitting out has been entrusted to fifty workers from Paris.[54]

48 GARF, F. 613, op. 1, D. 114, L. 1. Wollman may be referring to the Meissen bisque porcelain bust of Emperor Alexander I, another version of which is at the Zoubov Foundation in Geneva.

49 GARF, F. 644, op. 1, D. 264, L. 1-2.

50 Legrand 2016, 30.

51 RGIA, F. 526, op. 1, D. 355, L. 1-13.

52 RGIA, F. 468, op. 14, D. 3197, L. 2.

53 *Le Figaro*, January 16, 1913. The grand duke and countess were accompanied by comtesse Louis de Gontaut-Biron. *Le Figaro*, January 19, 1913. See also *Le Gaulois*, January 18, 1913.

54 *Gil Blas*, January 11, 1913.

The comtesse de Chevigné gave an "intimate" dinner for her friends' departure from Paris.[55]

In St. Petersburg, then at the Tsarskoye Selo construction site, we can imagine the couple's enthusiasm as they saw their future home near completion and themselves established in a Russian milieu. The end of exile was near. Euphoria was at its peak. The forthcoming celebrations to mark the tercentenary of the Romanov dynasty galvanized spirits. The troubles of 1905-6 were forgotten. Olga was delighted and optimistic to see a brilliant life developing with the imperial family in the discreet, elegant luxury of Tsarskoye Selo. On their return to France, in order to escape the construction work that was also taking place in Boulogne, and as the couple planned to send numerous works of art and pieces of furniture to Russia to furnish their new home, Olga and Paul spent several weeks in Italy, which included a happy stopover in Nice in March 1913.

It was at this point that Olga became involved in the many productions celebrating the Russian regime's tercentenary. She offered French readers a translation of the book that Russian professor Eltchaninow had dedicated to the reign of Nicholas II and published for a popular audience via the newspaper *Selsky Vestnik*.[56] The book was sold for the benefit of the Russian Benevolent Society in Paris, and was one of a number of works – dare one say of propaganda – that had flourished in the French publishing world since the signing of the Franco-Russian Alliance. The marquis de Ségur, who wrote the preface, noted that

> the eminent translator actively serves the fruitful and solid alliance that has already been consecrated by the decisive test of time. If we are to believe the old adage *mieux connaître pour mieux aimer* [know better to love better], she is rendering an appreciable service to the two countries that, in varying degrees, have some claim on her heart: her first homeland, Russia, to which her birth and august ties bind her doubly, and her second homeland, France, to which dear memories and shared friendships also bind her.[57]

The countess's foreword is equally forthright:

> I wanted my dear friends in France to get to know more closely the beautiful and noble figure of our Sovereign, as well as his private life, his labors and the great beneficial reforms with which He has endowed Russia in recent years. Those who read this book should not

55 *Le Gaulois*, January 20, 1913.

56 Eltchaninow 1913.

57 Marquis de Ségur, preface to Eltchaninow 1913, xvi.

> be surprised by its naive and simple style; this book was written for the use of the people; it is a truly popular edition. I did not wish to change anything in the text, so as to leave it with its primitive flavor, its essentially Russian character, and above all this true expression of the feelings of loyalty and attachment that the Russian people have for their Tsar and their homeland.[58]

What a change! Ten years later, the man who had condemned her to exile found himself praised by his former victim. A return to grace. As usual, the society columns wrote of this new act in the life of Countess von Hohenfelsen.[59] The grand duke began to visit Russia more regularly. He appeared at the glittering receptions in St. Petersburg in the winter of 1914. He posed with the best society at Countess Kleinmichel's costume ball in January.[60] This sumptuous reception was even the subject of a kind of report by Henry Dupuis-Mazuel in *Le Monde illustré*:

> People are going to extraordinary lengths to procure an invitation; the countess has already fallen out with three-quarters of Petersburg, as she cannot invite more than three hundred people.[61]

Countess Kleinmichel even states in her memoirs that this ball, to which she devotes a chapter, "became a social event through the impact it had."[62] Held in honor of her nieces, it was organized with the help of Alexander Polovtsov. In addition to Grand Duke Paul, the guests included Countess Marianna von Zarnekau (Zarnikov), Olga's youngest daughter by her first husband.

In June 1914, *Les Modes* announced the upheaval in Parisian social life caused by the couple's move to Russia for several months a year. But, says the paper:

> The Grand Duke and Countess von Hohenfelsen are still in their beautiful mansion in the Parc des Princes, and to their many friends, who were eager to pay their respects on Orthodox Easter Day, they have expressed their formal intention of coming to France every year, mainly in autumn. It is not without sadness that we see them revert from settled Parisians to august travelers, visiting the capital – as princes and foreigners of distinction are wont to do – but not staying for long. During their more than ten years of residence here,

58 Countess von Hohenfelsen, foreword to Eltchaninow 1913, v-vi.

59 *Le Petit Parisien*, June 20, 1913.

60 *Stolitsa i Usadba*, no. 4 (February 15, 1914): 21.

61 *Le Monde illustré*, April 18, 1914.

62 Kleinmichel 1927, 140.

> they had created an atmosphere of warmth and friendship around them, the memory of which will not soon fade. When they left, it was a resounding demonstration of these feelings.[63]

Indeed, as early as October 4, 1913, preparations were underway for the move. Marcel Boulanger had announced to Colonel Nicholas Petrokov (1872–?), at the grand duke's base in St. Petersburg, the dispatch from Boulogne of a first "padded train car," an expensive but safe means of transport for the objects, organized by Mory. The delivery of twenty-four crates was insured for a value of around 400,000 francs. It contained the Boulogne works of art, including four crates from Langweil with screens, carpets, and porcelain. The bronzes were part of the second consignment of thirty-six crates. Next came marbles, chandeliers, and decorative bronzes by Delisle, silks by Tassinari, and rugs by Hamot. The thirteenth and final car was shipped on April 7, 1914.[64] Marcel Boulanger, who had traveled to Tsarskoye Selo in the spring of 1914 to supervise the installation, had four final crates sent from France between July 11 and 18, 1914,[65] after the couple had already left Paris (in May) and moved into their new residence. *Le Gaulois* devoted a column in its "Mondanités" section to this sad move, entitled "The departure of the Grand Duke Paul of Russia and of the Countess von Hohenfelsen":

> This afternoon will see the departure of our beloved guests of more than ten years, H.I.H. the Grand Duke Paul of Russia and his charming wife the Countess von Hohenfelsen. After a long stay, during which they sowed friendship and won affection, the Grand Duke and Countess von Hohenfelsen are returning to Russia; from now on, they will live most of the year in their new palace at Peterhof [*sic*], but they will keep their pretty home in the Parc des Princes, and, to their many friends, whose deep and sincere regret they deeply cherish, they have promised to come and spend a few weeks with them each year. This point is undoubtedly a mitigation to the real disappointment caused by the definitive announcement of a departure that we would have liked to have seen set forward. […] For Grand Duke Paul, apart from his annual trips to Russia, Boulogne-sur-Seine was his main place of residence, where he had brought his household goods and family memories, and where the last children of his second marriage were born. In this charming home at the edge of the woods, adorned with objets d'art and surrounded by greenery, he enjoyed entertaining a group of friends that grew larger every day. Those whom the grand

63 *Les Modes*, no. 162 (June 1914): 5.

64 GARF, F. 613, op. 1, D. 92, L. 25-67.

65 GARF, F. 644, op. 1, D. 275, L. 1 and 2.

> duke and Countess von Hohenfelsen received in their first house on l'avenue d'Iéna remained faithful; others came as our hosts, much sought-after and much invited in Parisian society, extended the circle of their relations. Every week, the grand duke and his wife gave very exclusive dinners, sometimes followed by excellent music, especially when Russian singers were in Paris. On Sundays, the Countess von Hohenfelsen often entertained, from four to six o'clock. We all know the charm of her warm welcome and kind spirit, and the infinite appeal of her person. Their frequent guests included the prince and princesse Murat, princesse Louis Murat, the comtesse de Talleyrand-Périgord, the late and much-lamented comtesse Edmond de Pourtalès, the marquise de Jaucourt, Princess Baryatinsky, all the members of the Russian Embassy, the comte and comtesse d'Haussonville, the comtesse R. de Fitz-James, the marquis and marquise de Ganay, the vicomte and vicomtesse Vigier, Mrs. Moore, the comtesse Adh. de Chevigné, the comte and comtesse Arthur de Vogüé, the comte and comtesse A. Pastré, comte and comtesse Ch. de Vogüé, the comtesse de Guerne, née Ségur, M. and Mme de Reszke, the marquis de Laborde, the comte de Gabriac, M. de Navenne, M. Reynaldo Hahn, and many others from Russian and French high society. It was a charming center of elegance. Here was a whole elite saddened and expressing aloud their regrets for a separation that seemed cruel. "We shall be back every year," the Countess von Hohenfelsen told her close friends the day before yesterday… And everyone firmly believes and hopes so.[66]

Thus ended the Parisian life of Countess von Hohenfelsen, whose new palace in Russia became a reflection of the French culture assimilated during her long stay.

66 *Le Gaulois*, May 9, 1914.

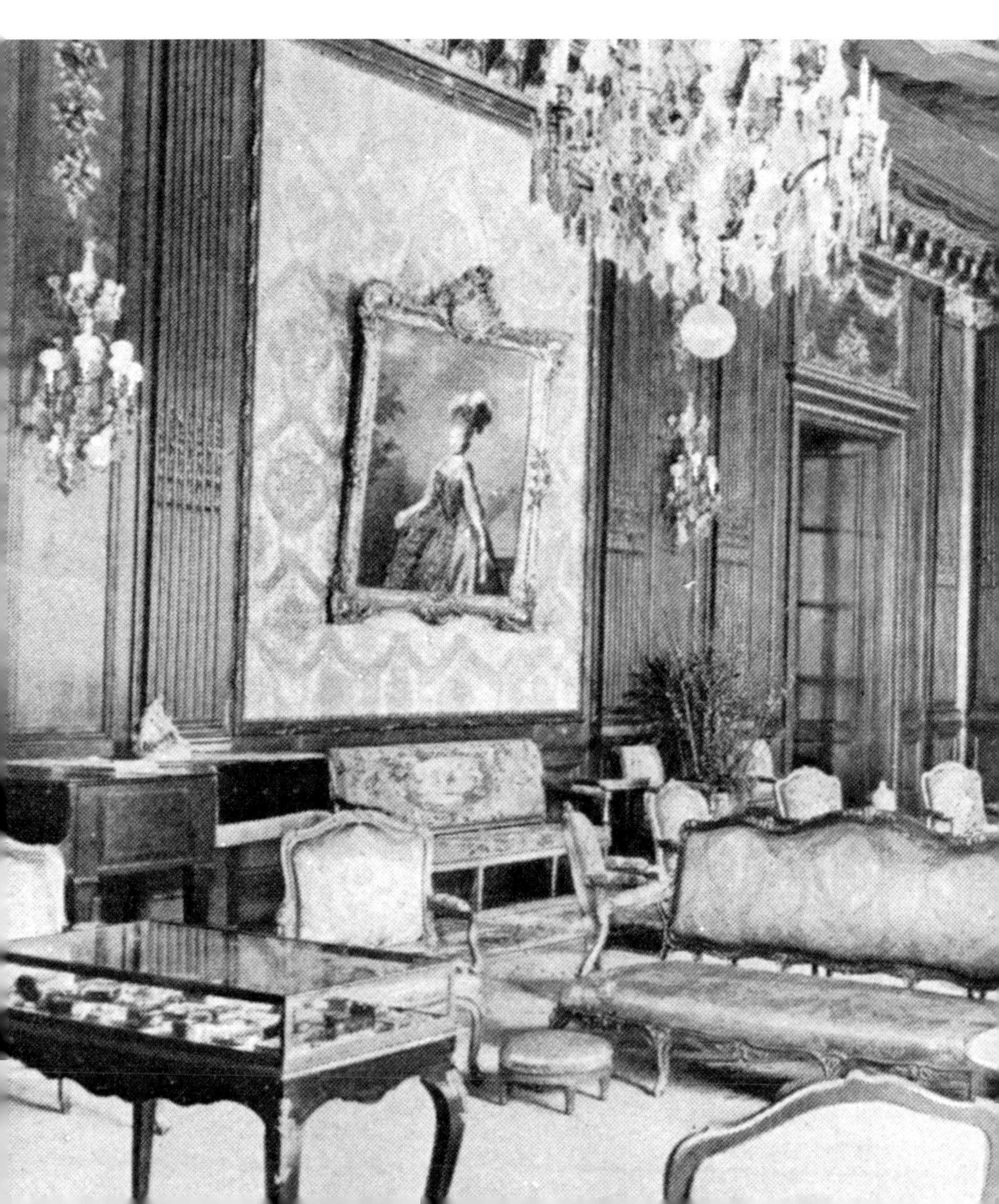

THE PALEY PALACE AT TSARSKOYE SELO: A PARISIAN PALACE IN THE HEART OF RUSSIA

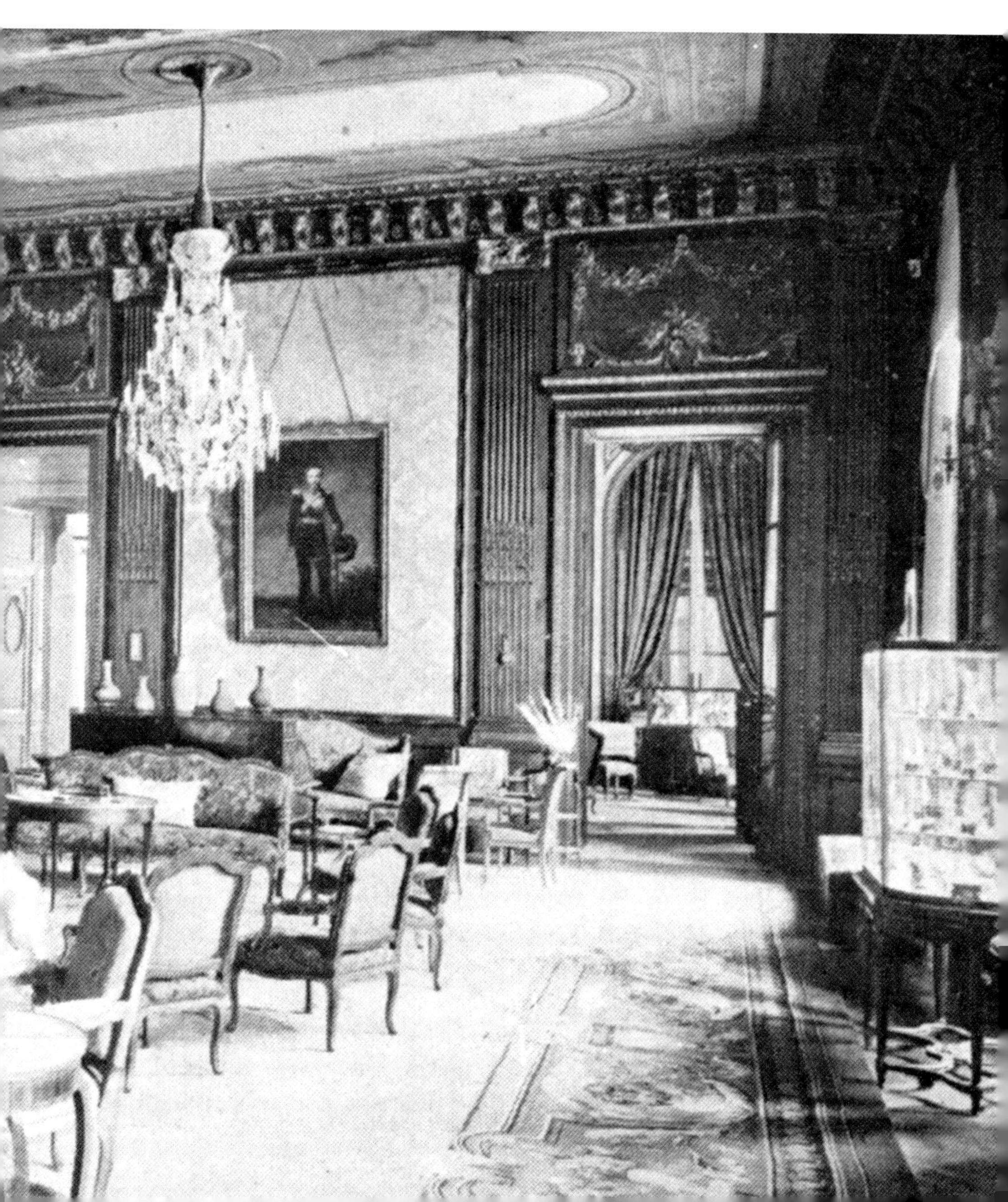

My father and stepmother were nearby in their new home and perfectly happy, especially my father, to be back in Russia. [...] My stepmother was renewing old friendships and making new ones. The Court was celebrating the visit of M. Poincaré, President of the French Republic.

Grand Duchess Maria Pavlovna of Russia

Raymond Poincaré visited Russia from July 13 to 23, 1914, for the summit meeting of the Franco-Russian Alliance, which was celebrating its silver anniversary at a time when the threat of war was growing in Europe. The grand duke took part in the festivities.[1] For the time being, there was no sign of future events just around the corner, and the couple settled into their new home in Tsarskoye Selo. Served by the railroad and located just a few kilometers from St. Petersburg, the fashionable resort was a sort of immense park with villas and country houses built around the imperial residence, comprising two immense palaces – the Catherine Palace and the Alexander Palace – their outbuildings (administration, theaters, pavilions, farms, churches, chapels, garrisons), and their perfectly manicured parks.

Behind a wrought-iron gate embellished with the grand duke's gilded monogram stood the two-story main building of the Paley Palace. It was reputed to have been built without a single Russian nail[2] (fig. 56).

The house, with its stone facade, was reminiscent of Parisian architecture conceived in the taste of Gabriel's early Neoclassicism. It was marked by a central pavilion and extended by two wings on either side, surmounted behind a balustrade by a mansard roof pierced by dormer windows. This style contrasted with that of the surrounding residences and palaces. Some had been designed in the ostentatious luxury of the Baroque, whether as original expressions, such as Rastrelli's Hermitage Pavilion in the nearby Imperial Park, or nineteenth-century revivals, like the nearby Yusupov villa. There were also numerous classical residences with white pediments and colonnades set against colorful walls, of which the nearby palace of Grand Duchess Vladimir was a fine expression. In addition, here were wooden villas with finely carved facades, luxurious interpretations of the traditional Russian dacha.

For the design of the gardens, Marcel Boulanger had considered the inevitable Achille Duchêne (1866-1947). After visiting the site in September 1913, the decorator had approached the famous gardener in Brussels. Achille and his father Henri Duchêne (1841-1902),[3] considered the restorers of the manner of Le Nôtre and of the French garden, disseminated the style throughout the world. In October, Duchêne accepted the proposal, as the work could be carried out by Russian workers under the direction of

1 Chambrun 1941, 2.

2 Gollerbakh ca. 1922, 9.

3 Arch. Nat. LH 19800035/740/84018.

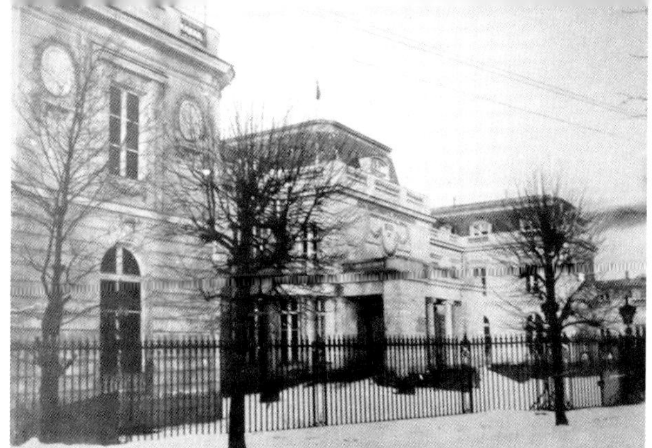

Fig. 56 Facade of the palace of Countess von Hohenfelsen and Grand Duke Paul, Tsarskoye Selo, ca. 1918. Period photograph.

one of his employees.[4] The war seems to have prevented final completion.[5] Indeed, in July 1914, Olga consulted Boni de Castellane on the subject, asking him to sketch a French garden.[6]

The facade of the house was animated on the first floor by lines, while on the upper floor, it was punctuated by large medallions with laurel tori over a corbel. The entrance was under a heavy porch with Ionic columns, topped on the noble facade by a carved table decorated with garlands. The decorative sculpture, as well as the main marble work, had been entrusted to the contractor N. A. Popov of St. Petersburg.[7]

The ground floor housed the reception apartments, while the first floor was reserved for private quarters and the attic for service accommodations, while the apartment of Colonel Petrokov, in charge of the grand duke's administration since 1911, was located in the right wing. This was connected to the outbuildings, a long building with a porch in its center. The house and its interior were a perfect example of Parisian architecture, taste, and collecting, or at least that of the cosmopolitan elite of the Belle Époque. As Marcel Boulanger pointed out, it was all about striving for perfection, sometimes beyond authenticity, as the know-how and models of the past were perfectly mastered by the Parisian art industries:

> You must understand, Madame la Comtesse, that I have a great responsibility for taste, and that I can only make progress on the basis of very careful work. We are making something new, so there is nothing to stop us from making it absolutely perfect.[8]

This could be a definition of Belle Époque decorating.

4 Boulanger to Olga von Hohenfelsen (Paley), October 20, 1913, GARF, F. 613, op. 1, D. 92, L. 32-33.

5 Boulanger to Olga von Hohenfelsen (Paley), July 22, 1914, *ibid.*, L. 97.

6 Mension-Rigau 2016 (Kindle ed.), loc. 2730.

7 GARF, F. 644, op. 1, D. 329, L. 1-40.

8 GARF, F. 613, op. 1, D. 92, L. 1, Correspondance Boulanger. Letter dated July 12, 1911.

Like the Camondo mansion,[9] built in the same years, Olga's new residence combined all the elements of modern comfort and technology with a decor that paid homage to French styles, illustrated by original old works as well as copies from models of the past. The concrete structure of the palace was built in 1911, to Schmidt's design, by Lorentsen & Co. of St. Petersburg.[10] In the same year, plumbing and heating work was carried out by C. Siegel, which was based in the same city.[11] The palace had a garage for the family's two automobiles, naphtha central heating, its own generator, telephone, vacuum suction system, elevator, and several bathrooms and shower rooms distributed throughout the house. Bathtubs and sanitaryware were chosen by Boulanger from Bamberger, Leroi & Co. in Frankfurt am Main,[12] known for its work on luxury liners during the same period. The kitchens were particularly well appointed, with cookware valued at over 10,000 rubles.[13]

A great deal of attention had been paid to the fluid and appropriate circulation of personnel between the various spaces and floors of the palace,[14] which had been designed to operate with sixty-four servants in impeccable liveries and uniforms.[15]

In a letter to Boni de Castellane dated May 20, 1914, the countess confided that all this work and all these decisions largely involved her:

> If you could see me at work from eight o'clock in the morning until dinnertime, you'd feel sorry for how tired and edgy I am. The odious thing we call "fine-tuning" appears in all its horror. Electricity, telephone, elevator, all sorts of little details need to be sorted out. Finally, after ten days, I start doing what I like best: putting the furniture in place and the knickknacks in the display cases. I think you'd be happy with me in this respect, but how much I have benefited from your lessons! How much I miss you and how often, for all things, I think of you.[16]

Eager to create an ideal work of art in the manner of a Moïse de Camondo in Paris, Boulanger was exacting about the interior decoration he planned with

9 Bertrand Rondot, "Entre plaisir et dévotion : Collectionner le XVIIIe siècle chez les Camondo," in Hoog 2009, 84. See also Gary 2007.

10 GARF, F. 644, op. 1, D. 327, L. 1-32. On the Russian contractors working on the site, see also RGIA, F. 526, op. 1, D. 217 and 219.

11 GARF, F. 644, op. 1, D. 328, L. 1-103.

12 GARF, F. 644, op. 1, D. 273, L. 1.

13 Paley 1923, 139.

14 GARF, F. 613, op. 1, D. 92, L. 9-11.

15 Paley 1923, 155.

16 Mension-Rigau 2016 (Kindle ed.), loc. 2723.

the countess's approval. In his topographical description of the decor in 1913 and 1914,[17] we can see how each space became a sort of period room, from the eighteenth century to the Empire. Boulanger's new decorations were "based on period documents," whether for ceilings, voussoirs, woodwork, or marble fireplaces. In the case of the reception room, characterized by its carved oak paneling "in the style of an old period document," he even seems to have used "old wood." The gilding is "done as in the period, that is, with water and color and with an antique-style patina," while the bronzes on the mantels were gilded with mercury. So copying was not only a stylistic activity but also a technical one. All suppliers complied with the same requirements.[18] Some of Delisle's bronzes and lighting fixtures refer to models from prestigious collections or famous artisans, and are described as "Wallace style," "duc d'Aumont style," and "Double collection style" for the chandeliers in the oak salon and dining room, or as "Delafosse" and "A.C. Boulle."[19]

From the moment a visitor entered, one was immersed in the atmosphere of a Parisian mansion, with a double layout between courtyard and garden. One passed through "a large double wrought-iron door with hammered copper ornaments in the old style," and in the space revealed, the oak doors featured "Versailles molding profiles." In each room, with a few exceptions, the furniture was by Boulanger, the bronzes by Delisle (pls. 33-36), the silks by Tassinari (pls. 37-40), and the carpets by Hamot, all enhanced by the collection of the countess and the grand duke.

The Louis XVI – style vestibule, with its stone stucco walls decorated with "large motifs of attributes, representing lion skin, shield motifs, capitals, rosettes, cornice decoration, all carved in stucco," opened onto the grand staircase with its "antique-style" banister, which extended to the right (fig. 57). A door beneath the staircase led to two small rooms: the Chinese salon and the everyday dining room. There was also direct access to the large reception room on the same axis, or to the gallery on the left. In the vestibule, embellished with green plants to give it a very 1900 touch, there were the first antique elements of the collection: a series of six columns "Corinthian style, rouge de Rance marble capitals, wood and Carrara marble, said columns sculpted on 4 faces, antique details," invoiced by Boulanger at 14,000 francs, for which he spent a further 1,620 francs in repair costs. The use of antique columns as ornamentation to structure reception areas was relatively common in high-class interiors of this period.

The first significant items in the collection were displayed in the gallery (fig. 58). Designed as a stylistic extension of the vestibule, it featured

17 GARF, F. 613, op. 1, D. 614, L. 193-206, 207-20. See also F. 644, op. 1, D. 347, L. 1-15.

18 On the palace's interior fittings, see Gollerbakh ca. 1922; Bott 2013b, 37-49; and Iraida Bott, "'Our Wonderful… Our Beloved Home': The Paley Palace at Tsarskoye Selo," in Bott 2013a, 19-26.

19 AD, invoice, February 18, 1914.

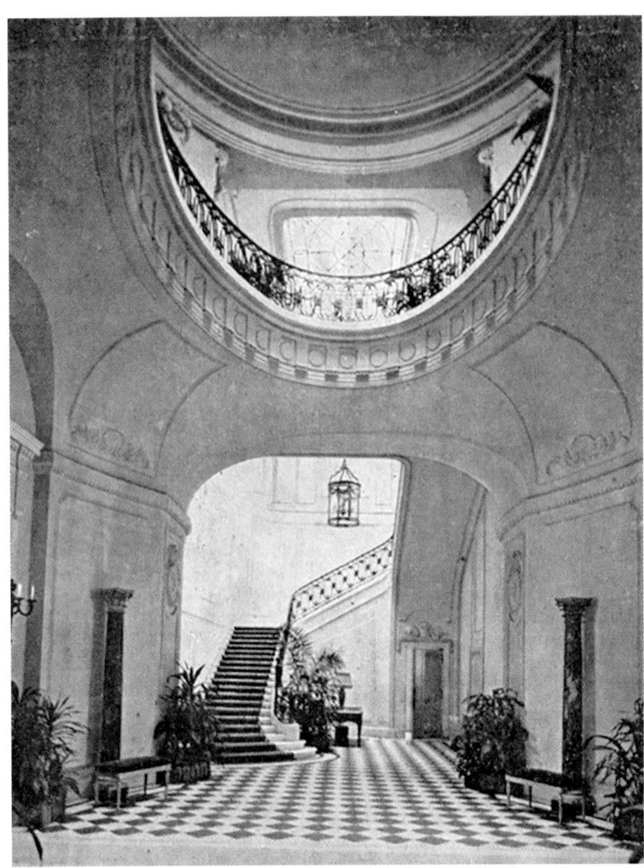

Fig. 57 (opposite) Vestibule, palace of Countess von Hohenfelsen and Grand Duke Paul, Tsarskoye Selo, ca. 1918. Hillwood Estate, Museum & Gardens, Archives and Special Collections, Washington, DC.

Fig. 58 (below) Gallery, palace of Countess von Hohenfelsen and Grand Duke Paul, Tsarskoye Selo, ca. 1918. Hillwood Estate, Museum & Gardens, Archives and Special Collections, Washington, DC.

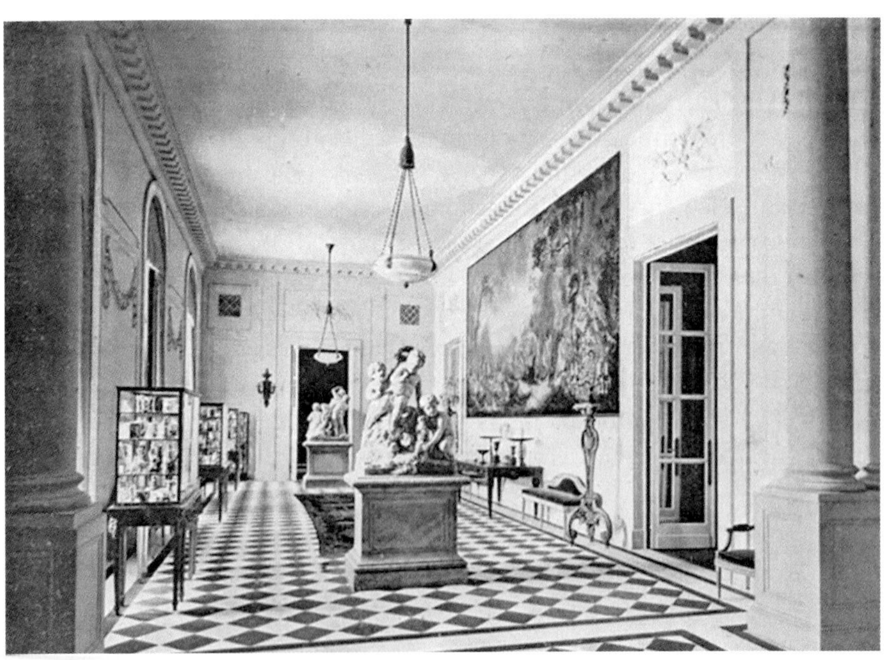

the eighteenth-century Brussels tapestry from Boulogne. Two monumental sculpted groups of children playing, evocative of garden art, were placed in the center.[20] This original choice of presentation was a success that Olga enthusiastically shared with Boni de Castellane in June 1914.[21] Beneath the tapestry, on a table, were decorative objects in lapis lazuli.[22] Alongside the windows, Boulanger had placed three tables to hold the display cases sent from France, to which were added two other bronze models copied from those in Boulogne. These displayed part of the countess's porcelain collections, each organized according to a special theme. The first showcase housed Chinese porcelain dating from the late sixteenth to the nineteenth century, including several mounted in French gilt bronze.[23] In the second showcase, mainly devoted to Chinese crazed pottery, the oldest piece dated from the fifteenth century.[24] The third showcase was devoted to celadons; the fourth to Western and Russian porcelain, with a particular focus on pieces from Vienna, Gardner, and Meissen; and the fifth exclusively to Meissen.[25]

This was followed by a rotunda, a passageway leading from one side to the other of the rooms in the wing, including the grand duke's "grand study" overlooking the courtyard and, on the other side, the library and the countess's study. The tapestry portrait of Empress Catherine I[26] probably hung in line with these, above a large gondola sofa by Boulanger (pl. 41). In the center of the room, Boulanger had placed a round table of his work, "all in fantasy pink satin violet wood, adorned with bronze," supporting a display case housing part of the ornamental and fine stone collections arranged on four shelves. It brought together some eighty works, including some from workshops in the Urals, fashioned in various marbles or jasper, sardonyx, amethyst, topaz, nephrite, and rock crystal: a menagerie of hares, frogs, elephants, roosters, birds, crocodiles, dogs, bears, and other multicolored and precious animals and objects.[27]

In the grand duke's study, which paid tribute to the reign of Louis XV "after period documents," the furniture designed by Boulanger included "two large bergères known as from Les Arts décoratifs,"[28] a model that was dear

20 Paley sale, Christie's, London, June 6-7, 1929, lot 155.

21 Mension-Rigau 2016 (Kindle ed.), loc. 2723. Letter dated June 12, 1914.

22 Paley sale, Christie's, London, June 6-7, 1929, lots 68-70.

23 TsGALI, F. 254, op. 1, D. 5, L. 13; Paley sale, Christie's, London, July 1st-2, 1929, lots 111-173.

24 *Ibid.*, L. 14.

25 Paley sale, Christie's, London, June 6-7, 1929, lots 157-227.

26 *Ibid.*, no. 151.

27 TsGALI, F. 254, op. 1, D. 1, L. 5; Paley sale, Christie's, July 1st-2, 1929, lots 222-234. As early as 1904, the countess is mentioned in the Cartier archives for the purchase of a carnelian hen; in 1911, the grand duke acquired a red rose in aventurine and red jasper. See Habsburg 2003, 447.

28 The model is a bergère "à oreilles," inv. 5408, which has been in the museum since 1890; equally famous is the armchair, inv. 5033, which entered the collections in 1888.

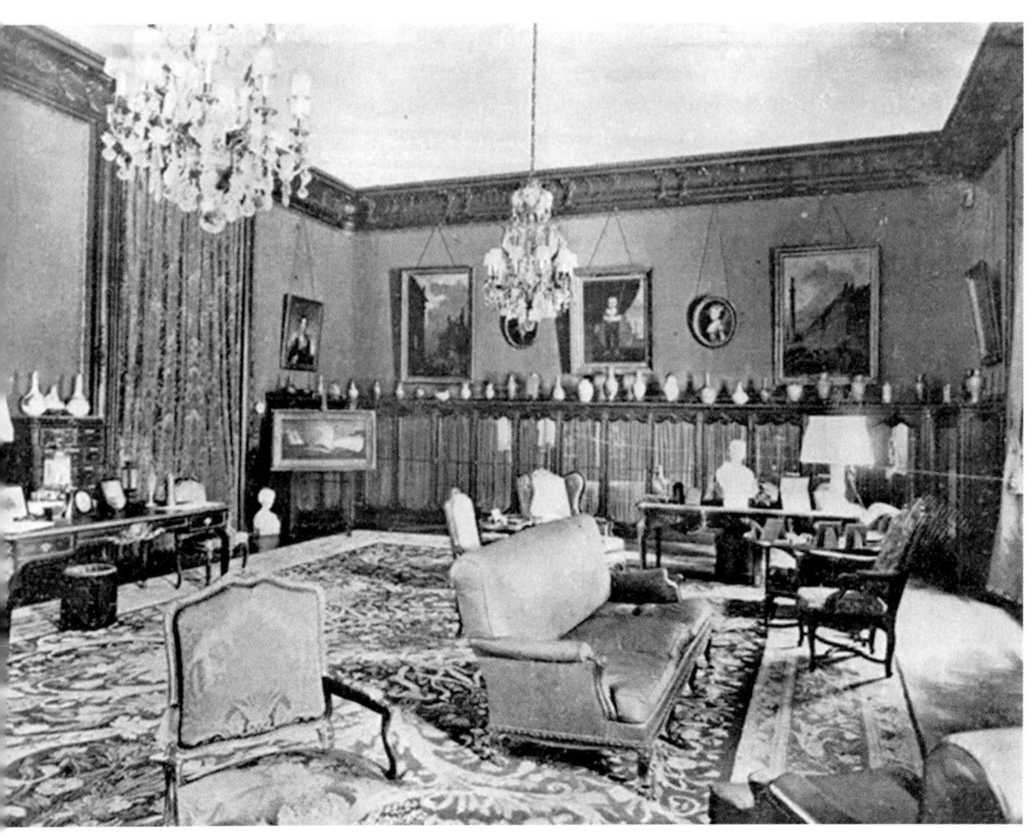

Fig. 59 Grand Duke Paul Alexandrovich's study, palace of Countess von Hohenfelsen and Grand Duke Paul, Tsarskoye Selo, ca. 1918. Hillwood Estate, Museum & Gardens, Archives and Special Collections, Washington, DC.

to the grand duke since he had chosen one from *L'Escalier de Cristal*, which remained in Boulogne and was sold in 1923[29] (fig. 59). The antique furniture, probably of Russian origin, dated from the reigns of Empress Elizabeth and Empress Catherine II, and they included an armchair and four small tables set on a comfortable carpet. Numerous Chinese porcelain vases were displayed on the low bookcases along the wall. This was one of the few rooms where contemporary art had found a place, illustrated by Henri Leys's *The Guild of the Archers Welcomes Margaret of Austria*, probably a youthful acquisition of the grand duke (pl. 42), and the portrait of his wife by Dagnan-Bouveret (see pl. 11). Other works on display included the two large landscapes by Hubert Robert that had adorned the grand duke's study in Boulogne (see pls. 15, 16), the Chardin placed on an easel (see pl. 31), and several Russian portraits (fig. 60), including those of Catherine II and Alexander I (see pl. 7,

29 Paley sale, Paris, December 5, 1923, lot 75.

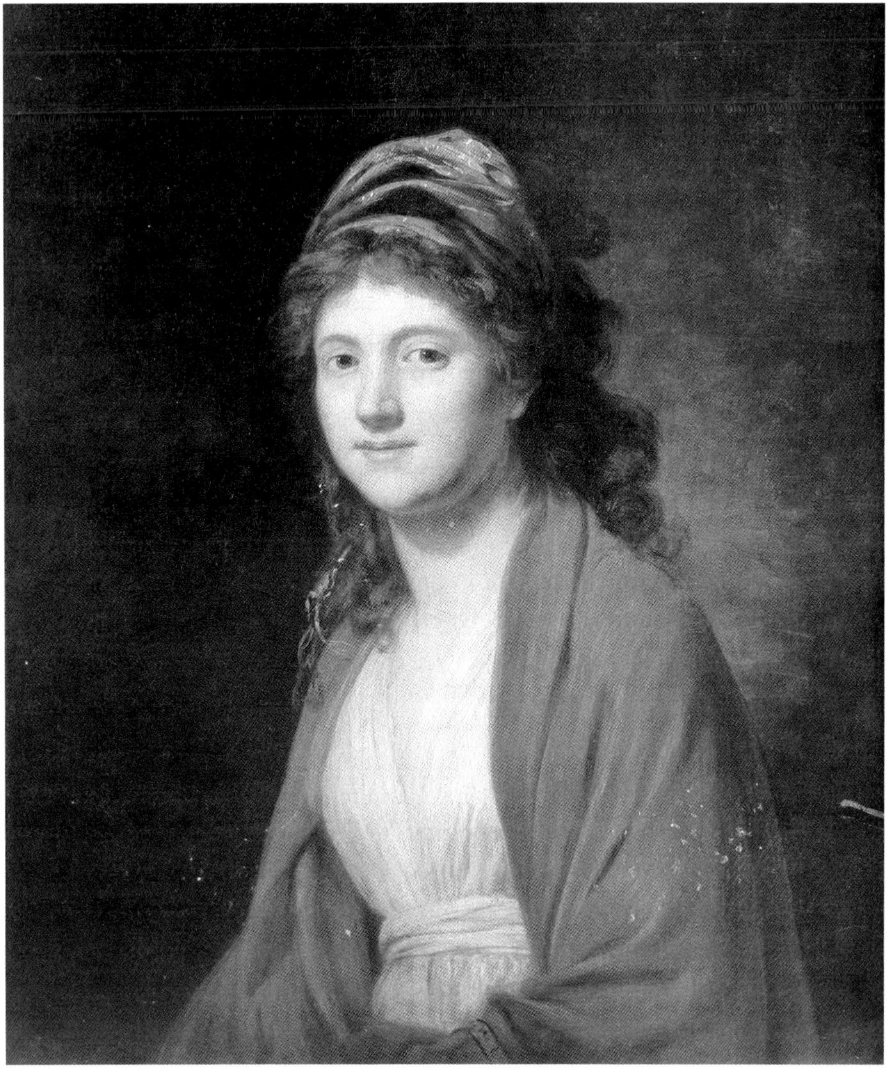

Fig. 60 Martin-Ferdinand Quadal. *Portrait of Princess Lobanov-Rostovsky*, 1798. Oil on canvas. Current location unknown. Frick Art Reference Library, New York.

fig. 22), as well as the George Dawe depicting Alexander II as a child in 1820 (see pl. 14) and the portrait of the same by Franz Krüger (pl. 43). After the outbreak of the Bolshevik Revolution, the palace was subjected to regular searches, and Olga recalls the mood when a troop came to rummage through the grand duke's study:

> My husband was sitting in his green leather armchair, in his usual place, reading. He had the strength of character to continue reading without taking his eyes off the newspaper. And yet, fifteen armed

> men were there, coming and going, opening his bookcase, lifting his books, talking, laughing.[30]

This and the following rooms, including the library stacked with shelves, housed several thousand volumes in Russian and foreign languages. This was one of the palace's other treasures, the fruit of the grand duke's love of books, with a rare collection dedicated to theater and music.

With its carved woodwork "based on documents of the period and treated in the antique style," the countess's study was designed after models of Henri Salembier (figs. 61, 62). Here too, only a few of the furnishings were antique, including a few lacquers, a coromandel screen, and the collection's centerpiece: the Taskin fortepiano discovered in Paris with Boni de Castellane (fig. 63; see pl. 32). Olga, delighted with the installation, told him she had no doubt that "the piano, with the Chantilly vase on top, will make all the women swoon."[31] Among the models that inspired the creation of the stylish furniture in this room are the cartonnier bureau with "Gouthière-style" bronzes and, above all, the armchair, which was a copy of the famous leather-upholstered wooden model sold with Jacques Doucet's collection in 1912, now in the Musée Nissim de Camondo.[32] This example shows once again the impact this sale had in spreading taste for the French eighteenth century.

In addition to Dagnan-Bouveret's portrait of the grand duke, the display reflected the countess's taste for old art, particularly portraits. These included the third Hubert Robert (*Bridge with Washerwomen*) (see pl. 10), the Guardi, the Lawrence, the Perronneau (see pl. 9), the Nattier (see fig. 18), the Boucher, the van Dyck (see pl. 19), and a group of miniatures depicting Russian sovereigns from Catherine II to Alexander I. Porcelains from Meissen, Nymphenburg, and Chelsea were positioned in display cabinets in front of the windows. Among these were the rare and precious perfume bottles that Olga had been collecting for years. The collection included over a hundred different models, evoking eighteenth-century toiletry practices and the refinement of the accessories of this period.[33] Made of porcelain, often mounted in gold, they came mainly from the Chelsea or Dresden manufactories. Chelsea, one of England's major porcelain factories, was renowned for its bone china figurines inspired by Continental models, notably from the famous Saxony factory. The few flasks known to come from the Hohenfelsen collection bear witness to production of this type, which, above and beyond their quality, illustrate the sense of whimsy and taste for festivities, music, and pastorals of

30 Paley 1923, 145.

31 Mension-Rigau 2016 (Kindle ed.), loc. 2730. Letter dated June 12, 1914.

32 Inv. 136. Doucet sale, Paris, June 5-8, 1912, no. 291.

33 AGE, F. I, op. 5, D. 89 (1919), L. 3; Paley sale, Christie's, London, July 1st-2, 1929, lots 1-53, 63-80.

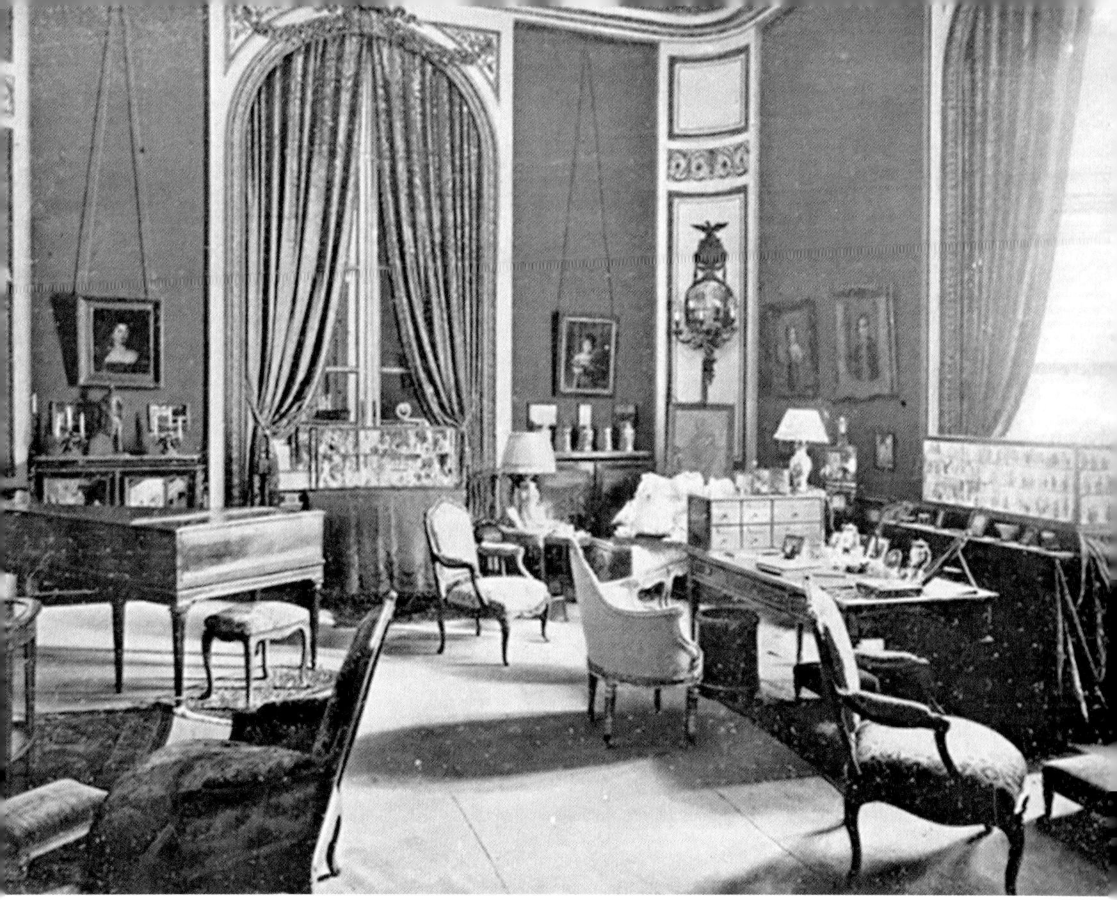

Fig. 61 (above) Small study, palace of Countess von Hohenfelsen and Grand Duke Paul, Tsarskoye Selo, ca. 1918. Hillwood Estate, Museum & Gardens, Archives and Special Collections, Washington, DC.

Fig. 62 (below) Bronze decorative pieces from the small study, palace of Countess von Hohenfelsen and Grand Duke Paul, Tsarskoye Selo. Current location unknown. Hillwood Estate, Museum & Gardens, Archives and Special Collections, Washington, DC.

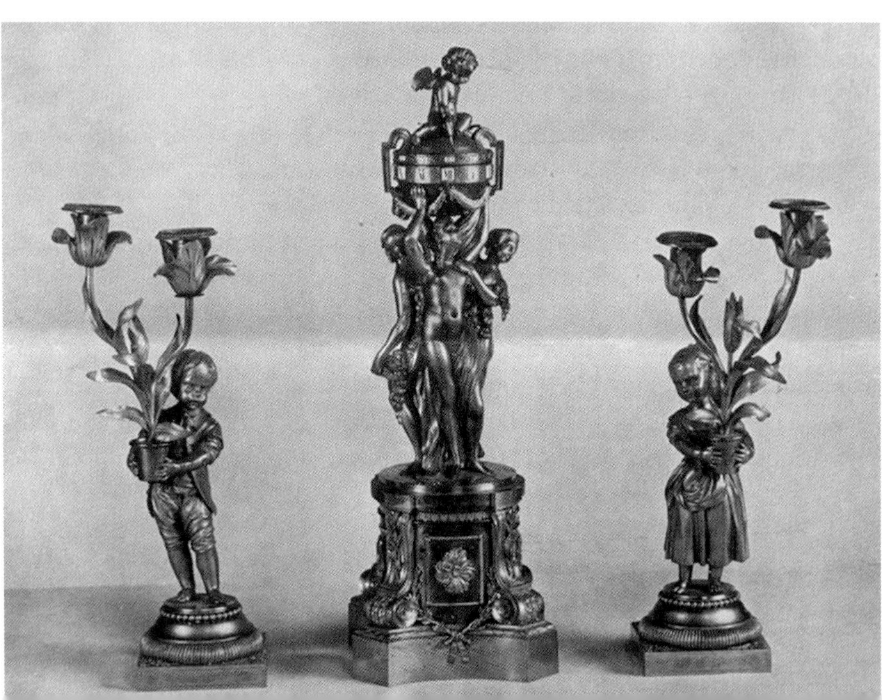

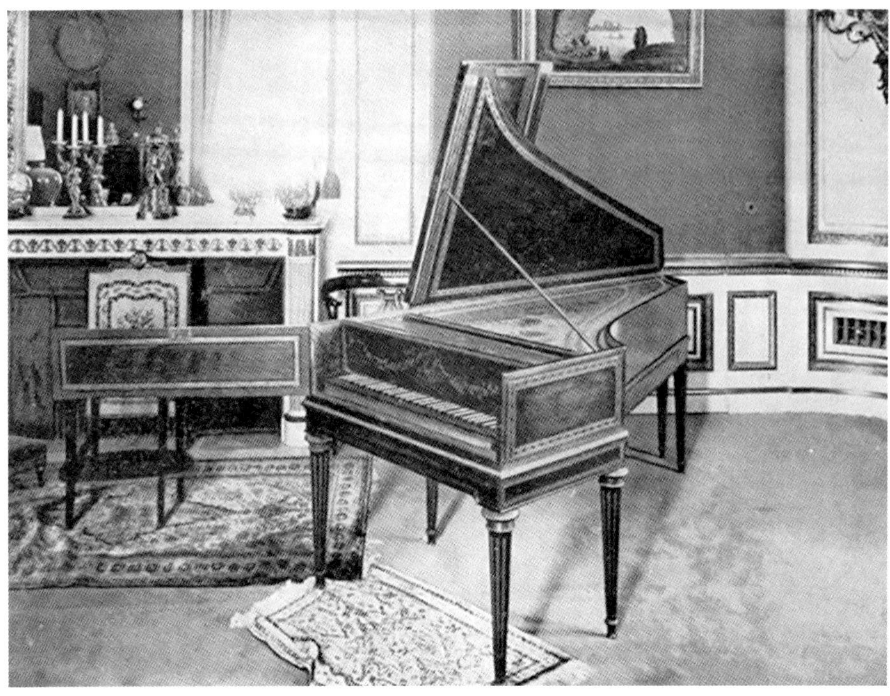

Fig. 63 Small study, palace of Countess von Hohenfelsen and Grand Duke Paul, Tsarskoye Selo (fortepiano by Taskin), ca. 1918. Hillwood Estate, Museum & Gardens, Archives and Special Collections, Washington, DC.

the gallant society of the mid-eighteenth century and those who admired and collected it in the Belle Époque. These flasks take the form of an abbot (pl. 44), a Harlequin getting drunk (pl. 45), a young couple writing in a flowery garden (pl. 46), a couple playing flute and guitar, a lute player, a hurdy-gurdy player (pl. 47), a masked child tapping a tambourine (pl. 48), a dovecote (pl. 49), a group of four hens (pl. 50), a golden-stemmed pear with a Watteau landscape (pl. 51) and a fish caught in a net.

This study is probably the room Olga describes as the "pink salon," where the grand duke used to read in the evenings and where she had "gathered together all the objects she loved."[34]

The row overlooking the garden continued through the main ceremonial rooms, starting with the oak salon, whose woodwork was inspired by models by the ornamentalist Jean-Charles Delafosse (fig. 64). The ceiling was formed of a large, five-part antique canvas depicting an allegory *di sotto in su*, which had been enlarged by a wide foliate frame.

The furniture, comprising several series of seats, was for the most part antique (see figs. 8, 17, 24) and had been completed and restored by

34 Paley 1923, 120.

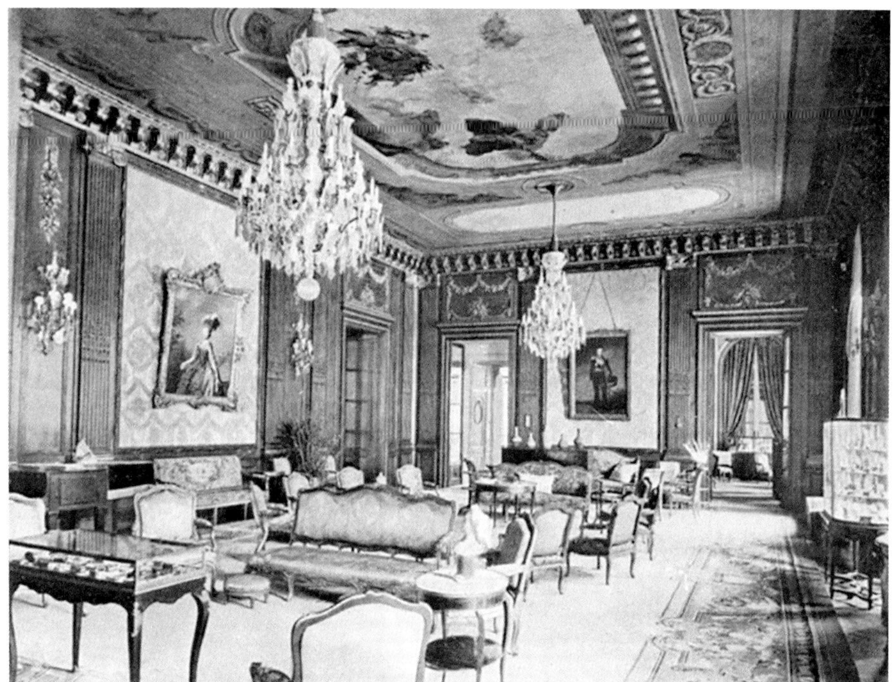

Fig. 64 Oak salon, palace of Countess von Hohenfelsen and Grand Duke Paul, Tsarskoye Selo, ca. 1918. Hillwood Estate, Museum & Gardens, Archives and Special Collections, Washington, DC.

Boulanger. All the gilding work for this salon, carried out using antique techniques, had been invoiced at 30,000 francs out of the estimated 150,000 francs for this room. Several canvases enhanced this highly accomplished decor, including the portrait of Empress Maria Feodorovna after Roslin (see pl. 30) and one of Emperor Alexander II by Dawe (pl. 53). Chinese porcelain was scattered around the room, while the display cabinets contained Chinese jades and gems, mostly from Langweil in Paris.[35] During a visit by revolutionaries in search of bottles of alcohol in December 1917, Olga mentioned this aspect of the collections that was dear to her:

> They found nothing in the large crimson drawing room with its antique woodwork. They stopped, curious, in front of the display case of Chinese jades, asking what it was. I had to do the honors again.[36]

The progression in the pomp and splendor of the rooms was also reflected in the stylistic choices of each space, with the two main reception rooms paying homage to the most accomplished expressions of Neoclassicism at the time

35 Paley sale, June 6-7, 1929, lots 243-294.

36 Paley 1923, 144.

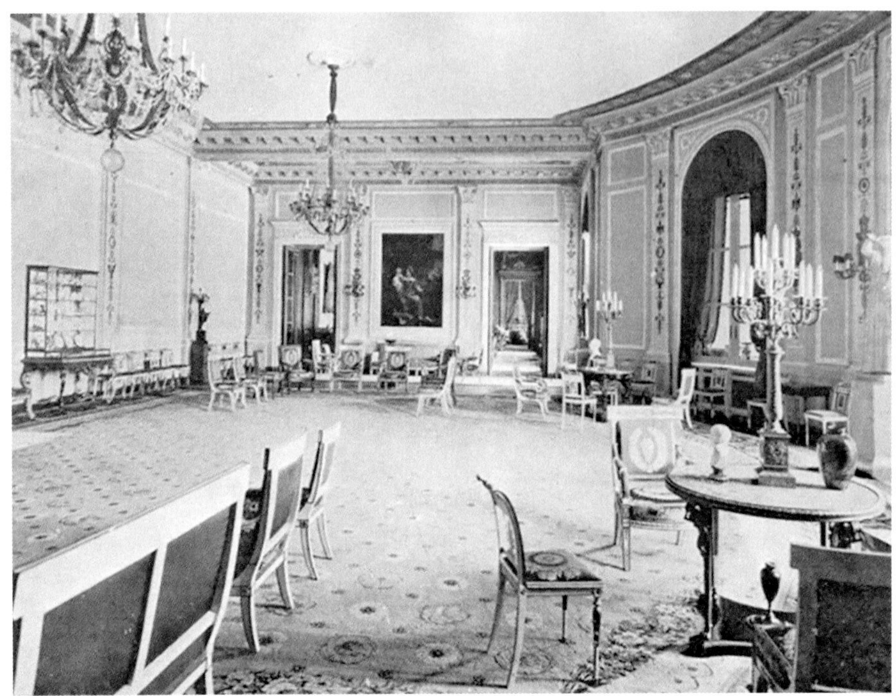

Fig. 65 Great hall, palace of Countess von Hohenfelsen and Grand Duke Paul, Tsarskoye Selo, ca. 1918. Hillwood Estate, Museum & Gardens, Archives and Special Collections, Washington, DC.

of the Directoire, Consulate, and Empire. They were a further demonstration of the success of neo-empire at the heart of the imperial family under the last Romanov.

During the same inspection that Olga recounts, in the "*Grand salon d'honneur*, Empire style,"[37] the "muddy boots" of the revolutionaries "were sinking into the beautiful cream carpet with rose garlands"[38] (fig. 65). The woodwork was punctuated by pilasters decorated with paintings on canvas. Empire tables and pedestal tables with bronze sirens or sphinxes were supplied by Boulanger, based on antique models by Weisweiler in particular. One of these tables had bothered Boulanger, who was still looking for an "Empire table" in June 1914. He suggested making one based on a model he had seen at the Hermitage.[39] It was undoubtedly in connection with this quest for a table that Olga asked Boni de Castellane in July 1914 to find her "a large console, either mahogany and bronze, or white and gold, or a round octagonal mahogany and bronze table, but very very large."[40]

37 GARF, F. 644, op. 1, D. 347, L. 1-15.

38 Paley 1923, 144.

39 Boulanger to Olga von Hohenfelsen (Paley), June 8, 1914, GARF, F. 613, op. 1, D. 92, L. 83.

40 Mension-Rigau 2016 (Kindle ed.), loc. 2730. Letter dated July 9, 1914.

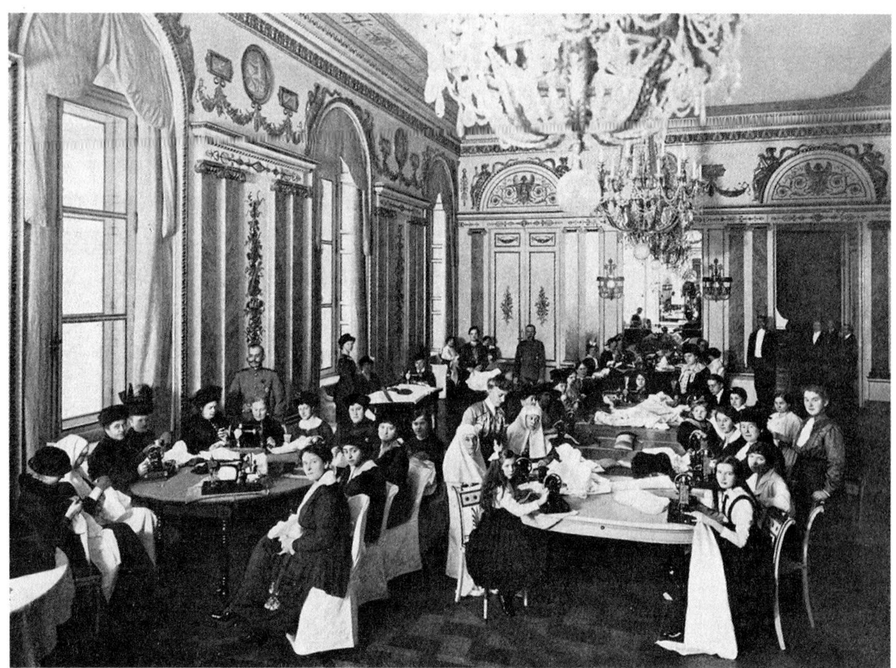

Fig. 66 Ballroom, palace of Countess von Hohenfelsen and Grand Duke Paul, Tsarskoye Selo, *Stolitsa i Usadba*, no. 29 (March 1, 1915). Hillwood Estate, Museum & Gardens, Archives and Special Collections, Washington, DC.

Added to this decor were antique pieces of furniture from the collection, including eight Directoire armchairs and twelve Empire chairs that served as models for the chairs delivered by Boulanger. The series acquired in Paris was reputed to have come from Marshal Davout (1770-1823). The Empire spirit of the premises was reinforced by the presence of gilded and patinated bronze candelabras and busts of Emperors Alexander I and Napoleon I. Also on display was George Dawe's portrait of Empress Alexandra Feodorovna, which came from the grand duke's historical collections and is now in the British Royal Collection (pl. 52). The two display cabinets contained the rest of the porcelain collection: mainly pieces from the Vienna and Sèvres manufactures, as well as various German productions, notably from Saxony (pls. 54-59).

The ballroom, a large empty space with similar decor to the previous room, featured several banquettes and sixty "light" chairs in gilded beechwood. The war prevented this space from being used for social purposes. The room was used as a meeting place for the good works of the countess, who can be seen busy in this room sewing with her daughters and the ladies of the best society for the army hospitals in a 1915 photograph[41] (fig. 66). In a letter to

41 *Stolitsa i Usadba*, no. 29 (March 1st, 1915).

her supplier Delisle in 1916, Olga notes: "had work over my head with my hospitals, my workroom and several charities I preside over!"[42] Nevertheless, it was in this ballroom that the family put up their Christmas tree in 1916: "a huge tree overloaded with sweets, fruit and gifts."[43] The following year, the situation was very different, notes Olga: "A modest little tree, placed in the rotunda, contrasted strangely with last year's superb tree. The gifts, too, were quite modest, for the grand duke's fortune had been noticeably affected."[44]

However, it was around the tree in 1916 that one of the most disturbing family reunions took place. It happened shortly after the assassination of Grigori Rasputin, in which Grand Duke Paul's son Dimitri was implicated. Dimitri's sister gives a precise account of this strange moment:

> Princess Paley's eldest sister, L. V. Golovina, and one of her daughters were sincere and fanatical supporters of Rasputin, as was my stepmother's eldest son, A. E. Pistohlkors, married to Vyrubova's sister. On the other hand, one of the princess's daughters, Marianna Zarnekau, a great friend of Dimitri's, was of the opposite party. All these people, a few days after Rasputin's murder, were gathered at the same table, along with the father and sister of one of the conspirators. The atmosphere was tense, very somber, and my stepmother tried in vain to find something to talk about, but nobody was interested. The atmosphere was not cheerful for the children, and my little half sisters anxiously scrutinized the faces around them. Finally, to end the scene, my father got up to light the Christmas tree.[45]

The large white dining room, which was next door, was also probably not used as Olga had originally envisaged (fig. 67). After the Revolution, formal dinners were rare. Maurice Paléologue describes one such evening:

> Tonight, I am dining at Tsarskoye Selo [...]. There's only the family. It is the first time I have been back to the house since the Revolution. The Grand Duke wears the general's uniform, with the Cross of St. George, but without the imperial cipher, without the aiguillettes of aide-de-camp general. He retains his calm, simple dignity, but his thin face is etched with sadness. The princess is tremulous with pain and exasperation. [...] As we pass through the salons to the table, the same thought stops us for a moment. We contemplate this sumptuous decor, these paintings, these tapestries, this profusion of furniture and

42 AD, Princess Paley to M. Delisle, July 6, 1916.

43 Paley 1923, 30.

44 *Ibid.*, 153.

45 Marie de Russie 1938, 298.

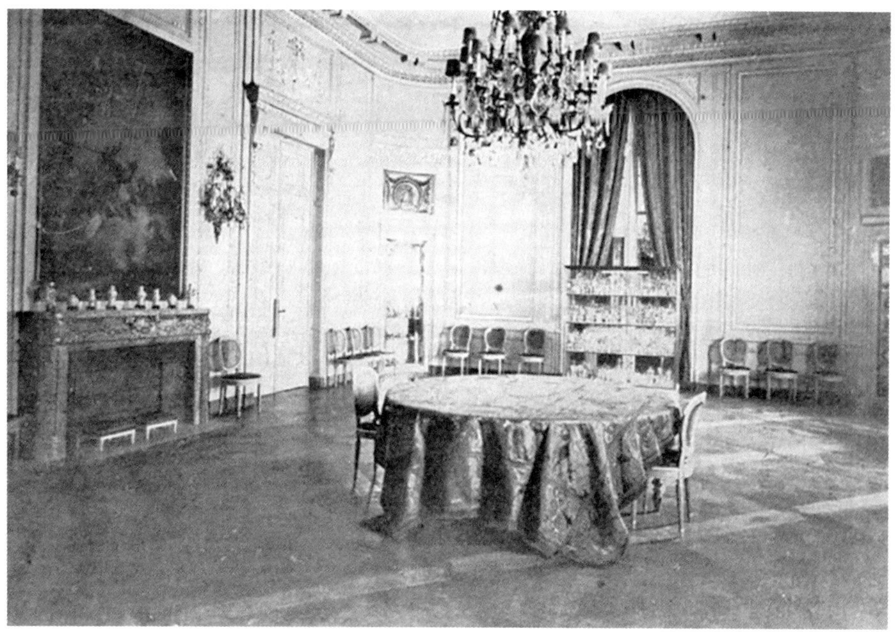

Fig. 67 Large dining room, palace of Countess von Hohenfelsen and Grand Duke Paul, Tsarskoye Selo, ca. 1918. Hillwood Estate, Museum & Gardens, Archives and Special Collections, Washington, DC.

> precious objects… What is the point of it all now? What will become of all these wonders and riches?[46]

On a visit to her father, Grand Duchess Maria noted at the same time:

> Tea was served in the dining room, but it was not like the tea parties of yesteryear. There were no cakes, buns, butter or cream for tea, and the bread was black. But in my agitation, it seemed to me that the cheerful atmosphere had remained the same.[47]

The room was in the Louis XVI style (Delafosse), with wood paneling painted "in three coats of oil on a white lead base in fine colors with a patina to give period tones." Four eighteenth-century overdoor panels, two by Leriche and two by Dyrk van der Aa,[48] were inserted in the rounded corners. A large dresser in violet brocatelle was designed in harmony with the marble of the mantelpiece. The "American mechanical closing" table could seat forty place settings when extended, and forty chairs had been supplied by Boulanger. A folding screen, as befits a dining room of the period, this one

46 Paléologue 1922, 3:319.

47 Marie de Russie 1938, 344.

48 Christie's, New York, May 23, 1997, lot 31.

in seventeenth-century Chinese lacquer, completed the furnishings. The display cabinets were lined with Sèvres porcelain, family silverware, and the grand duke's Russian crystal collection. All these objects were in place by December 1917, notes Olga: "Pieces of silver glittered in the display cases and seventeenth- and eighteenth-century crystals shone with all their brilliance."[49]

The grand duke's glassware was one of the highlights of the collection that Polovtsov, who was interested in all things related to the decorative arts as part of his duties at the Stieglitz Museum, had come to study, probably when it was still in the grand duke's palace in St. Petersburg.[50] This collection of more than a hundred pieces testified to the evolution of crystal production in Russia from the time of Peter the Great to the early nineteenth century, and included numerous stemmed glasses, sometimes covered and enhanced with gilding, whose bowls were engraved with the monograms of Russian sovereigns and/or their profiles (pl. 60).[51]

The family made regular use of the small Directoire dining room, whose sideboard had been composed from eighteenth-century decorative panels belonging to Baroness von André. The table could seat up to fourteen people.

The smoking room or Chinese drawing room, furnished with comfortable seats for smoking tobacco and drinking liqueurs, was decorated with antique panels and opened onto the vestibule and staircase leading to the private apartments upstairs.

The more sober, Louis XVI – style stucco imitation stone corridors and halls gave access to the bedrooms and bathrooms. Designed in the Salembier style, the furnishings, notably the twin beds in the countess's bedroom, were "Boulogne-style." It should be noted that "Monseigneur's room" had no bed.

In addition to a special piece of furniture for her shoes and an imposing wardrobe, the countess's bedroom was fitted with a Fichet safe, concealed behind the leaf of an interior cabinet.[52] Invoiced at 13,750 francs, it came from the famous Parisian locksmith's shop founded in 1825. It was here that the countess kept part of her jewelry, most of which came from Cartier (see pls. 27, 28; see figs. 46, 48-51). As for the historical jewels, which the grand duke had inherited from his parents, Emperor Alexander II and Empress Maria Alexandrovna, they were deposited at the bank in two safes. Estimated at 50 million francs, this treasure consisted of "necklaces, brooches, pendants, diadems of pearls, diamonds, sapphires and emeralds [...], [splendors that] shone with all their brilliance in their old caskets."[53]

49 Paley 1923, 143.

50 GARF, F. 613, op. 1, D. 391, L. 62.

51 AGE, F. I, op. 5, D. 89, 1919, L. 2; Paley sale, Christie's, London, July 1st-2, 1929, lots 174-206; Paris sale, June 16, 1960, lots 85-149.

52 GARF, F. 644, op. 1, D. 347, L. 1-15.

53 Paley 1923, 163-64.

Other treasures lurked within the palace walls: "The grand duke had a superb collection of sabers and swords of all periods and kinds. The finest specimens from Toledo stood side by side with cuirassiers' swords from the time of Catherine the Great, bearing engraved images of the Blessed Virgin,"[54] recalled Olga.

And, as in any house of this standing, there was a fine cellar – around ten thousand bottles – valued at 10 million francs.[55] These Madeira, Port, Sherry, Bordeaux, and Burgundy wines had been collected by the grand duke since the 1880s, and had been added to by bottles inherited from Grand Duke Alexei, who died in 1908. A diplomat called Louis de Robien described a dinner given by Grand Duke Paul on the occasion of his birthday in July 1917: "the wines were remarkable, and Chambrun praised a Musigny with which the grand duke had his French guests refill their glasses."[56]

Finally, the inventories drawn up after the Revolution, between 1919 and 1923, not only list the collections integrated into the decor, but they paint a picture of a palace in which every table, desk, and display case was used to showcase small antique and contemporary objects. These include antique medals and coins, gold and silver snuffboxes, cigarette cases and holders, precious ashtrays, table bells and charms, frames for photographs and miniatures, mechanical pencils and paperweights, clocks and watches, antique fans, small Chinese bronzes, icons with precious frames… A whole range of objects, often telling a personal story – gifts, photographs of a relative, souvenirs of travels – that made this decor a real home. Olga wrote to Boni de Castellane on June 12, 1914: "What am I going to do, great gods, now that my house is finished?"[57] Maria Pavlovna noted:

> The house in Tsarskoye Selo that my father and his wife had so lovingly built now looked finished. There were still a few details to be completed, but they would take care of them after the war was over. The collections brought from Paris were in place, and the display cabinets were filled with precious porcelain, Chinese trinkets, antique silverware, and magnificent cut glass. The walls were decorated with valuable paintings and portraits, and the rooms were filled with superb antique furniture. My father and his wife had chosen everything with care, each object recalling a pleasant memory, and they intended to spend the rest of their lives in this house.[58]

54 *Ibid.*, 125.

55 *Ibid.*, 140-41, 145.

56 Robien 2017, 109.

57 Mension-Rigau 2016 (Kindle ed.), loc. 2734.

58 Marie de Russie 1938, 233.

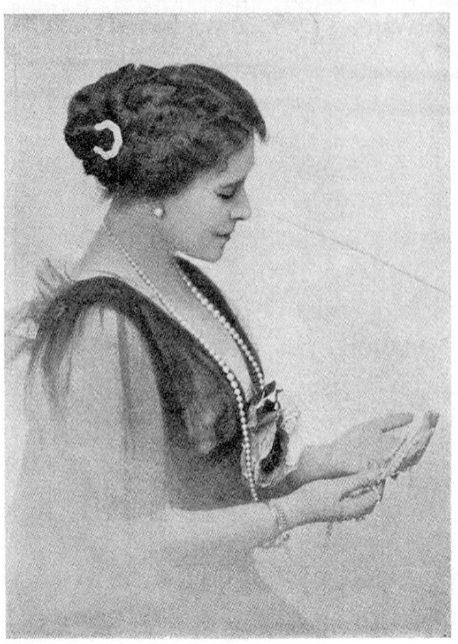

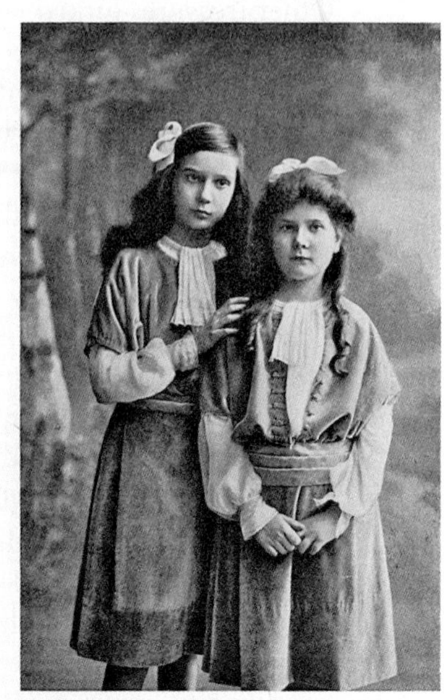

Fig. 68 Portraits of Countess von Hohenfelsen and of her daughters, *Stolitsa i Usadba*, no. 29 (March 1, 1915): 12. Hillwood Estate, Museum & Gardens Archives and Special Collections, Washington, DC.

The names linked to some of these objects – Cartier, Kendall, then Fabergé and Britsyn – gave an idea of life in Paris, then in Petersburg, which, had it not been for the war, would have taken the same form, with the name of Fabergé, Court jeweler, replacing that of Cartier by the end of 1914 in the countess's accounts.[59] Brisac, Empress Alexandra Feodorovna's couturier, also made an appearance, but Olga, who knew what she was talking about, judged the designer as "very expensive!"[60]

On her arrival in Paris, the countess had been introduced to the Parisian world via an attractive photographic portrait published in *Les Modes* in 1905[61] (see fig. 31). In 1915, it was *Stolitsa i Usadba*, the Russian equivalent of the select *Town & Country*, that officially introduced her to Petersburg society[62] (fig. 68). As usual, she poses as an elegant woman, holding and observing her long pearl necklace. Her daughters, Irina and Natalie, are also present. Olga's status has evolved: back in grace, she and her children soon

59 Several works by Fabergé reputed to have come from Grand Duke Paul were dispersed in Geneva in 1974. See Christie's, Geneva, May 1, 1974, lots 186, 189, 190, 192, 193, 197, 201, 205, 207, 210, 219, 220, 225-227.

60 GARF, F. 613, op. 1, D. 613, L. 94.

61 *Les Modes*, no. 50 (February 1905): 13.

62 *Stolitsa i Usadba*, no. 29 (March 1st, 1915): 12.

receive a princely title. She is now Princess Paley. The name refers to a maternal ancestor of the countess who had distinguished himself at the time of Peter the Great. In their report, *Le Gaulois* and *Le Figaro* took advantage of the opportunity to give news of the couple to the best of Parisian society.[63]

But times had changed, and *Stolitsa i Usadba*'s other photographs were dedicated to the family's good works in the context of the war, which was thought would not last very long. However, events turned life upside down for the couple, who had planned to return to Boulogne in the autumn and travel around Europe.[64]

"What a calamity..." wrote Marcel Boulanger to Olga in August 1914. His children and nephews had been sent to the front; his worksites had been closed, particularly in Vienna; and many of his workers had left for the war. One of them returned in extremis from the Tsarskoye Selo worksite, but the upholsterer Raffy, who was stranded, was taken in charge by the countess and the grand duke, as "the war may well last several months."[65] He did not return until August 1915, while the decorator and the countess continued to exchange views on installations and minor work until May 1916. War had set in. Olga worried and sometimes confided her torments to her French friends:

> It seems to me that a century, heavy and monotonous, has passed and flattened in me all my aspirations toward the beautiful, toward the ideal, toward hope! But there it is! Perhaps one day we'll find the old house in Boulogne and the affection of the friends who adored us there.[66]

Two of her children were involved in the war, especially her beloved Vladimir. But she remained hopeful. In July 1916, Olga wrote: "I have every reason to believe that this 'end' is near."[67]

In September 1916, not able to travel in Western Europe, the family found themselves in the Crimea for a short stay.[68]

Meanwhile, however, difficulties were mounting. The grand duke's capital was frozen by Deutsche Bank in Berlin, the economy collapsed, and all their projects were obliged to be paused. Construction of the chapel that architect Vasily Ivanovich Chodov was to have installed in the palace was postponed.[69]

63 *Le Gaulois*, September 18, 1915; *Le Figaro*, September 17, 1915.

64 Mension-Rigau 2016 (Kindle ed.), loc. 2748.

65 GARF, F. 613, op. 1, D. 92, L. 98. Letter dated August 22, 1914.

66 Mension-Rigau 2016 (Kindle ed.), loc. 3248-3255. Letter to Boni de Castellane, May 7, 1915.

67 AD, letter dated July 6, 1916.

68 Paley 1923, 3.

69 *Ibid.*, 152.

The private secretary Dupré's letters testify to the difficulties of managing the house at Boulogne. Complaints from suppliers multiplied,[70] not only regarding the house itself (coal, electricity, personnel, insurance), but also for delays in settling the balance of invoices issued before the war by antique dealers and merchants, such as Bernard, Hamburger, and Agnew & Sons.[71] Specific orders were difficult to fulfill. The price of perfumes rose in parallel to that of alcohol.[72] As for the bolero requested from Madame Daine, "this work will take quite a long time, as all the factories where this work is done are mobilized, and fancy work comes after orders for the troops. Madame Daine warned me that there would also be a 40% increase,"[73] states the last letter in the correspondence with Dupré, dated July 12, 1916.

As the revolution rumbled on, Olga was gripped by anxiety: "We hardly slept at all. Gunshots rang out from time to time, and I imagined our palace in flames, and all the beautiful collections looted and ransacked."[74] Finally, the February Revolution swept away the regime. The emperor, commander in chief of the army since 1915, was forced to abdicate on his way back from the Mogilev headquarters to St. Petersburg, renamed Petrograd after the outbreak of war. Grand Duke Paul had the difficult task of breaking the news to the empress, who was in extremes of worry at Tsarskoye Selo. Olga noted: "The fall of the empire, for we understood that it was the fall, appeared to us in all its horror."[75]

70 GARF, F. 644, op. 1, D. 270, L. 67.

71 *Ibid.*, L. 75.

72 *Ibid.*, L. 90.

73 *Ibid.*, L. 95.

74 Paley 1923, 43.

75 *Ibid.*, 54-55.

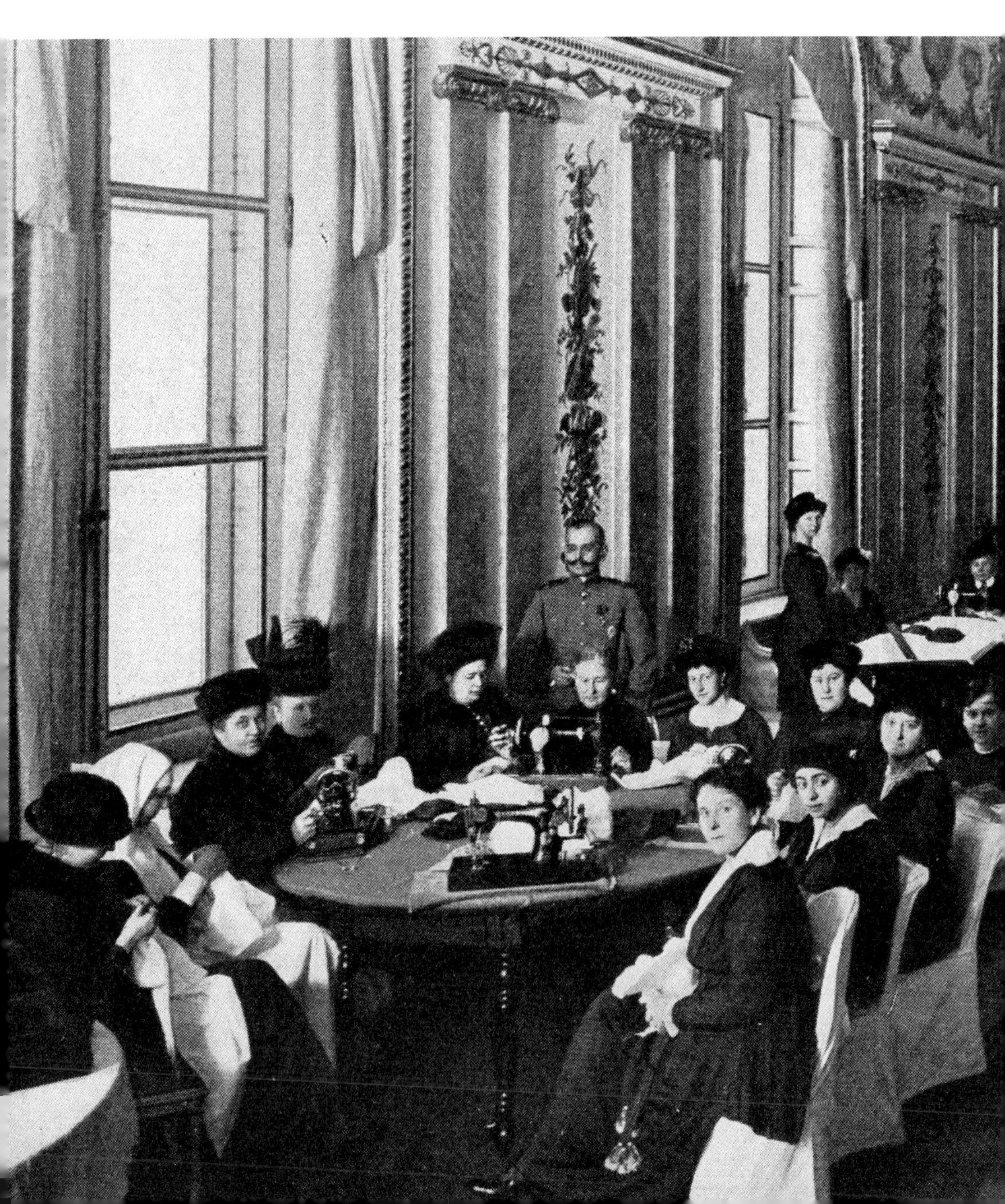

EPILOGUE

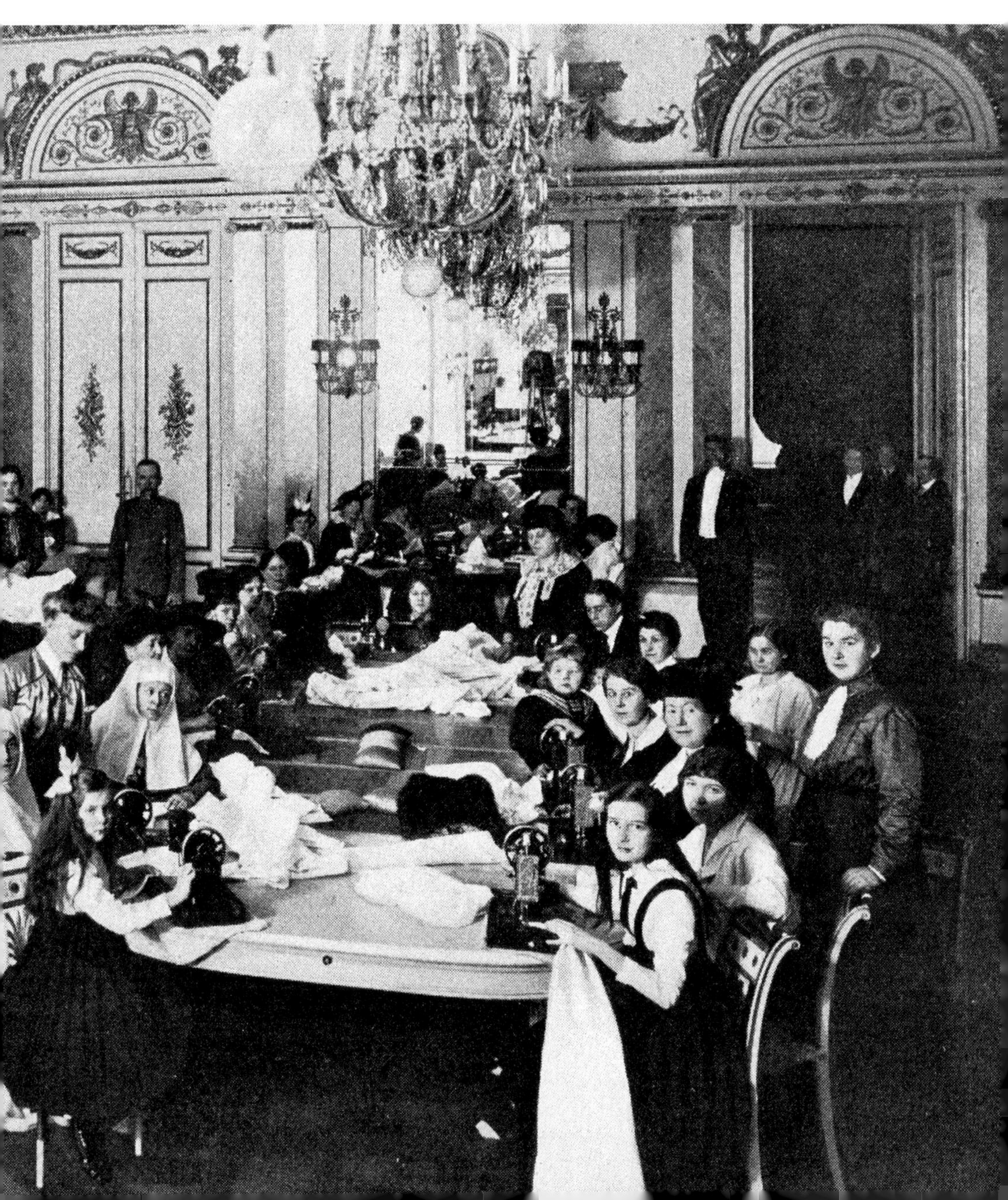

Like the furnishings and decorations freshly delivered for King Louis XVI and Queen Marie-Antoinette in the 1780s, those of the Paley Palace, an ideal vision of French decorative art from the eighteenth century to the Empire, were preserved as such for a time, but they disappeared with the Revolution.

Some initial requisitions were made. The grand duke's car, the one he kept in St. Petersburg, was seized by the provisional government. Ironically, it was subsequently used as a taxi for Lenin after he arrived by train at Finland Station in St. Petersburg from exile in April 1917.[1] But while the situation was already complicated, it got even worse for the family at Tsarskoye Selo when the Bolsheviks took power. From sixty-four servants, the palace staff fell to forty-eight after the first revolution, twenty-two after the October Revolution, three in July 1918, and none in December.[2] The grand duke suffered increasingly from his stomach ulcer. His worsening condition required daily visits from his faithful doctor Obnissky. Maria Pavlovna noted:

> Every time I visited my father in Tsarskoye Selo, I noticed yet another painful change. Little by little, he was forced to deprive himself of everything, despite the constant solicitude of Princess Paley, who employed all her energy to provide him with at least a shadow of the comfort to which he was accustomed.[3]

Impromptu searches and confiscations increased, followed by theft and looting. First and foremost, all weapons were confiscated, including bladed and antique weapons; their fate has been unknown since their seizure in November 1917.[4] The local soviet requisitioned cookware for its own use. As in most palaces, the cellars were condemned to disappear – the destruction of those in the Winter Palace has given rise to numerous descriptions[5] – and the bottles were destroyed one by one in the garden. Olga noted with disgust: "The smell alone was intoxicating. I stayed there, shivering with cold, rage and disgust, until four in the morning, when the last bottle was broken."[6]

To save on heating costs, the family closed part of the house and settled around the gallery, which, placed above the boiler, became the most pleasant room.[7] In January 1918, due to a shortage of naphtha, it was decided to

1 Paley 1923, 57.

2 *Ibid.*, 155-56.

3 Marie de Russie 1938, 372.

4 Paley 1923, 123-24.

5 Polovtsov 1919, 124; Paley 1923, 57.

6 Paley 1923, 145.

7 *Ibid.*, 138.

move into the nearby cottage belonging to Grand Duke Boris Vladimirovich, nephew of the grand duke, where the heating was supplied by wood and coal.

The first threat to the Paley Palace came from the local soviet, which was looking for a place into which it could move. Olga convinced Anatoly Lunacharsky (1875-1933), head of the People's Commissariat for Education, to save her residence. The house and its collections were initially preserved. The soviet was ordered to move into the neighboring palace, formerly owned by Grand Duchess Vladimir, which had been completely looted.[8]

At that moment, Alexander Polovtsov, Princess Paley's longtime friend, intervened. He had been involved in the preservation of artistic and historical monuments since the outbreak of the first revolution, along with historian Georgy Lukomsky (1884-1952). Already very active in the heritage organizations that developed during the reign of Nicholas II, they played a key role in safeguarding Russian heritage under the Provisional Government and then the Bolsheviks. Polovtsov became the first curator of the Pavlovsk residence and Lukomsky the first curator of the Tsarskoye Selo imperial estate. The painter Konstantin Korovin (1861-1939), who took part in the preservation operations, was sent to Tsarskoye Selo to inspect the Paley Palace, as the princess recounted in her *Souvenirs:*

> He went through the rooms, consulted me on my most beautiful paintings, on my rarest objects and we wrote a report, in which he said that it was essential, in the people's interest, to save the house of citizen Paley against any possible deterioration.[9]

In January, the palace became a museum, and Olga its official "guardian." She was busy putting furniture back in place and removing protective covers from furniture and paintings. An activity she had always enjoyed, tidying up her home, was now being done for the museum of French art and history that her home had become. In Lukomsky's first short guide to the Catherine Palace in Tsarskoye Selo, published in 1918, among the city's other sites he listed the "French Museum of Art and History (O. V. Paley Palace-Museum)," open Tuesdays and Thursdays from 3:00 p.m. to 6:00 p.m. and Sundays and holidays from 11:00 a.m. to 1:00 p.m.[10] Following the model of some German palace-museums, notably Sanssouci, visitors had to put on small felt slippers when they entered the house in order to visit the reception areas on the ground floor, the only ones open to the public.[11] Olga was a frequent visitor and guide. The upstairs became a storeroom, gradually housing collections

8 *Ibid.*, 149.

9 *Ibid.*, 150.

10 Lukomsky 1918, 96.

11 Paley 1923, 159.

from other residences in the city, which were transferred there between 1919 and 1920.[12] As early as 1919, after Polovtsov had immigrated to France in October 1918, he devoted a laudatory paragraph to the Paley Palace:

> Built only a few years ago, this vast building was filled with beautiful things, some of them family heirlooms, but mostly curios collected by the grand duke and princess. Some very fine paintings, including a famous van Dyck and two unusual panels by Hubert Robert, porcelain of exceptional quality, jades and vases from China, eighteenth-century furniture, some of it of the finest quality, along with family portraits, drawings and engravings, all making up a remarkable collection.[13]

Following the nationalization decrees, the princess was ousted and replaced by a certain Telepnev, who moved into the palace outbuildings with his family. Polovtsov notes:

> Lunacharsky wanted to give an official position to his protégé T., the ex-commander of the palaces, and to this end appointed him curator of the Paley Museum. All our complaints did nothing to help, and this character began systematically poisoning the existence of the princess and the palace curators, under whose care this little museum had been placed.[14]

Following this new change, Olga had to evacuate the premises. The kitchens, table linen, and household linen were assigned to schools, and the generator connected to the city system. All she could take with her were her personal objects, icons, photographs, dresses, and body linen, in addition to the belongings moved with the family to Grand Duke Boris's cottage, such as "silver trays, cutlery, the grand duke's toiletries, his clothes."[15] Then Telepnev was replaced by Boris Moïseevich Snessarenko. A distraught Olga noted: "I wandered sadly through this beautiful house, my own work, where so little happiness had reigned."[16] In July 1918, it appeared that the worst was happening: the grand duke was arrested.

The fate of the collection, so Parisian in many respects, was now out of Princess Paley's hands. The life of the museum took its course, inventories multiplied, and objects of a non-artistic nature were gradually transferred and, in some cases, sold from the 1920s on. During this period, a first guide was

12 Gollerbakh ca. 1922, 8; Antifeeva and Tshistikov 2000, 337.

13 Polovtsov 1919, 184-85.

14 *Ibid.*, 186.

15 Paley 1923, 253-54.

16 *Ibid.*, 254.

written and published by historian Erikh Gollerbakh, detailing the collection by school – French, Italian, British, Flemish, and Russian – and by technique – painting, sculpture, decorative arts – and then by room.[17]

As early as 1923, plans were afoot to sell off the palace and its collections. Their fate ushered in that of many other museums created in the aftermath of the Revolution. In February 1928, most of the collection was sold for £46,000 to Norman Weisz, an adventurer who did a lot of business with the Soviet government.[18] The ensemble was to be dispersed in several sales at Christie's in London. Princess Paley, who had immigrated to Paris at the time, was alerted and took legal action to stop the dispersal of her estate and assert her rights. Her stepdaughter recounted the event in her memoirs: "Princess Paley left for England, found the boat, found the crates, and put a stop to it. She then lodged a complaint against the buyers responsible."[19]

The princess lost the case. She appealed, but the court upheld the decision in 1929. Known as *Princess Paley v. Weisz*, the case is often used as a reference in questions of expropriation and restitution. Several sales took place in June and July 1929. The bidders were mainly dealers, some of whom, like Stettiner, had had Olga as a client. Polovtsov figured prominently among the buyers. Since emigrating, he had become an expert and dealer, selling many works of Russian provenance, notably to Henry Walters.[20] That he was one of the major buyers at these sales comes as no surprise, since he knew the collection well. Another buyer was the Parisian antique dealer Selmar Rosenau (1875-1953). He focused on porcelain scent bottles. He sold several to Léon Givaudan (1875-1936), the famous chemist and perfumer. Like many company directors of the time, he amassed a large collection of objects linked to the industry, of which he was an important representative. Still preserved by the company, the set includes several bottles from the Paley collection[21] (see pls. 44-51). Fernand Javal, owner of the Houbigant perfumery, was one of these entrepreneur-collectors. He, too, owned at least one bottle from the princess's collection, now in the Musée des arts décoratifs in Paris.[22]

For her part, the princess, who had very limited means, nevertheless bought a few pieces from her collection, including a portrait of Alexander II as a child by George Dawe (see pl. 14), several items of Saxon porcelain, a series of miniatures, and a few examples of biscuit ware featuring historical figures.[23]

17 Gollerbakh ca. 1922.

18 Antifeeva and Tshistikov 2000, 339; Iljine and Semyonova 2013, 110.

19 Marie de Russie 1937, 303.

20 Johnston 1999, 218.

21 Pillivuyt 1985.

22 Inv. 58054. Information supplied by Sophie Motsch.

23 Paley sale, Christie's, London, July 1st-2, 1929, lots 85, 96, 100, 218, 220, 242.

The rest of the collection, which included everything from palace decorations to furniture bronzes and silks,[24] was dispersed on the Soviet Union's domestic market. The fate of the collection is difficult to trace in detail, but some of the major works eventually found their way into museums and private collections around the world, from Tokyo to Springfield, Massachusetts, as well as St. Petersburg, Moscow, London, Paris, Rome, and Washington, DC. As for the palace, it housed various institutions before being rebuilt between 1952 and 1954 to give it a more Soviet touch, to house an engineering school, which is today more or less abandoned.

As for the jewels and precious objects that made the Paley collection famous, some of them had been put somewhere safe during the war. In her memoirs, Olga confides that she went to Finland in May 1917 with her friend Mikhail Aleksandrovich Stakhovich, who had become governor-general of Finland after the Revolution (since April 1917). He took her by special railway carriage to Helsinki with a crate full of jewelry and valuables.[25] It is conceivable that this was recovered when the princess fled. Other "treasures," however, were lost. Before the nationalization decrees were issued, Olga explained that she had deposited her personal papers with the Austrian embassy and "everything [she] still had in the way of jewelry and antique silver."[26]

With the collapse of Austria-Hungary and the looting of the country, these coffers seem to have disappeared. The jewels deposited in the bank's vaults were lost with nationalization, and they must have suffered the fate of most of the jewels that the Soviets then recovered: dismantled, melted down, and sold.

In her *Souvenirs*, Olga bitterly mentions her collection, which she had wanted so much to preserve:

> It was these collections, these riches, that caused our downfall, for instead of fleeing when there was still time, we remained nailed to these objects that were so dear to us. Could I have imagined that my most precious, most beloved treasure, the grand duke's life and Vladimir's life, would be sacrificed! Could I believe that the Russian people would raise sacrilegious hands against innocent people?[27]

First, her only son with the grand duke, Prince Vladimir, was arrested and sent to Siberia with other members of the imperial family, leading to a farewell

24 TsGALI, F. 254, op. 1, D. 4, L. 23.

25 Paley 1923, 91.

26 *Ibid.*, 260-61.

27 *Ibid.*, 44.

between father and son: "He [the grand duke] spoke of the hope he had that the cursed regime would not last and that one day we would find ourselves, all of us, happy and free, in our beloved France."[28]

News of Vladimir was scarce until this missive from July 1918:

> Everything that once interested me, [...] those dazzling ballets, those decadent paintings, that new music, all seem dull and tasteless to me now. I am looking for the truth, the truth alone, the light and the good.[29]

Then it was the grand duke's turn, imprisoned in the Peter and Paul Fortress in St. Petersburg. Olga's memory of this painful separation and what he told her remained intact:

> I do not know what I have left to live for, but I thank you with all my soul, with all the strength of my heart that loves you, that has never loved anyone but you, for these twenty-five years of happiness. Take good care of the little ones, it is your duty, and it is my wish.[30]

Olga complied. She arranged for Irina and Natalie to travel to Finland, while she remained in Petrograd, doing everything she could to free her husband and son. Their fate is known. On the night of July 16-17, 1918, the emperor and his family were massacred in Yekaterinburg. The next day, Vladimir, who was twenty-one, and the other members of the imperial family accompanying him into captivity were thrown into a mine at Alapayevsk in Siberia, into which the executioners threw grenades. Grand Duke Paul, who knew nothing of Vladimir's fate, was executed a few months later, on January 30, 1919, along with other grand dukes who were also prisoners. He was fifty-eight years old.

Olga was devastated:

> I stood there in a daze, unable to understand anything, unable to say a word. I felt life slipping away from me... All the radiant happiness of the past passed before my dazzled eyes. [...] and I don't remember a thing that day.[31]

Olga left Petrograd and joined her daughters in Finland, hoping to find Vladimir as well. There she learned that he, too, was a victim of the Revolution:

28 *Ibid.*, 188.
29 *Ibid.*, 211.
30 *Ibid.*, 221.
31 *Ibid.*, 300.

> And when, half-dead with grief, I arrived ten days later in Finland, to find the poor little girls, I learned of the martyred death of my son, my beautiful Vladimir, who was my whole life, my happiness, my joy![32]

Olga and her daughters departed for Paris. Olga was reunited with her stepdaughter, Maria Pavlovna, who, like her brother Dimitri, had escaped the worst.

> Her pain had completely transformed her; she was a pitifully broken creature who could barely speak, barely think. Her magnificent assurance, her former calm, had completely disappeared. She remained overwhelmed, crushed by her misfortunes; she abandoned herself to her misery, completely, passionately. Beneath the outward worldliness, there had always been something wild in her nature, something elemental, which was now taking over again.[33]

Olga devoted herself to her daughters and reconnected with a few old acquaintances, including the couturier Worth; the children's French teacher, Louise Patin;[34] and the painter Dagnan-Bouveret. The latter had lost his son in the war, and Olga shared his grief with him:

> More than any other of your friends, I sympathize with your pain, and express my deepest sympathy. Your dear son, however, died *for* his country; my two martyrs are victims of theirs, and the vision of their torment haunts me day and night. I am morally dead. Nevertheless, I have to live for the two little girls you saw when they were little [...] these memories plague my heart. My pilgrimages to Boulogne are real ordeals. I find all the memories there, and the image of that beautiful past rises up before me in all its implacable cruelty![35]

Olga arranged drawing lessons between her daughter Irina and the painter, with whom she shared an "eternal heartbreak," as she confided in another letter.[36] Boulogne was saddled with debts.[37] In order to wipe the slate clean of the past, which was too painful to bear, and to collect a nest egg, the decision

32 Princess Paley to Louise Patin, former French teacher of children at Tsarskoye Selo, November 24, 1919, Patin 1987, 244, ill. between 128 and 129.

33 Marie de Russie 1937, 122-23.

34 Patin 1987, 44.

35 Princess Paley to Dagnan-Bouveret, November 10, 1919, Archives départementales de la Haute-Saône, Vesoul, Fonds Dagnan-Bouveret.

36 Princess Paley to Dagnan-Bouveret, October 14, 1921, *ibid.*

37 Marie de Russie 1937, 138.

was taken to sell Boulogne and its contents in 1923.[38] The same year, Irina married Prince Feodor of Russia, son of Grand Duke Alexander and Grand Duchess Xenia, sister of Nicholas II (pls. 61, 62). In 1927, Natalie, perhaps less conventional, married fashion designer Lucien Lelong. Her life would become a novel, already partially written[39] (pl. 63). Olga kept her promise to Grand Duke Paul. She took care of her daughters. She was also involved in organizing charities for the Russian refugees who poured into France by the thousands. She helped her stepdaughter Maria Pavlovna manage and organize Kitmir, her embroidery business.[40]

Then came the Weisz affair, which brought back many memories through much-loved objects. Olga invested money and energy in asserting her rights, but the lawsuit was lost. Olga fell ill with a relapse of breast cancer.[41] The outcome was fatal:

> My stepmother died in early November 1929. She had longed for death for years, but when the time came, her inner strength fought desperately for life. Gradually, her grip loosened, but she gave in only at the last moment when her physical energy was completely exhausted.[42]

38 Paley sale, Paris, December 5, 1923.

39 Liaut 1996.

40 Albertini and Kurkdjian 2023.

41 Marie de Russie 1937, 315.

42 *Ibid.*, 316.

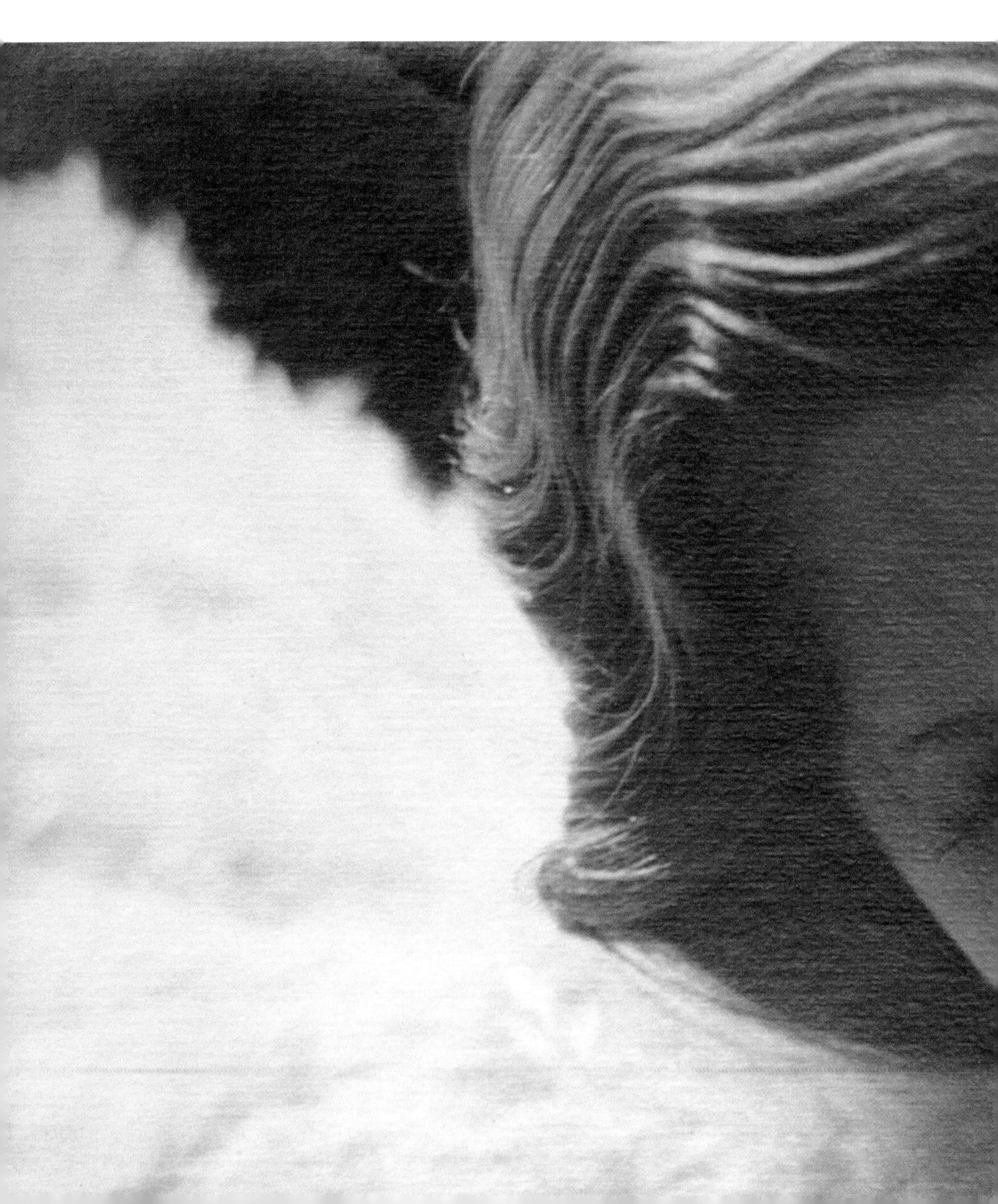

FROM EXILE TO AVANT-GARDE: THE LIFE OF PRINCESS NATALIE PALEY

by Megan J. Martinelli

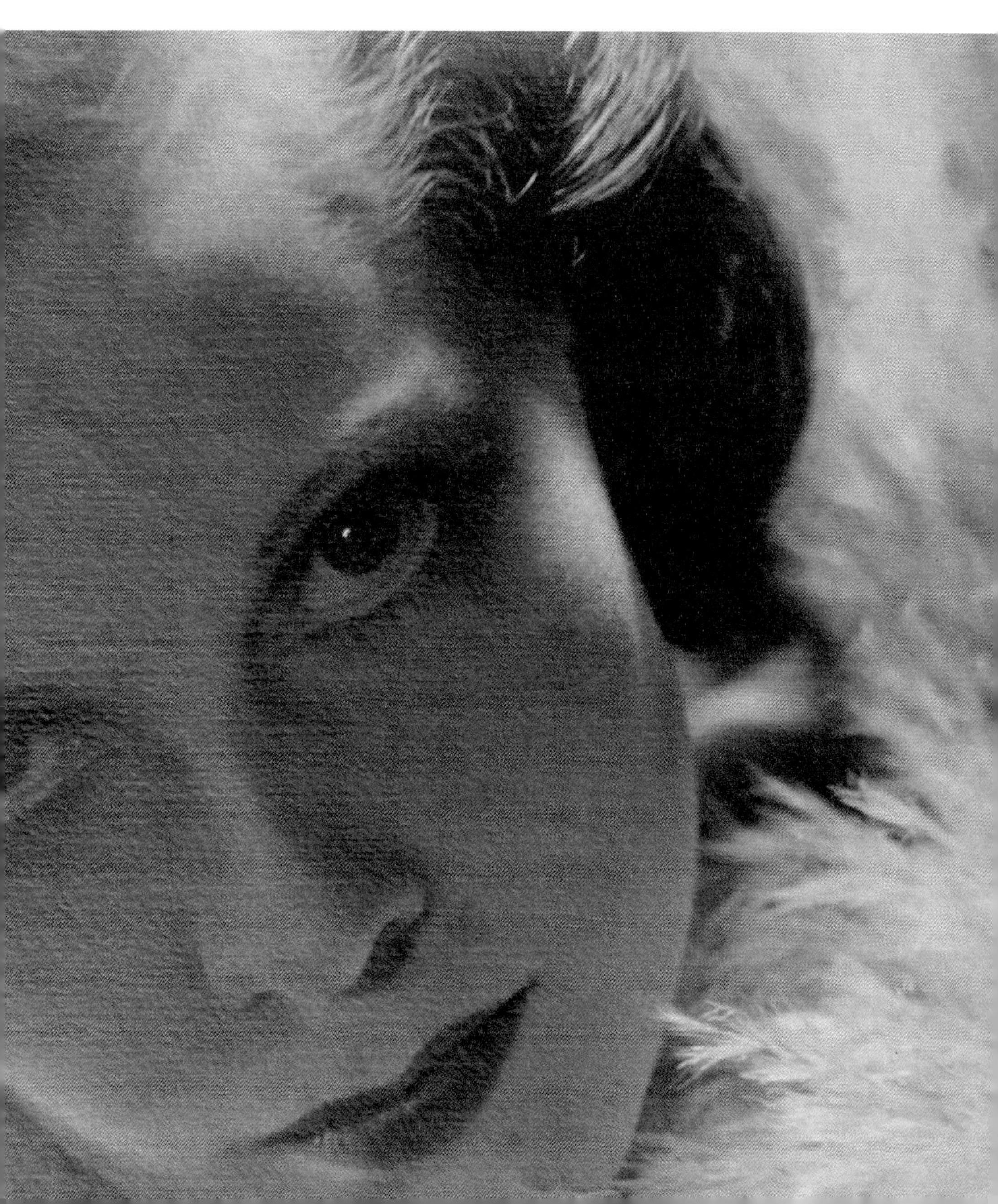

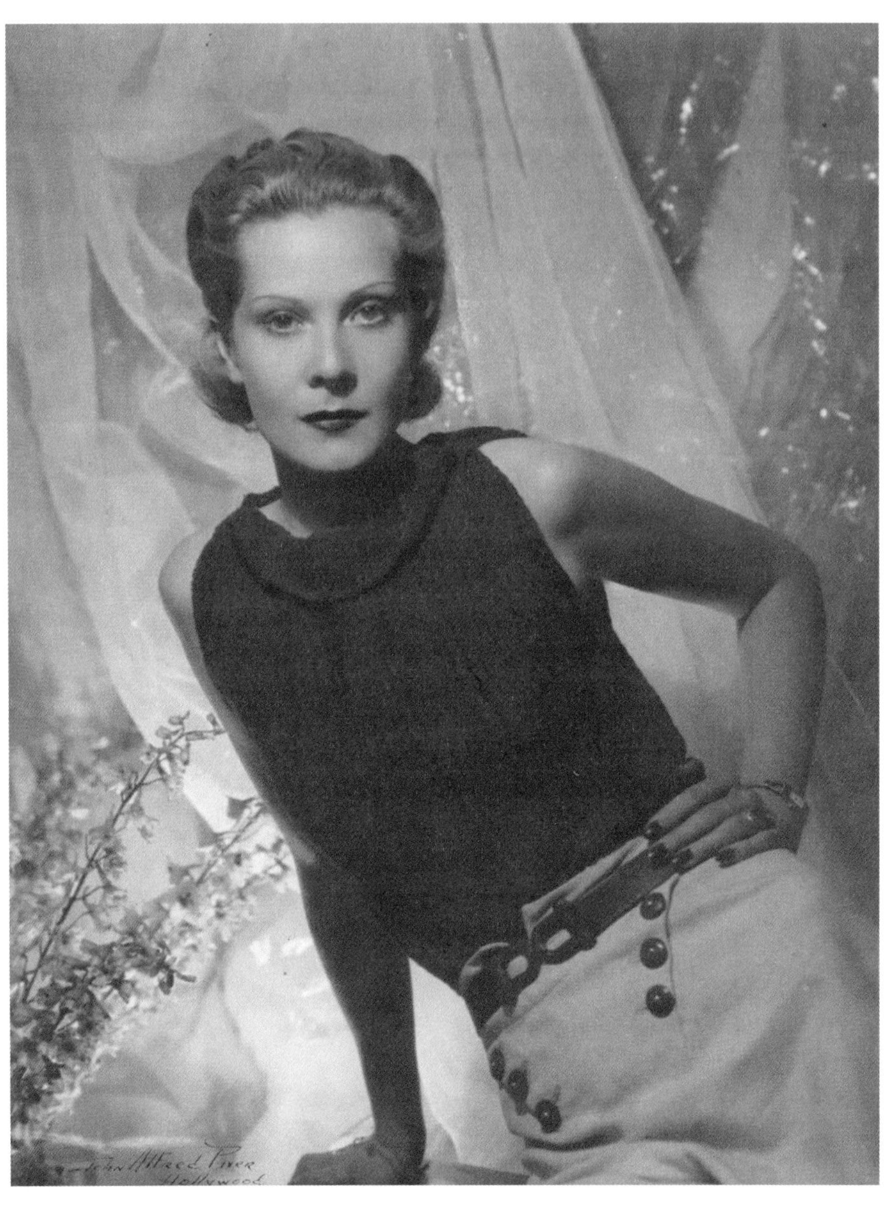

Fig. 69 Princess Natalie Paley, ca. 1935. Photograph by John Alfred Piver. Paley Family Collection, Hillwood Estate, Museum & Gardens Archives and Special Collections, Washington, DC.

Princess Natalie Paley (1905-1981), born in luxurious exile in Paris, was an enigmatic twentieth-century figure. Though nearly forgotten today, she was ever present in certain artistic circles of 1930s European creatives and mid-century New York café society. Paley inspired and nurtured photographers, painters, dancers, sculptors, actors, directors, designers, and writers with her beauty, cleverness, and sphinxlike presence (pl. 64). Throughout her life, she experienced tragedies and challenges but endured with a knack for elegant reinvention. The princess was a muse, model, fashion design collaborator, business director, actor, and producer's wife. She was a confidant to writers and poets; among them Jean Cocteau (1889-1963), Erich Maria Remarque (1898-1970), Antoine de Saint-Exupéry (1900-1944), and Noël Coward (1899-1973). Throughout her seventy-six years of life, she assumed many different names: she was everlastingly "Natasha" to friends, lovers, and family; Madame Lucien Lelong upon her 1927 marriage to the renowned French couturier, which formally ended in divorce ten years later; and Mrs. John C. Wilson, the wife of an American Broadway producer and bon vivant of Manhattan and Connecticut. Like most women whose lives were well lived and full of adventures, gossip and rumors regarding the princess abounded – contemporarily and to this day. For the purposes of this publication, references to her personal relationships are made only when they are confirmed via primary source materials, and when their passion inspired a body of culturally significant artistic work. This chapter traces her legacy and presence in twentieth-century innovation from French couture collections to Parisian and Hollywood film roles, to characters inspired by her personality, and Surrealist portraits capturing her beauty.

As the youngest of the three children from the forbidden union of Grand Duke Paul Alexandrovich of Russia and Olga von Pistohlkors, who came to be known as Countess Olga von Hohenfelsen, Princess Natalie Paley enjoyed a seemingly tranquil childhood in the background of her family's social prominence on the outskirts of Paris. Her mother's life, the subject of much of this book, supplied the foundation for Paley's childhood, though specific details about the younger daughter's experiences remain obscured. It is understood, of course, that the princess and her siblings bore witness to the elegant lifestyle of the grand duke and the countess from their nursey (fig. 70). Paley absorbed her mother's pursuit of aesthetic perfection in appearances. Her family's tradition of nurturing artists and writers persevered into the twentieth century through Paley's personal and professional relationships with creators. The loss of her talented elder brother, Vladimir, first temporarily to his formal military education as an imperial Russian royal in 1913, and then forever, when he was killed in the Russian Revolution, may have influenced the princess in her later relationships with artistic men.[1]

1 According to Jean-Noël Liaut, the princess's biographer, Paley "searched for his replacement all her life," and affectionately referred to him as "Bodia." See Liaut 2015, 32-24. The young

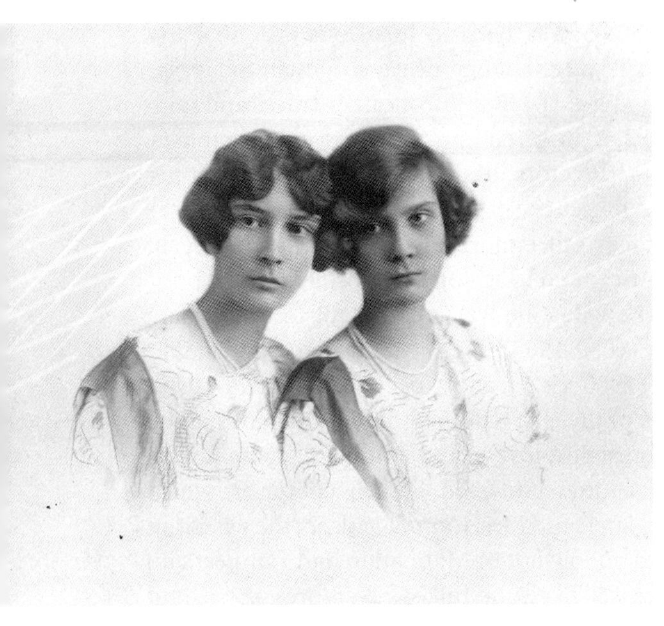

Fig. 70 Princess Irina Paley (left) and her younger sister by two years, Princess Natalie Paley, pose for a portrait, early 1920s. Photographed by C. Barl, Paris. Paley Family Collection, Hillwood Estate, Museum & Gardens Archives and Special Collections, Washington, DC.

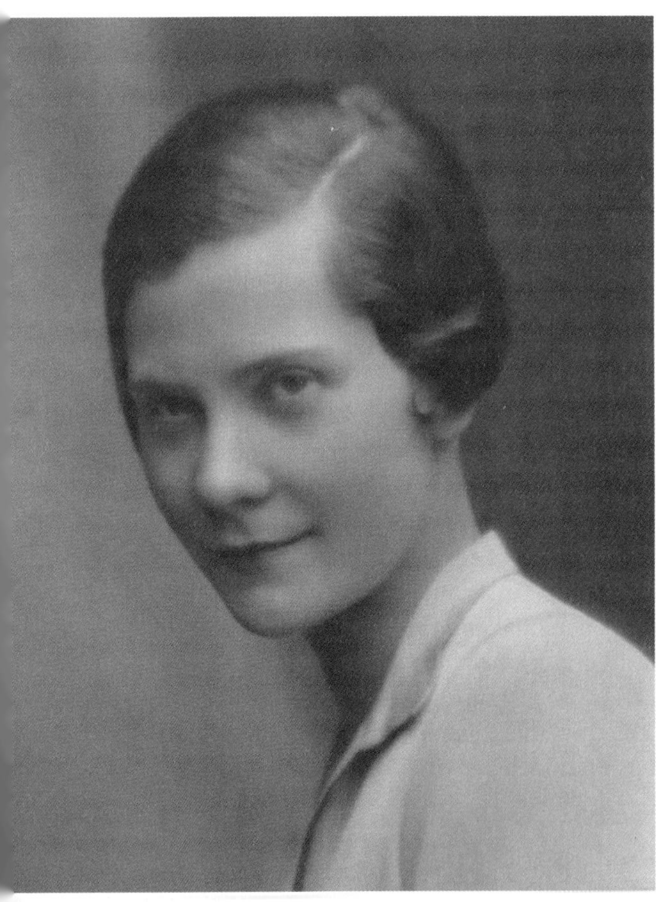

Fig. 71 Natalie Paley as a young woman, Paris, ca. 1925. Paley Family Collection, Hillwood Estate, Museum & Gardens Archives and Special Collections, Washington DC.

Paley carried the burden of the Revolution and the unnamed atrocities she experienced as a child throughout her life (fig. 71). Living in the United States at the outset of the Second World War, she lost touch with many of her glamorous, artistic friends, some of whom were gone forever. Her second husband, John C. Wilson (1899-1961), known as Jack, struggled through a decade-long health issue beginning in the late 1940s, culminating in his death at the age of sixty-two. Her later years were spent keeping them financially afloat as he faced career challenges in the theater world due to his illness. After Wilson's death, the princess herself survived him for twenty years, enduring her own health problems and watching as people she knew gradually passed away, but maintaining contact with surviving friends and members of the Wilson family. Though she is often remembered as a recluse in these years, she spent much of her life developing lasting friendships with important figures. Tracing her presence in twentieth-century fashion and art (including dance, film, fine arts, and literature) reveals a strong personality and cultural contributor who deserves better than reduction to a recluse, or to merely a beautiful woman ennobled by her royal title. The beauty and title, of course, contributed to her success and were utilized by Paley to her advantage, but this research reveals her talent and perseverance, a legacy worth celebrating.

Fashion and aesthetics were a critical part of Natalie Paley's formative years observing her mother, Princess Olga Paley. When the Paley women returned to Paris following the tragic ordeal of the Revolution, fashion emerged as an unexpected opportunity for income, public visibility, and reinvention. Grand Duchess Maria Pavlovna, elder half-sister of Natalie and Natalie's sister, Irina, succeeded in the 1920s with a Parisian house of embroidery named Kitmir after forging a connection to upstart couturier Gabrielle "Coco" Chanel (1883-1971) via her younger brother's love affair with the designer.[2]

Princess Olga Paley and her older daughter, Princess Irina, were devoted to aiding the Russian émigré population in France.[3] By 1926, the

dramatist's writings are partially preserved in the Paley Family Collection, Hillwood Estate, Museum & Gardens Archives and Special Collections.

2 Justine Picardie, *Coco Chanel: The Legend and the Life, New Edition* (New York: Dey Street Books, 2023), 142-148. Grand Duke Dimitri Pavlovich may have also helped his half sister Natalie Paley's entrée into the fashion world via his relationship with Chanel. His 1942 death of tuberculosis at a sanitarium in Switzerland was one of the sorrowful points of Paley's wartime experience. See Liaut 2015, 242-43. For more on Grand Duchess Maria's embroidery firm, see Albertini and Kurkdjian 2023.

3 The family of three princesses attracted the attention of the French and American press beginning in 1923 with Princess Irina's marriage to her cousin Prince Feodor Alexandrovich (1898-1968), which appeared in the *Vogue Paris*, July 1st, 1923. The following year, in its October 6 edition, *Women's Wear* reported extensively on Princess Olga's Russian Fete held at Le Pavillon Royal in Biarritz, a charitable event organized for émigrés.

Paley women's charitable efforts were prominently featured in *Women's Wear Daily*, *Vogue Paris*, and a local Biarritz publication titled *Biarritz illustré et Côte basque-Pyrénée*. Of particular interest in that year's coverage is the family's connection to the French couturier Lucien Lelong (1889-1952).

In June 1926, *Women's Wear* (its name until 1927) reported on a rooftop benefit to be held at the studio of Lelong, then located at 16, avenue Matignon. The article notes that the event would aid "the charity work carried on by Her Royal Highness, the Princess Paley." Scheduled for Saturday, June 5, 1926, the event was officially named "Fête des Trois Cents," for the exclusive cap on attendees that the couturier established.[4] Following the event, an illustrated report in the same publication notes that Lelong dressed all three Paley women in "sheer frocks and fringe."[5] (fig. 72) The summertime reportage on the princesses and their favorite young couturier concluded that September, when *Women's Wear* reported specifically on Princess Natalie Paley's ensemble, complete with an accompanying illustration, for that year's Russian Fete organized by her mother at Le Pavillon Royal near Biarritz.[6]

Several sources suggest that Natalie Paley began her modeling career with Yteb, a fashion atelier established by Baroness Elizabeth Hoyningen-Huene (1891-1973), the sister of Paley's future friend and collaborator, fashion photographer George Hoyningen-Huene (1900-1968).[7] It is also possible that Paley met Lelong via her half siblings' connections to fellow Parisian designer Chanel, mentioned earlier. Most likely, Lelong knew Paley's fashionable mother from her patronage of the family business in Paris prior to her return to Russia in 1914 for just a few years. During the late nineteenth century, Lelong's parents, Arthur and Éléonore, operated a small yet prestigious couture firm called A. E. Lelong, recognized for its court costumes, and noted to include Queen Victoria as a client. The couple gradually expanded their firm and even joined the Chambre Syndicale de la Couture. As their son came of age, he took an interest in the family business – but his initial participation was cut short by the onset of the First World War.[8]

Following his service as an intelligence officer, when he sustained injuries and received the Croix de Guerre, Lucien Lelong returned to resuscitate and lead the company.[9] A savvy businessperson, Lelong recognized the cultural popularity of Russian émigrés in Paris during the 1920s; Princess Olga

4 *Women's Wear*, June 2, 1926; Demornex 2008, 33.

5 *Women's Wear*, June 15, 1926.

6 *Women's Wear*, September 16, 1926.

7 Liaut 2015, 116; Vassiliev 2000, 439. The Hoyningen-Huenes were an international, aristocratic family, with an American mother and a Baltic-German father. Both siblings were raised in St. Petersburg at the Court of Nicholas II and shared Paley's experience of fleeing at the onset of the Russian Revolution. See Vassiliev 2000, 233-63.

8 Demornex 2008, 9.

9 *Ibid.*, 10.

Sheer Frocks and Fringe Designed to Be Worn at Lelong's Fete des Trois Cents

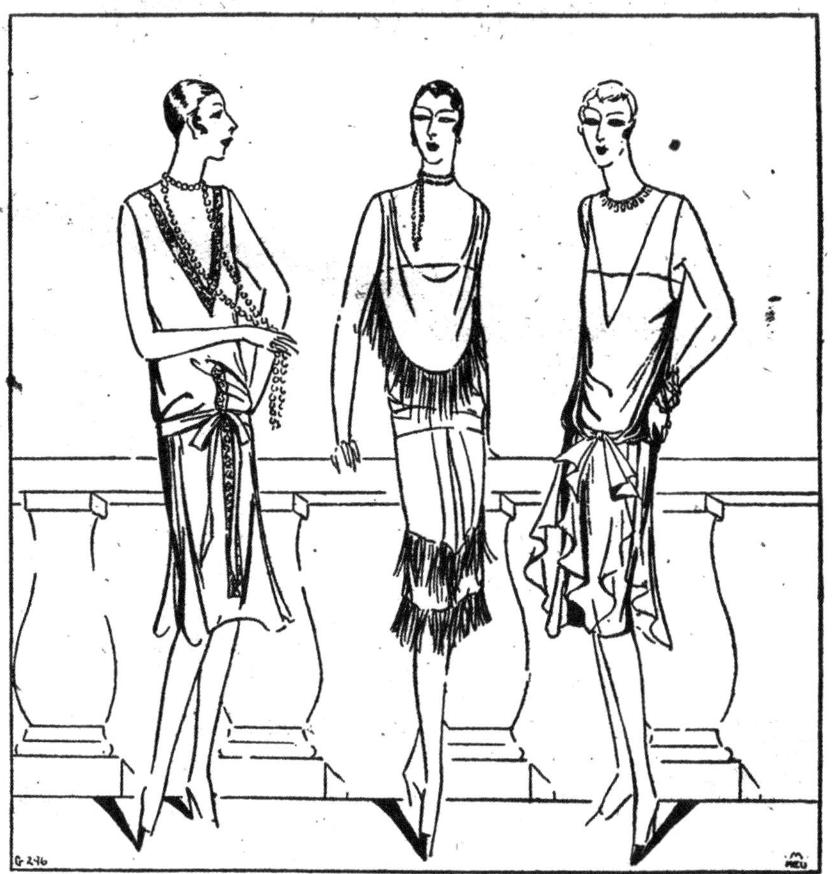

Left to Right:

BLUE Georgette Adorned With Silver Embroidery in a Frock Fashioned for Princess Theodore de Russie for the Charity Fete, Held on the Roof of the New Building Just Completed by Lucien Lelong, Which Limited the Guests to 300.

* * *

WHITE Silk Fringe Elaborates the Crepe Gown of Princess Nathalie Paley, While the Deep U Decolletage in Front Is of Interest.

PRINCESS PALEY, Who Organized the Fete, Favors a Black Chiffon Model Fashioned on Bloused Lines and Sometimes Embroidered in Strass.

From the Paris Bureau of WOMEN'S WEAR.

Fig. 72 All three Paley princesses wear Lucien Lelong fashions for the Fête des Trois Cents, hosted by Lelong, *Women's Wear*, June 15, 1926.

Paley and her young daughters were visible and influential figures.[10] Whatever the origin of the initial connection, Lelong asked Princess Natalie Paley to marry him, and the wedding was set for August 10, 1927, after months of speculation in the French and American fashion press (fig. 73).[11]

The bride's cream silk panne gown and Juliet-style headpiece and veil came from her husband's label, naturally, and the wedding took place at the Saint Alexander Nevsky Cathedral, in the 8th Arrondissement.[12] At the time of their marriage, Princess Paley was twenty-one years old and had large, expressive eyes, a fashionable curled bob hairstyle, and a delicate nose. Her features were especially suited to modeling hats – an accessory that would be part of her personal fashion oeuvre for decades to come.[13] Her debonair, thirty-seven-year-old husband, who was on his second marriage, had an appreciation for polo and tennis, and was part of an upper-class social circle. During the following decade, the 1930s, Lelong became one of the most popular couture labels, recognized for its sportswear and sophisticated evening wear. In 1932, the company became one of the first to introduce prêt-à-porter, and the business enjoyed success during the economic strife of the worldwide Depression because of a successful perfume line that had been added in 1926. Of course, these achievements were linked to his top model and creative consultant: the elegant "Madame Lucien Lelong."[14] (fig. 74)

Initially, the fashionable couple seemed content – apart from promoting the label on trips abroad, they attended the famous fancy dress balls of comte Étienne de Beaumont, traveled with large groups of aristocrats and creatives to St. Moritz and Venice's Lido Beach, and settled together in a new property Lelong built in Saint-Cloud, west of Paris (figs. 75-76).[15] In 1929, when Princess Olga passed away, she was buried in Lelong's family tomb. But by 1933, Paley was no longer identified as "Madame Lucien Lelong" in her numerous fashion periodical appearances. Gossip surrounding her "affairs" or close personal relationships with artists like Serge Lifar (1905-1986) and Jean

10 Lelong did not design, but he had a keen fashion and textile sense augmented by his genius for business and marketing acumen. He is remembered for hiring exceptional young designers to work under his label, a roster that included Christian Dior, Pierre Balmain, and Hubert de Givenchy. See Garnier 1987, 248-49.

11 *Women's Wear*, March 15 and May 14, 1927.

12 *Women's Wear*, August 10, 1927; the *Vogue Paris*, January 1st, 1928.

13 *Femina*, August 1st, 1926. Paley was famous for her collection of hats worn by the pool at Pebbles, her Fairfield, Connecticut, country house, as documented in snapshots from husband Jack Wilson's scrapbooks, today part of the John C. Wilson Papers, Yale Collection of American Literature, Beinecke Rare Book and Manuscript Library.

14 Garnier 1987, 248; Demornex 2008, 29, 39, 46; Liaut 2015, 125.

15 One of Natalie Paley's early 1930s scrapbooks containing snapshots of her, Lelong, and Coco Chanel sharing time together on the slopes of St. Moritz is preserved: Natalie Paley Photograph Albums, Photographs, and Correspondence, GEN MSS 574, Box 2. For more on the Saint-Cloud residence, see Liaut 2015, 126n.

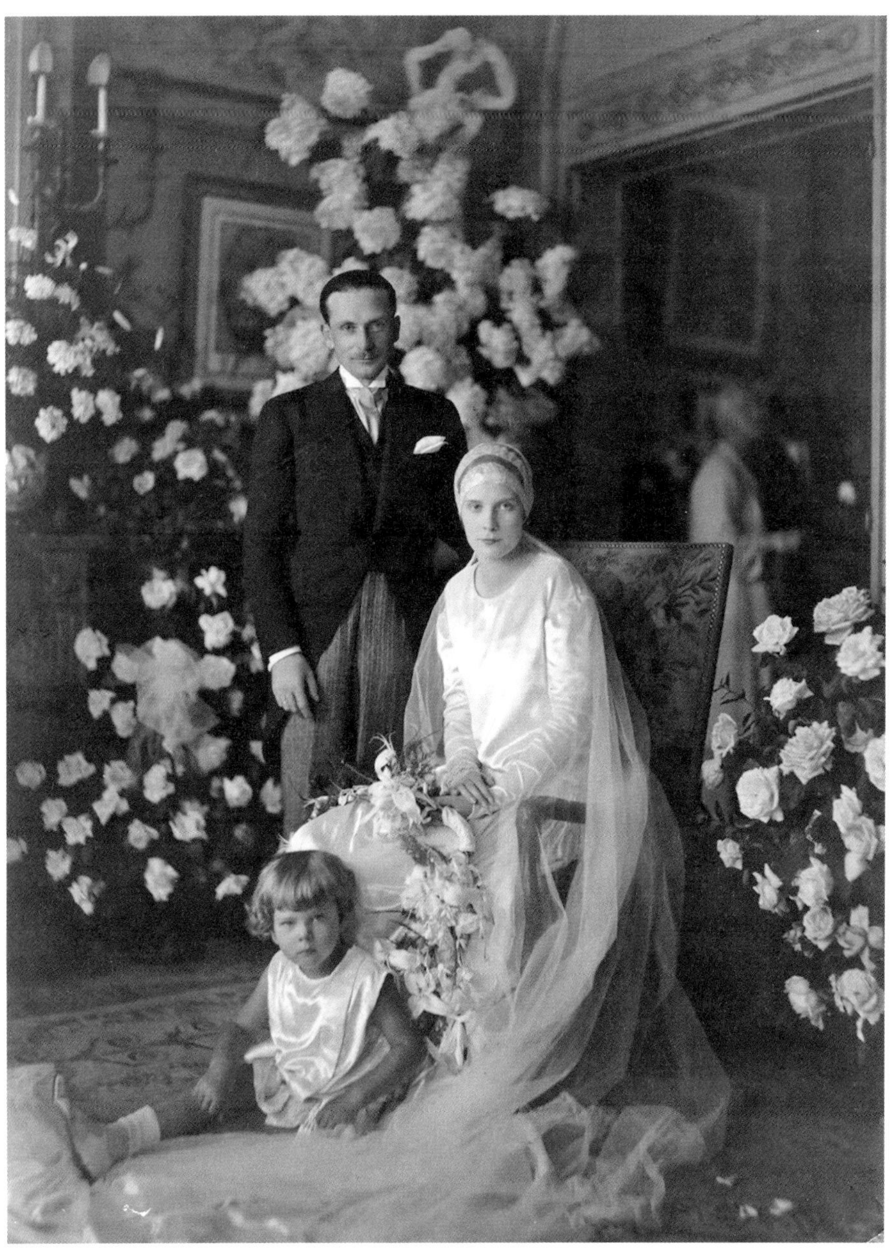

Fig. 73 Lelong and Paley pose for a wedding portrait, Paris, August 1927. Paley wears a bridal ensemble from Lelong. The boy at their feet is her nephew Prince Michael Feodorovich Romanoff. Paley Family Collection, Hillwood Estate, Museum & Gardens Archives and Special Collections, Washington, DC.

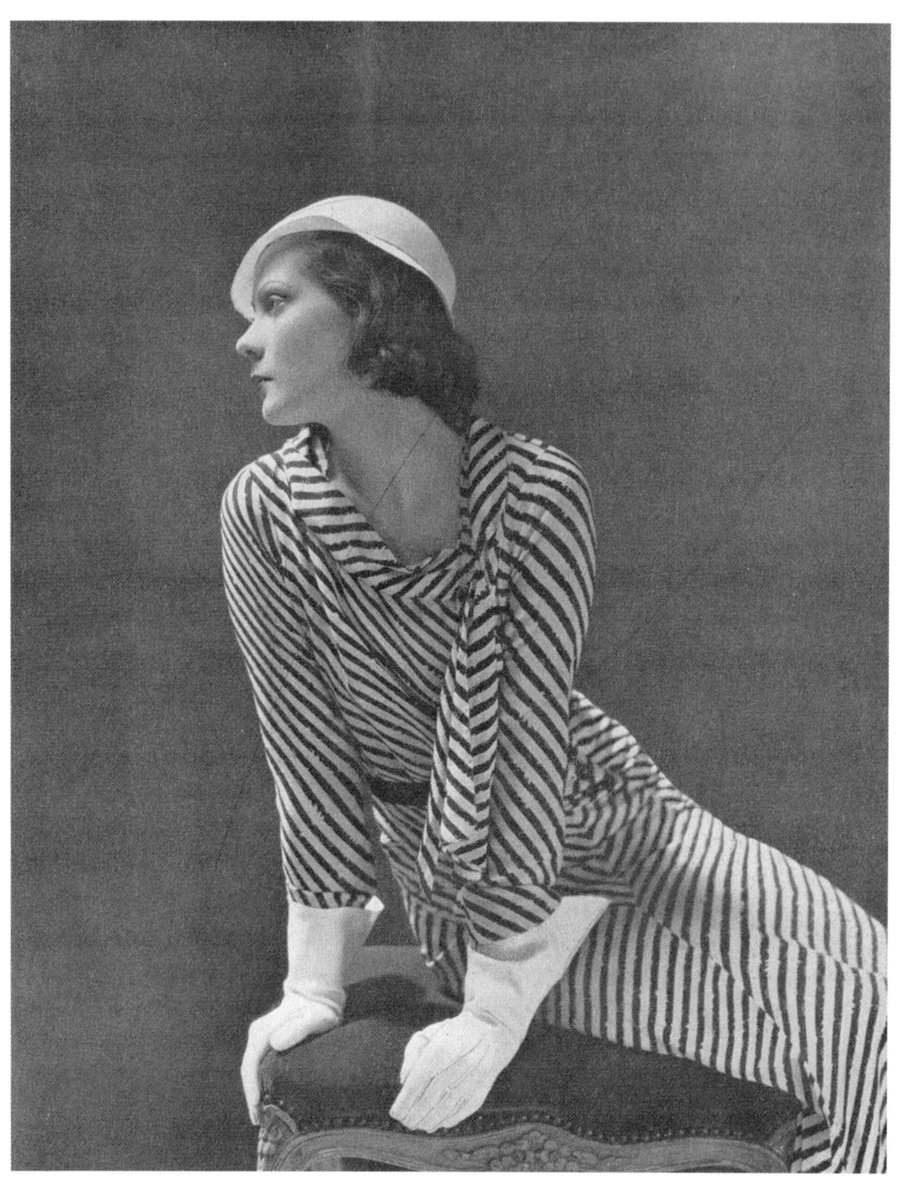

Fig. 74 Princess Paley makes an appearance as Madame Lucien Lelong, photographed by her friend George Hoyningen-Huene for *Vogue Paris*, August 1931 issue.

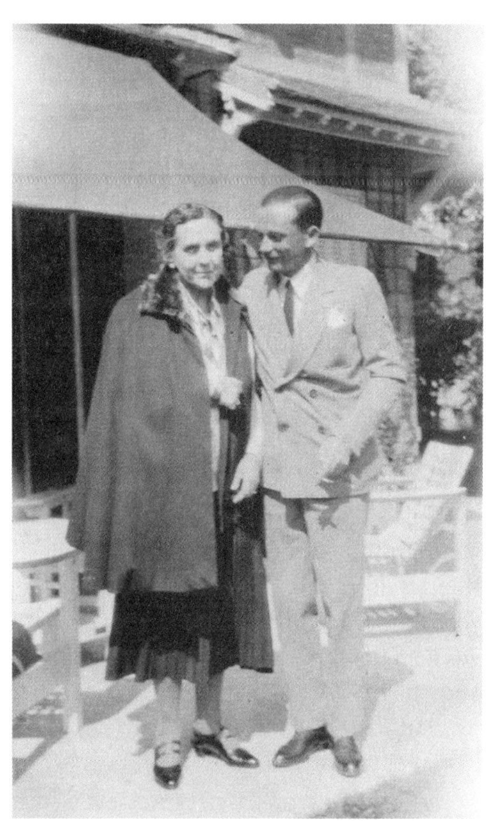

Fig. 75 Princess Olga Paley and Lucien Lelong, ca. 1928. Paley Family Collection, Hillwood Estate, Museum & Gardens Archives and Special Collections, Washington, DC.

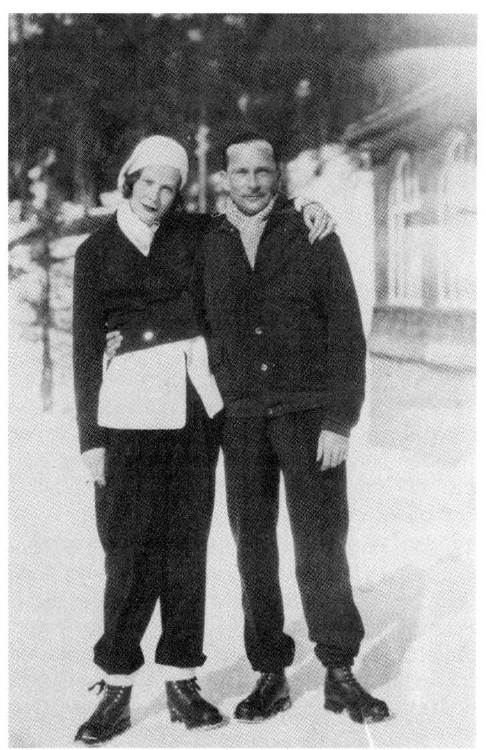

Fig. 76 Snapshot of Paley and Lelong during an early 1930s skiing trip with friends to St. Moritz. Natalie Paley Photograph Albums, Photographs, and Correspondence, Beinecke Rare Book and Manuscript Library, Yale University.

Cocteau (both of whom were notably gay) irritated Lelong and did not align with the discreet, elegant presence he expected her to embody. According to Liaut, they existed independently, with the princess busy nurturing her burgeoning film career and spending time abroad with friends including vicomtesse Marie de Noailles (1902-1970) and Princess Baba de Faucigny-Lucinge (1901-1945).[16]

After establishing herself socially and professionally in Los Angeles and New York, in 1937 the princess pursued a divorce from Lelong and made plans to remain in the United States for her marriage to theater producer Jack Wilson.[17] Lelong and Paley parted amicably. Paley kept Lelong's military identification bracelet, for instance – yet dispensed of her Lelong-labeled clothes, passing them off to her maids, likely less as a sign of derision and more a symbol of change: as one of the world's best-dressed women, she would not be wearing out-of-date styles![18] For his part, Lelong released a new fragrance, called N, in 1937, the year of their official divorce (pl. 65). That year, he sold his boat, the *Master Lou*, to Gilles de Monbrison – whose father would later become the second husband of Paley's sister, Princess Irina – and in 1947 even hired his former nephew, Prince Michael Feodorovich Romanoff (1924-2008), to work on his perfume line, the only extension of his label to endure.[19]

Aristocrats, society, and even royals held the greatest cachet in the pages of *Vogue* and *Harper's Bazaar* before celebrities associated with Hollywood films and musicians took hold as fashion models and brand ambassadors. When she made her *Vogue Paris* debut in 1928, Natalie Paley was identified first as Lelong's wife; then her royal lineage was revealed. Her portrait for the feature was taken by renowned American photographer Edward Steichen (1879-1973). Of course, she wore Lelong, paired with a Maria Guy cloche.[20]

16 These three women, including Paley, were defined by French and American *Vogue* editor Bettina Ballard (1903-1961) in her autobiography, *In My Fashion*, as "the women who make fashion" in 1930s Paris. Bettina Ballard *In My Fashion* (New York: David McKay Company, Inc 1960), 72.

17 Liaut 2015, 228-29.

18 Lelong's military ID bracelet remains in a private collection of Paley's family. The anecdote about the disbursement of her Lelong wardrobe comes from a conversation with Jean-Noël Liaut on January 6, 2023. Paley was a perennial awardee on the "International Best Dressed List" of fashion publicist Eleanor Lambert (1903-2003) from the mid-1940s to the early 1950s. See Tiffany 2011.

19 N is no longer produced, but according to Demornex, it was a scent defined as "cool, sharp… as bitter as a tonic with its astringent notes of wood, tea ylang-ylang, and damp leaves… an aristocratic coolness." Demornex 2008, 35. See also Lucien Lelong, Memorandum, June 24, 1937, Paley Family Collection, Hillwood Archives and Special Collections. Lelong was appointed president of Paris's Chambre Syndicale de la Couture in 1937, a role that defined his legacy in the fashion history as he is credited with saving the couture industry from relocation to Berlin under the Nazi occupation of part of France. Garnier 1987, 248.

20 *Vogue Paris*, January 1st, 1928.

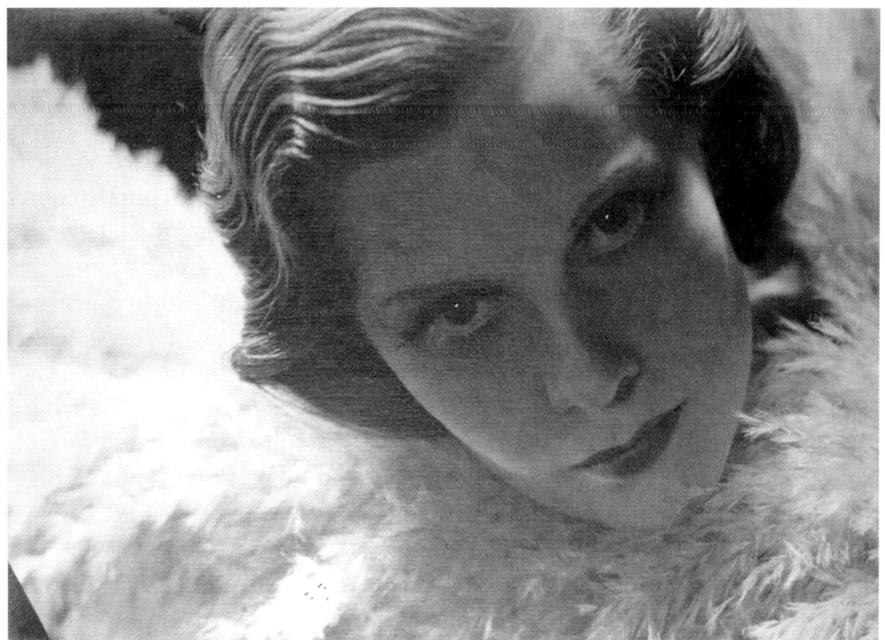

Fig. 77 Natalie Paley at the nascent stage of her film career, ca. 1933, Paley Family Collection, Hillwood Estate, Museum & Gardens Archives and Special Collections, Washington DC, photographed by Hoyningen-Huene.

Even if her marriage was destined to fizzle within years, Paley's affiliation with Lelong guaranteed the princess's relevance as a fashion model and arbiter of fashionable taste through the 1950s. Through her connection to Lelong, Paley met photographers Hoyningen-Huene, Horst P. Horst (1906-1999), and Cecil Beaton (1904-1980) – all of whom became frequent collaborators and friends.[21] She also had a tragic, often-romanticized past, making for compelling and dramatic copy. As interest in film stars mounted, Paley's brief but star – studded mid – 1930s stint as an actor further enhanced her relevance. As her biographer, Liaut, put it, "she became a goddess of the 1930s," ultimately appearing in a few French and American films and countless fashion photo shoots (fig. 77; see fig. 69).[22]

Paley's alignment with Hoyningen-Huene, his protégé Horst, and Beaton ensured her legendary status as an early to mid-twentieth-century fashion icon and propelled her into the next decade of success in the fashion industry. Hoyningen-Huene, who began studying with Steichen in Paris, photographed Paley for more than twenty years. Some of his earliest photos

21 Paley worked with other important twentieth-century photographers including Adolf de Meyer, Man Ray, Studio Dorvyne, André Durst, Louise Dahl-Wolfe, Erwin Blumenfeld, Georges Platt Lynes, and Peter Rose Pulham.

22 Liaut 2015, 108.

of her date to his years affiliated with *Vogue Paris*, from 1925 to 1934, when he captured her embodiment of Lelong's fashion label and several glamorous promotional photos for the 1933 French film she started in, *L'Épervier*, directed by Marcel L'Herbier (1888-1979) and costarring Charles Boyer (1899-1978). When Hoyningen-Huene made the transition to *Harper's Bazaar* in 1935, he continued to work with the princess as she completed her tenure as the face of Lelong ahead of their divorce.[23] During the late 1930s, Paley and Hoyningen-Huene shot editorials for New York – based labels like Bergdorf Goodman, Henri Bendel, Nettie Rosenstein, and Hattie Carnegie. In 1939, Condé Nast apparently forced her to choose between *Vogue*, which Nast owned, and *Harper's Bazaar*.[24] Yet Hoyningen-Huene's coverage of her new, fleeting endeavor in New York working with friends Niki de Gunzburg (1904-1981) and Barbara Karinska (1886-1983) still appeared in *Harper's Bazaar*, as did later fashion editorials of Paley in her capacity as spokesmodel for Mainbocher through the 1940s and 1950s (see pls. 66, 68).[25] Perhaps due to their shared experience of fleeing Russia as young people, the famous photographer and the princess seemed to trust each other, a connection revealed in their work. Hoyningen-Huene even cast his lover and mentee, the burgeoning German-born photographer Horst P. Horst, in his unnamed, unreleased experimental film opposite Paley, the springboard for the latter's cinematic aspirations (fig. 78).[26] He figured in Paley's American social life, spending time poolside at Pebbles, the country home she shared with her second husband, Jack Wilson.[27]

British-born photographer, artist, costume designer, and society personality Cecil Beaton also shared a connection to Natalie Paley in which their professional and personal lives overlapped. Paley featured in many of Beaton's caricature-like sketches of society and fashion leaders, some of which were published in *Vogue* during the 1930s and 1940s (see figs. 81, 82).[28] Several

23 Martineu 2018, 84; *Vogue Paris*, January 1st, 1933. See Liaut 2015, 198-204, for a discussion of this film, with exclusively Lelong costumes. Hoyningen-Huene, Signed Photographic Prints of Natalie Paley, 1932-1933, Paley Family Collection, Hillwood Archives and Special Collections. Paley continued to represent Lelong as shot by Hoyningen-Huene. See, for example, *Harper's Bazaar* 69 (May 1936):76, and 71 (June 1938): 38.

24 John C. Wilson to Noël Coward, November 8, 1939. Noël Coward Collection: Papers, 1911-2000, Cadbury Research Library, University of Birmingham.

25 See, for example, *Harper's Bazaar*, no. 2731 (December 1939): 68-71, and no. 2733 (February 1940): 42-47. For later examples of Paley and Hoyningen-Huene's editorial work for Mainbocher, see *Harper's Bazaar*, no. 2758 (November 1941): 66-67, no. 2765 (May 1942): 51, no. 2771 (November 1942): 32-33, no. 2776 (April 1943): 43, no. 2777 (May 1943): 49, and no. 2794 (October 1944):71.

26 Liaut 2015, 117, 123.

27 1941 Scrapbook, Vol. 2, Box 20, John C. Wilson Papers (YCAL MSS 1127).

28 *Vogue Paris*, January 1st, 1933. Beaton illustrated Paley while reporting on her attendance at a Toscanini concert at the Théâtre des Champs-Élysées with friends including Marie de Noailles, Elsa Schiaparelli, and Princess Baba de Faucigny-Lucinge. Examples of his later pencil

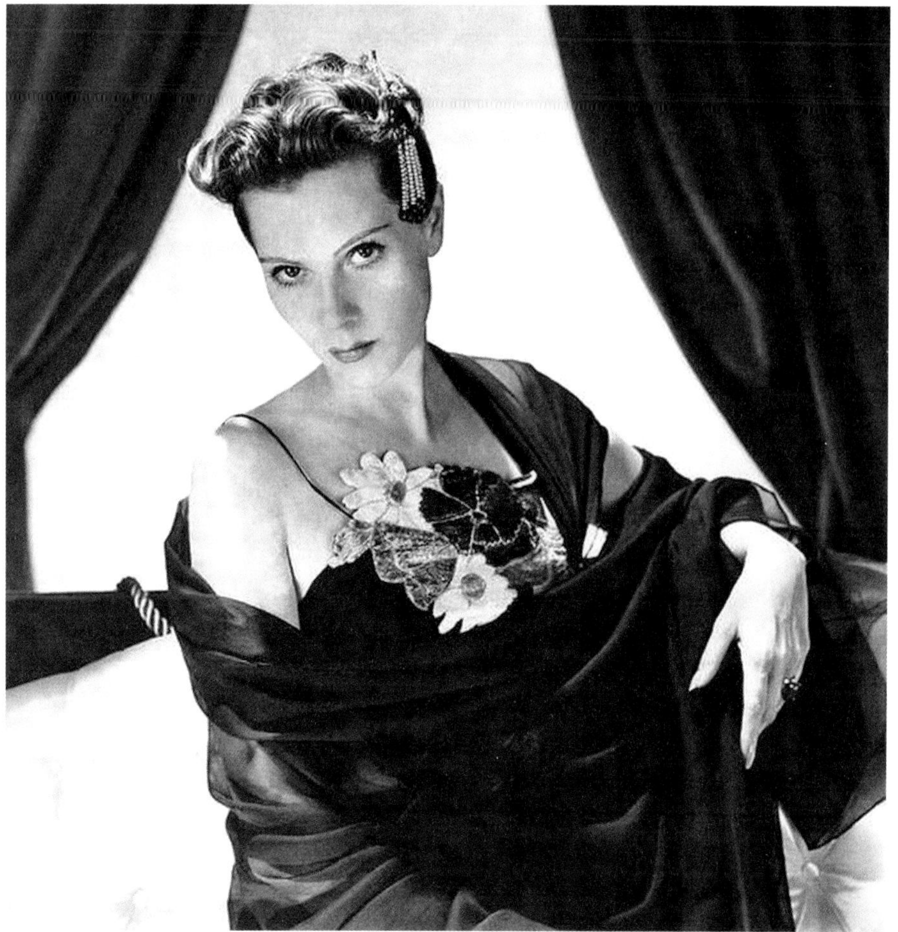

Fig. 78 Natalie Paley, photographed by her friend Horst P. Horst for *Vogue*, November 1942.

of his most exciting fashion editorial work featured her, notably his 1935 "New Edwardians" photo shoot for *Vogue*, her dramatic 1933 portrait in front of mattress springs, and a cover portrait for Britain's the *Sketch* (fig. 79).[29] He was also an early mutual friend of Jack Wilson (fig. 80) and his lover turned business partner in theater, Noël Coward.[30] Paley was a guest at Beaton's

sketches of the princess and husband Jack Wilson are today preserved in Hillwood's Paley Family Collection.

29 The latter two are in the collection of the National Portrait Gallery, London. Although the *Sketch* cover was dated Wednesday, February 14, 1940, a candid of Paley posing for Beaton is included in the 1938 Scrapbook, Vol. 1, Box 11, John C. Wilson Papers (YCAL MSS 1127).

30 Vickers 1987, 182. Their friendship, before Wilson's marriage to Paley, is also evident in Untitled Scrapbooks, 1930-1936, undated; 1933, undated (Box 1, 2), John C. Wilson Papers (YCAL MSS 1127).

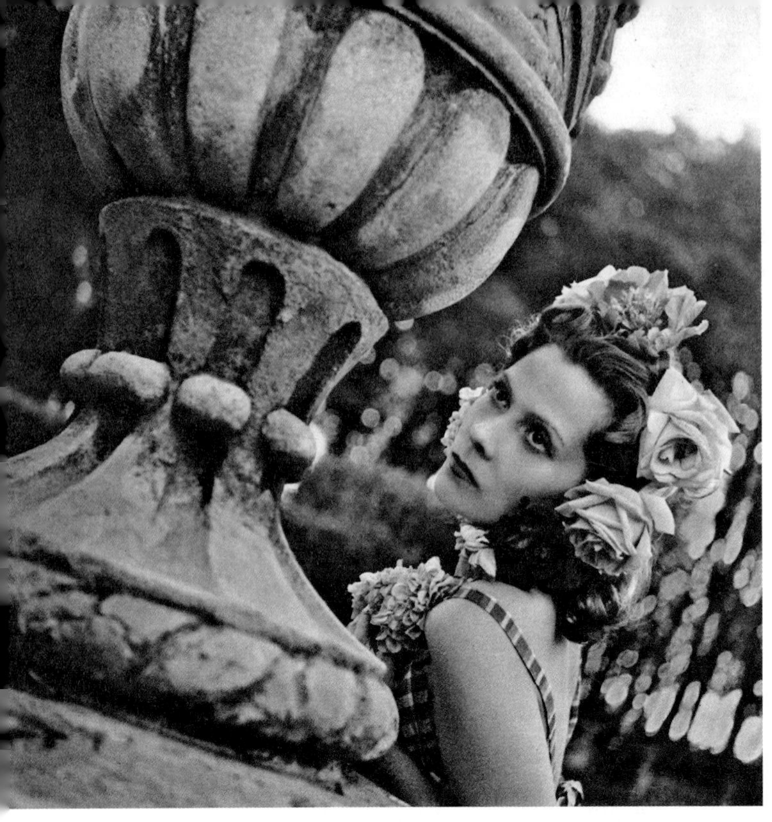

Fig. 79 Princess Natalie Paley, photographed by Cecil Beaton for the *Sketch*, February 14, 1940.

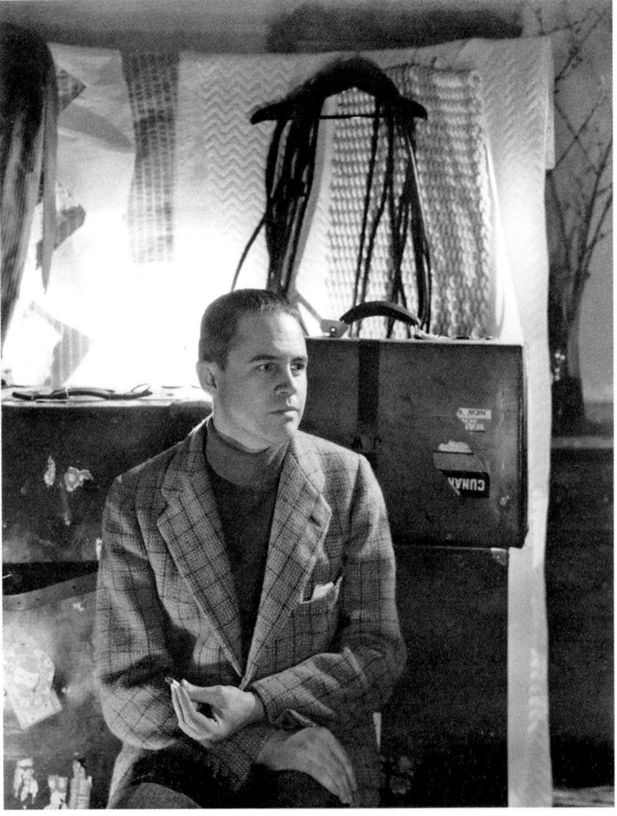

Fig. 80 Portrait of John C. "Jack" Wilson by Cecil Beaton, New York, late 1930s. Paley Family Collection, Hillwood Estate, Museum & Gardens Archives and Special Collections, Washington, DC.

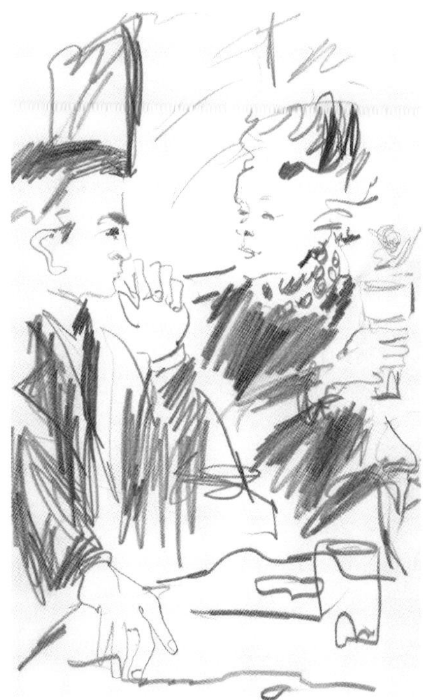

Fig. 81 Sketch by Beaton of Natalie Paley and her husband Jack Wilson, New York, late 1940s. Paley Family Collection, Hillwood Estate, Museum & Gardens Archives and Special Collections, Washington, DC.

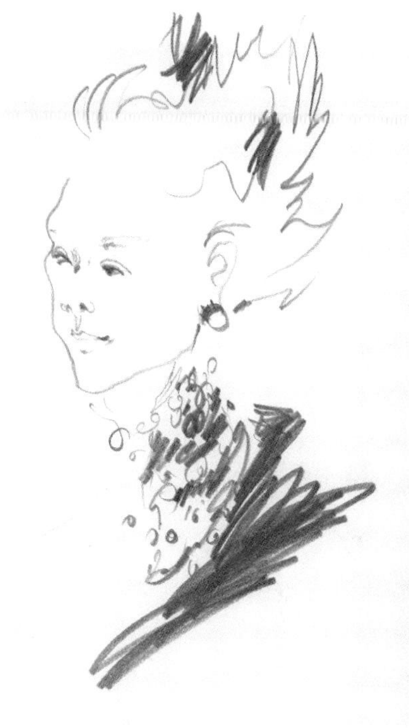

Fig. 82 Sketch by Beaton of Natalie Paley, New York, late 1940s. Paley Family Collection, Hillwood Estate, Museum & Gardens Archives and Special Collections, Washington, DC.

country estate, Ashcombe, with other glamorous aristocrats and actors, and even participated in an intimate, avant-garde photo shoot also featuring young, tattooed photographer Victor Kraft (1915-1976).[31] Beaton described Paley's beauty as "so rare and alluring" and considered her one of his closest friends, with whom he could confide his anxieties surrounding his relationship with Greta Garbo.[32]

Paley was so well-connected in the fashion industry that securing a position upon her relocation to New York was not a challenge, but certainly a requirement. As Wilson points out in his own biography, the princess was as tenacious as other survivors of the Revolution and sought to distinguish herself from the expected formality of her aristocratic upbringing via a career.[33] Still, correspondence between Wilson and Coward suggests that this may also

31 *Sketch*, June 27, 1934. One print from the Kraft-Paley series is held in the Metropolitan Museum of Art's photography collection.

32 Vickers 1987, 182, 318.

33 Wilson 2015, 97.

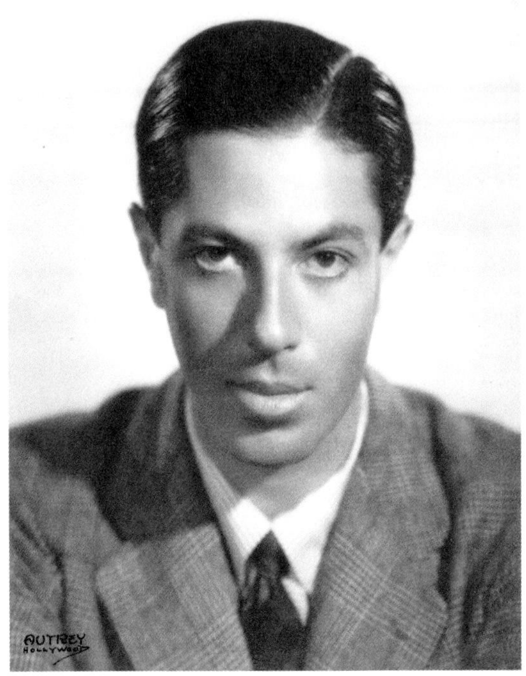

Fig. 83 Portrait of Natalie Paley's closest friend, Baron Niki de Gunzburg, Hollywood, late 1930s. Photographed by Max Munn Autrey. Paley Family Collection, Hillwood Estate, Museum & Gardens Archives and Special Collections, Washington, DC.

have been out of economic necessity.[34] The brief enterprise of costume designer and fellow Russian émigré Barbara Karinska's New York – based fashion atelier failed in less than a year, because its three partners – Paley, her best friend Niki de Gunzburg, and Karinska herself – were all creatives unable to manage product fulfillment and production (fig. 83).[35] Fortunately, a refugee from the Nazi occupation of France, American-born fashion designer Main Rousseau Bocher (1890-1976), who designed under his shortened name, "Mainbocher," arrived from Paris with a flourishing couture business. Paley was likely connected to the designer via her early days posing for *Vogue* in Paris, when the designer was then the editor; her friendship with Hoyningen-Huene; and her social circle including some of his aristocratic, illustrious clients.[36] Additionally, one of Mainbocher's earliest investors was Katherine "Kitty" Bache Miller (1896-1979), a philanthropist, art collector, and wife of

34 John C. Wilson to Noël Coward, November 2, 1939, December 8, 1939, December 27, 1939, May 19, 1943, John C. Wilson, 1936-1958 (COW/3/N/2/58), Noël Coward Collection: Papers, 1911-2000.

35 *Women's Wear Daily*, April 22, 1940, June 13, 1940); John C. Wilson to Noël Coward, June 26, 1940, July 24, 1940, John C. Wilson, 1936-1958 (COW/3/N/2/58), Noël Coward Collection: Papers, 1911-2000; Liaut 2015, 251-52.

36 See Slinkard 2016. Two signed portraits of Natalie Paley are in the collection of the Mainbocher Papers at the Irene Lewisohn Costume Reference Library at the Costume Institute, one written to her "favorite boss" and another addressed to "Uncle Main" featuring her beloved dachshund, Fan-Tan.

successful Broadway producer Gilbert Miller (1884-1969).[37] The Millers were close to Paley and Wilson through the 1940s.[38]

Prior to his relocation to New York, the designer cultivated an elite cadre of clients that famously included Wallis Simpson, the Duchess of Windsor, to whom he served only ice water in his salon at 12, avenue George V so they would not be preoccupied away from the designs. His experience as the *Vogue Paris*'s editor made him wary of fashion design piracy and copyists. He admired French couturiers Madeleine Vionnet and Augusta Bernard for their elegant restraint in eveningwear and expertise in draping (pl. 67).[39]

In terms of appearance, Paley's affiliation with Mainbocher was limited to being "the face" of the label, posing in his designs for magazines, and incorporating them into her wardrobe for social events, yet it seems she was more involved with client relationships and the day-to-day management of the firm (figs. 84, 85). The correspondence dating to the 1940s and 1950s between her husband, Jack Wilson, and erstwhile lover/business partner Coward, and held in the Noël Coward Collection: Papers, 1911-2000, Cadbury Research Library at the University of Birmingham, reveals a more involved, day-to-day role, for which Paley was compensated – not merely in gratis clothing, but on a salary relied upon by the couple.[40] According to a letter dated September 25, 1941, Paley was "very busy but blissfully happy" in her new role. Wilson went on to mention the salary and wardrobe, noting that the business was thriving because of her vast network of New York and Hollywood connections "flocking to the shop." A year later, she was equally perseverant; Wilson wrote on July 14, 1942, that Paley "has now become a sort of vital essential... caring very deeply about trying to keep its head above water." An update arrived following Paley's summer break that she would be managing the shop while Mainbocher traveled to Hollywood for an engagement with Twentieth Century-Fox. "She is very excited and a little nervous about the responsibility involved."[41] A letter dated May 17, 1943, noted that the princess was "frightfully busy... she seldom gets home before seven at night." Wilson elaborated further on her involvement with the firm in a May 19, 1943, letter that "she has done remarkably well there... [She has become] Main's irreplaceable right hand assistant.

37 Lee et al. 1975, 127.

38 John C. Wilson to Noël Coward, December 27, 1939, John C. Wilson, 1936-1958 (COW/3/N/2/58), Noël Coward Collection: Papers, 1911-2000.

39 Lee et al. 1975, 125-35.

40 This contrasts with a discussion of Paley's role at the designer in notes published in her second husband's memoir, Wilson 2015, 152. Elsewhere, Paley is identified as "manager," "client," and "première vendeuse"; see Lee et al. 1975, 166, 182.

41 John C. Wilson to Noël Coward, August 27, 1942, John C. Wilson, 1936-1958 (COW/3/N/2/58), Noël Coward Collection. In addition to film, Mainbocher designed for the stage, creating a costume for Wilson's productions of Coward's play *Blithe Spirit* (1941) and of the musical *One Touch of Venus* (1943), starring Mary Martin. See Slinkard 2016, 121-24.

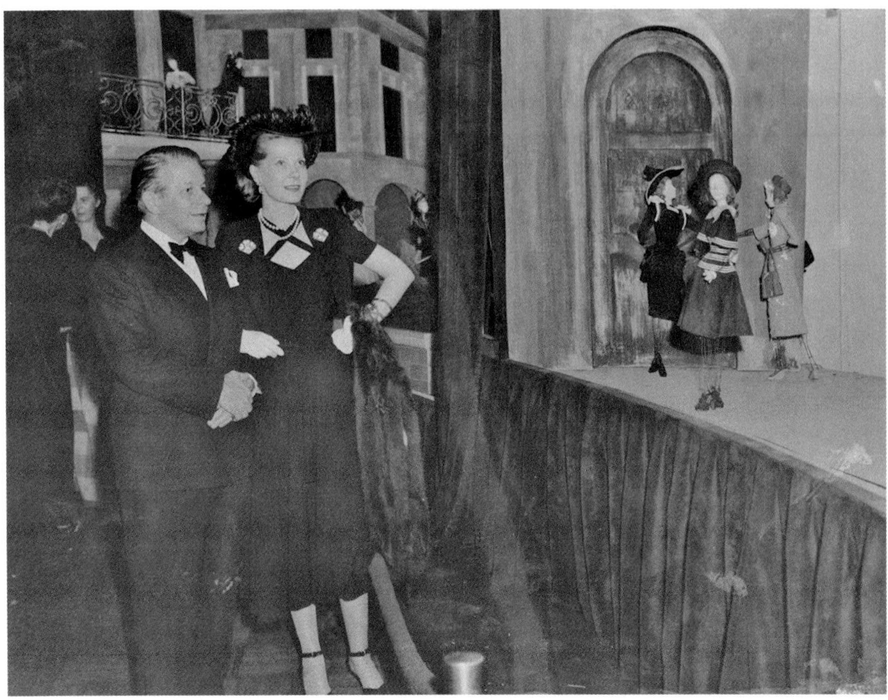

Fig. 84 Mainbocher and Natalie Paley attend the opening of the Théâtre de la Mode traveling exhibition of fashion dolls created by Parisian designers in New York, 1946. Scrapbooks, John C. Wilson Papers Yale Collection of American Literature, Beinecke Rare Book and Manuscript Library.

Every customer who comes into the shop asks for her and her well-known and completely false charm of manner… in addition to being exquisitely dressed for every occasion on the house, she has lately been receiving cheques of quite considerable importance."[42]

In contrast to Lelong's more subdued, androgynous designs of the 1920s and 1930s, Mainbocher's work in New York during the Second World War was slightly more exuberant – featuring jeweled collar sweaters, silk prints, hand-beaded cardigans, and his signature "cocktail aprons" to enliven preexisting ensembles at a time of war-related constraint. Paley wore his clothes well – they were suited to Broadway openings in the city and Fairfield cocktail parties alike. Paley's work with Mainbocher continued at least through the 1950s; she sent a distressed telegram to mutual friend Coward noting that his shop sustained a serious fire in May 1952.[43] Other fashionable figures and friends in New York during her chapter in the United States include

42 John C. Wilson to Noël Coward, May 17, 1943, May 19, 1943, John C. Wilson, 1936-1958 (COW/3/N/2/58), Noël Coward Collection.

43 Telegram, Natalie Paley to Noël Coward, May 17, 1952, New York, Telegram Logbooks (COW/4/I/1), John C. Wilson to Noël Coward, February 1st, 1955, John C. Wilson, 1936-1958 (COW/3/N/2/58), Noël Coward Collection. Mainbocher and his partner, sketch artist Douglas

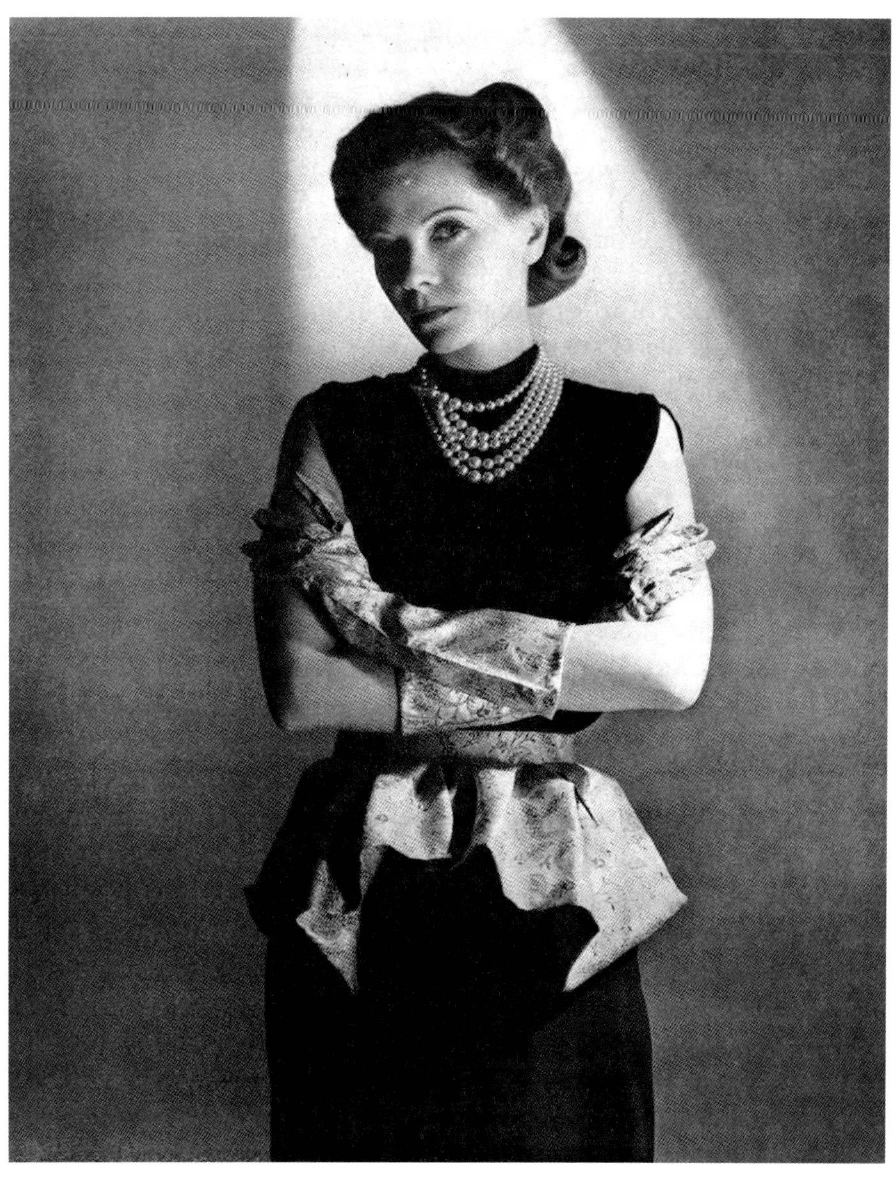

Fig. 85 Natalie Paley models an evening gown with gloves from Mainbocher, photographed by Hoyiningen-Huene for *Harper's Bazaar*, November 1942 issue.

fashion editor Diana Vreeland (1903-1989), jeweler Jean Schlumberger (1907-1987), and the Ukrainian-born designer Valentina Schlee (1899-1989), whose renowned Easter parties were regularly attended by Paley (fig. 86).[44] Italian jewelry designer Fulco di Verdura (1898-1978) and Baron Niki de Gunzburg were the princess's closest longtime friends (fig. 87).[45] Paley maintained friendships with stylish society figures, like Mary Cushing Astor Fosburgh, Mona Williams von Bismarck, Millicent Rogers, and Lady Iya Abdy. During and immediately after the war, Pebbles was host to two of fashion's greats – Elsa Schiaparelli (1890-1973), during the summers of 1940 and 1941, and Christian Dior (1905-1957), who visited with society friend Patricia Arturo Lopez Willshaw on Palm Sunday, 1950 (fig. 88).[46]

During the early twentieth century, the art and fashion worlds were inextricably linked, thus Natalie Paley's influence transcends the ateliers and fashion magazines to canvas, sculpture, illustration, and dance.[47] She is rumored to have been captured by Pablo Picasso (1881-1973) during the late 1920s while both were staying with French society figure Étienne de Beaumont.[48] Salvador Dalí (1904-1989), who was a friend from the 1930s to the 1950s, at the very least illustrated her Verdura jewelry for a *Vogue* editorial spread (fig. 89).[49] She was sculpted in porcelain and wood by Polish-born textile designer Sarah Lipska (1882-1973), who had designed for the Ballets Russes and House of Myrbor in Paris, and by Hungarian-born sculptor Nicolaus Koni (1911-2000).[50] A friend of Paley's from her Cecil Beaton circle, Elsa "Jack" von Reppert-Bismarck (1903-1971), made several charming

Pollard, were regular guests at Pebbles. According to Sarah Lee, Mainbocher remained open until 1971, but began to lose relevance and prestige during the 1960s. Lee et al. 1975, 165-66.

44 See Diana Vreeland and Christopher Hemphill, *Allure*. (repr., New York: Chronicle Books, 2010), 117-19, for a complete mis-telling of Paley's personal history. Vreeland and her husband were also frequent Pebbles guests during the 1940s.

45 Paley was often photographed in her Verdura jewelry in fashion editorials, and in personal snapshots preserved by Jack Wilson in his scrapbooks. See Corbett 2002. For more on Baron Niki de Gunzburg, who was editor at *Vogue*, *Harper's Bazaar*, and *Town & Country*, see Amy Fine Collins, "A Taste for Living," *Vanity Fair*, August 18, 2014, https://www.vanityfair.com/style/2014/09/niki-de-gunzburg-profile.

46 Scrapbooks, 1940, Vol. 2, Box 16; 1941, Vol. 2, Box 18; 1950, Vol. 2, Box 35, John C. Wilson Papers (YCAL MSS 1127).

47 Almost all the artists in Paley's circle were also costume designers for the performing arts, further connecting her to apparel and fashion.

48 See John Richardson, *A Life of Picasso: The Triumph Years* (New York: Alfred A. Knopf, 2010), 361-62. The work in question is today held in the collection of the Louvre Abu Dhabi and is titled *Portrait of a Lady*, 1928.

49 Liaut 2015, 223; Vickers 1987, 323. Souvenir photo of Prince Jean de Faucigny-Lucinge, Princess Paley, and Salvador Dalí at Birdland jazz club in New York, 1950s, Paley Family Papers, Hillwood Archives and Special Collections. See *Vogue*, October 1st, 1943.

50 For more on Lipska and Myrbor, see Laura Pirkelbauer and Cindy Kang, eds., *Marie Cuttoli: The Modern Thread from Miró to Man Ray* (Philadelphia: Barnes Foundation, 2020). Lipska's sculpture of Paley, ca. 1930, is in the collection of the Musée Sainte-Croix, Poitiers. Koni

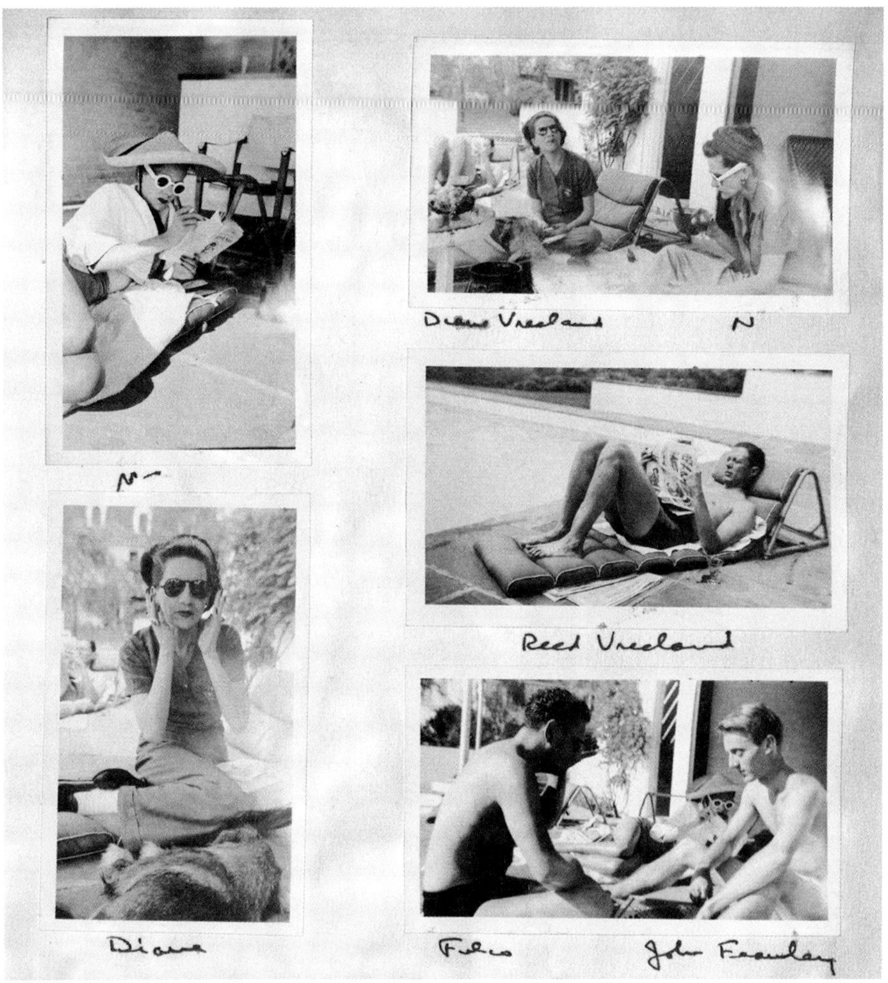

Fig. 86 One of Jack Wilson's scrapbook pages commemorating a 1939 pool party at Pebbles with Diana Vreeland and her husband, T. Reed Vreeland among other friends. Paley is identified as "N" in charming straw hat or headband and white sunglasses. Scrapbooks, John C. Wilson Papers, Yale Collection of American Literature, Beinecke Rare Book and Manuscript Library.

illustrations of Paley and Jack Wilson enjoying Manhattan life (today in a private collection).[51] Richard "Dicky" de Menocal (1919-1995), an associate of Horst P. Horst and younger brother to *Vogue* editor Babs Simpson (1913-2019), illustrated Paley in a Surrealist style in a mid-century work he titled *The Heart of Russia*, also held in a private collection.

sculpture seen in a clipping contained in the 1938 Scrapbook, Vol. 1, Box 11, John C. Wilson Papers (YCAL MSS 1127).

51 "Art: New Jack," *Time*, February 23, 1931, https://content.time.com/time/subscriber/article/0,33009,930356,00.html. See also Cecil Beaton, *Ashcombe: The Story of a Fifteen-Year Lease* (London: Batsford, 1949).

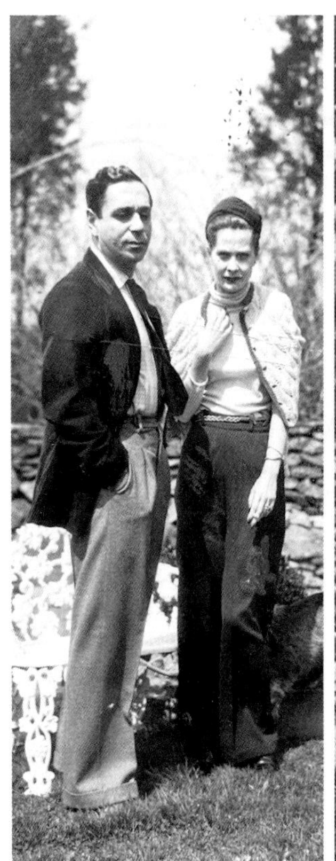
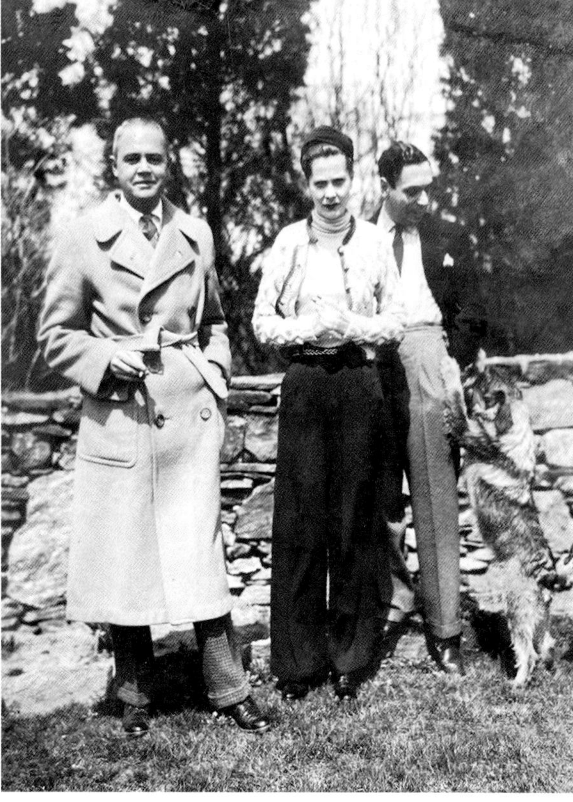

Fig. 87 Scrapbook snapshots featuring the Italian-born jewelry designer and close friend Fulco di Verdura on an April 1939 visit to Pebbles. Scrapbooks, John C. Wilson Papers, Yale Collection of American Literature, Beinecke Rare Book and Manuscript Library.

Paley was illustrated for *Vogue Paris* by another close friend, Christian "Bébé" Bérard (1902-1949), wearing a Caroline Reboux toque.[52] Her friendship with Bébé's rival, Surrealist Russian-born artist and costume designer Pavel Tchelitchew (1898-1957) was more fruitful in terms of known work representing Paley.[53] A 1931 portrait of Paley against a soft, glowing orange background represents the princess in a black beret and turtleneck, a look she favored in Venice during that time with Lelong.[54] In 1932, Tchelitchew also captured the princess as a sickly Ophelia, strewn with daisies and showing bladelike-cheekbones, today in the collection of the Yale University Art Gallery.[55] At least six other Tchelitchew studies and portraits of Paley have been sold in recent years

52 "La Mode et l'art," *Vogue Paris*, February 1st, 1936.

53 Liaut 2015, 171.

54 *Natalie Paley*, oil on canvas, in the collection of the Museum of Modern Art, New York.

55 The work was donated by Paley's friend Mary Cushing Astor Fosburgh (1906-1978) and previously was in Paley's own collection, displayed in her dressing room at Pebbles.

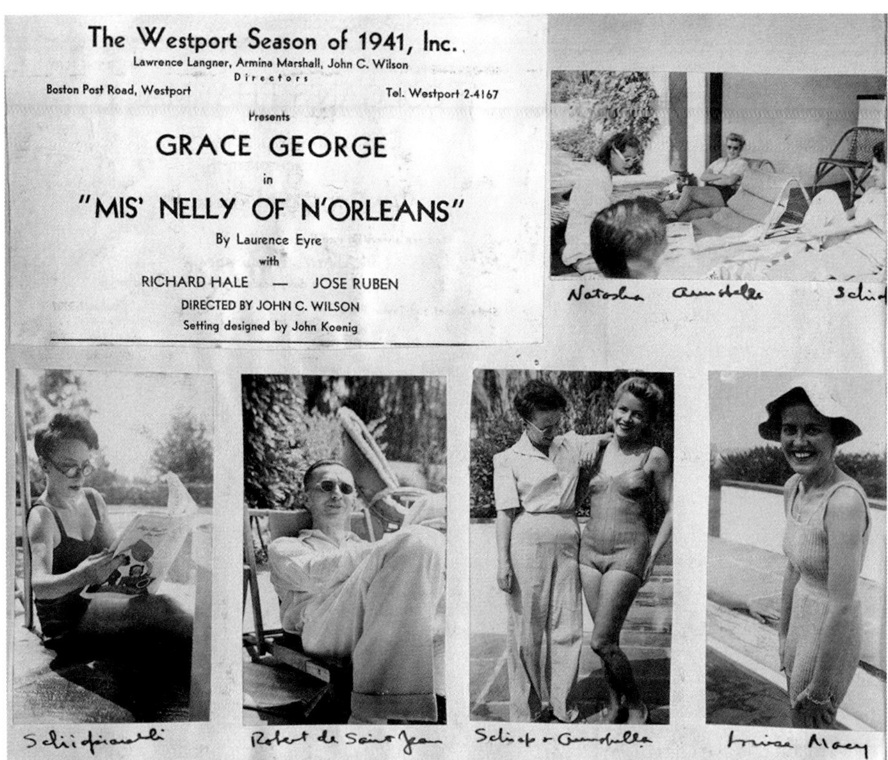

Fig. 88 Scrapbook snapshots of fashion designer Elsa Schiaparelli's 1941 visit to Pebbles. The party was joined by French journalist Robert de Saint-Jean, the mononymous French film star Annabella, and fashion editor Louise Gill Macy Hopkins Gates. Such snapshots are interspersed with Wilson's clippings pertaining to his theatrical career. John C. Wilson Papers, Yale Collection of American Literature, Beinecke Rare Book and Manuscript Library.

to private collectors. A striking illustration of Paley, titled *The Golden Wasp of Summer*, with curling locks strewn with wheat, features in a July 1940 *Harper's Bazaar*. Of course, Tchelitchew visited Pebbles, enjoying a May 1940 visit, perhaps inspired to complete the sketch just mentioned.[56]

During the early 1930s, while still married to Lelong, Paley met Ukrainian-born dancer and choreographer Serge Lifar on "the sands of Lido Beach," Venice (figs. 90, 91). Her artist and costume-designing friend from the same early 1930s set, British-born Oliver Messel (1904-1978), is also featured in Natalie Paley's photos at Lido beach, constructing the sandcastle "sets" she and rumored lover Lifar frolicked upon.[57] Liaut's publication carefully

56 Scrapbooks, 1940, Vol. 1, Box 15, John C. Wilson Papers (YCAL MSS 1127).

57 Photos of this Lido trip featuring Messel's sand sculpture "sets" are in Hillwood's Paley Family Papers today. They also feature Lifar dancing with Paley. These beachside escapades are further preserved in the Natalie Paley Photograph Albums, Photographs, and Correspondence, GEN MSS 574, Box 2. Messel's own scrapbooks from the period also feature the Lido Beach

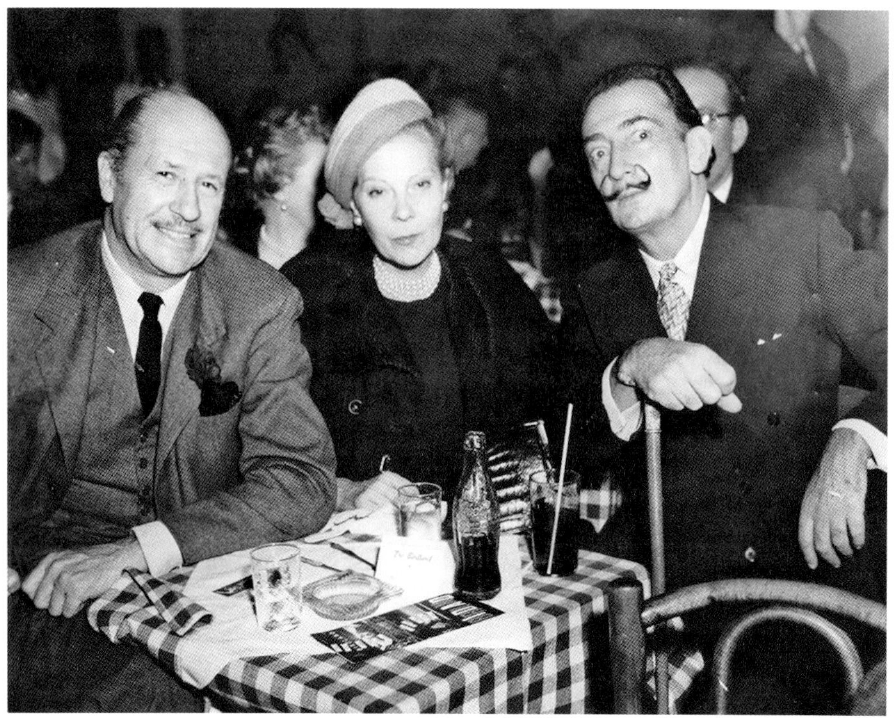

Fig. 89 Souvenir snapshot from Birdland jazz club, New York, ca. 1955. Pictured with Paley (center) are friends Prince Jean de Faucigny-Lucinge (left) and Salvador Dalí (right). Paley Family Collection, Hillwood Estate, Museum & Gardens Archives and Special Collections, Washington, DC.

details the two-year-long "affair" between Lifar and Paley, noting that her then husband, Lelong, was unconcerned.[58] Lifar choreographed a performance for de Beaumont's fancy dress Colonial Ball (a theme that would in every way assault and offend sensibilities of the twenty-first century) for which he, Paley, Verdura, and Baba de Faucigny-Lucinge wore costumes inspired by Cambodia.[59] According to Liaut, the two parted ways as Lifar focused on his choreography, yet he was still "devastated" when Paley focused her affections on Jean Cocteau. Lifar immortalized Paley in his 1932 ballet, *Sur le Borysthène*, with a character named "Natasha."[60]

photos: Photograph album containing photographs of Oliver Messel and his friends on holiday and photographs of Nymans, Personal Papers of Oliver Messel, Theatre Collection, University of Bristol.

58 Liaut 2015, 137-59. See also Serge Lifar and James Holman Mason, *Ma Vie-from Kiev to Kiev: An Autobiography* (New York: World Publishing, 1970).

59 Photos from this event are found in Hillwood's Paley Family Collection and in Natalie Paley Photograph Albums, Photographs, and Correspondence, GEN MSS 574, Box 2. See also Corbett 2002, 74.

60 Liaut 2015, 156, 159, 165. Paley and Lifar continued to correspond; his 1978 letters to Paley and signed portrait are in Hillwood's Paley Family Collection.

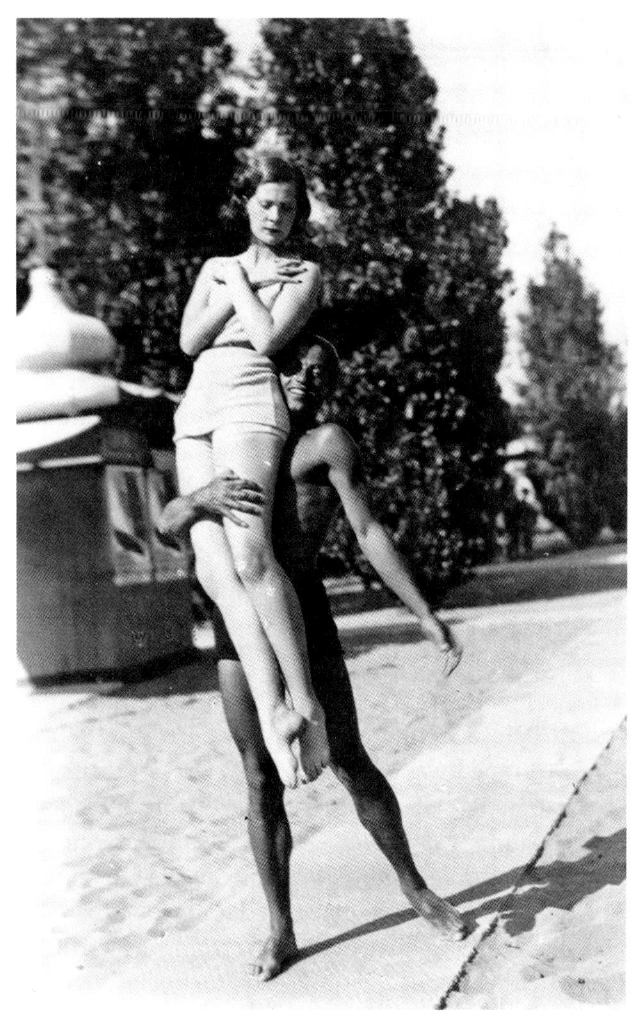

Fig. 90 Serge Lifar and Paley captured in a dance pose, Lido Beach, Venice, 1931. Paley Family Collection, Hillwood Estate, Museum & Gardens Archives and Special Collections, Washington, DC.

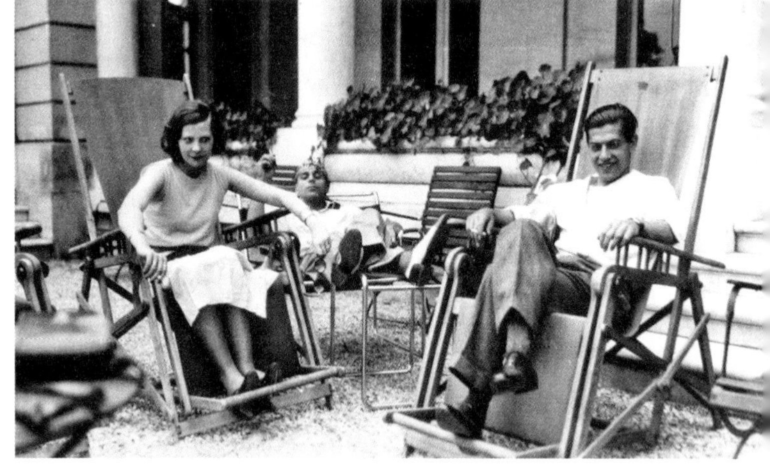

Fig. 91 Paley, an unidentified friend, and Lifar (right) relax in rocking chairs, Venice, 1931. Natalie Paley Photograph Albums, Photographs, and Correspondence, Beinecke Rare Book and Manuscript Library, Yale University.

For his part, Messel's friendship and connection to Paley continued into the mid-1930s, when she posed for his remarkable portrait of her surrounded by lilies (see pl. 63). The 1934 painting is held at Nymans, his country estate today preserved by the National Trust in the United Kingdom. Intriguing snapshots of Paley posing for the portrait in Messel's studio with branches and blossoms represent the collaborative connection between artist and subject.[61] Messel also connects to Paley's other artistic expression: film. He created the medieval-inspired costumes for her third feature film role, in *The Private Life of Don Juan* (1934, directed by Alexander Korda).[62] Messel and Paley met up once again in Hollywood when she was filming *Sylvia Scarlett* opposite Katharine Hepburn and Cary Grant in 1935 in a clique of superstar friends that also included Marlene Dietrich, director George Cukor, and Clark Gable.[63] Among her filmography, *Sylvia Scarlett* is the sole English-language example made in Hollywood, and the most accessible movie (fig. 92). Paley cheekily plays a version of herself, a complicated, wealthy Russian émigré with a taste for the luxurious and taken men. Off camera, she forged a close friendship with Hepburn, who literally saved her in a drowning scene, and her director, Cukor, with whom she stayed during filming.[64]

L'Épervier, *The Private Life of Don Juan*, and *Sylvia Scarlett* represent half of Paley's acting oeuvre, shot between 1933 and 1936. Paley's second film in France was *Le Prince Jean* (1934), directed by Jean de Marguenat. She also appeared in the French version of *Folies Bergère de Paris* (1935), titled *L'Homme des Folies Bergère*, costarring Maurice Chevalier, directed by Roy Del Ruth and shot simultaneously with the English-language version. The production took place in Hollywood between December 1934 and February 1935 and while it never achieved critical acclaim, the glamorous Paley, with bleached blonde hair, penciled brows, and fantastic costumes designed by Omar Kiam, stole the show in her dance scenes.[65] Her final appearance came in *Les Hommes nouveaux* (1936), directed for the second time by Marcel L'Herbier. Some argue that this may be her strongest role, but it was destined to be her last.[66] She is quoted in a 1936 article, "No place in the world has ever affected me like Hollywood. For me it was like

61 "Princess Natalia Pavlovna Paley (1905-1981) with Lilies," Nymans Estate, West Sussex, National Trust, UK. Photographs and negatives of Natasha Wilson, Photographs and Negatives of Oliver Messel's Friends and Acquaintances, Personal Papers of Oliver Messel, Theatre Collection, University of Bristol.

62 Liaut 2015, 212-13. Not a successful film. She had a minor role.

63 Photograph album titled "Oliver in Hollywood – Romeo and Juliet," Personal Papers of Oliver Messel, Theatre Collection, University of Bristol.

64 Liaut 2015, 221, 222.

65 Ibid., 220.

66 *Ibid.*, 224-26: Vassiliev 2000, 440.

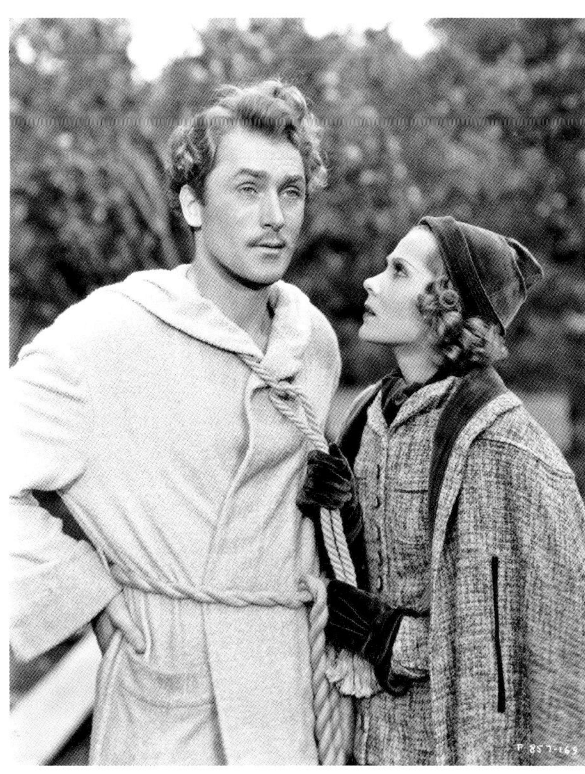

Fig. 92 Film still from *Sylvia Scarlett* (1935) with costar Brian Aherne. Natalie Paley Photograph Albums, Photographs, and Correspondence, Beinecke Rare Book and Manuscript Library, Yale University.

a nightmare."[67] When invited by Noël Coward to participate in an onstage revue in 1938, she respectfully declined, choosing to focus on her new family life and fashion career.[68]

The princess always seemed to be reading, whether it was a suitcase full of books during her convalescence in Switzerland at the time of her breakup with Cocteau or French scripts she was previewing as options for production by Wilson (fig. 93). She often read her friends' work and shared feedback.[69] Unsurprisingly, Princess Natalie Paley is immortalized in literature – whether in passionate letters between herself and Jean Cocteau, Antoine de Saint-Exupéry, and Erich Maria Remarque or in characters inspired by her. Her Cocteau "romance" began in 1932 and culminated in a summer-long exchange of lovelorn, dramatic letters invoking the legend of Tristan

67 "American Women Overdress, Says Princess Paley: Russian Beauty Vacations at Sasco Hill," Bridgeport, CT, August 2, 1936, clipping, Box 61, John C. Wilson Papers (YCAL MSS 1127).

68 John C. Wilson to Noël Coward, September 14, 1938, John C. Wilson, 1936-1958 (COW/3/N/2/58), Noël Coward Collection.

69 Liaut 2015, 184: John C. Wilson to Noël Coward, March 5, 1940, and Natalie Paley to Noël Coward, undated, 1954 (COW/3/N/2/58), Noël Coward Collection.

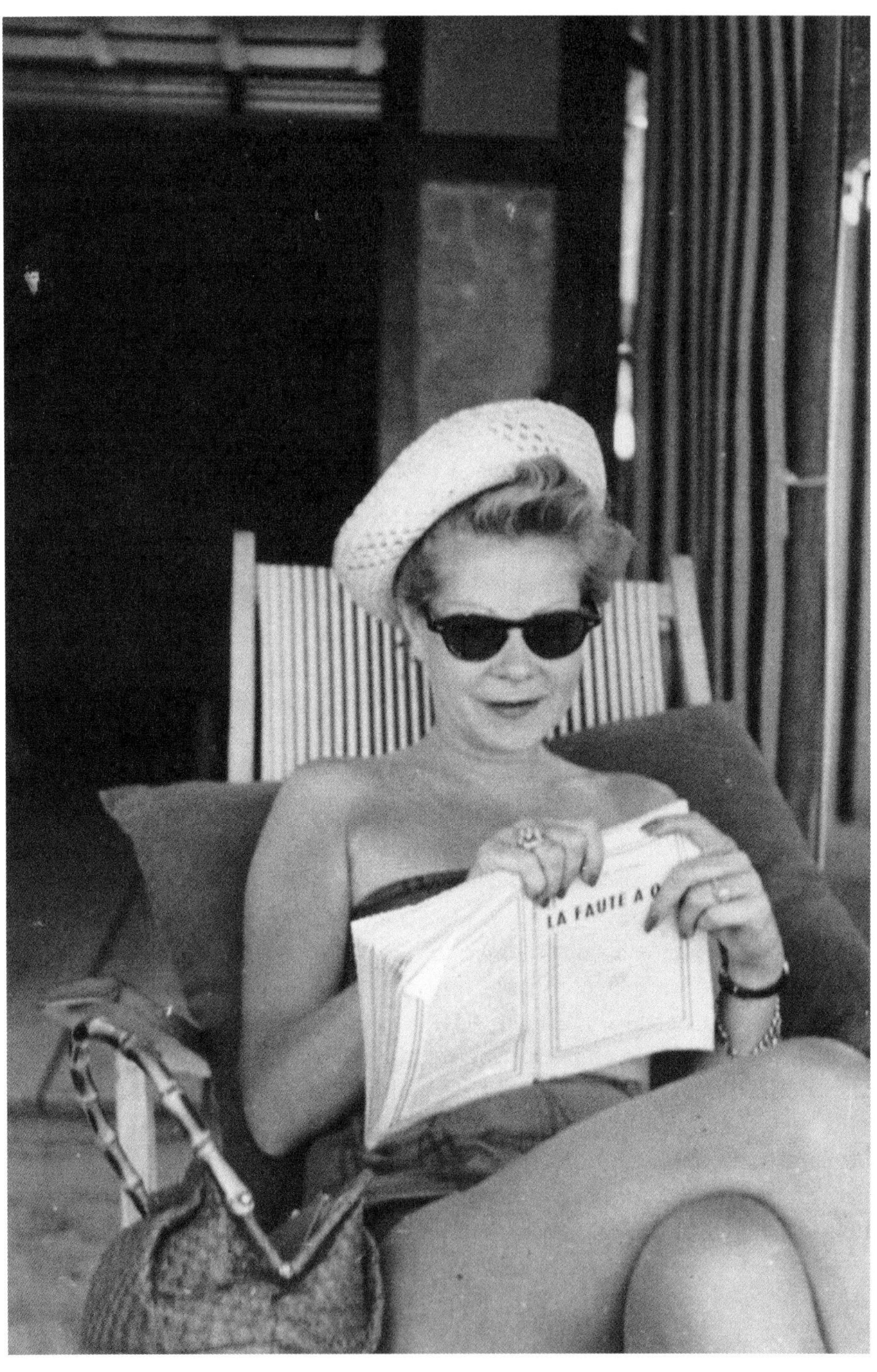

Fig. 93 Paley with a book, and yet another jaunty hat, in Wilson's 1952 scrapbook. John C. Wilson Papers, Yale Collection of American Literature, Beinecke Rare Book and Manuscript Library.

and Isolde (fig. 94).[70] Unlike her relationship with Lifar, this connection did concern her then husband, Lucien Lelong, who was disturbed by Cocteau's drug use and the open Parisian gossip about the relationship.[71] Her two later flirtations – with Saint-Exupéry and Remarque – occurred in the 1940s, at the time of her marriage to Jack Wilson. Paley reconnected with Saint-Exupéry in 1942 while he was in the United States; the two had met years earlier during Paley's brief French film career. As with Cocteau, they exchanged passionate letters, and one of his best-known works, *Le Petit Prince*, was completed during their dalliance.[72] Paley's equally tumultuous connection to Remarque between 1942 and 1943 was also an epistolary romance, partially represented in Hillwood's Paley Family Papers (figs. 95, 96). Paley retained a portrait of Remarque, which is in that collection today. Paley is immortalized as Natasha in his 1971 novel, *Shadows in Paradise*.[73] The princess also inspired two characters in her friend Noël Coward's work: one is the role of Joanna in his play *Present Laughter* (1939), and her relationship with Jack Wilson might have been the basis for a short story called "Nature Study," published in his 1939 collection, *To Step Aside*.[74]

Photos of her in Wilson's scrapbooks at Pebbles show her lounging, her nose in a book. She also enjoyed gardening, her dogs, and knitting. Spending time with friends and family was paramount to Paley. It is through her fascinating community that the princess encountered some of the incredible opportunities of her lifetime. Her network was vast, too large to be contained in a book chapter, and she was a complicated person, though often recalled as witty and generous by those who knew her (fig. 97). As this essay has illustrated, her influence in fashion, the arts, film, and literature form her legacy, even as she overcame the trauma of her childhood.

70 Most of this exchange is published. See David Gullentops, ed., *Jean Cocteau et le théâtre: Cahiers Jean Cocteau 13* (Paris: Non Lieu, 2015).

71 For greater details about the Cocteau-Paley relationship, see Liaut 2015, 168-90. Hillwood's Paley Family Collection includes a signed portrait of Cocteau. He immortalized Paley in *La Fin du Potomak*, published in 1940 by Gallimard, Paris. She also inspired "the Sphinx" in his 1934 play, *La Machine infernale*. He collaged a Hoyningen-Huene portrait of her into this character, a work on paper today preserved at the Centre Pompidou. Finally, the character of Nathalie in *L'Éternel Retour* (1943), a film written by Cocteau and directed by Jean Delannoy, was inspired by their romance.

72 Liaut 2015, 253-54. Paley and Saint-Exupéry's letters are also published, see Antoine de Saint-Exupéry, *Sept lettres à Natalie Paley* (Paris: Gallimard, 2007).

73 Liaut 2015, 255-57.

74 *Ibid.*, 236-37.

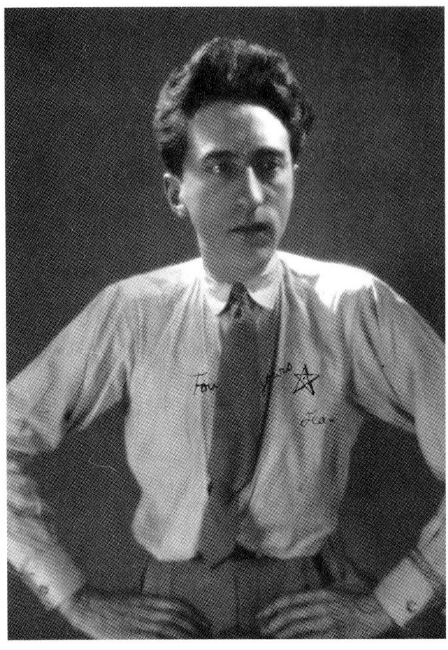

Fig. 94 Signed portrait of Jean Cocteau photographed by Sacha Masour, around 1935, Paley Family Collection, Hillwood Estate, Museum & Gardens Archives and Special Collections, Washington, DC.

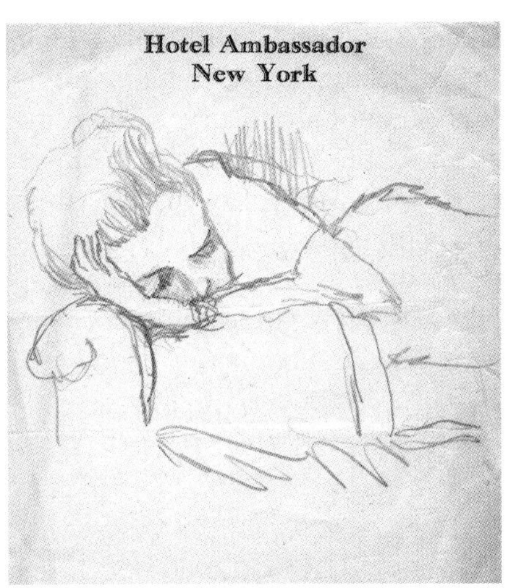

Fig. 95 Doodle from Erich Maria Remarque to Natalie Paley, New York, undated (1940s). Paley Family Collection, Hillwood Estate, Museum & Gardens Archives and Special Collections, Washington, DC.

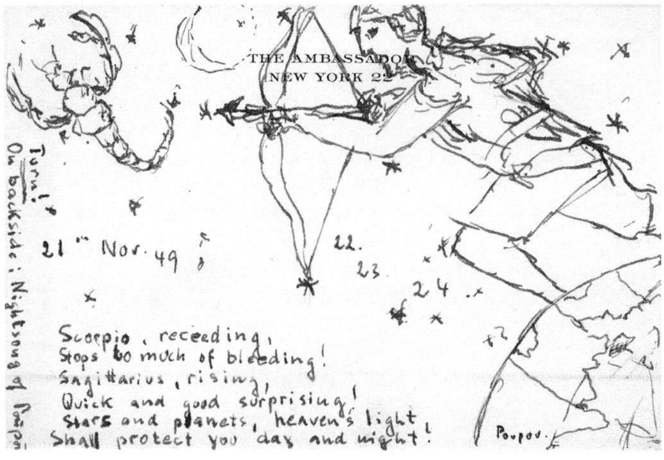

Fig. 96 Poem and doodle, Erich Maria Remarque to Natalie Paley, November 21, 1949. Paley Family Collection, Hillwood Estate, Museum & Gardens Archives and Special Collections, Washington, DC.

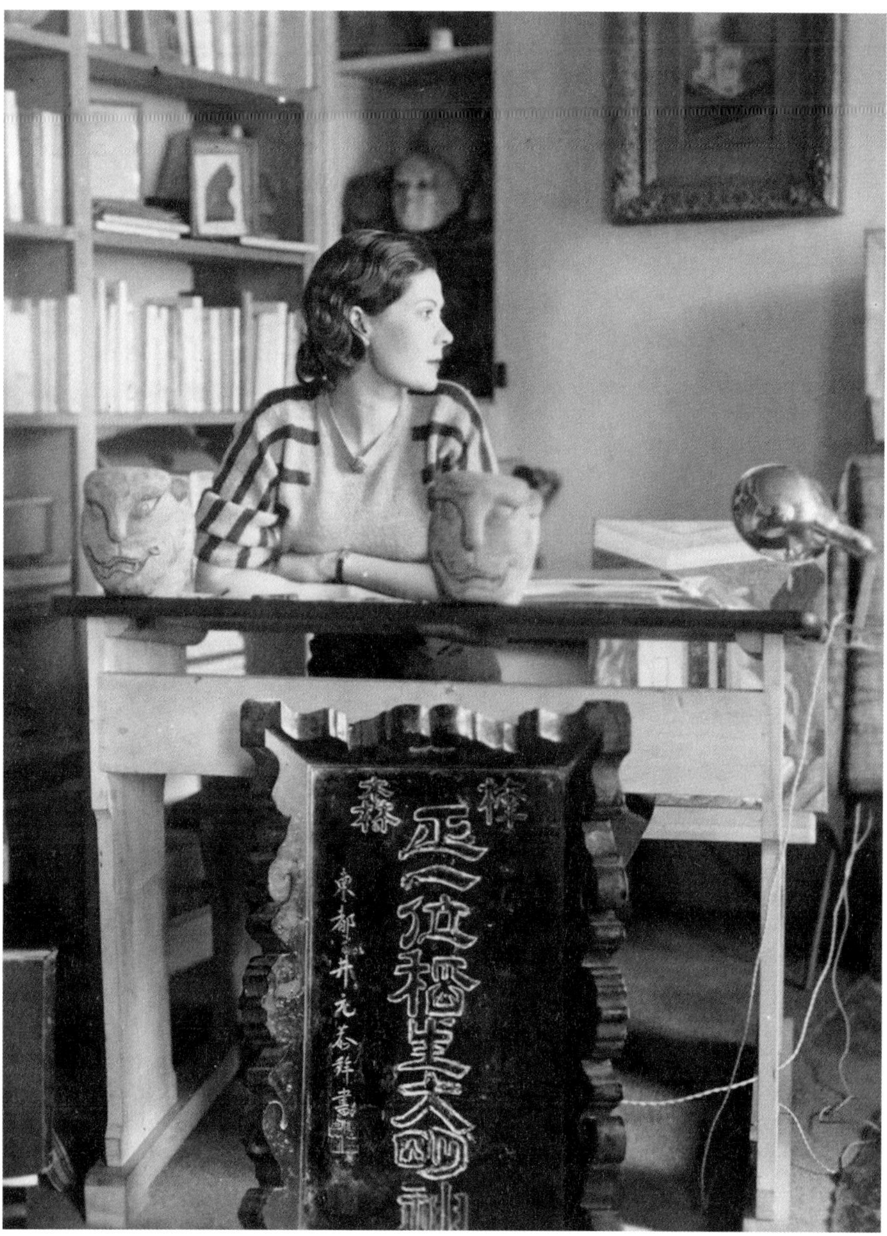

Fig. 97 Princess Natalie Paley at Jean Cocteau's desk, in his Paris apartment, ca. 1931. Paley Family Collection, Hillwood Estate, Museum & Gardens Archives and Special Collections, Washington, DC.

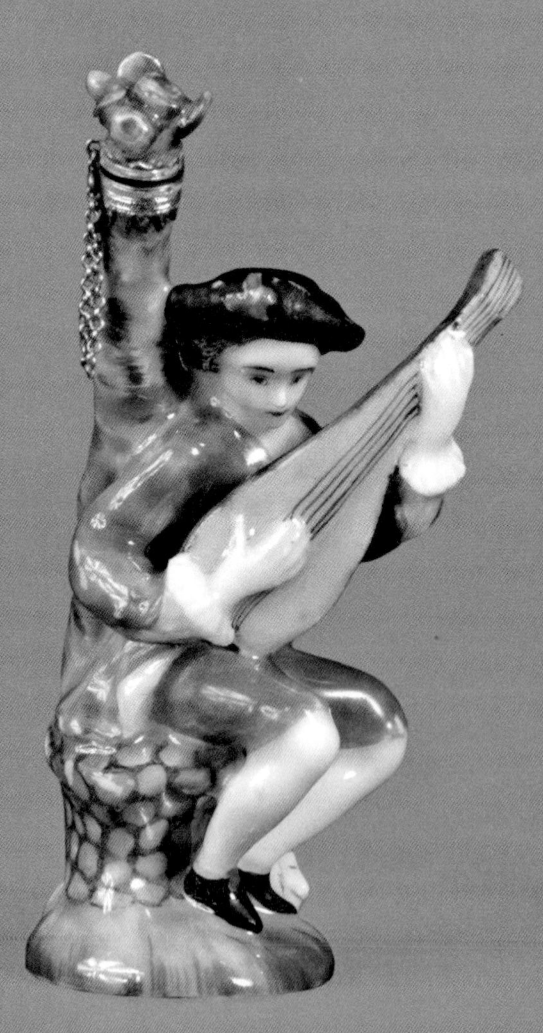

ANNEXES

PRINCIPAL WORKS FROM THE COLLECTION OF THE COUNTESS VON HOHENFELSEN AND GRAND DUKE PAUL

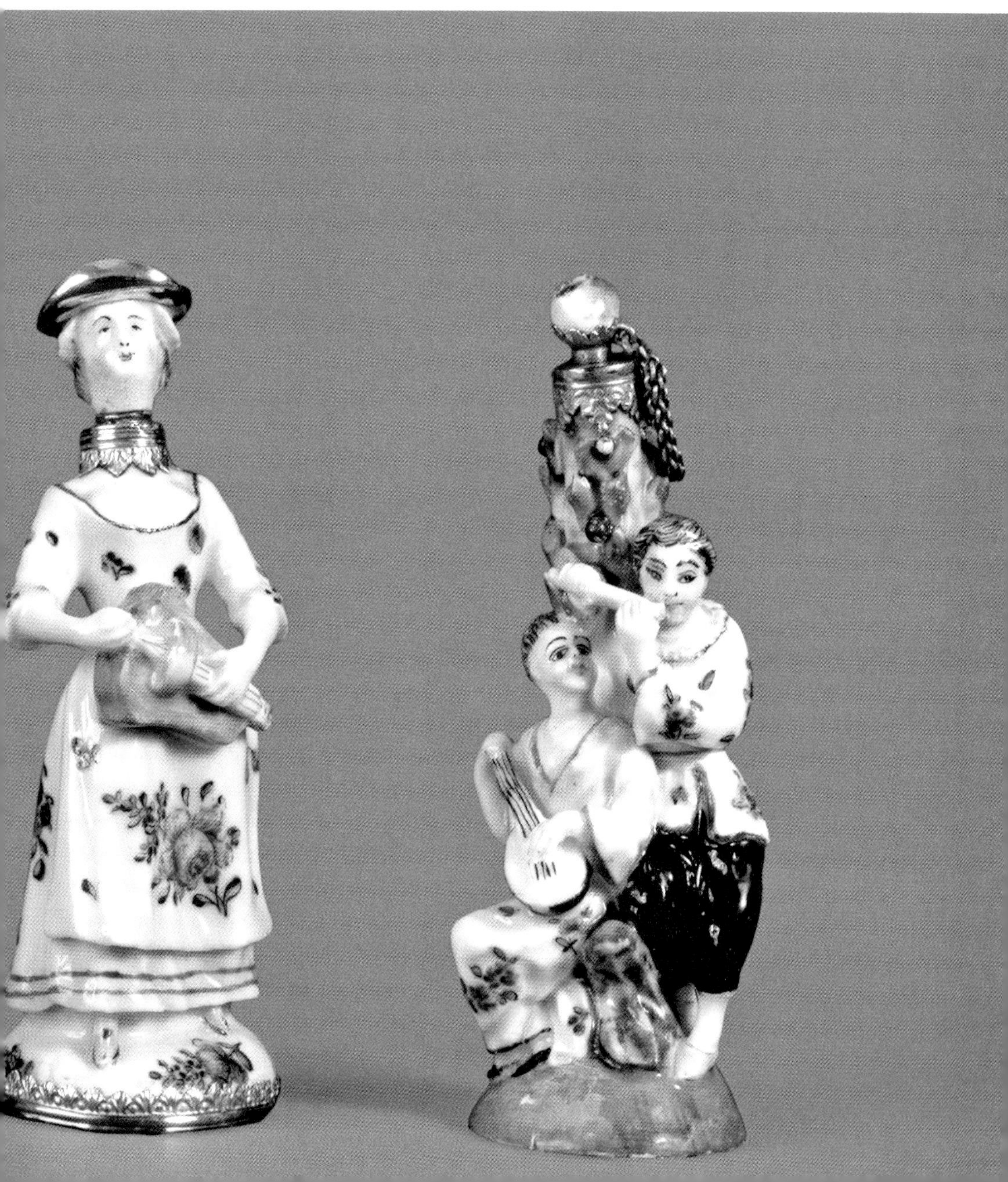

Paintings

***

French school

Jean-Marc Nattier (1685-1766)
Portrait of a Young Girl in a Blue and White Dress (Mademoiselle Marsollier, also known as Mlle *Lorimier de Chamilly)* (fig. 18)
1757
Oil on canvas
Gollerbakh ca. 1922, 15, 47. Salmon 1999, fig. 2, 206. Wintermute 1996, 97, pl. 13, 51.

Marquis Dodun de Keroman, château de Saint-Pierre-du-Fresne, Calvados; marquis Dafosse (?); Wildenstein & Co., Paris; Collection of the Grand Duke Paul and the Countess von Hohenfelsen, Boulogne (pink boudoir); Paley Palace, Tsarskoye Selo (small study); Paley sale, Christie's, London, June 21, 1929, lot 37. 21 ½ × 17 ½ in. (signed and dated); Smith; Albert H. Wiggin (1868-1951), New York; Muriel Wiggin Selden, daughter of the preceding; Lynde Selden (?–1972), husband of the preceding; Parke Bernet, New York, April 4, 1973, no. 149; M. Levitt, New York; Barbara Divver Fine Arts, New York (1991); Private collection, California; Private collection, New York. 23 ¼ × 20 in. / 61.5 × 50.5 cm; Sotheby's, New York, January 28, 1999, no. 287.

***

Jean-Baptiste-Siméon Chardin (1699-1779)
The Attributes of the Arts with a Bust of Mercury (pl. 31)
Before 1728
Oil on canvas
Signed lower right *Chardin*
Gollerbakh ca. 1922, 12, 43. Rosenberg 1982, 15, fig. 1, 16. Rosenberg and Temperini 1999, no. 9, 193-194.

Collection Laurent Laperlier (1805-1868), sale, Paris, Drouot, April 11-13, 1867, no. 28; acquired by the Grand Duke Paul and the Countess von Hohenfelsen from Guiraud, Paris, March 26, 1914; Paley Palace, Tsarskoye Selo (large study); State Hermitage Museum, 1924; Pushkin State Museum of Fine Arts, Moscow, 1927, inv. 1140 – 53 × 112 cm (20 7/8 × 44 1/8 in.).

***

François Boucher (1703-1770)
The Young Sinner
Colored chalk on brown paper
Gollerbakh ca. 1922, 43. Neil Jeffares, *Dictionary of Pastellists before 1800*, J.173.27 http://www.pastellists.com/Articles/Boucher.pdf [accessed April 2024].

Presented by Grand Duke Paul to the Countess von Hohenfelsen, January 24, 1910; Paley Palace, Tsarskoye Selo (large study); Paley sale, Christie's, London, June 21, 1929, lot 8. 27.9 × 39.4 cm (11 × 15 ½ in.) "Young man dressed in white and black, seated on the ground holding a rod."

***

François Boucher
Young Girl with Cat
Dressed in red and blue, holding a Pastel shawl
Gollerbakh ca. 1922, 12 (?), 47.
Neil Jeffares, *Dictionary of Pastellists before 1800*, J.173.596 http://www.pastellists.com/Articles/Boucher.pdf [accessed April 2024].

Presented by Grand Duke Paul to the Countess von Hohenfelsen, January 24, 1910; Collection of the Grand Duke Paul and the Countess von Hohenfelsen, Boulogne (entrance hall); Paley Palace, Tsarskoye Selo (small study); Paley sale, Christie's, London, June 21, 1929, lot 9. 14 × 11 ½ in. 35.6 × 29.2 cm (14 × 11 ½ in.). Pastel; Private collection.

***

Jean-Baptiste Perronneau (1715-1783)
Portrait of a Young Man in Gray Suit and Jacket (pl. 9)
Oil on canvas
Gollerbakh ca. 1922, 47.

Acquired by the Grand Duke Paul and the Countess von Hohenfelsen from Larcade, Paris, March 15, 1907 (6,000 francs); Collection of the Grand Duke Paul and the Countess von Hohenfelsen, Boulogne (salon Louis XVI); Paley Palace, Tsarskoye Selo (small study); Paley sale, Christie's, London, June 21, 1929, lot 38. 23 ½ × 19 ½ in.; Christie's, London, May 19, 1939, lot 129; Ader-Picard-Tajan, Paris, Drouot, November 30, 1990, lot 100. 61 × 50 cm; Christie's, New York, June 4, 2009, lot 47. 60.2 × 50 cm.

***

Pierre-Antoine Baudouin (1723-1769)
Lovers in a Cellar
Oil on canvas (oval)
Gollerbakh ca. 1922, 43.

Paley Palace, Tsarskoye Selo (large study); Paley sale, Christie's, London, June 21, 1929, lot 16. 31.1 × 25.4 cm (12 ¼ × 10 in.)

***

Jean-Baptiste Greuze (1725-1805)
Portrait (?)

Empress Maria Alexandrovna (?); Collection of the Grand Duke Paul (?); Paley Palace, Tsarskoye Selo.

***

Jean-Baptiste Greuze
The Return of the Prodigal Son
Sepia on paper
Gollerbakh ca. 1922, 13.

Magne Collection; Salze Collection; Paley sale, Christie's, London, June 21, 1929, lot 11. 36.8 × 49.5 cm (14 ½ × 19 ½ in.)

***

Hubert Robert (1733-1808)
Imaginary View of Rome with the Horse-Tamer of the Monte Cavallo and a Church (pl. 16)
1786
Oil on canvas
Gollerbakh ca. 1922, 15, 43.

Lazarev Collection; Princess Urusov; Collection of the Grand Duke Paul and the Countess von Hohenfelsen, Boulogne (library); Paley Palace, Tsarskoye Selo (large study); Paley sale, Christie's, London, June 21, 1929, lot 40. 63 × 41 ½ in.; Jacques Seligmann, Paris; Landon K. Throne, New York, 1931; Eugene Victor Thaw, New York; Xavier Fourcade, New York; Artemis, Brussel; The National Museum of Western Art, Tokyo, inv. p. 1977-0002. 161 × 107 cm (63 3/8 × 42 1/8 in.)

***

Hubert Robert
Imaginary View of Rome with Equestrian Statue (pl. 15)
1786
Oil on canvas
Signed ROBERT. PINXIT ANNO 1786

Gollerbakh ca. 1922, 15, 43.

Lazarev Collection; Princess Urusov; Collection of the Grand Duke Paul and the Countess von Hohenfelsen, Boulogne (library); Paley Palace, Tsarskoye Selo (large study); Paley sale, Christie's, London, June 21, 1929, lot 40. 63 × 41 ½ in; Jacques Seligmann, Paris; Landon K. Throne, New York, 1931; Eugene Victor Thaw, New York; Xavier Fourcade, New York; Artemis, Brussel; The National Museum of Western Art, Tokyo, inv. P. 1976-0002. 161 × 107 cm (63 3/8 × 42 1/8 in.)

***

Hubert Robert (?)
Landscape with Washerwomen and Fountain in a Park
Oil on canvas

Acquired by the Grand Duke Paul and the Countess von Hohenfelsen from Larcade, Paris, March 15, 1907 (13,000 francs) (?); Collection of the Grand Duke Paul and the Countess von Hohenfelsen, Boulogne (dining room).

***

Hubert Robert
Bridge with Washerwomen (pl. 10)
Oil on canvas
Gollerbakh ca. 1922, 15, 47.

Arthur Tooth & Sons, London, acquired after October 1907; Collection of the Grand Duke Paul and the Countess von Hohenfelsen, Boulogne (library); Paley Palace, Tsarskoye Selo (small study); Paley sale, Christie's, London, June 21, 1929, lot 41. 28 × 36 in.; Arthur Tooth & Sons, London, September 1929; Lascito Dimitri Sursock, duca di Cervinara, until 1962; Palazzo Barberini, Galleria nazionale d'arte antica, Rome, inv. 2479. 72 × 92 cm (28 3/8 × 36 1/4 in.).

***

Louis-Léopold Boilly (1761-1845)
The Husband's Return
Oil on panel
Gollerbakh ca. 1922, 13, 43 (copy).

Courtois sale, by Oudart, March 28, 1876, lot 4; Paley Palace, Tsarskoye Selo (large study); Paley sale, Christie's, London, June 21, 1929, lot 17. 36.8 × 44.5 cm (14 ½ × 17 ½ in.)

***

Leriche (?)
Four overdoors
Two by Leriche and two by Dyrk van der Aa (?)
Gollerbakh ca. 1922, 18, 63.

Acquired by the Grand Duke Paul and the Countess von Hohenfelsen from Laurent-Perdreau, March 19, 1914 (17,000 francs) – acquired with a marquetry table; Paley Palace, Tsarskoye Selo (large dining room); Paley sale, Christie's, London, June 21, 1929, lot 13: putti in clouds by D. van der Aa, signed and dated 1775. 281.9 × 175.3 cm (111 × 69 in.)

***

Anonymous, Louis XVI period
Six decorative panels
Gollerbakh ca. 1922, 69.

Acquired by the Grand Duke Paul and the Countess von Hohenfelsen from Baroness Alice von André, January 31, 1912 (14,000 francs). Paley Palace, Tsarskoye Selo (small dining room).

***

Narcisse Diaz de la Peña (1807-1876)
The Road through the Woods
Oil on panel

Paley sale, Christie's, London, June 21, 1929, lot 25. 36.8 × 45.7 cm (14 ½ × 18 in.)

***

Alfred de Dreux (1810-1860)
A Zouave on Horseback
Oil on canvas

Paley sale, Christie's, London, June 21, 1929, lot 26. 45.7 × 55.9 cm (18 × 22 in.)

***

Jean-Léon Gérôme (1824-1904)
Diana and Actaeon (pl. 6)
1895
Oil on canvas
Signed lower left J.L. GEROME
Ackerman 2000, no. 428, 342

Acquired by Boussod, Valadon & Cie, successors of Goupil & Cie, December 3, 1895 (8,000 francs); Sold to Grand Duke Paul, December 18, 1895 (12,000 francs); Collection of the Grand Duke Paul, St. Petersburg, English Embankment palace ("English rooms" – 1911); Paley Palace, Tsarskoye Selo (guest room); Bellini, Florence; Private collection, 1930-2013; Sotheby's, New York, November 8, 2013, lot 17. 64.1 × 99.7 cm (25 ¼ × 39 1/4 in.)

***

Jean-Jacques Henner (1829-1905)
In the Library
Oil on canvas

Acquired by Boussod, Valadon & Cie, successors of Goupil & Cie, Paris, April 4, 1886 (2,000 francs); sold to Grand Duke Paul in Paris (avenue de l'Opéra), June 23, 1887 (4,000 francs); Paley sale, Christie's, London, June 21, 1929, lot 31. 61 × 45.7 cm (24 × 18 in.) "Le Plat d'or."

***

Ferdinand Roybet (1840-1920)
A Soldier in Medieval Costume at Attention
Oil on panel

Paley sale, Christie's, London, June 21, 1929, lot 43. 39.4 × 25.4 cm (15 ½ × 10 in.)

***

Édouard Detaille (1848-1912)
Two Grenadiers after Fishing
Oil on canvas

Acquired in London by Boussod, Valadon & Cie, successors of Goupil & Cie, March 1, 1897 (3,600 francs); sold to Grand Duke Paul, June 19, 1897 (10,000 francs); Paley sale, Christie's, London, June 21, 1929, lot 24. 23.5 × 19.1 cm (9 ¼ × 7 ½ in.)

***

Édouard Detaille
Ural Cossacks
1884
Watercolor

Collection of the Grand Duke Paul and the Countess von Hohenfelsen, Boulogne; Paley sale, Paris, December 5, 1923, lot 8. 35 × 26 cm (13 ¾ × 10 1/4 in.)

***

Albert Lynch (1851-1912)
Diana (fig. 10)
1897
Oil on canvas

Acquired by Boussod, Valadon & Cie, successors of Goupil & Cie, July 21, 1897 (1,250 francs); sold to Grand Duke Paul, October 14, 1897 (4,000 francs); Drouot Estimation, Paris, June 22, 2007, lot 167 (?), *Diane surprise*. 64 × 80 cm; Tradart Deauville, November 27, 2016, lot 135. 65 × 81 cm.; Debureaux-Du Plessis, Paris, Drouot, February 24, 2017, lot 222. 65 × 81 cm.; Me Olivier Baron, Montargis, July 2, 2017, lot 261. 65 × 80.5 cm; Me Olivier Baron, Montargis, January 28, 2018, lot 248. 65 × 80.5 cm.; Pichon & Noudel-Deniau, Cannes, November 24, 2022, lot 143. 65 × 81 cm; Tajan, Paris, June 6, 2023, lot 3. 65.5 × 80 cm; Cannes Enchères, Cannes, December 15, 2023, lot 743. 65 × 81 cm; Cannes Enchères, Cannes, February 23, 2024, lot 707. 65 × 81 cm (25 5/8 × 31 7/8 in.)

***

Pascal Dagnan-Bouveret (1852-1929)
Portrait of Countess von Hohenfelsen (pl. 11)
1908
Oil on canvas
Gollerbakh ca. 1922, 19, 43.

Commissioned in 1907; Annual exhibition of the *Cercle de l'union artistique*, Paris, March 1908; SNBA, 1908, *Portrait de la comtesse H.*, no. 280; Collection of the Grand Duke Paul and the Countess von Hohenfelsen, Boulogne (Grand Duke's cabinet); Paley Collection, Tsarskoye Selo (large study); Antikvariat; State Hermitage Museum, 1931, inv. ГЭ-9474. 126 × 100 cm (49 5/8 × 39 3/8 in.)

***

Pascal Dagnan-Bouveret
Portrait of Grand Duke Paul
1910
Pastel
Gollerbakh ca. 1922, 19, 47.

Commissioned in 1910; Paley Palace, Tsarskoye Selo (small study).

***

Pascal Dagnan-Bouveret
Portrait of the Countess
Drawing

Commissioned in 1910 (?); Private collection.

***

François Flameng (1856-1923)
The Reception for Napoleon I on the Isola Bella in the 5th Year of his Reign (pl. 5)
1892
Oil on canvas
Page 2016, 25-26.

Acquired by Boussod, Valadon & Cie, successors of Goupil & Cie, November 4, 1892 (25,000 francs); Sold to Grand Duke Paul, July 6, 1894 (35,000 francs); Collection of the Grand Duke Paul and the Countess von Hohenfelsen, Boulogne; Paley sale, Paris, December 5, 1923, lot 14. 110 × 140 cm (gilded frame); Sotheby's New York, October 12, 1994, lot 110. 105.4 × 141 cm (41 ½ × 55 1/2 in.)

***

François Flameng
Venetian Scene
Watercolor (gold frame)

Collection of the Grand Duke Paul and the Countess von Hohenfelsen, Boulogne; Paley sale, Paris, December 5, 1923, lot 9. 17 × 12 cm (6 ¾ × 4 3/4 in.)

***

François Flameng
Episodes from the Life of Napoleon I.

Four colored engravings. First proof with autograph (mahogany and bronze frame)

Collection of the Grand Duke Paul and the Countess von Hohenfelsen, Boulogne; Paley sale, Paris, December 5, 1923, lots 2 to 5.

***

Austro-Hungarian School

Martin-Ferdinand Quadal (1736-1811)
Portrait of Princess Lobanov-Rostovsky (fig. 60)
1798
Oil on canvas
Work signed and dated
Gollerbakh ca. 1922, 15, 43.

Paley Palace, Tsarskoye Selo (large study); Paley sale, Christie's, London, June 21, 1929, lot 39. 28 × 23 in; Leger & Sons, London; Christie's, London, November 16, 1973, lot 93.

***

Heinrich von Angeli (1840-1925)
Portrait of Maria Alexandrovna
Oil on canvas

Collection of the Grand Duke Paul and the Countess von Hohenfelsen, Boulogne (grand duke's cabinet).

***

Swedish School

Alexander Roslin (1718-1793)
(after?)
Portrait of Empress Maria Feodorovna (pl. 30)
1777
Oil on canvas
Gollerbakh ca. 1922, 18, 55. Elsig 2012, no. 37, 128-29.

Acquired by the Grand Duke Paul and the Countess von Hohenfelsen from Bacri Frères, Paris, March 16, 1913 (30,000 francs); Paley Palace, Tsarskoye Selo (oak salon); Paley sale, Christie's, London, June 21, 1929, lot 42. 66 × 54 in; De Casseres; Comtesse de la Béraudière, American Art Association,

New York, December 11-13, 1930, no. 307; Paula de Koenigsberg, Buenos Aires; Countess Zubov, after 1945; Zubov Foundation, Geneva, inv. FZ 113. 152×120 cm (59 7/8×47 1/4 in.)

***

Russian Imperial School

Dimitri Levitsky (Ukrainian-born, 1735-1822)
Portrait of Platon Zubov in Dark-blue Uniform with Red Edging (fig. 21)
Oil on canvas

Collection of the Grand Duke Paul and the Countess von Hohenfelsen, Boulogne (grand duke's cabinet – in storage in 1911); Paley sale, Christie's, London, June 21, 1929, lot 35. 58.4×48.3 cm (23×19 in.); Weisz (£ 120.5)

***

Feodor Jakovlevich Alexeev (1753-1824)
View of the St. Petersburg Stock Exchange
Oil on canvas
Gollerbakh ca. 1922, 20, 43.

Paley Palace, Tsarskoye Selo (large study); Paley sale, Christie's, London, June 21, 1929, lot 14. 35.6×54.6 cm (14×21 ½ in.)

***

Stepan S. Shchukin (1754-1828)
Portrait of Grand Duchess Elena Pavlovna (fig. 19)
ca. 1800
Oil on canvas
Gollerbakh ca. 1922, 43.

Collection of the Grand Duke Paul and the Countess von Hohenfelsen, Boulogne (library); Paley Palace, Tsarskoye Selo (large study); Paley sale, Christie's, London, June 21, 1929, lot 44 (See Syke). 29×18 in; Johnson (£94.10); Arthur U. Newton, dealer, New York, 1929; Mrs. E. J. Ludvigh; Bonhams, London, June 8, 2011, lot 5 (after Stepan Shchukin). 57×47 cm (22 7/16×18 ½ in).

***

Vladimir Borovikovsky (?) (Ukrainian-born, 1757-1825)
Portrait of Architect N. A. Lvov

Gollerbakh ca. 1922, 20, 43.

Paley Palace, Tsarskoye Selo (large study).

***

Vladimir Borovikovsky (?)
Portrait of Maria A. Lvova, née Diakova Wife of the Architect
Gollerbakh ca. 1922, 12, 43.

Paley Palace, Tsarskoye Selo (large study).

***

Mikhail Shibanov (? – after 1789)
Portrait of Empress Catherine II (pl. 7)
ca. 1787-89
Oil on canvas
Gollerbakh ca. 1922, 20, 43 (after?). Guitaut and Patterson 2018, 44-45.

Sir W. A., May 14, 1900; Acquired by Grand Duke Paul from Thomas Agnew & Sons, London, October 25, 1901 (sold as Lampi / Drouais); Collection of the Grand Duke Paul and the Countess von Hohenfelsen, Boulogne (entrance hall); Paley Palace, Tsarskoye Selo (large study); Paley sale, Christie's, London, June 21, 1929, lot 49. 98 × 22 in; Collings (£714); Acquired by Queen Mary, 1929; Royal Collections, London, inv. RCIN 400964. 72.3 × 56.5 cm (28 ½ × 22 1/4 in.)

***

Konstantin Makovsky (1839-1915)
Portrait of Olga von Pistohlkors (pl. 1)
1886
Oil on canvas
Signed and dated lower left
Toscano 2014, 218, ill. p. 300.

Princess Olga Paley, thence by descente; Private collection; Hillwood Estate, Museum & Gardens, inv. 2022.2.1. 91.4 × 78.7 cm (36 × 31 in.)

***

Wilhelm Velten (1847-1929)
The Toast
Oil on panel

Paley sale, Christie's, London, June 21, 1929, lot 48. 21.6 × 29.2 cm (8 ½ × 11 ½ in.)

***

Franz Roubaud (1856-1928)
Caucasian Riders
Watercolor (gold frame)

Collection of the Grand Duke Paul and the Countess von Hohenfelsen, Boulogne; Paley sale, Paris, December 5, 1923, lot 10. 37 × 51 cm (14 5/8 × 20 1/8 in.)

***

Léon Bakst (1866-1924)
Russian Headdress
Watercolor (gold frame)

Collection of the Grand Duke Paul and the Countess von Hohenfelsen, Boulogne; Paley sale, Paris, December 5, 1923, lot 7. 30 × 20 cm (11 7/8 × 7 7/8 in.)

***

Serge S. Solomco (1867-1928)
Scene from the Russian Middle Ages
Watercolor (gold frame)

Collection of the Grand Duke Paul and the Countess von Hohenfelsen, Boulogne; Paley sale, Paris, December 5, 1923, lot 11. 16 × 34 cm (6 3/8 × 13 3/8 in.)

***

Serge S. Solomco
Russian Nun in a Landscape
Watercolor (gold frame)

Collection of the Grand Duke Paul and the Countess von Hohenfelsen, Boulogne; Paley sale, Paris, December 5, 1923, lot 12. 15 × 31 cm (6 × 12 1/4 in.)

***

Leonid Mikhailovich Brailovsky (Ukrainian-born, 1867-1937)
Russian Church Porch
Watercolor

Collection of the Grand Duke Paul and the Countess von Hohenfelsen, Boulogne; Paley sale, Paris, December 5, 1923, lot 6. 67 × 48 cm (26 3/8 × 18 7/8 in.)

***

Leonid Mikhailovich Brailovsky
Head of Peter the Great
Drawing – colored chalk

Paley sale, Christie's, London, June 21, 1929, lot 7. 50.8 × 38.1 cm (20 × 15 in.)

***

Belgian School

Henri Leys (1815-1869)
The Guild of the Archers Welcomes Margaret of Austria (pl. 42)
1860
Oil on panel
Gollerbakh ca. 1922, 18, 43.

Collection of the Grand Duke Paul, St. Petersburg, English Embankment palace; Paley Palace, Tsarskoye Selo (large study); Paley sale, Christie's, London, June 21, 1929, lot 36. 78.7 × 104.1 cm (31 × 41 in.); Royal Museum of Fine Arts, Antwerp, inv. 2111.

***

Constant Wauters (1826-1853)
Eighteenth-century Scene
1852
Oil on canvas (gold frame)

Collection of the Grand Duke Paul and the Countess von Hohenfelsen, Boulogne; Paley sale, Paris, December 5, 1923, lot 16. 65 × 84 cm (25 5/8 × 33 1/8 in.)

***

Constant Wauters
Portrait of Louis XVI Seated
Oil on canvas (gold frame)

Collection of the Grand Duke Paul and the Countess von Hohenfelsen, Boulogne; Paley sale, Paris, December 5, 1923, lot 17.

***

British School

Thomas Lawrence (1769-1830)
Portrait of a Young Woman in a Dark, Low-Cut Dress
Oil on canvas
Gollerbakh ca. 1922, 17, 47.

Collection of the Grand Duke Paul and the Countess von Hohenfelsen, Boulogne (library); Paley Palace, Tsarskoye Selo (small study); Paley sale, Christie's, London, June 21, 1929, lot 34. 52.1 × 43.2 cm (20 ½ × 17 in.)

***

George Dawe (1781-1829)
Portrait of Emperor Alexander I (fig. 22)
1825
Oil on canvas
Signed and dated "painted in St. Petersburg, 1825."
Gollerbakh ca. 1922, 17, 43.

Collection of the Grand Duke Paul and the Countess von Hohenfelsen, Boulogne (grand duke's study); Paley Palace, Tsarskoye Selo (large study); Paley sale, Christie's, London, June 21, 1929, lot 23. 86.4 × 58.4 cm (34 × 23 in.); Baldwin (£73.10).

***

George Dawe
Portrait of Alexander II as a Child, on a Terrace Holding a Pistol (pl. 14)
1820
Oil on canvas
Signed and dated lower left "Geo. Dawe R. A./Pinxt 1820."
Gollerbakh ca. 1922, 17, 43. Toscano 2014, 218.

Probably commissioned by Emperor Alexander I, 1820; Empress Maria Alexandrovna, Gatchina Palace; Paley Palace, Tsarskoye Selo (large study); Paley sale, Christie's, London, June 21, 1929, lot 22. 48 × 36 ½ in; Princess Paley (?) (£31.10); Natalie Paley; Private collection; Hillwood Estate, Museum & Gardens, inv. 2022.2.2. 133.7 × 109.1 cm (52 5/8 × 43 in.)

***

George Dawe
Portrait of Emperor Alexander II as a Child in Uniform against a Landscape Background (pl. 53)

ca. 1825
Oil on canvas
Gollerbakh ca. 1922, 17, 55 (after?).

Empress Maria Alexandrovna, Gatchina Palace; Collection of the Grand Duke Paul, St. Petersburg, English Embankment palace; Collection of the Grand Duke Paul and the Countess von Hohenfelsen, Boulogne (library) (?); Paley Palace, Tsarskoye Selo (oak salon); Paley sale, Christie's, London, June 21, 1929, lot 21. 70×46 in; Princess Paley (?) (£131.5); Private collection, Rueil-Malmaison; Christie's, London, November 26, 2018, lot 22. 180×120.3 cm (70 7/8×47 3/8 in.)

***

George Dawe
Charlotte (Alexandra Feodorovna), Empress of Russia, with Her Eldest Children, Alexander and Maria (pl. 52)
ca. 1821
Oil on canvas
Gollerbakh ca. 1922, 59 (after?). Guitaut and Patterson 2018, 154-55.

Adolphus Frederick, Duke of Cambridge; Purchased by Grand Duke Paul, 1889; Collection of the Grand Duke Paul, St. Petersburg, English Embankment palace (antechamber no. 2 – 1911); Paley Palace, Tsarskoye Selo (great hall); Paley sale, Christie's, London, June 21, 1929, lot 20. 109×73 in; Jones (£136.10); Purchased by Queen Mary, 1929; Royal Collections, London, inv. RCIN 404608. 276.9×185.4 cm (109×73 in.)

***

Arthur Hacker (1858-1919)
Circe
1893
Oil on canvas

Collection of the Grand Duke Paul, St. Petersburg, English Embankment palace ("English rooms" – 1911); Paley Palace, Tsarskoye Selo (guest room) (?); Paley sale, Christie's, London, June 21, 1929, lot 29. 116.8×184.2 cm (46×72 ½ in.) (presented at the Royal Academy in 1893).

Italian School

Francesco Guardi (1712-1793)
View of St. Mark's Square in Venice

Oil on canvas
Gollerbakh ca. 1922, 16, 47 (after Bellotto?).

Borden sale, New York, February 13, 1913; Acquired by Grand Duke Paul from Thomas Agnew & Sons, London, November 21, 1913 (45,000 francs); Paley Palace, Tsarskoye Selo (small study); Paley sale, Christie's, London, June 21, 1929, lot 28. 23.5 × 36.2 cm (9 ¼ × 14 ¼ in.)

***

Bernardo Bellotto (1721/22-1780)
"Canaletto"
View of the Church of San Giovanni e Paolo in Venice (pl. 8)
ca. 1741
Oil on canvas
Gollerbakh ca. 1922, 16. "Colleone Square in Venice" *Bernardo Bellotto and the Capitals of Europe*, Bowron 2001, no. 7, 60-63.

Christie's Massay-Mamidarny (?), March 16, 1907. 23 ½ × 38 ¼ in; Acquired by Grand Duke Paul from Thomas Agnew & Sons, London, June 22, 1908 (25,000 francs); Collection of the Grand Duke Paul and the Countess von Hohenfelsen, Boulogne (grand duke's study); Paley Palace, Tsarskoye Selo (small study?); Paley sale, Christie's, London, June 21, 1929, no. 18. 23 ½ × 38 in; Knoedler & Co., London; Marshall Field, Chicago, 1929; Michele and Donald D'Amour Museum of Fine Arts, Springfield, Massachusetts, The James Philip Gray Collection, inv. 36.03. Museum purchase, 1936. 68 × 98.4 cm (26 ¾ × 38 ¾ in.)

***

Tito Conti (1842-1924)
The Young Squire
Oil on canvas

Paley sale, Christie's, London, June 21, 1929, lot 19. 20.3 × 13.9 cm (8 × 5 ½ in.)

***

Federico Andreotti (1847-1930)
The Casket
Oil on canvas

Paley sale, Christie's, London, June 21, 1929, lot 15. 29.2 × 24.8 cm (11 ½ × 9 ¾ in.)

***

Tito Lessi (1858-1917)
The Epicurean
Drawing

Paley sale, Christie's, London, June 21, 1929, lot 12. 22.2 × 14 cm (8 ¾ × 5 ½ in.)

***

Polish School

Alfred von Kowalski (1849-1915)
Off Duty
Oil on panel

Paley sale, Christie's, London, June 21, 1929, lot 32. 21 × 26 cm (8 ¼ × 10 ¼ in.)

***

German School

Franz Krüger (1797-1857)
(after?)
Portrait of Grand Duke Alexander Nikolayevich in Blue Uniform and Silver Epaulets (pl. 43)
1833
Oil on canvas
Gollerbakh ca. 1922, 18, 43 (after?).

Paley Palace, Tsarskoye Selo (large study); Paley sale, Christie's, London, June 21, 1929, lot 33. 34 × 26 ½ in; Private collection, Rueil-Malmaison; Christie's, London, November 26, 2018, lot 23. 88 × 69.2 cm (34 ¾ × 27 ¼ in.)

***

Max Thedy (1858-1924)
The Happy Monkey
Oil on panel

Paley sale, Christie's, London, June 21, 1929, lot 45. 26 × 17.1 cm (10 ¼ × 6 ¾ in.)

***

Max Thedy
Portrait of a Man in a Black Suit and Hat
Oil on canvas

Paley sale, Christie's, London, June 21, 1929, lot 27. 63.5 × 49.5 cm (25 × 19 ½ in.)

***

Spanish School

Baldomero Galofré y Jiménez (1845-1902)
Spanish Scene
1896
Oil on panel (under glass; gilded frame)

Collection of the Grand Duke Paul and the Countess von Hohenfelsen, Boulogne; Paley sale, Paris, December 5, 1923, lot 15. 23 × 37 cm (9 × 14 ½ in.)

***

Flemish School

Anthony van Dyck (1599-1641)
The Blue Boy (pl. 19)
ca. 1638
Oil on canvas
Gollerbakh ca. 1922, 19, 47.

Collection of the Grand Duke Paul and Countess von Hohenfelsen, Boulogne (salon Louis XVI); Paley Palace, Tsarskoye Selo (small study also known as Salon Delafosse); Paley sale, Christie's, London, June 21, 1929, lot 47 (*Portrait of Charles II when a Boy*) 37 × 21 ½ in; W.L. Moody, Dallas, by 1931; C.F. Williams, Cincinnati, Ohio, by 1988; Christie's, New York, October 3, 2001, no. 82 (*Portrait of Charles, Lord Strange, later 8th Earl of Derby (1628-1672), at the Age of 10* – Inscribed "Aeta. Suae 10" upper right) 69.8 × 56.9 cm (27 ½ × 22 3/8 in.)

***

Nicolaes van Verendael (1640-1691)
Series of four round compositions on copper depicting fruit

Paley sale, Christie's, London, June 21, 1929, lot 49. Diam. 20.3 cm (8 in.)

***

Dutch School

Dyrk van der Aa (1731-1809)
Four overdoors
Two by Dyrk van der Aa (putti in clouds) and two by Leriche (?)
1775
Oil on canvas pasted on cardboard
Works signed and dated
Gollerbakh ca. 1922, 18, 63.

Collection of Ambassador von Weckherlin, The Hague; F. Muller, Amsterdam, November 26, 1912, lot (*The Harvest*) – 7,000 florins; Acquired by the Grand Duke Paul and the Countess von Hohenfelsen from Laurent-Perdreau, March 19, 1914 – 17,000 francs with a marquetry table; Paley Palace, Tsarskoye Selo (large dining room); Paley sale, Christie's, London, June 21, 1929, lot 13. 111 × 69 in; Rothschild; Sackville Gallery, London, 1930; J.C. Veder; F. Muller, Amsterdam, April 30-May 1935, no. 37; Princess Natalie Paley (?); Christie's, New York, May 23, 1997, lot 31 (Allegories of Summer and Autumn). 271.2 × 167.6 cm (106 ¾ × 66 in.)

***

Unidentified School

P. Franz Lamy
View of Petrograd
Colored engraving (gold frame)

Collection of the Grand Duke Paul and the Countess von Hohenfelsen, Boulogne; Paley sale, Paris, December 5, 1923, lot 1.

***

T. Haupheimer
The Artist
1878
Oil on panel

Paley sale, Christie's, London, June 21, 1929, lot 30. 25.4 × 19 cm (10 × 7 ½ in.)

***

Louizet
Moonlight over the Sea

1907
Pastel (plane-tree frame)

Collection of the Grand Duke Paul and the Countess von Hohenfelsen, Boulogne; Paley sale, Paris, December 5, 1923, lot 13. 31 × 24 cm (12 ¼ × 9 ½)

***

Louizet
Portrait
Gollerbakh ca. 1922, 43.

Paley Palace, Tsarskoye Selo (large study).

***

Louizet
View of Versailles
Gollerbakh, ca. 1922, 47.
Paley Palace, Tsarskoye Selo (small study).

***

Louizet
Allegory of Government
Gollerbakh ca. 1922, 55.

Paley Palace, Tsarskoye Selo (small study).

***

Miniatures

Paul I
Gollerbakh ca. 1922, 47.

Paley Palace, Tsarskoye Selo (small study).

***

Catherine
Gollerbakh ca. 1922, 47.

Paley Palace, Tsarskoye Selo (small study).

***

Alexander I
Gollerbakh ca. 1922, 47.

Paley Palace, Tsarskoye Selo (small study).

***

Maria Feodorovna
Gollerbakh ca. 1922, 47.

Paley Palace, Tsarskoye Selo (small study).

***

Elizabeth Alexeevna
Gollerbakh ca. 1922, 47.

Paley Palace, Tsarskoye Selo (small study).

***

Sculptures

Paul Troubetzkoy (1866-1938)
Bronze statue of Grand Duke Paul
Gollerbakh ca. 1922, 23.

Paley Palace, Tsarskoye Selo (on the Taskin fortepiano in the small study). A 1910 example is in the collections of the State Russian Museum in St. Petersburg, inv. BX-74637.

***

Paul Troubetzkoy
Statue of a young girl in white marble
Gollerbakh ca. 1922, 23.

Paley Palace, Tsarskoye Selo (main hall).

***

Barriol?
Group of Children Playing
Gollerbakh ca. 1922, 23.

Paley Palace, Tsarskoye Selo (gallery).

***

Barriol?
Group of Children Playing
Gollerbakh ca. 1922, 23.

Paley Palace, Tsarskoye Selo (gallery).

***

Bust of Maria Alexandrovna
Gollerbakh ca. 1922, 43.

Paley Palace, Tsarskoye Selo (large study).

***

Bust of Catherine II
Gollerbakh ca. 1922, 23.

Paley Palace, Tsarskoye Selo.

***

Small Marble Bust of Alexander I
Gollerbakh ca. 1922, 23, 59.

Collection of the Grand Duke Paul and the Countess von Hohenfelsen, Boulogne (entrance hall); Paley Palace, Tsarskoye Selo (main hall).

***

Bust of Napoleon
Gollerbakh ca. 1922, 23, 59.

Paley Palace, Tsarskoye Selo (main hall).

***

Markezi
Bust of Young Alexander II
1839
Gollerbakh ca. 1922, 70.

Paley Palace, Tsarskoye Selo (rotunda – niche).

***

Pair of sphinxes
Acquired by the Grand Duke Paul and the Countess von Hohenfelsen from Kraemer, Paris, March 17, 1909 (14,000 francs).

***

van den Meersen (?)
Sculpture

Acquired by the Grand Duke Paul and the Countess von Hohenfelsen from Mantorani (1911).

***

Decorative Arts

Furniture and decorative bronzes

Pascal Taskin (1723-1793)
Fortepiano (grand piano), 1788, reputed to have belonged to Marie-Antoinette "a L. XVI period piano in rosewood and marquetry, enriched with gilded bronzes and paintings."
(pl. 32)
Gollerbakh ca. 1922, 25, 47, ill. p. 51.
Jullian 1961, 47.

Acquired by the Grand Duke Paul and the Countess von Hohenfelsen from Georges Bernard, Paris, March 26, 1914 (70,000 francs with the Chantilly porcelain vase); Paley Palace, Tsarskoye Selo, (small study); Paley sale, Christie's, London, June 6, 1929, lot 91; Weiss; Sir Joseph Duveen, New York; Arturo Lopez-Willshaw, Paris; Cité de la musique, Paris, inv. D.OA.10298.

***

Furniture and Gobelins

Laurent, May 30, 1906 (25,000 francs).

***

One sofa and six armchairs
Upholstered with Regence tapestry (fig. 17)

Collection of the Grand Duke Paul and the Countess von Hohenfelsen, Boulogne (entrance hall); Paley Palace, Tsarskoye Selo (boudoir); Paley sale, Christie's, London, June 6-7, 1929, lot 109 (?) ill.; Stettiner.

***

Regence table with marble top

Collection of the Grand Duke Paul and the Countess von Hohenfelsen, Boulogne (entrance hall); Paley Palace, Tsarskoye Selo (boudoir).

***

Two antique wing chairs

Collection of the Grand Duke Paul and the Countess von Hohenfelsen, Boulogne (salon Louis XVI); Paley Palace, Tsarskoye Selo (small study also known as Salon Delafosse); Paley sale, Christie's, London, June 6-7, 1929, lot 113; Fabre.

***

Screen

Acquired by the Grand Duke Paul and the Countess von Hohenfelsen from Bacri Frères, Paris, March 15, 1913 (5,400 francs) – acquired with porcelain.

***

Chinese lacquer screen
Seventeenth century
Gollerbakh ca. 1922, 27.

Langweil (?), Paris; Palace Palace, Tsarskoye Selo (large dining room).

***

Chaise longue with original gilding covered with pink fabric
Gollerbakh ca. 1922, 26.

Paley Palace, Tsarskoye Selo (cabinet).

***

Armchair
Empress Elizabeth period (new upholstery)
Gollerbakh ca. 1922, 43.

Tauride Palace; Paley Palace, Tsarskoye Selo (large study).

***

Two kidney-shaped tables
Catherine II period

Gollerbakh ca. 1922, 43.

Paley Palace, Tsarskoye Selo (large study).

***

Two small Louis XVI tables
Gollerbakh ca. 1922, 43.

Paley Palace, Tsarskoye Selo (large study).

***

Louis XVI desk, France
Gollerbakh ca. 1922, 47.

Paley Palace, Tsarskoye Selo (small study).

***

Louis XVI chair, France
Gollerbakh ca. 1922, 47.

Paley Palace, Tsarskoye Selo (small study).

***

Chair
Empress Elizabeth period
Gollerbakh ca. 1922, 23, 47.

Paley Palace, Tsarskoye Selo (small study).

***

Two chairs and two armchairs from Marshal Davout's estate, France
Gollerbakh ca. 1922, 26, 59.

Paley Palace, Tsarskoye Selo (main hall).

***

Furniture

Acquired by the Grand Duke Paul and the Countess von Hohenfelsen from Laurent-Perdreau, Paris, June 18, 1912 (11,000 francs).

***

Furniture

Acquired by Grand Duke Paul and Countess von Hohenfelsen from Laurent-Perdreau, Paris, March 1913 (60,000 francs).

***

Furniture

Acquired by Grand Duke Paul and Countess von Hohenfelsen from Laurent-Perdreau, Paris, August 1913 (55,000 francs).

***

Louis XVI table with marquetry (?)

Acquired by the Grand Duke Paul and the Countess von Hohenfelsen from Laurent-Perdreau, Paris, March 19, 1914 (17,000 francs) – acquired with four overdoors.

***

Empire clock

Acquired by the Grand Duke Paul and the Countess von Hohenfelsen from Drey, Munich, August 3, 1910 (1,800 francs).

***

Ceramics

Vase in Chantilly porcelain "A very important vase in Chantilly soft paste decorated with landscapes and flowers in monochrome and garnished with a superb bouquet of flowers in polychrome porcelain."

Acquired by the Grand Duke Paul and the Countess von Hohenfelsen from Georges Bernard, Paris, March 26, 1914 (70,000 francs with Taskin piano); Paley Palace, Tsarskoye Selo; Paley sale, Christie's, London, June 6-7, 1929, lot 227; Lévy.

***

Manufacture de Lunéville
Renaud et Armide
Gollerbakh ca. 1922, 47.

Paley Palace, Tsarskoye Selo (small study).

***

Porcelain

Acquired by the Grand Duke Paul and the Countess von Hohenfelsen from Bacri Frères, Paris, March 15, 1913 (5,400 francs) – acquired with a folding screen.

***

Tapestries

The Triumph of Amphitrite?
Tapestry
Brussels, Flanders
Early eighteenth century
Signed lower left "B. F. v D. Borcht"
Gollerbakh ca. 1922, 23, 37.

Acquired by the Grand Duke Paul and the Countess von Hohenfelsen from Laurent, Paris, June 17, 1907 (?) "Tapestry for the future dining room and screen"; Collection of the Grand Duke Paul and the Countess von Hohenfelsen, Boulogne (stairs) "grande tapisserie Louis XV"; Paley Palace, Tsarskoye Selo (gallery); Paley sale, Christie's, London, June 6-7, 1929, lot 150. L. 777.2 cm (25 ft. 6 in.); Feibes (?).

***

Portrait of Empress Catherine I (pl. 41)
Imperial Tapestry Manufactory
After 1717
Silk and silver threads
Gollerbakh ca. 1922, 23, 70.

Paley Palace, Tsarskoye Selo (rotunda); Paley sale, Christie's, London, June 6-7, 1929, lot 151, 44 × 36 in; Alexander Polovtsov; Walters Art Museum, Baltimore, inv. 82.4. 123.2 × 96.5 cm (48 ½ × 38 in.)

BIBLIOGRAPHY

Unpublished Sources

Russian Archives

In notes citing any Russian archives, F. = Fund; op. = division; D. = document; and L. = page.

AGE: Archives of the State Hermitage Museum, St. Petersburg; Paley Collection

TsGALI: State Archive of Art and Literature, St. Petersburg; Paley Collection (254)

RGIA: Russian National Historical Archive, St. Petersburg
Cabinet of the Grand Dukes Sergei and Paul Alexandrovich (526)
Cabinet of His Imperial Majesty (468)

GARF: National Archives of the Russian Federation, Moscow
Romanov holdings, Princess Paley (613)
Romanov holdings, Grand Duke Paul Alexandrovich (644)

French Archives

- Public Archives
Arch. Nat.: Archives nationales, Paris
Légion d'honneur

Archives municipales, Boulogne-Billancourt
Permis de construire
Archives départementales de la Haute-Saône, Vesoul
Fonds Dagnan-Bouveret Correspondance (23) Princesse Paley

Archives de la Police, Paris EA 17° grand-duc Alexei

BNF: Bibliothèque nationale de France, manuscrit
Fonds Robert de Montesquiou – Correspondance avec Olga von Hohenfelsen

- Private Archives
AB: Archives Boucheron
AD: Archives Delisle
Archives Givaudan
Louis Vuitton Collection
ATC: Archives Tassinari & Chatel
Archives privées

- Documentary Sources
Musée du Louvre
Documentation du département des Objets d'art
Documentation du département de la Peinture Musée d'Orsay
Documentation

Other Holdings

NGA: Archives of the National Gallery, London
Agnew & Sons holdings
The J. Paul Getty Trust, Los Angeles
Goupil & Cie / Boussod, Valadon & Cie Stock Books

Printed Sources

- Sales Catalogs
Doucet sale, Paris, June 5-8, 1912.
Paris sale, galerie Georges Petit, June 18-19, 1917.
Paley sale, Paris, December 5, 1923.
Paley sale, Christie's, London, June 6-7, 1929.
Paley sale, Christie's, London, June 21, 1929.
Paley sale, Christie's, London, July 1-2, 1929.
Sotheby's sale, New York, October 12, 1994.
Sotheby's sale, New York, November 8, 2013.

- Museum Guides (before 1941)

Gollerbakh ca. 1922
Gollerbakh, Erikh. *Dvortsy-muzei: Sobraniye Paley v Detskom Sele*. Petrograd, ca. 1922.

Lukomsky 1918
Lukomsky, Georgy. *Catherine Palace Museum Summary Catalog*. Petrograd, 1918 (published in Russian).

- Press and Periodicals

L'Art et la mode, 1886.

Les Arts, 1905.

L'Aurore, 1905.

La Croix, 1905.

Le Figaro, 1904-15.

Le Gaulois, 1904-1915, 1917, 1919, 1921.

Gil Blas, 1901, 1906, 1910, 1912, 1913.

Le Matin, 1904-15.

Les Modes, 1905-14.

Le Monde illustré, 1914.

Le Petit Parisien, 1905, 1908, 1913.

Le Radical, 1905.

Le Rappel, 1904.

La Revue illustrée, 1906.

Starye Gody, 1912.

Stolitsa i Usadba, 1914-15.

Le Temps, 1898, 1905, 1913.

- Correspondence, Memoirs, Souvenirs, and Literary Sources

Castellane 1986
Castellane, Boni de. *Mémoires de Boni de Castellane*. Paris: Perrin, 1986.

Chambrun 1941
Chambrun, Charles de. *Lettres à Marie: Pétersbourg-Pétrograd, 1914-1918*. Paris: Plon, 1941.

Efimov and Kovalskaya 2009
Efimov, A. B., and E. Y. Kovalskaya, eds. *Velikaia kniaginia Elisaveta Feodorovna i imperator Nikolai II dokumenty i materialy (1884-1909)*. St. Petersburg: Aleteiia, 2009.

Grand Duke Gabriel 1955
Grand Duke Gabriel. *V mramornom dvortse iz khroniki nashei semi*. New York, 1955.

Gimpel 1963
Gimpel, René. *Journal d'un collectionneur marchand de tableaux*. Paris: Calmann-Lévy, 1963.

Kleinmichel 1927
Kleinmichel, Comtesse. *Souvenirs d'un monde englouti*. Paris: Calmann-Lévy, 1927.

Kleinpenning 2010
Kleinpenning, Petra H., ed. *The Correspondence of the Empress of Russia with Ernst Ludwig and Eleonore Grand Duke and Duchess of Hesse, 1878-1916*. Books on Demand, 2010.

Marie de Roumanie 2014
Marie de Roumanie. *Histoire de ma vie, 1875-1918*. Paris: Lacurne, 2014.

Marie de Russie 1937
SAI Marie de Russie. *Une princesse en exil*. Paris: Stock, 1937.

Marie de Russie 1938
SAI Marie de Russie. *Éducation d'une Princesse*. Paris: Stock, 1938.

Maylunas and Mironenko 1996
Maylunas, Andrei, and Sergei Mironenko. *A Lifelong Passion: Nicholas & Alexandra*. London: Phoenix Giant, 1996.

Mension-Rigau 2011
Mension-Rigau, Éric. *L'Ami du prince: Journal inédit d'Alfred de Gramont, 1892-1915*. Paris: Fayard, 2011.

Nicholas II 2011-13
Nicolas II, *Dnevniki imperatora Nikolaia II, 1894-1918*. Moscow: Rosspen, 2011-13, 4 vols.

Paléologue 1922
Paléologue, Maurice. *La Russie des Tsars pendant la Grande Guerre*. Paris: Plon, 1922, 3 vols.

Paley 1923
Paley, Princesse. *Souvenirs de Russie*. Paris: Plon, 1923.

Patin 1987
Patin, Louise. *Journal d'une institutrice française en Russie pendant la Révolution, 1917-1919*. Paris: La Table ronde, 1987.

Poiret 1930
Poiret, Paul. *En habillant l'époque*. Paris: Grasset, 1930.

Polovtsov 1919
Polovtsov, Alexander A. *Les Trésors d'art en Russie sous le régime bolcheviste.* Paris: Soc. française d'imprimerie et de librairie, 1919.

Polovtsov 1966
Polovtsov, Alexander A. *Dnevnik gosudarstvennogo sekretaria A. A. Polovtsova.* Moscow: Nauka, 1966, 2 vols.

Pringué 1948
Pringué, Gabriel-Louis. *30 ans de dîners en ville.* Paris: Revue Adam, 1948.

Proust 1999
Proust, Marcel. *À la recherche du temps perdu.* Paris: Gallimard (Quarto), 1999.

Proust 2009
Proust, Marcel. *Le Salon de Mme de…*, Paris: L'Herne, 2009.

Robien 2017
Robien, Louis de. *Journal d'un diplomate en Russie, 1917-1918.* Paris: La Librairie Vuibert, 2017.

Singer 2000
Singer, Winnaretta. *Souvenirs de Winnaretta Singer princesse Edmond de Polignac.* Paris: Fondation Singer-Polignac, 2000.

Talleyrand-Périgord 1912
Talleyrand-Périgord, Véra de. *Pensées nouvelles, souvenirs anciens.* Paris: L. Maretheux, 1912.

Toscano 2014
Toscano, Anna. *Michel Romanoff de Russie: Un destin français.* Paris: L'Harmattan, 2014.

Vogel 2005
Vogel, Nadine, ed. *Au temps de l'Alliance franco-russe: Correspondance entre le grand-duc Nicolas Mikhaïlovich et Frédéric Masson, 1897-1914.* Paris: Bernard Giovanangeli, 2005.

Waleffe 1947
Waleffe, Maurice de. *Quand Paris était un paradis: Mémoires.* Paris: Denoël, 1947.

Publications and Articles

Ackerman 2000

Ackerman, Gerald M. *Jean-Léon Gérôme.* Paris-Courbevoie: ACR Édition, 2000.

Albertini and Kurdjian 2023

Albertini, Nadia, and Sophie Kurkdjian. *Kitmir: Les Broderies russes de Mademoiselle Chanel.* Montreuil: Gourcuff Gradenigo, 2023.

Ameliokhina and Parshina 2011

Ameliokhina, Svetlana, and Anastasia Parshina, eds. *Poiret – King of Fashion.* Moscow: Musée national du Kremlin, 2011 (published in Russian).

Antifeeva and Tshistikov 2000

Antifeeva, M. A., and A. N. Tshistikov. "Dvorets Palei: Muzei I ego kollektsii," *Sudby muzeinykh kollektsii materialy VII Tsarskoselskoi nauchnoi konferentsii.* St. Petersburg, 2000, 335-40.

Barten 1989

Barten, Sigrid. *René Lalique: Schmuck und Objet d'art, 1890-1910.* Munich: Prestel, 1989.

Bibesco 1950

Bibesco, Princesse. *La Duchesse de Guermantes : Laure de Sade Comtesse de Chevigné.* Paris: Plon, 1950.

Bott 2013a

Bott, Iraida K., ed. *The Romanovs: Tsarskoye Selo-Cincinnati.* St. Petersburg: Tsarskoye Selo State Museum-Preserve, 2013.

Bott 2013b

Bott, Iraida K. *"Svetilniki iz Parizha," Postavshchiki Imperatorskogo dvora: sbornik nauchnykh statei XIX Tsarskoselskoi konferentsii.* St. Petersburg, 2013.

Bowlt, Tregulova, and Rosticher Giordano 2009

Bowlt, John E., Zelfira Tregulova, and Nathalie Rosticher Giordano, eds. *Étonne-moi! Serge Diaghilev et les Ballets russes.* Monaco: Nouveau Musée national Monaco-Skira, 2009.

Bowron 2001

Bowron, Edgar P., ed. *Bernardo Bellotto and the Capitals of Europe.* New Haven: Yale University Press, 2001.

Bravard 2013

Bravard, Alice. *Le Grand Monde parisien (1900-1939) : La Persistance du modèle aristocratique.* Paris: PUR, 2013.

Bruson and Leribault 2002

Bruson, Jean-Marie, and Christophe Leribault, eds. *Au temps de Marcel Proust : La Collection François-Gérard Seligman au Musée Carnavalet.* Paris: Paris musées, 2002.

Centorame and Andia 2005

Centorame, Bruno, and Béatrice de Andia, eds. *Autour de la Madeleine : Art, littérature et société.* Paris: Action artistique de la Ville de Paris, 2005.

Champier and Sandoz 1900

Champier, Victor, and Gustave-Roger Sandoz. *Le Palais-Royal d'après des documents inédits, 1629-1900.* Paris: Société de propagande des livres d'art, 1900.

Chimènes 2004

Chimènes, Myriam. *Mécènes et musiciens: Du salon au concert à Paris sous la IIIe République.* Paris: Fayard, 2004.

Dard, Leymarie, and McWilliam 2010

Dard, Olivier, Michel Leymarie, and Neil McWilliam, eds. *Le Maurrassisme et la Culture: L'Action française, culture, société, politique.* Villeneuve-d'Ascq: Presse Universitaire du Septentrion, 2010.

Elsig 2012

Elsig, Frédéric, ed. *Une question de goût : La collection Zoubov à Genève.* Geneva: 5 continents, 2012.

Eltchaninow 1913

Eltchaninow, Le Professeur. *Le Règne de S. M. l'empereur Nicolas II.* Paris: Hachette, 1913.

Eudel 1886
Eudel, Paul. *L'Hôtel Drouot et la curiosité en 1884-1885*. Paris: G. Charpentier et Cie, 1886.

Falluel 1985
Falluel, Fabienne, ed. *L'Éventail, miroir de la Belle Époque*. Paris: Palais Galliera, 1985.

Faroult and Voiriot, 2016
Faroult, Guillaume, and Catherine Voiriot, eds. *Hubert Robert 1733-1808. Un peintre visionnaire*. Paris: Somogy-Louvre éditions, 2016.

Ferrand 1993
Ferrand, Jacques. *Le Grand-Duc Paul Alexandrovich de Russie*. Paris: Jacques Ferrand, 1993.

Fogt and Kirikov 2011
Fogt, Erika, and Boris Kirikov. *Arkhitektor Karl Shmidt zhizn i tvorchestvo*. St. Petersburg: Kolo, 2011.

Francis, Gontier 1981
Francis, Claude, and Fernande Gontier. *Marcel Proust et les siens*. Paris: Plon, 1981.

Gabet 2011
Gabet, Olivier. *Un marchand entre deux empires – Élie Fabius et le monde de l'art*. Paris: Skira Flammarion, 2011.

Garnier 1987
Garnier, Guillaume, ed. *Paris-couture – Années trente*. Paris: Le Musée, 1987.

Gary 2007
Gary, Marie-Noël de, ed. *Musée Nissim de Camondo: La Demeure d'un collectionneur*. Paris: Les Arts décoratifs, 2007.

Gautier 1980
Gautier, Gilberte. *La rue de la Paix*. Paris: Julliard, 1980.

Gendre 2003
Gendre, Catherine, ed. *Versailles : Vie artistique, littéraire et mondaine. 1889-1939*. Paris: Somogy, 2003.

Georgel 2016
Georgel, Chantal, ed. *Jacques Doucet : Collectionneur et mécène*. Paris: INHA/ Les Arts Décoratifs, 2016.

Grange 2016
Grange, Cyril. *Une élite parisienne : Les Familles de la grande bourgeoisie juive (1870-1939)*. Paris: CNRS, 2016.

Guitaut and Patterson 2018
Guitaut, Caroline de, and Stephen Patterson. *Russia: Art, Royalty and the Romanovs*. London: Royal Collection Trust, 2018.

Habsburg 2003
Habsburg, Géza von, ed. *Fabergé | Cartier: Rivalen am Zarenhof*. Munich: Hirmer, 2003.

Havard 1884
Havard, Henry. *L'Art dans la maison*. Paris: Rouveyre et G. Blond, 1884.

Haye and Mendes 2014
Haye, Amy de la, and Valerie D. Mendes. *The House of Worth – Portrait of an Archive*. London: Victoria & Albert Museum, 2014.

Hillerin 2014
Hillerin, Laure. *La Comtesse de Greffulhe : L'Ombre de Guermantes*. Paris: Flammarion, 2014.

Hoog 2009
Hoog, Anne H., ed. *La Splendeur des Camondo : De Constantinople à Paris, 1806-1945*. Paris: Musée d'art et d'histoire du judaïsme, 2009.

Huesca 2001
Huesca, Roland. *Triomphes et scandales : La Belle Époque des Ballets russes*. Paris: Hermann, 2001.

Iljine and Semyonova 2013
Iljine, Nicolas V., and Natalya Semyonova, eds. *Selling Russia's Treasures*. New York: Abbeville Press, 2013.

Johnston 1999
Johnston, William R. *William and Henry Walters, the Reticent Collectors*. Baltimore: Johns Hopkins University Press, 1999.

Jullian 1961

Jullian, Philippe. *14, rue du Centre, Neuilly-sur-Seine*. Monaco: Jaspard, Polus & Cie, 1961.

Kisluk-Grosheide, Krohn, and Leben 2013

Kisluk-Grosheide, Daniëlle, Deborah L. Krohn, and Ulrich Leben, eds. *Salvaging the Past: Georges Hoentschel and French Decorative Arts from the Metropolitan Museum of Art*. New York: Bard Graduate Center, 2013.

Kostiuk 2010

Kostiuk, Olga, ed. *Since Tobacco You Love Too Much*. St. Petersburg: State Hermitage Museum, 2010.

La Ville lumière 1909

La Ville lumière: Anecdotes et documents. Paris: Direction et Administration, 1909.

Legrand 2016

Legrand, Sylvie. *Les Services aux oiseaux Buffon*. Paris: Gourcuff Gradenico – Les Arts Décoratifs, 2016.

Léri and Saillard 2013

Léri, Jean-Marc, and Olivier Saillard, eds. *Roman d'une garde-robe : Le Chic d'une Parisienne de la Belle Époque aux années 1930*. Paris: Paris-Musées, 2013.

Leribault 2014

Leribault, Christophe, ed. *Paris 1900 : La Ville spectacle*. Paris: Paris musées, 2014.

Letourmy 2005

Letourmy, Georgina. *Ernest Kees, éventailliste Parisien*. Paris: AHME-Musée de l'Éventail Hervé Hoguet, 2005.

Lheureux 2016

Lheureux, Rosine. *Une histoire des parfumeurs. France, 1850-1910*. Ceyzérieu: Champ Vallon, 2016.

Liaut 1996

Jean-Noël Liaut, *Une princesse déchirée : Natalie Paley* (Levallois-Perret: Filipacchi, 1996).

Mension-Rigau 2016
Mension-Rigau, Éric. *Boni de Castellane*. Paris: Perrin, 2016.

Meyer-Plantureux 2005
Meyer-Plantureux, Chantal. *Les Enfants de Shylock ou l'antisémitisme sur scène*. Paris: Éditions Complexe, 2005.

Molinier 1885
Molinier, Émile. *Guide du collectionneur: Dictionnaire des émailleurs*. Paris: Jules Rouam, 1885.

Moulin 1999
Moulin, Hélène, ed. *Hubert Robert et Saint-Pétersbourg : Les Commandes de la famille impériale et des princes russes entre 1773 et 1802*. Valence: Musée de Valence, 1999.

Munn, 2001
Munn, Geoffrey C. *Tiaras – A History of Splendour*. London: Antique Collectors' Club, 2001.

Nadelhoffer 1984
Nadelhoffer, Hans. *Cartier*. Paris: Éditions du Regard, 1984.

Page 2016
Page, Alexandre. *François Flameng (1856-1923), un artiste peintre dans la Grande Guerre*. Saarbrücken: Éditions universitaire européennes, 2016.

Painter 2008
Painter, George D. *Marcel Proust (1871-1922)*. Paris: Tallandier, 2008.

Pasols 2012
Pasols, Paul-Gérard. *Louis Vuitton : La Naissance du luxe moderne*. Paris: Éditions de La Martinière, 2012.

Penot 2017
Penot, Agnés. *La Maison Goupil : Galerie d'art internationale au XIX*[e] *siècle*. Paris: Mare & Martin, 2017.

Peshekhonova 2010
Peshekhonova, Larissa, ed. *The Art of René Lalique*. Moscow: Moscow Kremlin Museums, 2010.

Petrova 2009
Petrova, Evgenia, ed. *Diaghilev: The Beginning*. St. Petersburg: Palace Editions; State Russian Museum, 2009.

Pillivuyt 1985
Pillivuyt, Ghislaine. *Les Flacons de la seduction*. Paris: Bibliothèque des arts, 1985.

Pojarskaïa and Volodina 1990
Pojarskaïa, Militsa, and Tatiana Volodina, *L'Art des Ballets russes à Paris : Projet de décors et de costumes, 1908-1929*. Paris: Gallimard, 1990.

Robichon 2007
Robichon, François. *Édouard Detaille: Un siècle de gloire militaire*. Paris: Bernard Giovanangeli – Ministère de la Défense, 2007.

Roger-Milès 1910
Roger-Milès, Léon. *Les Créateurs de la mode*. Paris: Le Figaro, 1910.

Rosenberg 1982
Rosenberg, Pierre. "Ingres et Chardin." *Bulletin du musée Ingres*, no. 49 [December 1982]: 15.

Rosenberg and Temperini 1999
Rosenberg, Pierre, and Renaud Temperini. *Chardin*. Paris: Flammarion, 1999.

Rousset-Charny 1990
Rousset-Charny, Gérard. *Les Palais parisiens de la Belle Époque*. Alençon: Action artistique de la ville de Paris, 1990.

Saillard 2014
Saillard, Olivier, ed. *Fashion Mix : Mode d'ici; Créateurs d'ailleurs*. Paris: Flammarion, 2014.

Saillard 2015
Saillard, Olivier, ed. *La Mode retrouvée : Les Robes trésors de la comtesse Greffulhe*. Paris: Palais Galliera – Paris musées, 2015.

Salmon 1999
Salmon, Xavier, ed. *Jean-Marc Nattier (1685-1766)*. Paris: RMN, 1999.

Salomé and Dalon 2013
Salomé, Laurent, and Laure Dalon, eds. *Cartier, le style et l'histoire*. Paris: RMN, 2013.

Sassi 2009
Sassi, Daniel. *Jean-Adolphe-Pascal Dagnan-Bouveret : Les Couleurs de sa vie*. Quincey: D. Sassi, 2009.

Sirop 1989
Sirop, Dominique. *Paquin*. Paris: Adam Biro, 1989.

Verlaine 2013
Verlaine, Julie. *Femmes collectionneuses d'art et mécènes*. Paris: Hazan, 2013.

Vever 1906-8
Vever, Henri. *La Bijouterie française au* XIXe *siècle*. 3 vols. Paris: H. Floury, 1906-8.

Vogtherr, Preti, and Faroult 2014
Vogtherr, Christoph, Monica Preti, and Guillaume Faroult, eds. *Delicious Decadence: The Rediscovery of French Eighteenth-Century Painting in the Nineteenth Century*. Farnham, UK: Ashgate, 2014.

Weisberg 2002
Weisberg, Gabriel P. *Against the Modern: Dagnan-Bouveret and the Transformation of the Academic Tradition*. New York: Dahesh Museum of Art, 2002.

Wintermute 1996
Wintermute, Alan. *The French Portrait*. New York: Colnaghi, 1996.

Worth 1928
Worth, Jean-Philippe. *A Century of Fashion*. Boston: Little, Brown, 1928.

Zeisler, 2014a
Zeisler, Wilfried. "De l'orfèvrerie parisienne du dernier quart du XIXe siècle à la Première Guerre mondiale : La maison Keller." *Revue de l'Art*, no. 185 [2014-3]: 19-26.

Zeisler 2014b
Zeisler, Wilfried. *L'Objet d'art et de luxe français en Russie (1881-1917) : Fournisseurs, clients, collections et influences*. Paris: Mare et Martin, 2014.

Additional Bibliography (2025)

– Unpublished Sources

United States Archives

Mainbocher Collection. The Irene Lewisohn Costume Reference Library at the Costume Institute, The Metropolitan Museum of Art.

Paley Family Collection. Russian History Collection, Hillwood Estate, Museum & Gardens Archives and Special Collections.

Natalie Paley Photograph Albums, Photographs, and Correspondence. General Collection (GEN MSS), Beinecke Rare Book and Manuscript Library, Yale University.

Series 1. Scrapbooks, 1919-1961. John C. Wilson Papers (YCAL MSS 1127). Yale Collection of American Literature, Beinecke Rare Book and Manuscript Library.

UK Archives

John C. Wilson, 1936-1958 (COW/3/N/2/58). Noël Coward Collection: Papers, 1911-2000. Cadbury Research Library. University of Birmingham.

The Personal Papers of Oliver Messel. Theatre Collection. University of Bristol.

– Press and Periodicals

Femina, 1926.

Vogue Paris, 1923-1936.

Harper's Bazaar, 1936-1944.

Sketch, 1934.

Time, 1931.

Women's Wear, 1924-1927.

Women's Wear Daily, 1940.

Publications

Corbett 2002

Corbett, Patricia. *Verdura: The Life and Work of a Master Jeweler*. New York: Harry N. Abrams, 2002.

Demornex 2008

Demornex, Jacqueline. *Lucien Lelong*. London: Thames & Hudson, 2008.

Garnier 1987

Garnier, Guillaume, ed. *Paris-couture – Années trente*. Paris: Le Musée, 1987.

Lee et al. 1975

Lee, Sarah, and Fashion Institute of Technology. *American Fashion: The Life and Lines of Adrian, Mainbocher, McCardell, Norell, Trigère*. New York: Quadrangle/New York Times, 1975.

Liaut 2015

Liaut, Jean-Noël. *Natalie Paley: Princesse en exile*. Paris: Bartillat, New Edition, 2015.

Martineu 2018

Martineu, Paul. "Style in the Face of Crisis, 1930-1946." In *Icons of Style: A Century of Fashion*. Los Angeles: Getty Publications, 2018.

Slinkard 2016

Slinkard, Petra *Making Mainbocher: The First American Couturier*. Chicago: Chicago History Museum, 2016.

Tiffany 2011

Tiffany, John A. *Eleanor Lambert: Still Here*. New York: Pointed Leaf Press, 2011.

Vassiliev 2000

Vassiliev, Alexander. *Beauty in Exile*. New York: Harry N. Abrams, 2000.

Vickers 1987
Vickers, Hugo *Cecil Beaton: A Biography*. New York: Plume, 1987.

Wilson 2015
Wilson, John C. *Noel, Tallulah, Cole, and Me: A Memoir of Broadway's Golden Age*. Edited with commentary by Thomas S. Hischak and Jack Macauley. Lanham, MD: Roman & Littlefield Publishers, 2015.

INDEX

C

D

E

F

G

H

J

K

L

M

N

O

P

R

PHOTOGRAPHIC CREDITS

© Hillwood Estate, Museum & Gardens, photographed by Mark Finkenstaedt: pls. 1, 3, 4, 14, 55, 59, 60, 61, 65.

© Private collection: pls. 22, 23.

© Photographs by the author / Private collection: pls. 12, 13, 17, 18, 20, 21; figs. 1, 3, 4, 5, 6, 7, 10, 13, 14, 15, 16, 20, 23, 25, 26, 27, 28, 29, 31, 32, 33, 34, 35, 36, 38, 39, 40, 41, 42, 56.

Source: Hillwood Estate, Museum & Gardens, Archives and Special Collections: figs. 8, 9, 17, 24, 30, 37, 43, 44, 53, 57, 58, 59, 61, 62, 63, 64, 65, 66, 67, 68, 70, 71, 73, 75, 89, 90, 95, 96, 97, pl. 26.

Source: Hillwood Estate, Museum & Gardens, Archives and Special Collections, photographed by John Alfred Piver: fig. 69.

© George Hoyningen-Huene Estate Archives. Image source Hillwood Estate, Museum & Gardens, Archives and Special Collections: figs. 77.

© Cecil Beaton, Condé Nast. Image source Hillwood Estate, Museum & Gardens, Archives and Special Collections: figs. 80, 81, 82.

Source: Hillwood Estate, Museum & Gardens, Archives and Special Collections, photographed by Max Munn Autrey: fig. 83.

Source: Hillwood Estate, Museum & Gardens, Archives and Special Collections, photographed by Sacha Masour: fig. 94.

© Georges de Pistolkors Papers, Holy Trinity Orthodox Seminary / Russian History Museum, Jordanville, NY: figs. 2, 11, 12.

Tretyakov Gallery, Moscow, RussiaPhoto © Fine Art Images/Bridgeman Images: pl. 2.

Private Collection Photo © Christie's Images/Bridgeman Images: pls. 5, 9, 19, 43, 53.

Private Collection/Bridgeman Images: pl. 6.

Royal Collection Trust / © His Majesty King Charles III 2023: pls. 7, 52.

© Michele and Donald D'Amour Museum of Fine Arts, Springfield, Massachusetts. The James Philip Gray Collection. Photography by John Polak: pl. 8.

Gallerie Nazionali di Arte Antica, Roma (MiC) – Bibliotheca Hertziana, Istituto Max Planck per la storia dell'arte/Enrico Fontolan: pl. 10.

© State Hermitage Museum, St. Petersburg, Russia/Bridgeman Images: pl. 11.

Courtesy of the Frick Art Reference Library: fig. 18.

Courtesy of the Frick Art Reference Library, photo by A.C. Cooper, London: figs. 19, 21, 22, 60.

© Photo: NMWA / DNPartcom: pl. 15.

National Museum of Western Art, Tokyo, Japan Photo © Fine Art Images/ Bridgeman Images: pl. 16.

© Hillwood Estate, Museum & Gardens, photographed by Brian Searby: pls. 24, 25.

© Louis Vuitton Collection, Paris: fig. 45.

Archives Cartier © Cartier: figs. 46, 47, 48, 49, 50, 51.

Vincent Wulveryck, Collection Cartier © Cartier: pl. 27.

Photo: Vincent Wulveryck, Cartier Collection © Cartier: pl. 28.

Photo Boissonnas & Taponier, Cartier Archives © Cartier: fig. 52.

© Archives Delisle, Paris: figs. 54, 55, pls. 33, 34, 35, 36.

© Tassinari & Chatel, Paris: pls. 29, 37, 38, 39, 40.

© Fondation Zoubov / Photo. André Longchamp: pl. 30.

Scala / Art Resource, NY: pl. 31.

Dépôt du Musée du Louvre au Musée de la musique / Cliché Anglès: pl. 32.

The Walters Art Museum, Baltimore: pl. 41.

KMSKA/artinflanders.be, photo by Hugo Maertens, public domain: pl. 42.

© Collection Givaudan / photo G. Routhier: pls. 44, 45, 46, 47, 48, 49, 50, 51.

© Hillwood Estate, Museum & Gardens, photographed by Edward Owen: pl. 54.

© Metropolitan Museum of Art, New York City: pl. 56.

Fitzwilliam Museum, University of Cambridge, UKPhoto: © Fitzwilliam Museum, University of Cambridge, UK/Bridgeman Images: pls. 57, 58.

© Hillwood Estate, Museum & Gardens, photographed by Connor Beaty: pl. 62.

Credit to property of the National Trust. Estate of Oliver Messel, CBE. © National Trust / Charles Thomas: pl. 63.

Digital Image © CNAC/MNAM, Dist. RMN-Grand Palais / Art Resource, NY. © ARS / Comité Cocteau, Paris / ADAGP, Paris 2024: pl. 64.

© George Hoyningen-Huene Estate Archives. Image credit Harper's Bazaar, Hearst Magazine Media, Inc: pls. 66, 68, 85.

© Hillwood Estate, Museum & Gardens, photographed by Alex Braun: pl. 67.

© 1926, Penske Media Corporation. All rights reserved: fig. 72.

© George Hoyningen-Huene Estate Archives. Image courtesy of Bibliothèque nationale de France: fig. 74.

Source: Natalie Paley Photograph Albums, Photographs, and Correspondence. General Collection, Beinecke Rare Book and Manuscript Library, Yale University: figs. 76, 91, 92.

Source: John C. Wilson Papers. Yale Collection of American Literature, Beinecke Rare Book and Manuscript Library: figs. 84, 86, 87, 88, 93.

Horst P. Horst, Vogue, © Condé Nast: fig. 78.

Cecil Beaton, Vogue © Condé Nast: fig. 79.

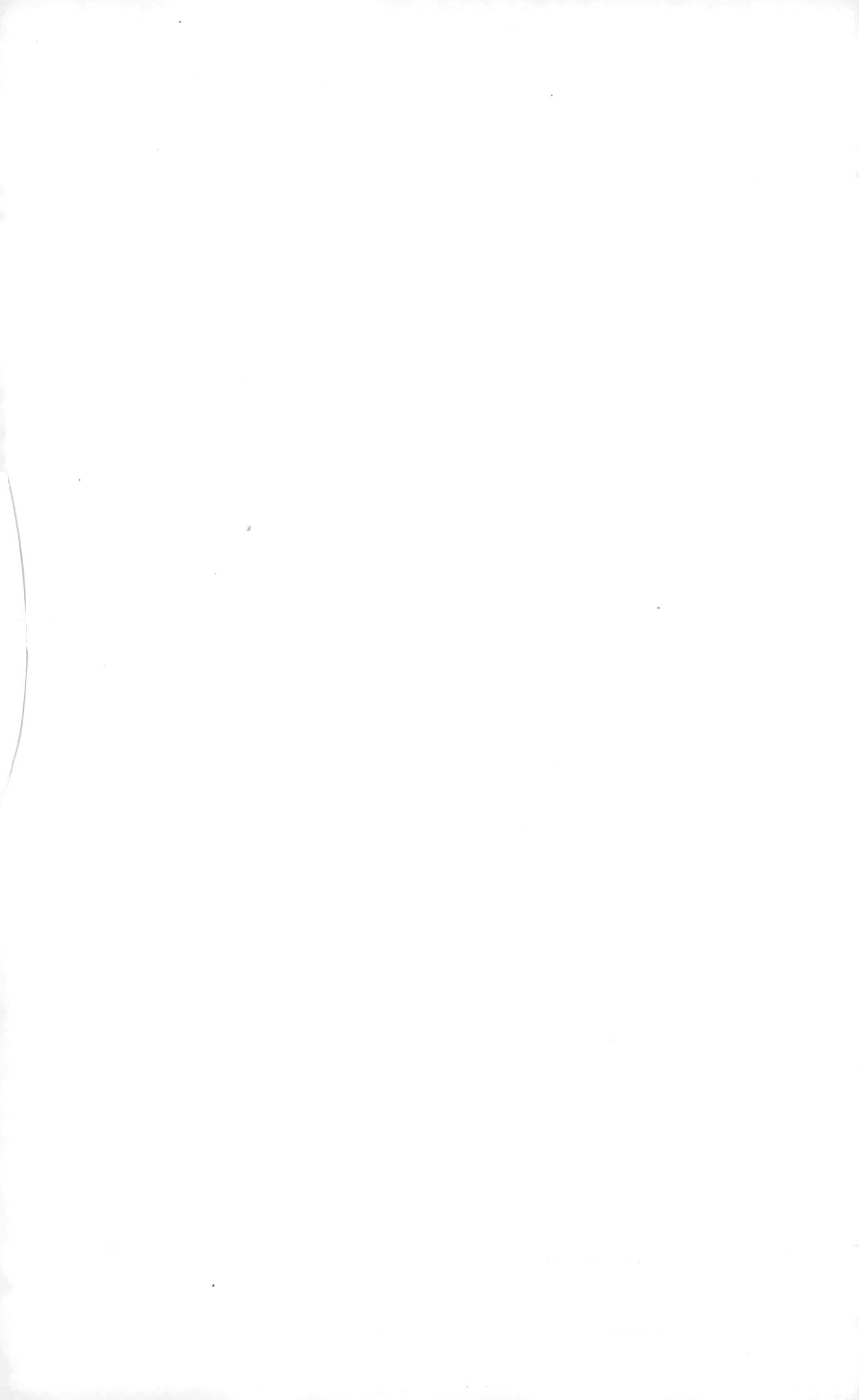

TABLE OF CONTENTS

Hillwood Estate, Museum & Gardens
4155 Linnean Avenue
NW Washington, D.C. 20008
www.hillwoodmuseum.org

Deputy Director and Chief Curator: Wilfried Zeisler
Exhibitions and Collections Project Manager: Rachel Burns
Editor: Richard Slovak

16, rue Danton
94270 Le Kremlin-Bicêtre
www.mareetmartin.com

Chairman: Gaël Martin
Editorial Director: Alain Bonnet
Production Manager: Nastasiea Hadoux
English Translator: Lucian Comoy
English Proofreader: Roberta Pertegato
Photoengraving: Rmax

ISBN Mare & Martin : 978-2-36222-123-1
ISBN Giles ltd : 978-1-917273-06-0

Printed in February 2025 in the European Union
Legal deposit: March 2025